GnuTLS Reference Manual

A catalogue record for this book is available from the Hong Kong Public Libraries.

Published in Hong Kong by Samurai Media Limited.

Email: info@samuraimedia.org

ISBN 978-988-8381-64-7

Contents

Preface   **xiii**

1. Introduction to GnuTLS   **1**
  1.1. Downloading and installing 1
  1.2. Installing for a software distribution 2
  1.3. Overview 3

2. Introduction to TLS and DTLS   **5**
  2.1. TLS Layers 5
  2.2. The Transport Layer 5
  2.3. The TLS record protocol 6
    2.3.1. Encryption algorithms used in the record layer 6
    2.3.2. Compression algorithms used in the record layer 8
    2.3.3. Weaknesses and countermeasures 8
    2.3.4. On record padding 9
  2.4. The TLS alert protocol 9
  2.5. The TLS handshake protocol 10
    2.5.1. TLS ciphersuites 11
    2.5.2. Authentication 11
    2.5.3. Client authentication 11
    2.5.4. Resuming sessions 11
  2.6. TLS extensions 12
    2.6.1. Maximum fragment length negotiation 12
    2.6.2. Server name indication 12
    2.6.3. Session tickets 13
    2.6.4. HeartBeat 13
    2.6.5. Safe renegotiation 14
    2.6.6. OCSP status request 15
    2.6.7. SRTP 16
    2.6.8. Application Layer Protocol Negotiation (ALPN) 17
    2.6.9. Extensions and Supplemental Data 18
  2.7. How to use TLS in application protocols 18
    2.7.1. Separate ports 18
    2.7.2. Upward negotiation 18
  2.8. On SSL 2 and older protocols 20

3. Authentication methods   **21**
  3.1. Certificate authentication 21
    3.1.1. X.509 certificates 21
    3.1.2. OpenPGP certificates 36
    3.1.3. Advanced certificate verification 38
    3.1.4. Digital signatures 39

Contents

3.2. More on certificate authentication 41
    3.2.1. PKCS #10 certificate requests 41
    3.2.2. PKIX certificate revocation lists 44
    3.2.3. OCSP certificate status checking 47
    3.2.4. Managing encrypted keys 51
    3.2.5. Invoking certtool 55
    3.2.6. Invoking ocsptool 72
    3.2.7. Invoking danetool 76
3.3. Shared-key and anonymous authentication 82
    3.3.1. SRP authentication 82
    3.3.2. PSK authentication 85
    3.3.3. Anonymous authentication 87
3.4. Selecting an appropriate authentication method 88
    3.4.1. Two peers with an out-of-band channel 88
    3.4.2. Two peers without an out-of-band channel 88
    3.4.3. Two peers and a trusted third party 89

4. Abstract keys types and Hardware security modules   **95**
4.1. Abstract key types 95
    4.1.1. Public keys 96
    4.1.2. Private keys 98
    4.1.3. Operations 100
4.2. System and application-specific keys 103
    4.2.1. System-specific keys 103
    4.2.2. Application-specific keys 103
4.3. Smart cards and HSMs 105
    4.3.1. Initialization 105
    4.3.2. Accessing objects that require a PIN 107
    4.3.3. Reading objects 108
    4.3.4. Writing objects 111
    4.3.5. Using a PKCS #11 token with TLS 112
    4.3.6. Invoking p11tool 112
    4.3.7. p11tool help/usage (``--help'') 113
    4.3.8. token-related-options options 115
    4.3.9. object-list-related-options options 115
    4.3.10. keygen-related-options options 116
    4.3.11. write-object-related-options options 117
    4.3.12. other-options options 119
    4.3.13. p11tool exit status 121
    4.3.14. p11tool See Also 121
    4.3.15. p11tool Examples 121
4.4. Trusted Platform Module (TPM) 122
    4.4.1. Keys in TPM 122
    4.4.2. Key generation 123
    4.4.3. Using keys 124
    4.4.4. Invoking tpmtool 125

4.4.5. tpmtool help/usage ("`--help`") 126
4.4.6. debug option (-d) 127
4.4.7. generate-rsa option 127
4.4.8. user option 127
4.4.9. system option 127
4.4.10. test-sign option 128
4.4.11. sec-param option 128
4.4.12. inder option 128
4.4.13. outder option 128
4.4.14. tpmtool exit status 128
4.4.15. tpmtool See Also 128
4.4.16. tpmtool Examples 129

5. How to use GnuTLS in applications   **131**
5.1. Introduction 131
    5.1.1. General idea 131
    5.1.2. Error handling 132
    5.1.3. Common types 133
    5.1.4. Debugging and auditing 133
    5.1.5. Thread safety 134
    5.1.6. Sessions and fork 135
    5.1.7. Callback functions 135
5.2. Preparation 136
    5.2.1. Headers 136
    5.2.2. Initialization 136
    5.2.3. Version check 136
    5.2.4. Building the source 137
5.3. Session initialization 138
5.4. Associating the credentials 138
    5.4.1. Certificates 138
    5.4.2. SRP 144
    5.4.3. PSK 146
    5.4.4. Anonymous 148
5.5. Setting up the transport layer 148
    5.5.1. Asynchronous operation 151
    5.5.2. DTLS sessions 153
5.6. TLS handshake 154
5.7. Data transfer and termination 155
5.8. Buffered data transfer 157
5.9. Handling alerts 158
5.10. Priority strings 160
5.11. Selecting cryptographic key sizes 163
5.12. Advanced topics 167
    5.12.1. Session resumption 167
    5.12.2. Certificate verification 170
    5.12.3. Re-authentication 173

Contents

5.12.4. Parameter generation 174
5.12.5. Deriving keys for other applications/protocols 175
5.12.6. Channel bindings 176
5.12.7. Interoperability 177
5.12.8. Compatibility with the OpenSSL library 177

6. GnuTLS application examples   179
6.1. Client examples 179
6.1.1. Simple client example with X.509 certificate support 179
6.1.2. Simple client example with SSH-style certificate verification 182
6.1.3. Simple client example with anonymous authentication 184
6.1.4. Simple datagram TLS client example 186
6.1.5. Obtaining session information 189
6.1.6. Using a callback to select the certificate to use 191
6.1.7. Verifying a certificate 196
6.1.8. Using a smart card with TLS 198
6.1.9. Client with resume capability example 201
6.1.10. Simple client example with SRP authentication 204
6.1.11. Simple client example using the C++ API 207
6.1.12. Helper functions for TCP connections 208
6.1.13. Helper functions for UDP connections 209
6.2. Server examples 211
6.2.1. Echo server with X.509 authentication 211
6.2.2. Echo server with OpenPGP authentication 214
6.2.3. Echo server with SRP authentication 218
6.2.4. Echo server with anonymous authentication 221
6.2.5. DTLS echo server with X.509 authentication 224
6.3. OCSP example 232
6.4. Miscellaneous examples 237
6.4.1. Checking for an alert 237
6.4.2. X.509 certificate parsing example 238
6.4.3. Listing the ciphersuites in a priority string 240
6.4.4. PKCS #12 structure generation example 242

7. Other included programs   245
7.1. Invoking gnutls-cli 245
7.2. Invoking gnutls-serv 253
7.3. Invoking gnutls-cli-debug 258

8. Internal Architecture of GnuTLS   263
8.1. The TLS Protocol 263
8.2. TLS Handshake Protocol 264
8.3. TLS Authentication Methods 265
8.4. TLS Extension Handling 265
8.5. Cryptographic Backend 271

A. Upgrading from previous versions   275

B. Support   **279**

   B.1. Getting Help 279

   B.2. Commercial Support 279

   B.3. Bug Reports 280

   B.4. Contributing 280

   B.5. Certification 281

C. Supported Ciphersuites   **283**

D. Error Codes and Descriptions   **289**

GNU Free Documentation License   **295**

Bibliography   **303**

List of Tables

2.1. Supported ciphers. 7
2.2. Supported MAC algorithms. 7
2.3. Supported compression algorithms 8
2.4. The TLS alert table 10
2.5. Supported SRTP profiles 16

3.1. Supported key exchange algorithms. 22
3.2. X.509 certificate fields. 22
3.3. Supported X.509 certificate extensions. 29
3.4. The `gnutls_certificate_status_t` enumeration. 90
3.5. The `gnutls_certificate_verify_flags` enumeration. 91
3.6. Key purpose object identifiers. 92
3.7. OpenPGP certificate fields. 92
3.8. The types of (sub)keys required for the various TLS key exchange methods. . . 92
3.9. Certificate revocation list fields. 93
3.10. The most important OCSP response fields. 93
3.11. The revocation reasons 94
3.12. Encryption flags 94

4.1. The `gnutls_pin_flag_t` enumeration. 107

5.1. Environment variables used by the library. 134
5.2. Key exchange algorithms and the corresponding credential types. 140
5.3. Supported initial keywords. 161
5.4. The supported algorithm keywords in priority strings. 163
5.5. Special priority string keywords. 164
5.6. More priority string keywords. 165
5.7. Key sizes and security parameters. 166
5.8. The DANE verification status flags. 173

C.1. The ciphersuites table 287

D.1. The error codes table 294

List of Figures

2.1. The TLS protocol layers. 6

3.1. An example of the X.509 hierarchical trust model. 23
3.2. An example of the OpenPGP trust model. 36

4.1. PKCS #11 module usage. 105

5.1. High level design of GnuTLS. 132

8.1. TLS protocol use case. 263
8.2. GnuTLS handshake state machine. 264
8.3. GnuTLS handshake process sequence. 264
8.4. GnuTLS cryptographic back-end design. 272

Preface

This document demonstrates and explains the GnuTLS library API. A brief introduction to the protocols and the technology involved is also included so that an application programmer can better understand the GnuTLS purpose and actual offerings. Even if GnuTLS is a typical library software, it operates over several security and cryptographic protocols which require the programmer to make careful and correct usage of them. Otherwise it is likely to only obtain a false sense of security. The term of security is very broad even if restricted to computer software, and cannot be confined to a single cryptographic library. For that reason, do not consider any program secure just because it uses GnuTLS; there are several ways to compromise a program or a communication line and GnuTLS only helps with some of them.

Although this document tries to be self contained, basic network programming and public key infrastructure (PKI) knowledge is assumed in most of it. A good introduction to networking can be found in [35], to public key infrastructure in [14] and to security engineering in [5].

Updated versions of the GnuTLS software and this document will be available from `http://www.gnutls.org/`.

Introduction to GnuTLS

In brief GnuTLS can be described as a library which offers an API to access secure communication protocols. These protocols provide privacy over insecure lines, and were designed to prevent eavesdropping, tampering, or message forgery.

Technically GnuTLS is a portable ANSI C based library which implements the protocols ranging from SSL 3.0 to TLS 1.2 (see chapter 2, for a detailed description of the protocols), accompanied with the required framework for authentication and public key infrastructure. Important features of the GnuTLS library include:

- Support for TLS 1.2, TLS 1.1, TLS 1.0 and SSL 3.0 protocols.

- Support for Datagram TLS 1.0 and 1.2.

- Support for handling and verification of X.509 and OpenPGP certificates.

- Support for password authentication using TLS-SRP.

- Support for keyed authentication using TLS-PSK.

- Support for TPM, PKCS #11 tokens and smart-cards.

The GnuTLS library consists of three independent parts, namely the "TLS protocol part", the "Certificate part", and the "Cryptographic back-end" part. The "TLS protocol part" is the actual protocol implementation, and is entirely implemented within the GnuTLS library. The "Certificate part" consists of the certificate parsing, and verification functions and it uses functionality from the libtasn1 library. The "Cryptographic back-end" is provided by the nettle and gmplib libraries.

1.1. Downloading and installing

GnuTLS is available for download at: http://www.gnutls.org/download.html

GnuTLS uses a development cycle where even minor version numbers indicate a stable release and a odd minor version number indicate a development release. For example, GnuTLS 1.6.3 denote a stable release since 6 is even, and GnuTLS 1.7.11 denote a development release since 7 is odd.

GnuTLS depends on `nettle` and `gmplib`, and you will need to install it before installing GnuTLS. The `nettle` library is available from `http://www.lysator.liu.se/~nisse/nettle/`, while `gmplib` is available from `http://www.gmplib.org/`. Don't forget to verify the cryptographic signature after downloading source code packages.

The package is then extracted, configured and built like many other packages that use Autoconf. For detailed information on configuring and building it, refer to the "INSTALL" file that is part of the distribution archive. Typically you invoke `./configure` and then `make check install`. There are a number of compile-time parameters, as discussed below.

Several parts of GnuTLS require ASN.1 functionality, which is provided by a library called libtasn1. A copy of libtasn1 is included in GnuTLS. If you want to install it separately (e.g., to make it possibly to use libtasn1 in other programs), you can get it from `http://www.gnu.org/software/libtasn1/`.

The compression library, `libz`, the PKCS #11 helper library `p11-kit`, the TPM library `trousers`, as well as the IDN library `libidn`[1] are optional dependencies. Check the README file in the distribution on how to obtain these libraries.

A few `configure` options may be relevant, summarized below. They disable or enable particular features, to create a smaller library with only the required features. Note however, that although a smaller library is generated, the included programs are not guaranteed to compile if some of these options are given.

```
--disable-srp-authentication
--disable-psk-authentication
--disable-anon-authentication
--disable-openpgp-authentication
--disable-dhe
--disable-ecdhe
--disable-openssl-compatibility
--disable-dtls-srtp-support
--disable-alpn-support
--disable-heartbeat-support
--disable-libdane
--without-p11-kit
--without-tpm
--without-zlib
```

For the complete list, refer to the output from `configure --help`.

1.2. Installing for a software distribution

When installing for a software distribution, it is often desirable to preconfigure GnuTLS with the system-wide paths and files. There two important configuration options, one sets the trust

---

[1]Needed to use RFC6125 name comparison in internationalized domains.

store in system, which are the CA certificates to be used by programs by default (if they don't override it), and the other sets to DNSSEC root key file used by unbound for DNSSEC verification.

For the latter the following configuration option is available, and if not specified GnuTLS will try to auto-detect the location of that file.

```
--with-unbound-root-key-file
```

To set the trust store the following options are available.

```
--with-default-trust-store-file
--with-default-trust-store-dir
--with-default-trust-store-pkcs11
```

The first option is used to set a PEM file which contains a list of trusted certificates, while the second will read all certificates in the given path. The recommended option is the last, which allows to use a PKCS #11 trust policy module. That module not only provides the trusted certificates, but allows the categorization of them using purpose, e.g., CAs can be restricted for e-mail usage only, or administrative restrictions of CAs, for examples by restricting a CA to only issue certificates for a given DNS domain using NameConstraints. A publicly available PKCS #11 trust module is p11-kit's trust module[2].

1.3. Overview

In this document we present an overview of the supported security protocols in chapter 2, and continue by providing more information on the certificate authentication in section 3.1, and shared-key as well anonymous authentication in section 3.3. We elaborate on certificate authentication by demonstrating advanced usage of the API in section 3.2. The core of the TLS library is presented in chapter 5 and example applications are listed in chapter 6. In chapter 7 the usage of few included programs that may assist debugging is presented. The last chapter is chapter 8 that provides a short introduction to GnuTLS' internal architecture.

---

[2]http://p11-glue.freedesktop.org/doc/p11-kit/trust-module.html

Introduction to TLS and DTLS

TLS stands for "Transport Layer Security" and is the successor of SSL, the Secure Sockets Layer protocol [13] designed by Netscape. TLS is an Internet protocol, defined by IETF[1], described in [10]. The protocol provides confidentiality, and authentication layers over any reliable transport layer. The description, above, refers to TLS 1.0 but applies to all other TLS versions as the differences between the protocols are not major.

The DTLS protocol, or "Datagram TLS" [29] is a protocol with identical goals as TLS, but can operate under unreliable transport layers such as UDP. The discussions below apply to this protocol as well, except when noted otherwise.

2.1. TLS Layers

TLS is a layered protocol, and consists of the record protocol, the handshake protocol and the alert protocol. The record protocol is to serve all other protocols and is above the transport layer. The record protocol offers symmetric encryption, data authenticity, and optionally compression. The alert protocol offers some signaling to the other protocols. It can help informing the peer for the cause of failures and other error conditions. section 2.4, for more information. The alert protocol is above the record protocol.

The handshake protocol is responsible for the security parameters' negotiation, the initial key exchange and authentication. section 2.5, for more information about the handshake protocol. The protocol layering in TLS is shown in Figure 2.1.

2.2. The Transport Layer

TLS is not limited to any transport layer and can be used above any transport layer, as long as it is a reliable one. DTLS can be used over reliable and unreliable transport layers. GnuTLS supports TCP and UDP layers transparently using the Berkeley sockets API. However, any transport layer can be used by providing callbacks for GnuTLS to access the transport layer (for details see section 5.5).

---

[1]IETF, or Internet Engineering Task Force, is a large open international community of network designers, operators, vendors, and researchers concerned with the evolution of the Internet architecture and the smooth operation of the Internet. It is open to any interested individual.

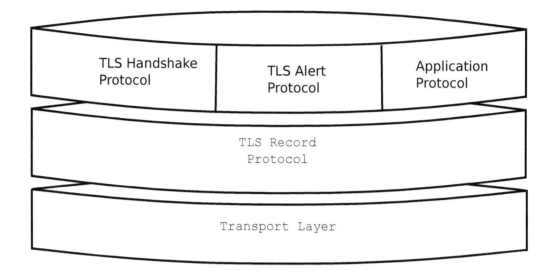

Figure 2.1.: The TLS protocol layers.

2.3. The TLS record protocol

The record protocol is the secure communications provider. Its purpose is to encrypt, authenticate and —optionally— compress packets. The record layer functions can be called at any time after the handshake process is finished, when there is need to receive or send data. In DTLS however, due to re-transmission timers used in the handshake out-of-order handshake data might be received for some time (maximum 60 seconds) after the handshake process is finished.

The functions to access the record protocol are limited to send and receive functions, which might, given the importance of this protocol in TLS, seem awkward. This is because the record protocol's parameters are all set by the handshake protocol. The record protocol initially starts with NULL parameters, which means no encryption, and no MAC is used. Encryption and authentication begin just after the handshake protocol has finished.

2.3.1. Encryption algorithms used in the record layer

Confidentiality in the record layer is achieved by using symmetric block encryption algorithms like 3DES, AES or stream algorithms like ARCFOUR_128. Ciphers are encryption algorithms that use a single, secret, key to encrypt and decrypt data. Block algorithms in CBC mode also provide protection against statistical analysis of the data. Thus, if you're using the TLS protocol, a random number of blocks will be appended to data, to prevent eavesdroppers from guessing the actual data size.

The supported in GnuTLS ciphers and MAC algorithms are shown in Table 2.1 and Table 2.2.

6

Algorithm	Description
AES_CBC	AES or RIJNDAEL is the block cipher algorithm that replaces the old DES algorithm. Has 128 bits block size and is used in CBC mode.
AES_GCM	This is the AES algorithm in the authenticated encryption GCM mode. This mode combines message authentication and encryption and can be extremely fast on CPUs that support hardware acceleration.
AES_CCM	This is the AES algorithm in the authenticated encryption CCM mode. This mode combines message authentication and encryption and is often used by systems without AES or GCM acceleration support.
AES_CCM_8	This is the AES algorithm in the authenticated encryption CCM mode with a truncated to 64-bit authentication tag. This mode is for communication with restricted systems.
CAMELLIA_CBC	This is an 128-bit block cipher developed by Mitsubishi and NTT. It is one of the approved ciphers of the European NESSIE and Japanese CRYPTREC projects.
CHACHA20_-POLY1305	CHACHA20-POLY1305 is an authenticated encryption algorithm based on CHACHA20 cipher and POLY1305 MAC. CHACHA20 is a refinement of SALSA20 algorithm, an approved cipher by the European ESTREAM project. POLY1305 is Wegman-Carter, one-time authenticator. The combination provides a fast stream cipher suitable for systems where a hardware AES accelerator is not available.
3DES_CBC	This is the DES block cipher algorithm used with triple encryption (EDE). Has 64 bits block size and is used in CBC mode.
ARCFOUR_128	ARCFOUR-128 is a compatible algorithm with RSA's RC4 algorithm, which is considered to be a trade secret. It is a fast cipher but considered weak today, and thus it is not enabled by default.

Table 2.1.: Supported ciphers.

Algorithm	Description
MAC_MD5	This is an HMAC based on MD5 a cryptographic hash algorithm designed by Ron Rivest. Outputs 128 bits of data.
MAC_SHA1	An HMAC based on the SHA1 cryptographic hash algorithm designed by NSA. Outputs 160 bits of data.
MAC_SHA256	An HMAC based on SHA256. Outputs 256 bits of data.
MAC_AEAD	This indicates that an authenticated encryption algorithm, such as GCM, is in use.

Table 2.2.: Supported MAC algorithms.

2.3.2. Compression algorithms used in the record layer

The TLS record layer also supports compression. The algorithms implemented in GnuTLS can be found in the table below. The included algorithms perform really good when text, or other compressible data are to be transferred, but offer nothing on already compressed data, such as compressed images, zipped archives etc. These compression algorithms, may be useful in high bandwidth TLS tunnels, and in cases where network usage has to be minimized. It should be noted however that compression increases latency.

The record layer compression in GnuTLS is implemented based on [15]. The supported algorithms are shown below.

```
enum gnutls_compression_method_t:
    GNUTLS_COMP_UNKNOWN          Unknown compression method.
    GNUTLS_COMP_NULL            The NULL compression method (no compression).
    GNUTLS_COMP_DEFLATE         The DEFLATE compression method from zlib.
    GNUTLS_COMP_ZLIB            Same as GNUTLS_COMP_DEFLATE.
```

Table 2.3.: Supported compression algorithms

Note that compression enables attacks such as traffic analysis, or even plaintext recovery under certain circumstances. To avoid some of these attacks GnuTLS allows each record to be compressed independently (i.e., stateless compression), by using the "%STATELESS_COMPRESSION" priority string, in order to be used in cases where the attacker controlled data are pt in separate records.

2.3.3. Weaknesses and countermeasures

Some weaknesses that may affect the security of the record layer have been found in TLS 1.0 protocol. These weaknesses can be exploited by active attackers, and exploit the facts that

1. TLS has separate alerts for "decryption_failed" and "bad_record_mac"

2. The decryption failure reason can be detected by timing the response time.

3. The IV for CBC encrypted packets is the last block of the previous encrypted packet.

Those weaknesses were solved in TLS 1.1 [9] which is implemented in GnuTLS. For this reason we suggest to always negotiate the highest supported TLS version with the peer[2]. For a detailed discussion of the issues see the archives of the TLS Working Group mailing list and [23].

---

[2]If this is not possible then please consult subsection 5.12.7.

2.3.4. On record padding

The TLS protocol allows for extra padding of records in CBC ciphers, to prevent statistical analysis based on the length of exchanged messages (see [10] section 6.2.3.2). GnuTLS appears to be one of few implementations that take advantage of this feature: the user can provide some plaintext data with a range of lengths she wishes to hide, and GnuTLS adds extra padding to make sure the attacker cannot tell the real plaintext length is in a range smaller than the user-provided one. Use `gnutls_record_send_range` to send length-hidden messages and `gnutls_record_can_use_length_hiding` to check whether the current session supports length hiding. Using the standard `gnutls_record_send` will only add minimal padding.

The TLS implementation in the Symbian operating system, frequently used by Nokia and Sony-Ericsson mobile phones, cannot handle non-minimal record padding. What happens when one of these clients handshake with a GnuTLS server is that the client will fail to compute the correct MAC for the record. The client sends a TLS alert (`bad_record_mac`) and disconnects. Typically this will result in error messages such as 'A TLS fatal alert has been received', 'Bad record MAC', or both, on the GnuTLS server side.

If compatibility with such devices is a concern, not sending length-hidden messages solves the problem by using minimal padding.

If you implement an application that has a configuration file, we recommend that you make it possible for users or administrators to specify a GnuTLS protocol priority string, which is used by your application via `gnutls_priority_set`. To allow the best flexibility, make it possible to have a different priority string for different incoming IP addresses.

2.4. The TLS alert protocol

The alert protocol is there to allow signals to be sent between peers. These signals are mostly used to inform the peer about the cause of a protocol failure. Some of these signals are used internally by the protocol and the application protocol does not have to cope with them (e.g. `GNUTLS_A_CLOSE_NOTIFY`), and others refer to the application protocol solely (e.g. `GNUTLS_A_-USER_CANCELLED`). An alert signal includes a level indication which may be either fatal or warning. Fatal alerts always terminate the current connection, and prevent future re-negotiations using the current session ID. All alert messages are summarized in the table below.

The alert messages are protected by the record protocol, thus the information that is included does not leak. You must take extreme care for the alert information not to leak to a possible attacker, via public log files etc.

Alert	ID	Description
GNUTLS_A_CLOSE_NOTIFY	0	Close notify
GNUTLS_A_UNEXPECTED_MESSAGE	10	Unexpected message
GNUTLS_A_BAD_RECORD_MAC	20	Bad record MAC
GNUTLS_A_DECRYPTION_FAILED	21	Decryption failed

GNUTLS_A_RECORD_OVERFLOW	22	Record overflow
GNUTLS_A_DECOMPRESSION_FAILURE	30	Decompression failed
GNUTLS_A_HANDSHAKE_FAILURE	40	Handshake failed
GNUTLS_A_SSL3_NO_CERTIFICATE	41	No certificate (SSL 3.0)
GNUTLS_A_BAD_CERTIFICATE	42	Certificate is bad
GNUTLS_A_UNSUPPORTED_CERTIFICATE	43	Certificate is not supported
GNUTLS_A_CERTIFICATE_REVOKED	44	Certificate was revoked
GNUTLS_A_CERTIFICATE_EXPIRED	45	Certificate is expired
GNUTLS_A_CERTIFICATE_UNKNOWN	46	Unknown certificate
GNUTLS_A_ILLEGAL_PARAMETER	47	Illegal parameter
GNUTLS_A_UNKNOWN_CA	48	CA is unknown
GNUTLS_A_ACCESS_DENIED	49	Access was denied
GNUTLS_A_DECODE_ERROR	50	Decode error
GNUTLS_A_DECRYPT_ERROR	51	Decrypt error
GNUTLS_A_EXPORT_RESTRICTION	60	Export restriction
GNUTLS_A_PROTOCOL_VERSION	70	Error in protocol version
GNUTLS_A_INSUFFICIENT_SECURITY	71	Insufficient security
GNUTLS_A_INTERNAL_ERROR	80	Internal error
GNUTLS_A_INAPPROPRIATE_FALLBACK	86	Inappropriate fallback
GNUTLS_A_USER_CANCELED	90	User canceled
GNUTLS_A_NO_RENEGOTIATION	100	No renegotiation is allowed
GNUTLS_A_UNSUPPORTED_EXTENSION	110	An unsupported extension was sent
GNUTLS_A_CERTIFICATE_UNOBTAINABLE	111	Could not retrieve the specified certificate
GNUTLS_A_UNRECOGNIZED_NAME	112	The server name sent was not recognized
GNUTLS_A_UNKNOWN_PSK_IDENTITY	115	The SRP/PSK username is missing or not known
GNUTLS_A_NO_APPLICATION_PROTOCOL	120	No supported application protocol could be negotiated

Table 2.4.: The TLS alert table

2.5. The TLS handshake protocol

The handshake protocol is responsible for the ciphersuite negotiation, the initial key exchange, and the authentication of the two peers. This is fully controlled by the application layer, thus your program has to set up the required parameters. The main handshake function is `gnutls_handshake`. In the next paragraphs we elaborate on the handshake protocol, i.e., the ciphersuite negotiation.

2.5.1. TLS ciphersuites

The handshake protocol of TLS negotiates cipher suites of a special form illustrated by the `TLS_DHE_RSA_WITH_3DES_CBC_SHA` cipher suite name. A typical cipher suite contains these parameters:

- The key exchange algorithm. `DHE_RSA` in the example.

- The Symmetric encryption algorithm and mode `3DES_CBC` in this example.

- The MAC[3] algorithm used for authentication. `MAC_SHA` is used in the above example.

The cipher suite negotiated in the handshake protocol will affect the record protocol, by enabling encryption and data authentication. Note that you should not over rely on TLS to negotiate the strongest available cipher suite. Do not enable ciphers and algorithms that you consider weak.

All the supported ciphersuites are listed in Appendix C.

2.5.2. Authentication

The key exchange algorithms of the TLS protocol offer authentication, which is a prerequisite for a secure connection. The available authentication methods in GnuTLS follow.

- Certificate authentication: Authenticated key exchange using public key infrastructure and certificates (X.509 or OpenPGP).

- SRP authentication: Authenticated key exchange using a password.

- PSK authentication: Authenticated key exchange using a pre-shared key.

- Anonymous authentication: Key exchange without peer authentication.

2.5.3. Client authentication

In the case of ciphersuites that use certificate authentication, the authentication of the client is optional in TLS. A server may request a certificate from the client using the `gnutls_certificate_server_set_request` function. We elaborate in subsection 5.4.1.

2.5.4. Resuming sessions

The TLS handshake process performs expensive calculations and a busy server might easily be put under load. To reduce the load, session resumption may be used. This is a feature of the TLS protocol which allows a client to connect to a server after a successful handshake, without the expensive calculations. This is achieved by re-using the previously established

---

[3]MAC stands for Message Authentication Code. It can be described as a keyed hash algorithm. See RFC2104.

keys, meaning the server needs to store the state of established connections (unless session tickets are used – subsection 2.6.3).

Session resumption is an integral part of GnuTLS, and subsection 5.12.1, subsection 6.1.9 illustrate typical uses of it.

2.6. TLS extensions

A number of extensions to the TLS protocol have been proposed mainly in [6]. The extensions supported in GnuTLS are discussed in the subsections that follow.

2.6.1. Maximum fragment length negotiation

This extension allows a TLS implementation to negotiate a smaller value for record packet maximum length. This extension may be useful to clients with constrained capabilities. The functions shown below can be used to control this extension.

---

size_t **gnutls_record_get_max_size** (*gnutls_session_t* **session**)

ssize_t **gnutls_record_set_max_size** (*gnutls_session_t* **session**, *size_t* **size**)

2.6.2. Server name indication

A common problem in HTTPS servers is the fact that the TLS protocol is not aware of the hostname that a client connects to, when the handshake procedure begins. For that reason the TLS server has no way to know which certificate to send.

This extension solves that problem within the TLS protocol, and allows a client to send the HTTP hostname before the handshake begins within the first handshake packet. The functions `gnutls_server_name_set` and `gnutls_server_name_get` can be used to enable this extension, or to retrieve the name sent by a client.

---

int **gnutls_server_name_set** (*gnutls_session_t* **session**, *gnutls_server_name_type_t* **type**, *const void* * **name**, *size_t* **name_length**)

int **gnutls_server_name_get** (*gnutls_session_t* **session**, *void* * **data**, *size_t* * **data_length**, *unsigned int* * **type**, *unsigned int* **indx**)

2.6.3. Session tickets

To resume a TLS session, the server normally stores session parameters. This complicates deployment, and can be avoided by delegating the storage to the client. Because session parameters are sensitive they are encrypted and authenticated with a key only known to the server and then sent to the client. The Session Tickets extension is described in RFC 5077 [33].

A disadvantage of session tickets is that they eliminate the effects of forward secrecy when a server uses the same key for long time. That is, the secrecy of all sessions on a server using tickets depends on the ticket key being kept secret. For that reason server keys should be rotated and discarded regularly.

Since version 3.1.3 GnuTLS clients transparently support session tickets, unless forward secrecy is explicitly requested (with the PFS priority string).

2.6.4. HeartBeat

This is a TLS extension that allows to ping and receive confirmation from the peer, and is described in [27]. The extension is disabled by default and `gnutls_heartbeat_enable` can be used to enable it. A policy may be negotiated to only allow sending heartbeat messages or sending and receiving. The current session policy can be checked with `gnutls_heartbeat_allowed`. The requests coming from the peer result to `GNUTLS_E_HEARTBEAT_PING_RECEIVED` being returned from the receive function. Ping requests to peer can be send via `gnutls_heartbeat_ping`.

---

int **gnutls_heartbeat_allowed** (*gnutls_session_t* **session**, *unsigned int* **type**)

void **gnutls_heartbeat_enable** (*gnutls_session_t* **session**, *unsigned int* **type**)

---

int **gnutls_heartbeat_ping** (*gnutls_session_t* **session**, *size_t* **data_size**, *unsigned int* **max_tries**, *unsigned int* **flags**)

int **gnutls_heartbeat_pong** (*gnutls_session_t* **session**, *unsigned int* **flags**)

void **gnutls_heartbeat_set_timeouts** (*gnutls_session_t* **session**, *unsigned* *int* **retrans_timeout**, *unsigned int* **total_timeout**)

unsigned int **gnutls_heartbeat_get_timeout** (*gnutls_session_t* **session**)

2.6.5. Safe renegotiation

TLS gives the option to two communicating parties to renegotiate and update their security parameters. One useful example of this feature was for a client to initially connect using anonymous negotiation to a server, and the renegotiate using some authenticated ciphersuite. This occurred to avoid having the client sending its credentials in the clear.

However this renegotiation, as initially designed would not ensure that the party one is renegotiating is the same as the one in the initial negotiation. For example one server could forward all renegotiation traffic to an other server who will see this traffic as an initial negotiation attempt.

This might be seen as a valid design decision, but it seems it was not widely known or understood, thus today some application protocols use the TLS renegotiation feature in a manner that enables a malicious server to insert content of his choice in the beginning of a TLS session.

The most prominent vulnerability was with HTTPS. There servers request a renegotiation to enforce an anonymous user to use a certificate in order to access certain parts of a web site. The attack works by having the attacker simulate a client and connect to a server, with server-only authentication, and send some data intended to cause harm. The server will then require renegotiation from him in order to perform the request. When the proper client attempts to contact the server, the attacker hijacks that connection and forwards traffic to the initial server that requested renegotiation. The attacker will not be able to read the data exchanged between the client and the server. However, the server will (incorrectly) assume that the initial request sent by the attacker was sent by the now authenticated client. The result is a prefix plain-text injection attack.

The above is just one example. Other vulnerabilities exists that do not rely on the TLS renegotiation to change the client's authenticated status (either TLS or application layer).

While fixing these application protocols and implementations would be one natural reaction, an extension to TLS has been designed that cryptographically binds together any renegotiated handshakes with the initial negotiation. When the extension is used, the attack is detected and the session can be terminated. The extension is specified in [30].

GnuTLS supports the safe renegotiation extension. The default behavior is as follows. Clients will attempt to negotiate the safe renegotiation extension when talking to servers. Servers will accept the extension when presented by clients. Clients and servers will permit an initial handshake to complete even when the other side does not support the safe renegotiation extension. Clients and servers will refuse renegotiation attempts when the extension has not been negotiated.

Note that permitting clients to connect to servers when the safe renegotiation extension is not enabled, is open up for attacks. Changing this default behavior would prevent interoperability against the majority of deployed servers out there. We will reconsider this default behavior in the future when more servers have been upgraded. Note that it is easy to configure clients to always require the safe renegotiation extension from servers.

To modify the default behavior, we have introduced some new priority strings (see section 5.10). The %UNSAFE_RENEGOTIATION priority string permits (re-)handshakes even when the safe renegotiation extension was not negotiated. The default behavior is `%PARTIAL_RENEGOTIATION` that will prevent renegotiation with clients and servers not supporting the extension. This is secure for servers but leaves clients vulnerable to some attacks, but this is a trade-off between security and compatibility with old servers. The `%SAFE_RENEGOTIATION` priority string makes clients and servers require the extension for every handshake. The latter is the most secure option for clients, at the cost of not being able to connect to legacy servers. Servers will also deny clients that do not support the extension from connecting.

It is possible to disable use of the extension completely, in both clients and servers, by using the `%DISABLE_SAFE_RENEGOTIATION` priority string however we strongly recommend you to only do this for debugging and test purposes.

The default values if the flags above are not specified are:

- Server: %PARTIAL_RENEGOTIATION
- Client: %PARTIAL_RENEGOTIATION

For applications we have introduced a new API related to safe renegotiation. The `gnutls_safe_renegotiation_status` function is used to check if the extension has been negotiated on a session, and can be used both by clients and servers.

2.6.6. OCSP status request

The Online Certificate Status Protocol (OCSP) is a protocol that allows the client to verify the server certificate for revocation without messing with certificate revocation lists. Its drawback is that it requires the client to connect to the server's CA OCSP server and request the status of the certificate. This extension however, enables a TLS server to include its CA OCSP server response in the handshake. That is an HTTPS server may periodically run `ocsptool` (see subsection 3.2.6) to obtain its certificate revocation status and serve it to the clients. That way a client avoids an additional connection to the OCSP server.

---

void **gnutls_certificate_set_ocsp_status_request_function** (*gnutls_certificate_credentials_t* **sc,** *gnutls_status_request_ocsp_func* **ocsp_func,** *void* *** ptr**)

int **gnutls_certificate_set_ocsp_status_request_file** (*gnutls_certificate_credentials_t* **sc,** *const char* *** response_file,** *unsigned int* **flags**)

int **gnutls_ocsp_status_request_enable_client** (*gnutls_session_t* **session,** *gnutls_datum_t* *** responder_id,** *size_t* **responder_id_size,** *gnutls_datum_t* *** extensions**)

int **gnutls_ocsp_status_request_is_checked** (*gnutls_session_t* **session,** *unsigned int* **flags**)

A server is required to provide the OCSP server's response using the **gnutls_certificate_** set_ocsp_status_request_file. The response may be obtained periodically using the following command.

```
1  ocsptool --ask --load-cert server_cert.pem --load-issuer the_issuer.pem
2          --load-signer the_issuer.pem --outfile ocsp.response
```

Since version 3.1.3 GnuTLS clients transparently support the certificate status request.

2.6.7. SRTP

The TLS protocol was extended in [22] to provide keying material to the Secure RTP (SRTP) protocol. The SRTP protocol provides an encapsulation of encrypted data that is optimized for voice data. With the SRTP TLS extension two peers can negotiate keys using TLS or DTLS and obtain keying material for use with SRTP. The available SRTP profiles are listed below.

enum **gnutls_srtp_profile_t**:	
GNUTLS_SRTP_AES128_CM_HMAC_-SHA1_80	128 bit AES with a 80 bit HMAC-SHA1
GNUTLS_SRTP_AES128_CM_HMAC_-SHA1_32	128 bit AES with a 32 bit HMAC-SHA1
GNUTLS_SRTP_NULL_HMAC_SHA1_80	NULL cipher with a 80 bit HMAC-SHA1
GNUTLS_SRTP_NULL_HMAC_SHA1_32	NULL cipher with a 32 bit HMAC-SHA1

Table 2.5.: Supported SRTP profiles

To enable use the following functions.

int **gnutls_srtp_set_profile** (*gnutls_session_t* **session**, *gnutls_srtp_profile_t* **profile**)

int **gnutls_srtp_set_profile_direct** (*gnutls_session_t* **session**, *const char* * **profiles**, *const char* ** **err_pos**)

To obtain the negotiated keys use the function below.

Other helper functions are listed below.

> *int* **gnutls_srtp_get_keys** (*gnutls_session_t* **session**, *void* * **key_material**, *unsigned int* **key_material_size**, *gnutls_datum_t* * **client_key**, *gnutls_datum_t* * **client_salt**, *gnutls_datum_t* * **server_key**, *gnutls_datum_t* * **server_salt**)
>
> **Description:** `This is a helper function to generate the keying material for SRTP. It requires the space of the key material to be pre-allocated (should be at least 2x the maximum key size and salt size).` The **client_key**, **client_salt**, **server_key** and **server_salt** are `convenience datums that point inside the key material. They may be` **NULL**.
>
> **Returns:** `On success the size of the key material is returned, otherwise,` **GNUTLS_E_SHORT_MEMORY_BUFFER** `if the buffer given is not sufficient, or a negative error code. Since 3.1.4`

> *int* **gnutls_srtp_get_selected_profile** (*gnutls_session_t* **session**, *gnutls_srtp_profile_t* * **profile**)
>
> *const char* * **gnutls_srtp_get_profile_name** (*gnutls_srtp_profile_t* **profile**)
>
> *int* **gnutls_srtp_get_profile_id** (*const char* * **name**, *gnutls_srtp_profile_t* * **profile**)

2.6.8. Application Layer Protocol Negotiation (ALPN)

The TLS protocol was extended in `RFC7301` to provide the application layer a method of negotiating the application protocol version. This allows for negotiation of the application protocol during the TLS handshake, thus reducing round-trips. The application protocol is described by an opaque string. To enable, use the following functions.

> *int* **gnutls_alpn_set_protocols** (*gnutls_session_t* **session**, *const gnutls_datum_t* * **protocols**, *unsigned* **protocols_size**, *unsigned int* **flags**)
>
> *int* **gnutls_alpn_get_selected_protocol** (*gnutls_session_t* **session**, *gnutls_datum_t* * **protocol**)

Note that these functions are intended to be used with protocols that are registered in the Application Layer Protocol Negotiation IANA registry. While you can use them for other protocols (at the risk of collisions), it is preferable to register them.

2.6.9. Extensions and Supplemental Data

It is possible to transfer supplemental data during the TLS handshake, following [34]. This is for "custom" protocol modifications for applications which may want to transfer additional data (e.g. additional authentication messages). Such an exchange requires a custom extension to be registered. The provided API for this functionality is low-level and described in section 8.4.

2.7. How to use TLS in application protocols

This chapter is intended to provide some hints on how to use TLS over simple custom made application protocols. The discussion below mainly refers to the TCP/IP transport layer but may be extended to other ones too.

2.7.1. Separate ports

Traditionally SSL was used in application protocols by assigning a new port number for the secure services. By doing this two separate ports were assigned, one for the non-secure sessions, and one for the secure sessions. This method ensures that if a user requests a secure session then the client will attempt to connect to the secure port and fail otherwise. The only possible attack with this method is to perform a denial of service attack. The most famous example of this method is "HTTP over TLS" or HTTPS protocol [28].

Despite its wide use, this method has several issues. This approach starts the TLS Handshake procedure just after the client connects on the —so called— secure port. That way the TLS protocol does not know anything about the client, and popular methods like the host advertising in HTTP do not work[4]. There is no way for the client to say "I connected to YYY server" before the Handshake starts, so the server cannot possibly know which certificate to use.

Other than that it requires two separate ports to run a single service, which is unnecessary complication. Due to the fact that there is a limitation on the available privileged ports, this approach was soon deprecated in favor of upward negotiation.

2.7.2. Upward negotiation

Other application protocols[5] use a different approach to enable the secure layer. They use something often called as the "TLS upgrade" method. This method is quite tricky but it is more flexible. The idea is to extend the application protocol to have a "STARTTLS" request, whose purpose it to start the TLS protocols just after the client requests it. This approach does not require any extra port to be reserved. There is even an extension to HTTP protocol to support this method [17].

---

[4]See also the Server Name Indication extension on subsection 2.6.2.
[5]See LDAP, IMAP etc.

The tricky part, in this method, is that the "STARTTLS" request is sent in the clear, thus is vulnerable to modifications. A typical attack is to modify the messages in a way that the client is fooled and thinks that the server does not have the "STARTTLS" capability. See a typical conversation of a hypothetical protocol:

(client connects to the server)

CLIENT: HELLO I'M MR. XXX

SERVER: NICE TO MEET YOU XXX

CLIENT: PLEASE START TLS

SERVER: OK

*** TLS STARTS

CLIENT: HERE ARE SOME CONFIDENTIAL DATA

And an example of a conversation where someone is acting in between:

(client connects to the server)

CLIENT: HELLO I'M MR. XXX

SERVER: NICE TO MEET YOU XXX

CLIENT: PLEASE START TLS

(here someone inserts this message)

SERVER: SORRY I DON'T HAVE THIS CAPABILITY

CLIENT: HERE ARE SOME CONFIDENTIAL DATA

As you can see above the client was fooled, and was naïve enough to send the confidential data in the clear, despite the server telling the client that it does not support "STARTTLS".

How do we avoid the above attack? As you may have already noticed this situation is easy to avoid. The client has to ask the user before it connects whether the user requests TLS or not. If the user answered that he certainly wants the secure layer the last conversation should be:

(client connects to the server)

CLIENT: HELLO I'M MR. XXX

SERVER: NICE TO MEET YOU XXX

CLIENT: PLEASE START TLS

(here someone inserts this message)

SERVER: SORRY I DON'T HAVE THIS CAPABILITY

CLIENT: BYE

(the client notifies the user that the secure connection was not possible)

This method, if implemented properly, is far better than the traditional method, and the security properties remain the same, since only denial of service is possible. The benefit is that the server may request additional data before the TLS Handshake protocol starts, in order to send the correct certificate, use the correct password file, or anything else!

2.8. On SSL 2 and older protocols

One of the initial decisions in the GnuTLS development was to implement the known security protocols for the transport layer. Initially TLS 1.0 was implemented since it was the latest at that time, and was considered to be the most advanced in security properties. Later the SSL 3.0 protocol was implemented since it is still the only protocol supported by several servers and there are no serious security vulnerabilities known.

One question that may arise is why we didn't implement SSL 2.0 in the library. There are several reasons, most important being that it has serious security flaws, unacceptable for a modern security library. Other than that, this protocol is barely used by anyone these days since it has been deprecated since 1996. The security problems in SSL 2.0 include:

- Message integrity compromised. The SSLv2 message authentication uses the MD5 function, and is insecure.

- Man-in-the-middle attack. There is no protection of the handshake in SSLv2, which permits a man-in-the-middle attack.

- Truncation attack. SSLv2 relies on TCP FIN to close the session, so the attacker can forge a TCP FIN, and the peer cannot tell if it was a legitimate end of data or not.

- Weak message integrity for export ciphers. The cryptographic keys in SSLv2 are used for both message authentication and encryption, so if weak encryption schemes are negotiated (say 40-bit keys) the message authentication code uses the same weak key, which isn't necessary.

Other protocols such as Microsoft's PCT 1 and PCT 2 were not implemented because they were also abandoned and deprecated by SSL 3.0 and later TLS 1.0.

3

Authentication methods

The initial key exchange of the TLS protocol performs authentication of the peers. In typical scenarios the server is authenticated to the client, and optionally the client to the server.

While many associate TLS with X.509 certificates and public key authentication, the protocol supports various authentication methods, including pre-shared keys, and passwords. In this chapter a description of the existing authentication methods is provided, as well as some guidance on which use-cases each method can be used at.

3.1. Certificate authentication

The most known authentication method of TLS are certificates. The PKIX [16] public key infrastructure is daily used by anyone using a browser today. GnuTLS supports both X.509 certificates [16] and OpenPGP certificates using a common API.

The key exchange algorithms supported by certificate authentication are shown in Table 3.1.

3.1.1. X.509 certificates

The X.509 protocols rely on a hierarchical trust model. In this trust model Certification Authorities (CAs) are used to certify entities. Usually more than one certification authorities exist, and certification authorities may certify other authorities to issue certificates as well, following a hierarchical model.

One needs to trust one or more CAs for his secure communications. In that case only the certificates issued by the trusted authorities are acceptable. The framework is illustrated on Figure 3.1.

X.509 certificate structure

An X.509 certificate usually contains information about the certificate holder, the signer, a unique serial number, expiration dates and some other fields [16] as shown in Table 3.2.

The certificate's *subject or issuer name* is not just a single string. It is a Distinguished name and in the ASN.1 notation is a sequence of several object identifiers with their corresponding

Key exchange	Description
RSA	The RSA algorithm is used to encrypt a key and send it to the peer. The certificate must allow the key to be used for encryption.
DHE_RSA	The RSA algorithm is used to sign ephemeral Diffie-Hellman parameters which are sent to the peer. The key in the certificate must allow the key to be used for signing. Note that key exchange algorithms which use ephemeral Diffie-Hellman parameters, offer perfect forward secrecy. That means that even if the private key used for signing is compromised, it cannot be used to reveal past session data.
ECDHE_RSA	The RSA algorithm is used to sign ephemeral elliptic curve Diffie-Hellman parameters which are sent to the peer. The key in the certificate must allow the key to be used for signing. It also offers perfect forward secrecy. That means that even if the private key used for signing is compromised, it cannot be used to reveal past session data.
DHE_DSS	The DSA algorithm is used to sign ephemeral Diffie-Hellman parameters which are sent to the peer. The certificate must contain DSA parameters to use this key exchange algorithm. DSA is the algorithm of the Digital Signature Standard (DSS).
ECDHE_ECDSA	The Elliptic curve DSA algorithm is used to sign ephemeral elliptic curve Diffie-Hellman parameters which are sent to the peer. The certificate must contain ECDSA parameters (i.e., EC and marked for signing) to use this key exchange algorithm.

Table 3.1.: Supported key exchange algorithms.

Field	Description
version	The field that indicates the version of the certificate.
serialNumber	This field holds a unique serial number per certificate.
signature	The issuing authority's signature.
issuer	Holds the issuer's distinguished name.
validity	The activation and expiration dates.
subject	The subject's distinguished name of the certificate.
extensions	The extensions are fields only present in version 3 certificates.

Table 3.2.: X.509 certificate fields.

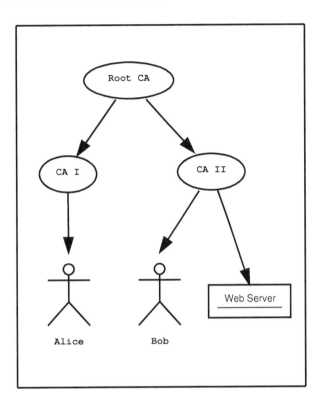

Figure 3.1.: An example of the X.509 hierarchical trust model.

values. Some of available OIDs to be used in an X.509 distinguished name are defined in "gnutls/x509.h".

The *Version* field in a certificate has values either 1 or 3 for version 3 certificates. Version 1 certificates do not support the extensions field so it is not possible to distinguish a CA from a person, thus their usage should be avoided.

The *validity* dates are there to indicate the date that the specific certificate was activated and the date the certificate's key would be considered invalid.

In GnuTLS the X.509 certificate structures are handled using the **gnutls_x509_crt_t** type and the corresponding private keys with the **gnutls_x509_privkey_t** type. All the available functions for X.509 certificate handling have their prototypes in "gnutls/x509.h". An example program to demonstrate the X.509 parsing capabilities can be found in subsection 6.4.2.

Importing an X.509 certificate

The certificate structure should be initialized using **gnutls_x509_crt_init**, and a certificate structure can be imported using **gnutls_x509_crt_import**.

---

int **gnutls_x509_crt_init** (*gnutls_x509_crt_t* * **cert**)

int **gnutls_x509_crt_import** (*gnutls_x509_crt_t* **cert**, *const gnutls_datum_t* * **data**, *gnutls_x509_crt_fmt_t* **format**)

void **gnutls_x509_crt_deinit** (*gnutls_x509_crt_t* **cert**)

In several functions an array of certificates is required. To assist in initialization and import the following two functions are provided.

---

int **gnutls_x509_crt_list_import** (*gnutls_x509_crt_t* * **certs**, *unsigned int* * **cert_max**, *const gnutls_datum_t* * **data**, *gnutls_x509_crt_fmt_t* **format**, *unsigned int* **flags**)

int **gnutls_x509_crt_list_import2** (*gnutls_x509_crt_t* ** **certs**, *unsigned int* * **size**, *const gnutls_datum_t* * **data**, *gnutls_x509_crt_fmt_t* **format**, *unsigned int* **flags**)

In all cases after use a certificate must be deinitialized using `gnutls_x509_crt_deinit`. Note that although the functions above apply to `gnutls_x509_crt_t` structure, similar functions exist for the CRL structure `gnutls_x509_crl_t`.

X.509 certificate names

X.509 certificates allow for multiple names and types of names to be specified. CA certificates often rely on X.509 distinguished names (see section 3.1.1) for unique identification, while end-user and server certificates rely on the 'subject alternative names'. The subject alternative names provide a typed name, e.g., a DNS name, or an email address, which identifies the owner of the certificate. The following functions provide access to that names.

---

int **gnutls_x509_crt_get_subject_alt_name2** (*gnutls_x509_crt_t* **cert**, *unsigned int* **seq**, *void* * **san**, *size_t* * **san_size**, *unsigned int* * **san_type**, *unsigned int* * **critical**)

int **gnutls_x509_crt_set_subject_alt_name** (*gnutls_x509_crt_t* **crt**, *gnutls_x509_subject_alt_name_t* **type**, *const void* * **data**, *unsigned int* **data_size**, *unsigned int* **flags**)

24

---

int **gnutls_subject_alt_names_init** (*gnutls_subject_alt_names_t* * **sans**)

int **gnutls_subject_alt_names_get** (*gnutls_subject_alt_names_t* **sans**, *unsigned int* **seq**, *unsigned int* * **san_type**, *gnutls_datum_t* * **san**, *gnutls_datum_t* * **othername_oid**)

int **gnutls_subject_alt_names_set** (*gnutls_subject_alt_names_t* **sans**, *unsigned int* **san_type**, *const gnutls_datum_t* * **san**, *const char* * **othername_oid**)

Note however, that server certificates often used the Common Name (CN), part of the certificate DistinguishedName to place a single DNS address. That practice is discouraged (see [32]), because only a single address can be specified, and the CN field is free-form making matching ambiguous.

X.509 distinguished names

The "subject" of an X.509 certificate is not described by a single name, but rather with a distinguished name. This in X.509 terminology is a list of strings each associated an object identifier. To make things simple GnuTLS provides **gnutls_x509_crt_get_dn2** which follows the rules in [41] and returns a single string. Access to each string by individual object identifiers can be accessed using **gnutls_x509_crt_get_dn_by_oid**.

---

int **gnutls_x509_crt_get_dn2** (*gnutls_x509_crt_t* **cert**, *gnutls_datum_t* * **dn**)

Description: This function will allocate buffer and copy the name of the Certificate. The name will be in the form "C=xxxx,O=yyyy,CN=zzzz" as described in RFC4514. The output string will be ASCII or UTF-8 encoded, depending on the certificate data.

Returns: On success, **GNUTLS_E_SUCCESS** (0) is returned, otherwise a negative error value.

---

int **gnutls_x509_crt_get_dn** (*gnutls_x509_crt_t* **cert**, *char* * **buf**, *size_t* * **buf_size**)

int **gnutls_x509_crt_get_dn_by_oid** (*gnutls_x509_crt_t* **cert**, *const char* * **oid**, *int* **indx**, *unsigned int* **raw_flag**, *void* * **buf**, *size_t* * **buf_size**)

int **gnutls_x509_crt_get_dn_oid** (*gnutls_x509_crt_t* **cert**, *int* **indx**, *void* * **oid**, *size_t* * **oid_size**)

Similar functions exist to access the distinguished name of the issuer of the certificate.

---

int **gnutls_x509_crt_get_issuer_dn** (*gnutls_x509_crt_t* **cert**, *char* * **buf**, *size_t* * **buf_size**)

int **gnutls_x509_crt_get_issuer_dn2** (*gnutls_x509_crt_t* **cert**, *gnutls_datum_t* * **dn**)

int **gnutls_x509_crt_get_issuer_dn_by_oid** (*gnutls_x509_crt_t* **cert**, *const char* * **oid**, *int* **indx**, *unsigned int* **raw_flag**, *void* * **buf**, *size_t* * **buf_size**)

int **gnutls_x509_crt_get_issuer_dn_oid** (*gnutls_x509_crt_t* **cert**, *int* **indx**, *void* * **oid**, *size_t* * **oid_size**)

int **gnutls_x509_crt_get_issuer** (*gnutls_x509_crt_t* **cert**, *gnutls_x509_dn_t* * **dn**)

The more powerful `gnutls_x509_crt_get_subject` and `gnutls_x509_dn_get_rdn_ava` provide efficient but low-level access to the contents of the distinguished name structure.

---

int **gnutls_x509_crt_get_subject** (*gnutls_x509_crt_t* **cert**, *gnutls_x509_dn_t* * **dn**)

int **gnutls_x509_crt_get_issuer** (*gnutls_x509_crt_t* **cert**, *gnutls_x509_dn_t* * **dn**)

---

int **gnutls_x509_dn_get_rdn_ava** (*gnutls_x509_dn_t* **dn**, *int* **irdn**, *int* **iava**, *gnutls_x509_ava_st* * **ava**)

Description: Get pointers to data within the DN. The format of the ava structure is shown below. struct gnutls_x509_ava_st gnutls_datum_t oid; gnutls_datum_t value; unsigned long value_tag; ; The X.509 distinguished name is a sequence of sequences of strings and this is what the irdn and iava indexes model. Note that ava will contain pointers into the dn structure which in turns points to the original certificate. Thus you should not modify any data or deallocate any of those. This is a low-level function that requires the caller to do the value conversions when necessary (e.g. from UCS-2).

Returns: Returns 0 on success, or an error code.

X.509 extensions

X.509 version 3 certificates include a list of extensions that can be used to obtain additional information on the subject or the issuer of the certificate. Those may be e-mail addresses, flags that indicate whether the belongs to a CA etc. All the supported X.509 version 3 extensions are shown in Table 3.3.

The certificate extensions access is split into two parts. The first requires to retrieve the extension, and the second is the parsing part.

To enumerate and retrieve the DER-encoded extension data available in a certificate the following two functions are available.

---

int **gnutls_x509_crt_get_extension_info** (*gnutls_x509_crt_t* **cert**, *int* **indx**, *void* * **oid**, *size_t* * **oid_size**, *unsigned int* * **critical**)

int **gnutls_x509_crt_get_extension_data2** (*gnutls_x509_crt_t* **cert**, *unsigned* **indx**, *gnutls_datum_t* * **data**)

int **gnutls_x509_crt_get_extension_by_oid2** (*gnutls_x509_crt_t* **cert**, *const char* * **oid**, *int* **indx**, *gnutls_datum_t* * **output**, *unsigned int* * **critical**)

After a supported DER-encoded extension is retrieved it can be parsed using the APIs in `x509-ext.h`. Complex extensions may require initializing an intermediate structure that holds the parsed extension data. Examples of simple parsing functions are shown below.

---

int **gnutls_x509_ext_import_basic_constraints** (*const gnutls_datum_t* * **ext**, *unsigned int* * **ca**, *int* * **pathlen**)

int **gnutls_x509_ext_export_basic_constraints** (*unsigned int* **ca**, *int* **pathlen**, *gnutls_datum_t* * **ext**)

int **gnutls_x509_ext_import_key_usage** (*const gnutls_datum_t* * **ext**, *unsigned int* * **key_usage**)

int **gnutls_x509_ext_export_key_usage** (*unsigned int* **usage**, *gnutls_datum_t* * **ext**)

More complex extensions, such as Name Constraints, require an intermediate structure, in that case `gnutls_x509_name_constraints_t` to be initialized in order to store the parsed extension data.

---

int **gnutls_x509_ext_import_name_constraints** (*const* *gnutls_datum_t* * **ext,** *gnutls_x509_name_constraints_t* **nc,** *unsigned int* **flags**)

int **gnutls_x509_ext_export_name_constraints** (*gnutls_x509_name_constraints_t* **nc,** *gnutls_datum_t* * **ext**)

After the name constraints are extracted in the structure, the following functions can be used to access them.

---

int **gnutls_x509_name_constraints_get_permitted** (*gnutls_x509_name_constraints_t* **nc,** *unsigned* **idx,** *unsigned* * **type,** *gnutls_datum_t* * **name**)

int **gnutls_x509_name_constraints_get_excluded** (*gnutls_x509_name_constraints_t* **nc,** *unsigned* **idx,** *unsigned* * **type,** *gnutls_datum_t* * **name**)

int **gnutls_x509_name_constraints_add_permitted** (*gnutls_x509_name_constraints_t* **nc,** *gnutls_x509_subject_alt_name_t* **type,** *const gnutls_datum_t* * **name**)

int **gnutls_x509_name_constraints_add_excluded** (*gnutls_x509_name_constraints_t* **nc,** *gnutls_x509_subject_alt_name_t* **type,** *const gnutls_datum_t* * **name**)

---

unsigned **gnutls_x509_name_constraints_check** (*gnutls_x509_name_constraints_t* **nc,** *gnutls_x509_subject_alt_name_t* **type,** *const gnutls_datum_t* * **name**)

unsigned **gnutls_x509_name_constraints_check_crt** (*gnutls_x509_name_constraints_t* **nc,** *gnutls_x509_subject_alt_name_t* **type,** *gnutls_x509_crt_t* **cert**)

Other utility functions are listed below.

---

int **gnutls_x509_name_constraints_init** (*gnutls_x509_name_constraints_t* * **nc**)

void **gnutls_x509_name_constraints_deinit** (*gnutls_x509_name_constraints_t* **nc**)

Similar functions exist for all of the other supported extensions, listed in Table 3.3.

Note, that there are also direct APIs to access extensions that may be simpler to use for non-complex extensions. They are available in **x509.h** and some examples are listed below.

Extension	OID	Description
Subject key id	2.5.29.14	An identifier of the key of the subject.
Key usage	2.5.29.15	Constraints the key's usage of the certificate.
Private key usage period	2.5.29.16	Constraints the validity time of the private key.
Subject alternative name	2.5.29.17	Alternative names to subject's distinguished name.
Issuer alternative name	2.5.29.18	Alternative names to the issuer's distinguished name.
Basic constraints	2.5.29.19	Indicates whether this is a CA certificate or not, and specify the maximum path lengths of certificate chains.
Name constraints	2.5.29.30	A field in CA certificates that restricts the scope of the name of issued certificates.
CRL distribution points	2.5.29.31	This extension is set by the CA, in order to inform about the issued CRLs.
Certificate policy	2.5.29.32	This extension is set to indicate the certificate policy as object identifier and may contain a descriptive string or URL.
Authority key identifier	2.5.29.35	An identifier of the key of the issuer of the certificate. That is used to distinguish between different keys of the same issuer.
Extended key usage	2.5.29.37	Constraints the purpose of the certificate.
Authority information access	1.3.6.1.5.5.7.1.1	Information on services by the issuer of the certificate.
Proxy Certification Information	1.3.6.1.5.5.7.1.14	Proxy Certificates includes this extension that contains the OID of the proxy policy language used, and can specify limits on the maximum lengths of proxy chains. Proxy Certificates are specified in [37].

Table 3.3.: Supported X.509 certificate extensions.

---

int **gnutls_x509_crt_get_basic_constraints** (*gnutls_x509_crt_t* **cert**, *unsigned int* * **critical**, *unsigned int* * **ca**, *int* * **pathlen**)

int **gnutls_x509_crt_set_basic_constraints** (*gnutls_x509_crt_t* **crt**, *unsigned int* **ca**, *int* **pathLenConstraint**)

int **gnutls_x509_crt_get_key_usage** (*gnutls_x509_crt_t* **cert**, *unsigned int* * **key_usage**, *unsigned int* * **critical**)

int **gnutls_x509_crt_set_key_usage** (*gnutls_x509_crt_t* **crt**, *unsigned int* **usage**)

Accessing public and private keys

Each X.509 certificate contains a public key that corresponds to a private key. To get a unique identifier of the public key the **gnutls_x509_crt_get_key_id** function is provided. To export the public key or its parameters you may need to convert the X.509 structure to a **gnutls_pubkey_t**. See subsection 4.1.1 for more information.

---

int **gnutls_x509_crt_get_key_id** (*gnutls_x509_crt_t* **crt**, *unsigned int* **flags**, *unsigned char* * **output_data**, *size_t* * **output_data_size**)

Description: This function will return a unique ID that depends on the public key parameters. This ID can be used in checking whether a certificate corresponds to the given private key. If the buffer provided is not long enough to hold the output, then *output_data_size is updated and GNUTLS_E_SHORT_MEMORY_BUFFER will be returned. The output will normally be a SHA-1 hash output, which is 20 bytes.

Returns: In case of failure a negative error code will be returned, and 0 on success.

The private key parameters may be directly accessed by using one of the following functions.

---

int **gnutls_x509_privkey_get_pk_algorithm2** (*gnutls_x509_privkey_t* **key**, *unsigned int* * **bits**)

int **gnutls_x509_privkey_export_rsa_raw2** (*gnutls_x509_privkey_t* **key**, *gnutls_datum_t* * **m**, *gnutls_datum_t* * **e**, *gnutls_datum_t* * **d**, *gnutls_datum_t* * **p**, *gnutls_datum_t* * **q**, *gnutls_datum_t* * **u**, *gnutls_datum_t* * **e1**, *gnutls_datum_t* * **e2**)

int **gnutls_x509_privkey_export_ecc_raw** (*gnutls_x509_privkey_t* **key**, *gnutls_ecc_curve_t* * **curve**, *gnutls_datum_t* * **x**, *gnutls_datum_t* * **y**, *gnutls_datum_t* * **k**)

int **gnutls_x509_privkey_export_dsa_raw** (*gnutls_x509_privkey_t* **key**, *gnutls_datum_t* * **p**, *gnutls_datum_t* * **q**, *gnutls_datum_t* * **g**, *gnutls_datum_t* * **y**, *gnutls_datum_t* * **x**)

int **gnutls_x509_privkey_get_key_id** (*gnutls_x509_privkey_t* **key**, *unsigned int* **flags**, *unsigned char* * **output_data**, *size_t* * **output_data_size**)

Verifying X.509 certificate paths

Verifying certificate paths is important in X.509 authentication. For this purpose the following functions are provided.

---

int **gnutls_x509_trust_list_add_cas** (*gnutls_x509_trust_list_t* **list**, *const gnutls_x509_crt_t* * **clist**, *unsigned* **clist_size**, *unsigned int* **flags**)

Description: This function will add the given certificate authorities to the trusted list. The list of CAs must not be deinitialized during this structure's lifetime. If the flag GNUTLS_TL_NO_DUPLICATES is specified, then the provided clist entries that are duplicates will not be added to the list and will be deinitialized.

Returns: The number of added elements is returned.

The verification function will verify a given certificate chain against a list of certificate authorities and certificate revocation lists, and output a bit-wise OR of elements of the gnutls_certificate_status_t enumeration shown in Table 3.4. The GNUTLS_CERT_INVALID flag is always set on a verification error and more detailed flags will also be set when appropriate.

An example of certificate verification is shown in subsection 6.1.7. It is also possible to have a set of certificates that are trusted for a particular server but not to authorize other certificates. This purpose is served by the functions gnutls_x509_trust_list_add_named_crt and gnutls_x509_trust_list_verify_named_crt.

int **gnutls_x509_trust_list_add_named_crt** (*gnutls_x509_trust_list_t* **list**, *gnutls_x509_crt_t* **cert**, *const void ** **name**, *size_t* **name_size**, *unsigned int* **flags**)

Description: This function will add the given certificate to the trusted list and associate it with a name. The certificate will not be be used for verification with gnutls_x509_trust_list_verify_crt() but with gnutls_x509_trust_list_verify_named_crt() or gnutls_x509_trust_list_verify_crt2() - the latter only since GnuTLS 3.4.0 and if a hostname is provided. In principle this function can be used to set individual "server" certificates that are trusted by the user for that specific server but for no other purposes. The certificate must not be deinitialized during the lifetime of the trusted list.

Returns: On success, **GNUTLS_E_SUCCESS** (0) is returned, otherwise a negative error value.

---

int **gnutls_x509_trust_list_add_crls** (*gnutls_x509_trust_list_t* **list**, *const gnutls_x509_crl_t* *** crl_list**, *int* **crl_size**, *unsigned int* **flags**, *unsigned int* **verification_flags**)

Description: This function will add the given certificate revocation lists to the trusted list. The list of CRLs must not be deinitialized during this structure's lifetime. This function must be called after gnutls_x509_trust_list_add_cas() to allow verifying the CRLs for validity. If the flag **GNUTLS_TL_NO_DUPLICATES** is given, then any provided CRLs that are a duplicate, will be deinitialized and not added to the list (that assumes that gnutls_x509_trust_list_deinit() will be called with all=1).

Returns: The number of added elements is returned.

---

int **gnutls_x509_trust_list_verify_crt** (*gnutls_x509_trust_list_t* **list**, *gnutls_x509_crt_t* *** cert_list**, *unsigned int* **cert_list_size**, *unsigned int* **flags**, *unsigned int ** **voutput**, *gnutls_verify_output_function* **func**)

Description: This function will try to verify the given certificate and return its status. The **voutput** parameter will hold an OR'ed sequence of gnutls_certificate_status_t flags. The details of the verification are the same as in gnutls_x509_trust_list_verify_crt2().

Returns: On success, **GNUTLS_E_SUCCESS** (0) is returned, otherwise a negative error value.

int **gnutls_x509_trust_list_verify_crt2** (*gnutls_x509_trust_list_t* **list**, *gnutls_x509_crt_t* *** cert_list**, *unsigned int* **cert_list_size**, *gnutls_typed_vdata_st* *** data**, *unsigned int* **elements**, *unsigned int* **flags**, *unsigned int* *** voutput**, *gnutls_verify_output_function* **func**)

Description: This function will attempt to verify the given certificate and return its status. The voutput parameter will hold an OR'ed sequence of gnutls_certificate_status_t flags. When a chain of cert_list_size with more than one certificates is provided, the verification status will apply to the first certificate in the chain that failed verification. The verification process starts from the end of the chain (from CA to end certificate). Additionally a certificate verification profile can be specified from the ones in gnutls_certificate_verification_profiles_t by ORing the result of GNUTLS_PROFILE_TO_VFLAGS() to the verification flags. The acceptable data types are **GNUTLS_DT_DNS_HOSTNAME** and **GNUTLS_DT_KEY_PURPOSE_OID**. The former accepts as data a null-terminated hostname, and the latter a null-terminated object identifier (e.g., **GNUTLS_KP_TLS_WWW_SERVER**). If a DNS hostname is provided then this function will compare the hostname in the certificate against the given. If names do not match the **GNUTLS_CERT_UNEXPECTED_OWNER** status flag will be set. In addition it will consider certificates provided with gnutls_x509_trust_list_add_named_crt(). If a key purpose OID is provided and the end-certificate contains the extended key usage PKIX extension, it will be required to match the provided OID or be marked for any purpose, otherwise verification will fail with **GNUTLS_CERT_PURPOSE_MISMATCH** status.

Returns: On success, **GNUTLS_E_SUCCESS** (0) is returned, otherwise a negative error value. Note that verification failure will not result to an error code, only **voutput** will be updated.

---

int **gnutls_x509_trust_list_verify_named_crt** (*gnutls_x509_trust_list_t* **list**, *gnutls_x509_crt_t* **cert**, *const void* *** name**, *size_t* **name_size**, *unsigned int* **flags**, *unsigned int* *** voutput**, *gnutls_verify_output_function* **func**)

Description: This function will try to find a certificate that is associated with the provided name --see gnutls_x509_trust_list_add_named_crt(). If a match is found the certificate is considered valid. In addition to that this function will also check CRLs. The voutput parameter will hold an OR'ed sequence of gnutls_certificate_status_t flags. Additionally a certificate verification profile can be specified from the ones in gnutls_certificate_verification_profiles_t by ORing the result of GNUTLS_PROFILE_TO_VFLAGS() to the verification flags.

Returns: On success, **GNUTLS_E_SUCCESS** (0) is returned, otherwise a negative error value.

int **gnutls_x509_trust_list_add_trust_file** (*gnutls_x509_trust_list_t* **list**, *const char* * **ca_file**, *const char* * **crl_file**, *gnutls_x509_crt_fmt_t* **type**, *unsigned int* **tl_flags**, *unsigned int* **tl_vflags**)

Description: This function will add the given certificate authorities to the trusted list. PKCS #11 URLs are also accepted, instead of files, by this function. A PKCS #11 URL implies a trust database (a specially marked module in p11-kit); the URL "pkcs11:" implies all trust databases in the system. Only a single URL specifying trust databases can be set; they cannot be stacked with multiple calls.

Returns: The number of added elements is returned.

---

int **gnutls_x509_trust_list_add_trust_mem** (*gnutls_x509_trust_list_t* **list**, *const gnutls_datum_t* * **cas**, *const gnutls_datum_t* * **crls**, *gnutls_x509_crt_fmt_t* **type**, *unsigned int* **tl_flags**, *unsigned int* **tl_vflags**)

Description: This function will add the given certificate authorities to the trusted list.

Returns: The number of added elements is returned.

Verifying a certificate in the context of TLS session

When operating in the context of a TLS session, the trusted certificate authority list may also be set using:

int **gnutls_x509_trust_list_add_system_trust** (*gnutls_x509_trust_list_t* **list**, *unsigned int* **tl_flags**, *unsigned int* **tl_vflags**)

Description: This function adds the system's default trusted certificate authorities to the trusted list. Note that on unsupported systems this function returns **GNUTLS_-E_UNIMPLEMENTED_FEATURE**. This function implies the flag **GNUTLS_TL_NO_-DUPLICATES**.

Returns: The number of added elements or a negative error code on error.

---

int **gnutls_certificate_set_x509_trust_file** (*gnutls_certificate_credentials_t* **cred**, *const char* * **cafile**, *gnutls_x509_crt_fmt_t* **type**)

int **gnutls_certificate_set_x509_trust_dir** (*gnutls_certificate_credentials_t* **cred**, *const char* * **ca_dir**, *gnutls_x509_crt_fmt_t* **type**)

int **gnutls_certificate_set_x509_crl_file** (*gnutls_certificate_credentials_t* **res**, *const char* * **crlfile**, *gnutls_x509_crt_fmt_t* **type**)

int **gnutls_certificate_set_x509_system_trust** (*gnutls_certificate_credentials_t* **cred**)

These functions allow the specification of the trusted certificate authorities, either via a file, a directory or use the system-specified certificate authories. Unless the authorities are application specific, it is generally recommended to use the system trust storage (see **gnutls_certificate_set_x509_system_trust**).

Unlike the previous section it is not required to setup a trusted list, and there are two approaches to verify the peer's certificate and identity. The recommended in GnuTLS 3.5.0 and later is via the **gnutls_session_set_verify_cert**, but for older GnuTLS versions you may use an explicit callback set via **gnutls_certificate_set_verify_function** and then utilize **gnutls_certificate_verify_peers3** for verification. The reported verification status is identical to the verification functions described in the previous section.

Note that in certain cases it is required to check the marked purpose of the end certificate (e.g. **GNUTLS_KP_TLS_WWW_SERVER**); in these cases the more advanced **gnutls_session_set_verify_cert2** and **gnutls_certificate_verify_peers** should be used instead.

There is also the possibility to pass some input to the verification functions in the form of flags. For **gnutls_x509_trust_list_verify_crt2** the flags are passed directly, but for **gnutls_certificate_verify_peers3**, the flags are set using **gnutls_certificate_set_verify_flags**. All the available flags are part of the enumeration **gnutls_certificate_verify_flags** shown in Table 3.5.

Verifying a certificate using PKCS #11

Some systems provide a system wide trusted certificate storage accessible using the PKCS #11 API. That is, the trusted certificates are queried and accessed using the PKCS #11 API, and trusted certificate properties, such as purpose, are marked using attached extensions. One example is the p11-kit trust module[1].

These special PKCS #11 modules can be used for GnuTLS certificate verification if marked as trust policy modules, i.e., with **trust-policy: yes** in the p11-kit module file. The way

---

[1]see http://p11-glue.freedesktop.org/trust-module.html.

to use them is by specifying to the file verification function (e.g., `gnutls_certificate_set_-x509_trust_file`), a pkcs11 URL, or simply `pkcs11:` to use all the marked with trust policy modules.

The trust modules of p11-kit assign a purpose to trusted authorities using the extended key usage object identifiers. The common purposes are shown in Table 3.6. Note that typically according to [8] the extended key usage object identifiers apply to end certificates. Their application to CA certificates is an extension used by the trust modules.

With such modules, it is recommended to use the verification functions `gnutls_x509_trust_-list_verify_crt2`, or `gnutls_certificate_verify_peers`, which allow to explicitly specify the key purpose. The other verification functions which do not allow setting a purpose, would operate as if `GNUTLS_KP_TLS_WWW_SERVER` was requested from the trusted authorities.

3.1.2. OpenPGP certificates

The OpenPGP key authentication relies on a distributed trust model, called the "web of trust". The "web of trust" uses a decentralized system of trusted introducers, which are the same as a CA. OpenPGP allows anyone to sign anyone else's public key. When Alice signs Bob's key, she is introducing Bob's key to anyone who trusts Alice. If someone trusts Alice to introduce keys, then Alice is a trusted introducer in the mind of that observer. For example in Figure 3.2, David trusts Alice to be an introducer and Alice signed Bob's key thus Dave trusts Bob's key to be the real one.

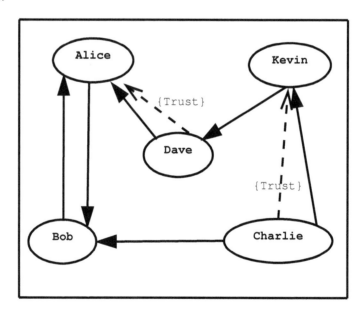

Figure 3.2.: An example of the OpenPGP trust model.

There are some key points that are important in that model. In the example Alice has to sign Bob's key, only if she is sure that the key belongs to Bob. Otherwise she may also make Dave falsely believe that this is Bob's key. Dave has also the responsibility to know who to trust. This model is similar to real life relations.

Just see how Charlie behaves in the previous example. Although he has signed Bob's key - because he knows, somehow, that it belongs to Bob - he does not trust Bob to be an introducer. Charlie decided to trust only Kevin, for some reason. A reason could be that Bob is lazy enough, and signs other people's keys without being sure that they belong to the actual owner.

OpenPGP certificate structure

In GnuTLS the OpenPGP certificate structures [7] are handled using the `gnutls_openpgp_crt_t` type. A typical certificate contains the user ID, which is an RFC 2822 mail and name address, a public key, possibly a number of additional public keys (called subkeys), and a number of signatures. The various fields are shown in Table 3.7.

The additional subkeys may provide key for various different purposes, e.g. one key to encrypt mail, and another to sign a TLS key exchange. Each subkey is identified by a unique key ID. The keys that are to be used in a TLS key exchange that requires signatures are called authentication keys in the OpenPGP jargon. The mapping of TLS key exchange methods to public keys is shown in Table 3.8.

The corresponding private keys are stored in the `gnutls_openpgp_privkey_t` type. All the prototypes for the key handling functions can be found in "`gnutls/openpgp.h`".

Verifying an OpenPGP certificate

The verification functions of OpenPGP keys, included in GnuTLS, are simple ones, and do not use the features of the "web of trust". For that reason, if the verification needs are complex, the assistance of external tools like GnuPG and GPGME[2] is recommended.

In GnuTLS there is a verification function for OpenPGP certificates, the `gnutls_openpgp_crt_verify_ring`. This checks an OpenPGP key against a given set of public keys (keyring) and returns the key status. The key verification status is the same as in X.509 certificates, although the meaning and interpretation are different. For example an OpenPGP key may be valid, if the self signature is ok, even if no signers were found. The meaning of verification status flags is the same as in the X.509 certificates (see Table 3.5).

Verifying a certificate in the context of a TLS session

Similarly with X.509 certificates, one needs to specify the OpenPGP keyring file in the credentials structure. The certificates in this file will be used by `gnutls_certificate_verify_peers3` to verify the signatures in the certificate sent by the peer.

---

[2]http://www.gnupg.org/related_software/gpgme/

---

int **gnutls_openpgp_crt_verify_ring** (*gnutls_openpgp_crt_t* **key**, *gnutls_openpgp_keyring_t* **keyring**, *unsigned int* **flags**, *unsigned int* * **verify**)

Description: Verify all signatures in the key, using the given set of keys (keyring). The key verification output will be put in **verify** and will be one or more of the *gnutls_certificate_status_t* enumerated elements bitwise or'd. Note that this function does not verify using any "web of trust". You may use GnuPG for that purpose, or any other external PGP application.

Returns: GNUTLS_E_SUCCESS on success, or an error code.

---

int **gnutls_openpgp_crt_verify_self** (*gnutls_openpgp_crt_t* **key**, *unsigned int* **flags**, *unsigned int* * **verify**)

Description: Verifies the self signature in the key. The key verification output will be put in **verify** and will be one or more of the gnutls_certificate_status_t enumerated elements bitwise or'd.

Returns: GNUTLS_E_SUCCESS on success, or an error code.

3.1.3. Advanced certificate verification

The verification of X.509 certificates in the HTTPS and other Internet protocols is typically done by loading a trusted list of commercial Certificate Authorities (see `gnutls_certificate_set_x509_system_trust`), and using them as trusted anchors. However, there are several examples (eg. the Diginotar incident) where one of these authorities was compromised. This risk can be mitigated by using in addition to CA certificate verification, other verification methods. In this section we list the available in GnuTLS methods.

---

int **gnutls_certificate_set_openpgp_keyring_file** (*gnutls_certificate_credentials_t* **c**, *const char* * **file**, *gnutls_openpgp_crt_fmt_t* **format**)

Description: The function is used to set keyrings that will be used internally by various OpenPGP functions. For example to find a key when it is needed for an operations. The keyring will also be used at the verification functions.

Returns: On success, GNUTLS_E_SUCCESS (0) is returned, otherwise a negative error value.

Verifying a certificate using trust on first use authentication

It is possible to use a trust on first use (TOFU) authentication method in GnuTLS. That is the concept used by the SSH programs, where the public key of the peer is not verified, or verified in an out-of-bound way, but subsequent connections to the same peer require the public key to remain the same. Such a system in combination with the typical CA verification of a certificate, and OCSP revocation checks, can help to provide multiple factor verification, where a single point of failure is not enough to compromise the system. For example a server compromise may be detected using OCSP, and a CA compromise can be detected using the trust on first use method. Such a hybrid system with X.509 and trust on first use authentication is shown in subsection 6.1.2.

See subsection 5.12.2 on how to use the available functionality.

Verifying a certificate using DANE (DNSSEC)

The DANE protocol is a protocol that can be used to verify TLS certificates using the DNS (or better DNSSEC) protocols. The DNS security extensions (DNSSEC) provide an alternative public key infrastructure to the commercial CAs that are typically used to sign TLS certificates. The DANE protocol takes advantage of the DNSSEC infrastructure to verify TLS certificates. This can be in addition to the verification by CA infrastructure or may even replace it where DNSSEC is fully deployed. Note however, that DNSSEC deployment is fairly new and it would be better to use it as an additional verification method rather than the only one.

The DANE functionality is provided by the `libgnutls-dane` library that is shipped with GnuTLS and the function prototypes are in **gnutls/dane.h**. See subsection 5.12.2 for information on how to use the library.

Note however, that the DANE RFC mandates the verification methods one should use in addition to the validation via DNSSEC TLSA entries. GnuTLS doesn't follow that RFC requirement, and the term DANE verification in this manual refers to the TLSA entry verification. In GnuTLS any other verification methods can be used (e.g., PKIX or TOFU) on top of DANE.

3.1.4. Digital signatures

In this section we will provide some information about digital signatures, how they work, and give the rationale for disabling some of the algorithms used.

Digital signatures work by using somebody's secret key to sign some arbitrary data. Then anybody else could use the public key of that person to verify the signature. Since the data may be arbitrary it is not suitable input to a cryptographic digital signature algorithm. For this reason and also for performance cryptographic hash algorithms are used to preprocess the input to the signature algorithm. This works as long as it is difficult enough to generate two different messages with the same hash algorithm output. In that case the same signature could be used as a proof for both messages. Nobody wants to sign an innocent message of donating 1 euro to Greenpeace and find out that they donated 1.000.000 euros to Bad Inc.

For a hash algorithm to be called cryptographic the following three requirements must hold:

1. Preimage resistance. That means the algorithm must be one way and given the output of the hash function $H(x)$, it is impossible to calculate x.

2. 2nd preimage resistance. That means that given a pair x, y with $y = H(x)$ it is impossible to calculate an x' such that $y = H(x')$.

3. Collision resistance. That means that it is impossible to calculate random x and x' such $H(x') = H(x)$.

The last two requirements in the list are the most important in digital signatures. These protect against somebody who would like to generate two messages with the same hash output. When an algorithm is considered broken usually it means that the Collision resistance of the algorithm is less than brute force. Using the birthday paradox the brute force attack takes 2 *textasciicircum*(hash size)/2 operations. Today colliding certificates using the MD5 hash algorithm have been generated as shown in [20].

There has been cryptographic results for the SHA-1 hash algorithms as well, although they are not yet critical. Before 2004, MD5 had a presumed collision strength of 2 *textasciicircum*64, but it has been showed to have a collision strength well under 2 *textasciicircum*50. As of November 2005, it is believed that SHA-1's collision strength is around 2 *textasciicircum*63. We consider this sufficiently hard so that we still support SHA-1. We anticipate that SHA-256/386/512 will be used in publicly-distributed certificates in the future. When 2 *textasciicircum*63 can be considered too weak compared to the computer power available sometime in the future, SHA-1 will be disabled as well. The collision attacks on SHA-1 may also get better, given the new interest in tools for creating them.

Trading security for interoperability

If you connect to a server and use GnuTLS' functions to verify the certificate chain, and get a `GNUTLS_CERT_INSECURE_ALGORITHM` validation error (see section 3.1.1), it means that somewhere in the certificate chain there is a certificate signed using `RSA-MD2` or `RSA-MD5`. These two digital signature algorithms are considered broken, so GnuTLS fails verifying the certificate. In some situations, it may be useful to be able to verify the certificate chain anyway, assuming an attacker did not utilize the fact that these signatures algorithms are broken. This section will give help on how to achieve that.

It is important to know that you do not have to enable any of the flags discussed here to be able to use trusted root CA certificates self-signed using `RSA-MD2` or `RSA-MD5`. The certificates in the trusted list are considered trusted irrespective of the signature.

If you are using **gnutls_certificate_verify_peers3** to verify the certificate chain, you can call **gnutls_certificate_set_verify_flags** with the flags:

• GNUTLS_VERIFY_ALLOW_SIGN_RSA_MD2

• GNUTLS_VERIFY_ALLOW_SIGN_RSA_MD5

as in the following example:

```
1   gnutls_certificate_set_verify_flags (x509cred,
2                               GNUTLS_VERIFY_ALLOW_SIGN_RSA_MD5);
```

This will signal the verifier algorithm to enable `RSA-MD5` when verifying the certificates.

If you are using `gnutls_x509_crt_verify` or `gnutls_x509_crt_list_verify`, you can pass the `GNUTLS_VERIFY_ALLOW_SIGN_RSA_MD5` parameter directly in the `flags` parameter.

If you are using these flags, it may also be a good idea to warn the user when verification failure occur for this reason. The simplest is to not use the flags by default, and only fall back to using them after warning the user. If you wish to inspect the certificate chain yourself, you can use `gnutls_certificate_get_peers` to extract the raw server's certificate chain, `gnutls_x509_crt_list_import` to parse each of the certificates, and then `gnutls_x509_crt_get_signature_algorithm` to find out the signing algorithm used for each certificate. If any of the intermediary certificates are using `GNUTLS_SIGN_RSA_MD2` or `GNUTLS_SIGN_RSA_MD5`, you could present a warning.

3.2. More on certificate authentication

Certificates are not the only structures involved in a public key infrastructure. Several other structures that are used for certificate requests, encrypted private keys, revocation lists, GnuTLS abstract key structures, etc., are discussed in this chapter.

3.2.1. PKCS #10 certificate requests

A certificate request is a structure, which contain information about an applicant of a certificate service. It usually contains a private key, a distinguished name and secondary data such as a challenge password. GnuTLS supports the requests defined in PKCS #10 [25]. Other formats of certificate requests are not currently supported.

A certificate request can be generated by associating it with a private key, setting the subject's information and finally self signing it. The last step ensures that the requester is in possession of the private key.

---

int **gnutls_x509_crq_set_version** (*gnutls_x509_crq_t* **crq**, *unsigned int* **version**)

int **gnutls_x509_crq_set_dn** (*gnutls_x509_crq_t* **crq**, *const char* * **dn**, *const char* ** **err**)

int **gnutls_x509_crq_set_dn_by_oid** (*gnutls_x509_crq_t* **crq**, *const char* * **oid**, *unsigned int* **raw_flag**, *const void* * **data**, *unsigned int* **sizeof_data**)

int **gnutls_x509_crq_set_key_usage** (*gnutls_x509_crq_t* **crq**, *unsigned int* **usage**)

int **gnutls_x509_crq_set_key_purpose_oid** (*gnutls_x509_crq_t* **crq**, *const void* * **oid**, *unsigned int* **critical**)

int **gnutls_x509_crq_set_basic_constraints** (*gnutls_x509_crq_t* **crq**, *unsigned int* **ca**, *int* **pathLenConstraint**)

The `gnutls_x509_crq_set_key` and `gnutls_x509_crq_sign2` functions associate the request with a private key and sign it. If a request is to be signed with a key residing in a PKCS #11 token it is recommended to use the signing functions shown in section 4.1.

---

int **gnutls_x509_crq_set_key** (*gnutls_x509_crq_t* **crq**, *gnutls_x509_privkey_t* **key**)

Description: This function will set the public parameters from the given private key to the request.

Returns: On success, **GNUTLS_E_SUCCESS** (0) is returned, otherwise a negative error value.

---

int **gnutls_x509_crq_sign2** (*gnutls_x509_crq_t* **crq**, *gnutls_x509_privkey_t* **key**, *gnutls_digest_algorithm_t* **dig**, *unsigned int* **flags**)

Description: This function will sign the certificate request with a private key. This must be the same key as the one used in gnutls_x509_crt_set_key() since a certificate request is self signed. This must be the last step in a certificate request generation since all the previously set parameters are now signed.

Returns: **GNUTLS_E_SUCCESS** on success, otherwise a negative error code. **GNUTLS_E_ASN1_VALUE_NOT_FOUND** is returned if you didn't set all information in the certificate request (e.g., the version using gnutls_x509_crq_set_version()).

The following example is about generating a certificate request, and a private key. A certificate request can be later be processed by a CA which should return a signed certificate.

```
1   /* This example code is placed in the public domain. */
2
3   #ifdef HAVE_CONFIG_H
4   #include <config.h>
5   #endif
6
7   #include <stdio.h>
8   #include <stdlib.h>
9   #include <string.h>
10  #include <gnutls/gnutls.h>
11  #include <gnutls/x509.h>
12  #include <gnutls/abstract.h>
13  #include <time.h>
14
15  /* This example will generate a private key and a certificate
16   * request.
17   */
18
19  int main(void)
20  {
21          gnutls_x509_crq_t crq;
22          gnutls_x509_privkey_t key;
23          unsigned char buffer[10 * 1024];
24          size_t buffer_size = sizeof(buffer);
25          unsigned int bits;
26
27          gnutls_global_init();
28
29          /* Initialize an empty certificate request, and
30           * an empty private key.
31           */
32          gnutls_x509_crq_init(&crq);
33
34          gnutls_x509_privkey_init(&key);
35
36          /* Generate an RSA key of moderate security.
37           */
38          bits =
39              gnutls_sec_param_to_pk_bits(GNUTLS_PK_RSA,
40                                          GNUTLS_SEC_PARAM_MEDIUM);
41          gnutls_x509_privkey_generate(key, GNUTLS_PK_RSA, bits, 0);
42
43          /* Add stuff to the distinguished name
44           */
45          gnutls_x509_crq_set_dn_by_oid(crq, GNUTLS_OID_X520_COUNTRY_NAME,
46                                        0, "GR", 2);
47
48          gnutls_x509_crq_set_dn_by_oid(crq, GNUTLS_OID_X520_COMMON_NAME,
49                                        0, "Nikos", strlen("Nikos"));
50
51          /* Set the request version.
52           */
53          gnutls_x509_crq_set_version(crq, 1);
54
55          /* Set a challenge password.
```

```
56        */
57        gnutls_x509_crq_set_challenge_password(crq,
58                                      "something to remember here");
59
60        /* Associate the request with the private key
61         */
62        gnutls_x509_crq_set_key(crq, key);
63
64        /* Self sign the certificate request.
65         */
66        gnutls_x509_crq_sign2(crq, key, GNUTLS_DIG_SHA1, 0);
67
68        /* Export the PEM encoded certificate request, and
69         * display it.
70         */
71        gnutls_x509_crq_export(crq, GNUTLS_X509_FMT_PEM, buffer,
72                          &buffer_size);
73
74        printf("Certificate Request: \n%s", buffer);
75
76
77        /* Export the PEM encoded private key, and
78         * display it.
79         */
80        buffer_size = sizeof(buffer);
81        gnutls_x509_privkey_export(key, GNUTLS_X509_FMT_PEM, buffer,
82                          &buffer_size);
83
84        printf("\n\nPrivate key: \n%s", buffer);
85
86        gnutls_x509_crq_deinit(crq);
87        gnutls_x509_privkey_deinit(key);
88
89        return 0;
90
91 }
```

3.2.2. PKIX certificate revocation lists

A certificate revocation list (CRL) is a structure issued by an authority periodically containing a list of revoked certificates serial numbers. The CRL structure is signed with the issuing authorities' keys. A typical CRL contains the fields as shown in Table 3.9. Certificate revocation lists are used to complement the expiration date of a certificate, in order to account for other reasons of revocation, such as compromised keys, etc.

Each CRL is valid for limited amount of time and is required to provide, except for the current issuing time, also the issuing time of the next update.

The basic CRL structure functions follow.

---

int **gnutls_x509_crl_init** (*gnutls_x509_crl_t* * **crl**)

int **gnutls_x509_crl_import** (*gnutls_x509_crl_t* **crl**, *const gnutls_datum_t* * **data**, *gnutls_x509_crt_fmt_t* **format**)

int **gnutls_x509_crl_export** (*gnutls_x509_crl_t* **crl**, *gnutls_x509_crt_fmt_t* **format**, *void* * **output_data**, *size_t* * **output_data_size**)

int **gnutls_x509_crl_export** (*gnutls_x509_crl_t* **crl**, *gnutls_x509_crt_fmt_t* **format**, *void* * **output_data**, *size_t* * **output_data_size**)

Reading a CRL

The most important function that extracts the certificate revocation information from a CRL is `gnutls_x509_crl_get_crt_serial`. Other functions that return other fields of the CRL structure are also provided.

---

int **gnutls_x509_crl_get_crt_serial** (*gnutls_x509_crl_t* **crl**, *int* **indx**, *unsigned char* * **serial**, *size_t* * **serial_size**, *time_t* * **t**)

Description: This function will retrieve the serial number of the specified, by the index, revoked certificate. Note that this function will have performance issues in large sequences of revoked certificates. In that case use gnutls_x509_crl_iter_crt_serial().

Returns: On success, **GNUTLS_E_SUCCESS** (0) is returned, otherwise a negative error value.

45

---

int **gnutls_x509_crl_get_version** (*gnutls_x509_crl_t* **crl**)

int **gnutls_x509_crl_get_issuer_dn** (*const gnutls_x509_crl_t* **crl**, *char ** **buf**, *size_t ** **sizeof_buf**)

int **gnutls_x509_crl_get_issuer_dn2** (*gnutls_x509_crl_t* **crl**, *gnutls_datum_t ** **dn**)

time_t **gnutls_x509_crl_get_this_update** (*gnutls_x509_crl_t* **crl**)

time_t **gnutls_x509_crl_get_next_update** (*gnutls_x509_crl_t* **crl**)

int **gnutls_x509_crl_get_crt_count** (*gnutls_x509_crl_t* **crl**)

Generation of a CRL

The following functions can be used to generate a CRL.

---

int **gnutls_x509_crl_set_version** (*gnutls_x509_crl_t* **crl**, *unsigned int* **version**)

int **gnutls_x509_crl_set_crt_serial** (*gnutls_x509_crl_t* **crl**, *const void ** **serial**, *size_t* **serial_size**, *time_t* **revocation_time**)

---

int **gnutls_x509_crl_set_crt** (*gnutls_x509_crl_t* **crl**, *gnutls_x509_crt_t* **crt**, *time_t* **revocation_time**)

int **gnutls_x509_crl_set_next_update** (*gnutls_x509_crl_t* **crl**, *time_t* **exp_time**)

int **gnutls_x509_crl_set_this_update** (*gnutls_x509_crl_t* **crl**, *time_t* **act_time**)

The `gnutls_x509_crl_sign2` and `gnutls_x509_crl_privkey_sign` functions sign the revocation list with a private key. The latter function can be used to sign with a key residing in a PKCS #11 token.

Few extensions on the CRL structure are supported, including the CRL number extension and the authority key identifier.

int **gnutls_x509_crl_sign2** (*gnutls_x509_crl_t* **crl**, *gnutls_x509_crt_t* **issuer**, *gnutls_x509_privkey_t* **issuer_key**, *gnutls_digest_algorithm_t* **dig**, *unsigned int* **flags**)

Description: This function will sign the CRL with the issuer's private key, and will copy the issuer's information into the CRL. This must be the last step in a certificate CRL since all the previously set parameters are now signed.

Returns: On success, **GNUTLS_E_SUCCESS** (0) is returned, otherwise a negative error value.

---

int **gnutls_x509_crl_privkey_sign** (*gnutls_x509_crl_t* **crl**, *gnutls_x509_crt_t* **issuer**, *gnutls_privkey_t* **issuer_key**, *gnutls_digest_algorithm_t* **dig**, *unsigned int* **flags**)

Description: This function will sign the CRL with the issuer's private key, and will copy the issuer's information into the CRL. This must be the last step in a certificate CRL since all the previously set parameters are now signed.

Returns: On success, **GNUTLS_E_SUCCESS** (0) is returned, otherwise a negative error value. Since 2.12.0

---

int **gnutls_x509_crl_set_number** (*gnutls_x509_crl_t* **crl**, *const void* * **nr**, *size_t* **nr_size**)

int **gnutls_x509_crl_set_authority_key_id** (*gnutls_x509_crl_t* **crl**, *const void* * **id**, *size_t* **id_size**)

3.2.3. OCSP certificate status checking

Certificates may be revoked before their expiration time has been reached. There are several reasons for revoking certificates, but a typical situation is when the private key associated with a certificate has been compromised. Traditionally, Certificate Revocation Lists (CRLs) have been used by application to implement revocation checking, however, several problems with CRLs have been identified [31].

The Online Certificate Status Protocol, or OCSP [24], is a widely implemented protocol which performs certificate revocation status checking. An application that wish to verify the identity of a peer will verify the certificate against a set of trusted certificates and then check whether the certificate is listed in a CRL and/or perform an OCSP check for the certificate.

Note that in the context of a TLS session the server may provide an OCSP response that will be used during the TLS certificate verification (see `gnutls_certificate_verify_peers2`).

You may obtain this response using `gnutls_ocsp_status_request_get`.

Before performing the OCSP query, the application will need to figure out the address of the OCSP server. The OCSP server address can be provided by the local user in manual configuration or may be stored in the certificate that is being checked. When stored in a certificate the OCSP server is in the extension field called the Authority Information Access (AIA). The following function extracts this information from a certificate.

---

int **gnutls_x509_crt_get_authority_info_access** (*gnutls_x509_crt_t* **crt**, *unsigned int* **seq**, *int* **what**, *gnutls_datum_t * ***data**, *unsigned int * ***critical**)

There are several functions in GnuTLS for creating and manipulating OCSP requests and responses. The general idea is that a client application creates an OCSP request object, stores some information about the certificate to check in the request, and then exports the request in DER format. The request will then need to be sent to the OCSP responder, which needs to be done by the application (GnuTLS does not send and receive OCSP packets). Normally an OCSP response is received that the application will need to import into an OCSP response object. The digital signature in the OCSP response needs to be verified against a set of trust anchors before the information in the response can be trusted.

The ASN.1 structure of OCSP requests are briefly as follows. It is useful to review the structures to get an understanding of which fields are modified by GnuTLS functions.

```
 1  OCSPRequest        ::=      SEQUENCE {
 2      tbsRequest                   TBSRequest,
 3      optionalSignature  [0]       EXPLICIT Signature OPTIONAL }
 4
 5  TBSRequest         ::=      SEQUENCE {
 6      version            [0]       EXPLICIT Version DEFAULT v1,
 7      requestorName      [1]       EXPLICIT GeneralName OPTIONAL,
 8      requestList                  SEQUENCE OF Request,
 9      requestExtensions  [2]       EXPLICIT Extensions OPTIONAL }
10
11  Request            ::=      SEQUENCE {
12      reqCert                      CertID,
13      singleRequestExtensions      [0] EXPLICIT Extensions OPTIONAL }
14
15  CertID             ::=      SEQUENCE {
16      hashAlgorithm      AlgorithmIdentifier,
17      issuerNameHash     OCTET STRING, -- Hash of Issuer's DN
18      issuerKeyHash      OCTET STRING, -- Hash of Issuers public key
19      serialNumber       CertificateSerialNumber }
```

The basic functions to initialize, import, export and deallocate OCSP requests are the following.

---

int **gnutls_ocsp_req_init** (*gnutls_ocsp_req_t* * **req**)

void **gnutls_ocsp_req_deinit** (*gnutls_ocsp_req_t* **req**)

int **gnutls_ocsp_req_import** (*gnutls_ocsp_req_t* **req**, *const gnutls_datum_t* * **data**)

int **gnutls_ocsp_req_export** (*gnutls_ocsp_req_t* **req**, *gnutls_datum_t* * **data**)

int **gnutls_ocsp_req_print** (*gnutls_ocsp_req_t* **req**, *gnutls_ocsp_print_formats_t* **format**, *gnutls_datum_t* * **out**)

To generate an OCSP request the issuer name hash, issuer key hash, and the checked certificate's serial number are required. There are two interfaces available for setting those in an OCSP request. The is a low-level function when you have the issuer name hash, issuer key hash, and certificate serial number in binary form. The second is more useful if you have the certificate (and its issuer) in a `gnutls_x509_crt_t` type. There is also a function to extract this information from existing an OCSP request.

---

int **gnutls_ocsp_req_add_cert_id** (*gnutls_ocsp_req_t* **req**, *gnutls_digest_algorithm_t* **digest**, *const gnutls_datum_t* * **issuer_name_hash**, *const gnutls_datum_t* * **issuer_key_hash**, *const gnutls_datum_t* * **serial_number**)

int **gnutls_ocsp_req_add_cert** (*gnutls_ocsp_req_t* **req**, *gnutls_digest_algorithm_t* **digest**, *gnutls_x509_crt_t* **issuer**, *gnutls_x509_crt_t* **cert**)

int **gnutls_ocsp_req_get_cert_id** (*gnutls_ocsp_req_t* **req**, *unsigned* **indx**, *gnutls_digest_algorithm_t* * **digest**, *gnutls_datum_t* * **issuer_name_hash**, *gnutls_datum_t* * **issuer_key_hash**, *gnutls_datum_t* * **serial_number**)

Each OCSP request may contain a number of extensions. Extensions are identified by an Object Identifier (OID) and an opaque data buffer whose syntax and semantics is implied by the OID. You can extract or set those extensions using the following functions.

---

int **gnutls_ocsp_req_get_extension** (*gnutls_ocsp_req_t* **req**, *unsigned* **indx**, *gnutls_datum_t* * **oid**, *unsigned int* * **critical**, *gnutls_datum_t* * **data**)

int **gnutls_ocsp_req_set_extension** (*gnutls_ocsp_req_t* **req**, *const char* * **oid**, *unsigned int* **critical**, *const gnutls_datum_t* * **data**)

A common OCSP Request extension is the nonce extension (OID 1.3.6.1.5.5.7.48.1.2), which is used to avoid replay attacks of earlier recorded OCSP responses. The nonce extension carries a value that is intended to be sufficiently random and unique so that an attacker will not be able to give a stale response for the same nonce.

---

int **gnutls_ocsp_req_get_nonce** (*gnutls_ocsp_req_t* **req**, *unsigned int* * **critical**, *gnutls_datum_t* * **nonce**)

int **gnutls_ocsp_req_set_nonce** (*gnutls_ocsp_req_t* **req**, *unsigned int* **critical**, *const gnutls_datum_t* * **nonce**)

int **gnutls_ocsp_req_randomize_nonce** (*gnutls_ocsp_req_t* **req**)

The OCSP response structures is a complex structure. A simplified overview of it is in Table 3.10. Note that a response may contain information on multiple certificates.

We provide basic functions for initialization, importing, exporting and deallocating OCSP responses.

---

int **gnutls_ocsp_resp_init** (*gnutls_ocsp_resp_t* * **resp**)

void **gnutls_ocsp_resp_deinit** (*gnutls_ocsp_resp_t* **resp**)

int **gnutls_ocsp_resp_import** (*gnutls_ocsp_resp_t* **resp**, *const gnutls_datum_t* * **data**)

int **gnutls_ocsp_resp_export** (*gnutls_ocsp_resp_t* **resp**, *gnutls_datum_t* * **data**)

int **gnutls_ocsp_resp_print** (*gnutls_ocsp_resp_t* **resp**, *gnutls_ocsp_print_formats_t* **format**, *gnutls_datum_t* * **out**)

The utility function that extracts the revocation as well as other information from a response is shown below.

The possible revocation reasons available in an OCSP response are shown below.

Note, that the OCSP response needs to be verified against some set of trust anchors before it can be relied upon. It is also important to check whether the received OCSP response corresponds to the certificate being checked.

int **gnutls_ocsp_resp_get_single** (*gnutls_ocsp_resp_t* **resp**, *unsigned* **indx**, *gnutls_digest_algorithm_t* * **digest**, *gnutls_datum_t* * **issuer_name_hash**, *gnutls_datum_t* * **issuer_key_hash**, *gnutls_datum_t* * **serial_number**, *unsigned int* * **cert_status**, *time_t* * **this_update**, *time_t* * **next_update**, *time_t* * **revocation_time**, *unsigned int* * **revocation_reason**)

Description: This function will return the certificate information of the indx'ed response in the Basic OCSP Response resp. The information returned corresponds to the OCSP SingleResponse structure except the final singleExtensions. Each of the pointers to output variables may be NULL to indicate that the caller is not interested in that value.

Returns: On success, **GNUTLS_E_SUCCESS** (0) is returned, otherwise a negative error code is returned. If you have reached the last CertID available **GNUTLS_E_REQUESTED_DATA_NOT_AVAILABLE** will be returned.

---

int **gnutls_ocsp_resp_verify** (*gnutls_ocsp_resp_t* **resp**, *gnutls_x509_trust_list_t* **trustlist**, *unsigned int* * **verify**, *unsigned int* **flags**)

int **gnutls_ocsp_resp_verify_direct** (*gnutls_ocsp_resp_t* **resp**, *gnutls_x509_crt_t* **issuer**, *unsigned int* * **verify**, *unsigned int* **flags**)

int **gnutls_ocsp_resp_check_crt** (*gnutls_ocsp_resp_t* **resp**, *unsigned int* **indx**, *gnutls_x509_crt_t* **crt**)

3.2.4. Managing encrypted keys

Transferring or storing private keys in plain may not be a good idea, since any compromise is irreparable. Storing the keys in hardware security modules (see section 4.3) could solve the storage problem but it is not always practical or efficient enough. This section describes ways to store and transfer encrypted private keys.

There are methods for key encryption, namely the PKCS #8, PKCS #12 and OpenSSL's custom encrypted private key formats. The PKCS #8 and the OpenSSL's method allow encryption of the private key, while the PKCS #12 method allows, in addition, the bundling of accompanying data into the structure. That is typically the corresponding certificate, as well as a trusted CA certificate.

High level functionality

Generic and higher level private key import functions are available, that import plain or encrypted keys and will auto-detect the encrypted key format.

int **gnutls_privkey_import_x509_raw** (*gnutls_privkey_t* **pkey**, *const gnutls_datum_t* * **data**, *gnutls_x509_crt_fmt_t* **format**, *const char* * **password**, *unsigned int* **flags**)

Description: This function will import the given private key to the abstract *gnutls_privkey_t* type. The supported formats are basic unencrypted key, PKCS8, PKCS12, and the openssl format.

Returns: On success, **GNUTLS_E_SUCCESS** (0) is returned, otherwise a negative error value.

---

int **gnutls_x509_privkey_import2** (*gnutls_x509_privkey_t* **key**, *const gnutls_datum_t* * **data**, *gnutls_x509_crt_fmt_t* **format**, *const char* * **password**, *unsigned int* **flags**)

Description: This function will import the given DER or PEM encoded key, to the native *gnutls_x509_privkey_t* format, irrespective of the input format. The input format is auto-detected. The supported formats are basic unencrypted key, PKCS8, PKCS12, and the openssl format. If the provided key is encrypted but no password was given, then **GNUTLS_E_DECRYPTION_FAILED** is returned. Since GnuTLS 3.4.0 this function will utilize the PIN callbacks if any.

Returns: On success, **GNUTLS_E_SUCCESS** (0) is returned, otherwise a negative error value.

Any keys imported using those functions can be imported to a certificate credentials structure using `gnutls_certificate_set_key`, or alternatively they can be directly imported using `gnutls_certificate_set_x509_key_file2`.

PKCS #8 structures

PKCS #8 keys can be imported and exported as normal private keys using the functions below. An addition to the normal import functions, are a password and a flags argument. The flags can be any element of the `gnutls_pkcs_encrypt_flags_t` enumeration. Note however, that GnuTLS only supports the PKCS #5 PBES2 encryption scheme. Keys encrypted with the obsolete PBES1 scheme cannot be decrypted.

---

int **gnutls_x509_privkey_import_pkcs8** (*gnutls_x509_privkey_t* **key**, *const gnutls_datum_t* * **data**, *gnutls_x509_crt_fmt_t* **format**, *const char* * **password**, *unsigned int* **flags**)

int **gnutls_x509_privkey_export_pkcs8** (*gnutls_x509_privkey_t* **key**, *gnutls_x509_crt_fmt_t* **format**, *const char* * **password**, *unsigned int* **flags**, *void* * **output_data**, *size_t* * **output_data_size**)

int **gnutls_x509_privkey_export2_pkcs8** (*gnutls_x509_privkey_t* **key**, *gnutls_x509_crt_fmt_t* **format**, *const char* * **password**, *unsigned int* **flags**, *gnutls_datum_t* * **out**)

PKCS #12 structures

A PKCS #12 structure [18] usually contains a user's private keys and certificates. It is commonly used in browsers to export and import the user's identities. A file containing such a key can be directly imported to a certificate credentials structure by using `gnutls_certificate_set_x509_simple_pkcs12_file`.

In GnuTLS the PKCS #12 structures are handled using the `gnutls_pkcs12_t` type. This is an abstract type that may hold several `gnutls_pkcs12_bag_t` types. The bag types are the holders of the actual data, which may be certificates, private keys or encrypted data. A bag of type encrypted should be decrypted in order for its data to be accessed.

To reduce the complexity in parsing the structures the simple helper function `gnutls_pkcs12_simple_parse` is provided. For more advanced uses, manual parsing of the structure is required using the functions below.

---

int **gnutls_pkcs12_get_bag** (*gnutls_pkcs12_t* **pkcs12**, *int* **indx**, *gnutls_pkcs12_bag_t* **bag**)

int **gnutls_pkcs12_verify_mac** (*gnutls_pkcs12_t* **pkcs12**, *const char* * **pass**)

int **gnutls_pkcs12_bag_decrypt** (*gnutls_pkcs12_bag_t* **bag**, *const char* * **pass**)

int **gnutls_pkcs12_bag_get_count** (*gnutls_pkcs12_bag_t* **bag**)

---

int **gnutls_pkcs12_simple_parse** (*gnutls_pkcs12_t* **p12**, *const char* * **password**, *gnutls_x509_privkey_t* * **key**, *gnutls_x509_crt_t* ** **chain**, *unsigned int* * **chain_len**, *gnutls_x509_crt_t* ** **extra_certs**, *unsigned int* * **extra_certs_len**, *gnutls_x509_crl_t* * **crl**, *unsigned int* **flags**)

Description: This function parses a PKCS12 structure in pkcs12 and extracts the private key, the corresponding certificate chain, any additional certificates and a CRL. The extra_certs and extra_certs_len parameters are optional and both may be set to **NULL**. If either is non-**NULL**, then both must be set. The value for extra_certs is allocated using gnutls_malloc(). Encrypted PKCS12 bags and PKCS8 private keys are supported, but only with password based security and the same password for all operations. Note that a PKCS12 structure may contain many keys and/or certificates, and there is no way to identify which key/certificate pair you want. For this reason this function is useful for PKCS12 files that contain only one key/certificate pair and/or one CRL. If the provided structure has encrypted fields but no password is provided then this function returns **GNUTLS_E_DECRYPTION_FAILED**. Note that normally the chain constructed does not include self signed certificates, to comply with TLS' requirements. If, however, the flag **GNUTLS_PKCS12_SP_INCLUDE_SELF_SIGNED** is specified then self signed certificates will be included in the chain. Prior to using this function the PKCS #12 structure integrity must be verified using gnutls_pkcs12_verify_mac().

Returns: On success, **GNUTLS_E_SUCCESS** (0) is returned, otherwise a negative error value.

---

int **gnutls_pkcs12_bag_get_data** (*gnutls_pkcs12_bag_t* **bag**, *int* **indx**, *gnutls_datum_t* * **data**)

int **gnutls_pkcs12_bag_get_key_id** (*gnutls_pkcs12_bag_t* **bag**, *int* **indx**, *gnutls_datum_t* * **id**)

int **gnutls_pkcs12_bag_get_friendly_name** (*gnutls_pkcs12_bag_t* **bag**, *int* **indx**, *char* ** **name**)

The functions below are used to generate a PKCS #12 structure. An example of their usage is shown at subsection 6.4.4.

int **gnutls_pkcs12_set_bag** (*gnutls_pkcs12_t* **pkcs12**, *gnutls_pkcs12_bag_t* **bag**)

int **gnutls_pkcs12_bag_encrypt** (*gnutls_pkcs12_bag_t* **bag**, *const char* * **pass**, *unsigned int* **flags**)

int **gnutls_pkcs12_generate_mac** (*gnutls_pkcs12_t* **pkcs12**, *const char* * **pass**)

---

int **gnutls_pkcs12_bag_set_data** (*gnutls_pkcs12_bag_t* **bag**, *gnutls_pkcs12_bag_type_t* **type**, *const gnutls_datum_t* * **data**)

int **gnutls_pkcs12_bag_set_crl** (*gnutls_pkcs12_bag_t* **bag**, *gnutls_x509_crl_t* **crl**)

int **gnutls_pkcs12_bag_set_crt** (*gnutls_pkcs12_bag_t* **bag**, *gnutls_x509_crt_t* **crt**)

int **gnutls_pkcs12_bag_set_key_id** (*gnutls_pkcs12_bag_t* **bag**, *int* **indx**, *const gnutls_datum_t* * **id**)

int **gnutls_pkcs12_bag_set_friendly_name** (*gnutls_pkcs12_bag_t* **bag**, *int* **indx**, *const char* * **name**)

OpenSSL encrypted keys

Unfortunately the structures discussed in the previous sections are not the only structures that may hold an encrypted private key. For example the OpenSSL library offers a custom key encryption method. Those structures are also supported in GnuTLS with `gnutls_x509_privkey_import_openssl`.

3.2.5. Invoking certtool

Tool to parse and generate X.509 certificates, requests and private keys. It can be used interactively or non interactively by specifying the template command line option.

The tool accepts files or URLs supported by GnuTLS. In case PIN is required for the URL access you can provide it using the environment variables GNUTLS_PIN and GNUTLS_SO_PIN.

This section was generated by **AutoGen**, using the `agtexi-cmd` template and the option descriptions for the `certtool` program. This software is released under the GNU General Public License, version 3 or later.

int **gnutls_x509_privkey_import_openssl** (*gnutls_x509_privkey_t* **key**, *const gnutls_datum_t* * **data**, *const char* * **password**)

Description: This function will convert the given PEM encrypted to the native gnutls_-x509_privkey_t format. The output will be stored in key. The password should be in ASCII. If the password is not provided or wrong then **GNUTLS_E_DECRYPTION_FAILED** will be returned. If the Certificate is PEM encoded it should have a header of "PRIVATE KEY" and the "DEK-Info" header.

Returns: On success, **GNUTLS_E_SUCCESS** (0) is returned, otherwise a negative error value.

certtool help/usage ("--help")

This is the automatically generated usage text for certtool.

The text printed is the same whether selected with the **help** option ("--help") or the **more-help** option ("--more-help"). **more-help** will print the usage text by passing it through a pager program. **more-help** is disabled on platforms without a working **fork(2)** function. The **PAGER** environment variable is used to select the program, defaulting to "**more**". Both will exit with a status code of 0.

```
1   certtool - GnuTLS certificate tool
2   Usage:  certtool [ -<flag> [<val>] | --<name>[{=| }<val>] ]...
3
4      -d, --debug=num            Enable debugging
5                                 - it must be in the range:
6                                   0 to 9999
7      -V, --verbose              More verbose output
8                                 - may appear multiple times
9          --infile=file          Input file
10                                 - file must pre-exist
11         --outfile=str          Output file
12     -s, --generate-self-signed  Generate a self-signed certificate
13     -c, --generate-certificate  Generate a signed certificate
14         --generate-proxy       Generates a proxy certificate
15         --generate-crl         Generate a CRL
16     -u, --update-certificate   Update a signed certificate
17     -p, --generate-privkey     Generate a private key
18     -q, --generate-request     Generate a PKCS #10 certificate request
19                                 - prohibits the option 'infile'
20     -e, --verify-chain         Verify a PEM encoded certificate chain
21         --verify               Verify a PEM encoded certificate chain using a trusted list
22         --verify-crl           Verify a CRL using a trusted list
23                                 - requires the option 'load-ca-certificate'
24         --verify-hostname=str  Specify a hostname to be used for certificate chain verification
25         --verify-email=str     Specify a email to be used for certificate chain verification
26                                 - prohibits the option 'verify-hostname'
27         --verify-purpose=str   Specify a purpose OID to be used for certificate chain verification
28         --generate-dh-params   Generate PKCS #3 encoded Diffie-Hellman parameters
```

29	`--get-dh-params`	Get the included PKCS #3 encoded Diffie-Hellman parameters
30	`--dh-info`	Print information PKCS #3 encoded Diffie-Hellman parameters
31	`--load-privkey=str`	Loads a private key file
32	`--load-pubkey=str`	Loads a public key file
33	`--load-request=str`	Loads a certificate request file
34	`--load-certificate=str`	Loads a certificate file
35	`--load-ca-privkey=str`	Loads the certificate authority's private key file
36	`--load-ca-certificate=str`	Loads the certificate authority's certificate file
37	`--load-crl=str`	Loads the provided CRL
38	`--load-data=str`	Loads auxilary data
39	`--password=str`	Password to use
40	`--null-password`	Enforce a NULL password
41	`--empty-password`	Enforce an empty password
42	`--hex-numbers`	Print big number in an easier format to parse
43	`--cprint`	In certain operations it prints the information in C-friendly format
44	`-i, --certificate-info`	Print information on the given certificate
45	`--fingerprint`	Print the fingerprint of the given certificate
46	`--key-id`	Print the key ID of the given certificate
47	`--certificate-pubkey`	Print certificate's public key
48	`--pgp-certificate-info`	Print information on the given OpenPGP certificate
49	`--pgp-ring-info`	Print information on the given OpenPGP keyring structure
50	`-l, --crl-info`	Print information on the given CRL structure
51	`--crq-info`	Print information on the given certificate request
52	`--no-crq-extensions`	Do not use extensions in certificate requests
53	`-!, --p12-info`	Print information on a PKCS #12 structure
54	`-", --p12-name=str`	The PKCS #12 friendly name to use
55	`-#, --p7-generate`	Generate a PKCS #7 structure
56	`-$, --p7-sign`	Signs using a PKCS #7 structure
57	`-%, --p7-detached-sign`	Signs using a detached PKCS #7 structure
58	`-&, --p7-time`	Will include a timestamp in the PKCS #7 structure
59	`-', --p7-info`	Print information on a PKCS #7 structure
60	`-(, --p7-verify`	Verify the provided PKCS #7 structure
61	`-), --p8-info`	Print information on a PKCS #8 structure
62	`-*, --smime-to-p7`	Convert S/MIME to PKCS #7 structure
63	`-k, --key-info`	Print information on a private key
64	`-+, --pgp-key-info`	Print information on an OpenPGP private key
65	`-,, --pubkey-info`	Print information on a public key
66	`--, --v1`	Generate an X.509 version 1 certificate (with no extensions)
67	`-., --to-p12`	Generate a PKCS #12 structure
68		- requires the option 'load-certificate'
69	`-/, --to-p8`	Generate a PKCS #8 structure
70	`-8, --pkcs8`	Use PKCS #8 format for private keys
71	`-0, --rsa`	Generate RSA key
72	`-1, --dsa`	Generate DSA key
73	`-2, --ecc`	Generate ECC (ECDSA) key
74	`-3, --ecdsa`	an alias for the 'ecc' option
75	`-4, --hash=str`	Hash algorithm to use for signing
76	`-5, --inder`	Use DER format for input certificates, private keys, and DH parameters
77		- disabled as '--no-inder'
78	`-6, --inraw`	an alias for the 'inder' option
79	`-7, --outder`	Use DER format for output certificates, private keys, and DH parameters
80		- disabled as '--no-outder'
81	`-8, --outraw`	an alias for the 'outder' option
82	`-9, --bits=num`	Specify the number of bits for key generate
83	`-:, --curve=str`	Specify the curve used for EC key generation
84	`-;, --sec-param=str`	Specify the security level [low, legacy, medium, high, ultra]
85	`-<, --disable-quick-random`	No effect
86	`-=, --template=str`	Template file to use for non-interactive operation

```
87    ->, --stdout-info              Print information to stdout instead of stderr
88    -?, --ask-pass                 Enable interaction for entering password when in batch mode.
89    -@, --pkcs-cipher=str          Cipher to use for PKCS #8 and #12 operations
90    -A, --provider=str             Specify the PKCS #11 provider library
91    -v, --version[=arg]            output version information and exit
92    -h, --help                     display extended usage information and exit
93    -!, --more-help                extended usage information passed thru pager
94
95  Options are specified by doubled hyphens and their name or by a single
96  hyphen and the flag character.
97
98  Tool to parse and generate X.509 certificates, requests and private keys.
99  It can be used interactively or non interactively by specifying the
100 template command line option.
101
102 The tool accepts files or URLs supported by GnuTLS.  In case PIN is
103 required for the URL access you can provide it using the environment
104 variables GNUTLS_PIN and GNUTLS_SO_PIN.
105
```

debug option (-d)

This is the "enable debugging" option. This option takes a number argument. Specifies the debug level.

generate-crl option

This is the "generate a crl" option. This option generates a CRL. When combined with –load-crl it would use the loaded CRL as base for the generated (i.e., all revoked certificates in the base will be copied to the new CRL).

generate-request option (-q)

This is the "generate a pkcs #10 certificate request" option.

This option has some usage constraints. It:

* must not appear in combination with any of the following options: infile.

Will generate a PKCS #10 certificate request. To specify a private key use –load-privkey.

verify-chain option (-e)

This is the "verify a pem encoded certificate chain" option. The last certificate in the chain must be a self signed one. It can be combined with –verify-purpose or –verify-hostname.

verify option

This is the "verify a pem encoded certificate chain using a trusted list" option. The trusted certificate list can be loaded with –load-ca-certificate. If no certificate list is provided, then the system's certificate list is used. Note that during verification multiple paths may be explored. On a successful verification the successful path will be the last one. It can be combined with –verify-purpose or –verify-hostname.

verify-crl option

This is the "verify a crl using a trusted list" option.

This option has some usage constraints. It:

- must appear in combination with the following options: load-ca-certificate.

The trusted certificate list must be loaded with –load-ca-certificate.

verify-hostname option

This is the "specify a hostname to be used for certificate chain verification" option. This option takes a string argument. This is to be combined with one of the verify certificate options.

verify-email option

This is the "specify a email to be used for certificate chain verification" option. This option takes a string argument.

This option has some usage constraints. It:

- must not appear in combination with any of the following options: verify-hostname.

This is to be combined with one of the verify certificate options.

verify-purpose option

This is the "specify a purpose oid to be used for certificate chain verification" option. This option takes a string argument. This object identifier restricts the purpose of the certificates to be verified. Example purposes are 1.3.6.1.5.5.7.3.1 (TLS WWW), 1.3.6.1.5.5.7.3.4 (EMAIL) etc. Note that a CA certificate without a purpose set (extended key usage) is valid for any purpose.

get-dh-params option

This is the "get the included pkcs #3 encoded diffie-hellman parameters" option. Returns stored DH parameters in GnuTLS. Those parameters are used in the SRP protocol. The parameters returned by fresh generation are more efficient since GnuTLS 3.0.9.

load-privkey option

This is the "loads a private key file" option. This option takes a string argument. This can be either a file or a PKCS #11 URL

load-pubkey option

This is the "loads a public key file" option. This option takes a string argument. This can be either a file or a PKCS #11 URL

load-certificate option

This is the "loads a certificate file" option. This option takes a string argument. This can be either a file or a PKCS #11 URL

load-ca-privkey option

This is the "loads the certificate authority's private key file" option. This option takes a string argument. This can be either a file or a PKCS #11 URL

load-ca-certificate option

This is the "loads the certificate authority's certificate file" option. This option takes a string argument. This can be either a file or a PKCS #11 URL

password option

This is the "password to use" option. This option takes a string argument. You can use this option to specify the password in the command line instead of reading it from the tty. Note, that the command line arguments are available for view in others in the system. Specifying password as " is the same as specifying no password.

null-password option

This is the "enforce a null password" option. This option enforces a NULL password. This is different than the empty or no password in schemas like PKCS #8.

empty-password option

This is the "enforce an empty password" option. This option enforces an empty password. This is different than the NULL or no password in schemas like PKCS #8.

cprint option

This is the "in certain operations it prints the information in c-friendly format" option. In certain operations it prints the information in C-friendly format, suitable for including into C programs.

fingerprint option

This is the "print the fingerprint of the given certificate" option. This is a simple hash of the DER encoding of the certificate. It can be combined with the –hash parameter. However, it is recommended for identification to use the key-id which depends only on the certificate's key.

key-id option

This is the "print the key id of the given certificate" option. This is a hash of the public key of the given certificate. It identifies the key uniquely, remains the same on a certificate renewal and depends only on signed fields of the certificate.

p12-info option

This is the "print information on a pkcs #12 structure" option. This option will dump the contents and print the metadata of the provided PKCS #12 structure.

p12-name option

This is the "the pkcs #12 friendly name to use" option. This option takes a string argument. The name to be used for the primary certificate and private key in a PKCS #12 file.

p7-generate option

This is the "generate a pkcs #7 structure" option. This option generates a PKCS #7 certificate container structure. To add certificates in the structure use –load-certificate and –load-crl.

p7-sign option

This is the "signs using a pkcs #7 structure" option. This option generates a PKCS #7 structure containing a signature for the provided data. The data are stored within the structure. The signer certificate has to be specified using –load-certificate and –load-privkey.

p7-detached-sign option

This is the "signs using a detached pkcs #7 structure" option. This option generates a PKCS #7 structure containing a signature for the provided data. The signer certificate has to be specified using –load-certificate and –load-privkey.

p7-time option

This is the "will include a timestamp in the pkcs #7 structure" option. This option will include a timestamp in the generated signature

p7-verify option

This is the "verify the provided pkcs #7 structure" option. This option verifies the signed PKCS #7 structure. The certificate list to use for verification can be specified with –load-ca-certificate. When no certificate list is provided, then the system's certificate list is used. Alternatively a direct signer can be provided using –load-certificate. A key purpose can be enforced with the –verify-purpose option, and the –load-data option will utilize detached data.

p8-info option

This is the "print information on a pkcs #8 structure" option. This option will print information about encrypted PKCS #8 structures. That option does not require the decryption of the structure.

pubkey-info option

This is the "print information on a public key" option. The option combined with –load-request, –load-pubkey, –load-privkey and –load-certificate will extract the public key of the object in question.

to-p12 option

This is the "generate a pkcs #12 structure" option.

This option has some usage constraints. It:

- must appear in combination with the following options: load-certificate.

It requires a certificate, a private key and possibly a CA certificate to be specified.

rsa option

This is the "generate rsa key" option. When combined with –generate-privkey generates an RSA private key.

dsa option

This is the "generate dsa key" option. When combined with –generate-privkey generates a DSA private key.

ecc option

This is the "generate ecc (ecdsa) key" option. When combined with –generate-privkey generates an elliptic curve private key to be used with ECDSA.

ecdsa option

This is an alias for the `ecc` option, section 3.2.5.

hash option

This is the "hash algorithm to use for signing" option. This option takes a string argument. Available hash functions are SHA1, RMD160, SHA256, SHA384, SHA512.

inder option

This is the "use der format for input certificates, private keys, and dh parameters " option.

This option has some usage constraints. It:

- can be disabled with –no-inder.

The input files will be assumed to be in DER or RAW format. Unlike options that in PEM input would allow multiple input data (e.g. multiple certificates), when reading in DER format a single data structure is read.

inraw option

This is an alias for the `inder` option, section 3.2.5.

outder option

This is the "use der format for output certificates, private keys, and dh parameters" option.

This option has some usage constraints. It:

- can be disabled with –no-outder.

The output will be in DER or RAW format.

outraw option

This is an alias for the `outder` option, section 3.2.5.

curve option

This is the "specify the curve used for ec key generation" option. This option takes a string argument. Supported values are secp192r1, secp224r1, secp256r1, secp384r1 and secp521r1.

sec-param option

This is the "specify the security level [low, legacy, medium, high, ultra]" option. This option takes a string argument "`Security parameter`". This is alternative to the bits option.

ask-pass option

This is the "enable interaction for entering password when in batch mode." option. This option will enable interaction to enter password when in batch mode. That is useful when the template option has been specified.

pkcs-cipher option

This is the "cipher to use for pkcs #8 and #12 operations" option. This option takes a string argument "`Cipher`". Cipher may be one of 3des, 3des-pkcs12, aes-128, aes-192, aes-256, rc2-40, arcfour.

provider option

This is the "specify the pkcs #11 provider library" option. This option takes a string argument. This will override the default options in /etc/gnutls/pkcs11.conf

certtool exit status

One of the following exit values will be returned:

- 0 (EXIT_SUCCESS) Successful program execution.

- 1 (EXIT_FAILURE) The operation failed or the command syntax was not valid.

certtool See Also

p11tool (1)

certtool Examples

Generating private keys

To create an RSA private key, run:

```
1  $ certtool --generate-privkey --outfile key.pem --rsa
```

To create a DSA or elliptic curves (ECDSA) private key use the above command combined with 'dsa' or 'ecc' options.

Generating certificate requests

To create a certificate request (needed when the certificate is issued by another party), run:

```
1  certtool --generate-request --load-privkey key.pem \
2      --outfile request.pem
```

If the private key is stored in a smart card you can generate a request by specifying the private key object URL.

```
1  $ ./certtool --generate-request --load-privkey "pkcs11:..." \
2      --load-pubkey "pkcs11:..." --outfile request.pem
```

Generating a self-signed certificate

To create a self signed certificate, use the command:

```
1 $ certtool --generate-privkey --outfile ca-key.pem
2 $ certtool --generate-self-signed --load-privkey ca-key.pem \
3    --outfile ca-cert.pem
```

Note that a self-signed certificate usually belongs to a certificate authority, that signs other certificates.

Generating a certificate

To generate a certificate using the previous request, use the command:

```
1 $ certtool --generate-certificate --load-request request.pem \
2    --outfile cert.pem --load-ca-certificate ca-cert.pem \
3    --load-ca-privkey ca-key.pem
```

To generate a certificate using the private key only, use the command:

```
1 $ certtool --generate-certificate --load-privkey key.pem \
2    --outfile cert.pem --load-ca-certificate ca-cert.pem \
3    --load-ca-privkey ca-key.pem
```

Certificate information

To view the certificate information, use:

```
1 $ certtool --certificate-info --infile cert.pem
```

PKCS #12 structure generation

To generate a PKCS #12 structure using the previous key and certificate, use the command:

```
1 $ certtool --load-certificate cert.pem --load-privkey key.pem \
2    --to-p12 --outder --outfile key.p12
```

Some tools (reportedly web browsers) have problems with that file because it does not contain the CA certificate for the certificate. To work around that problem in the tool, you can use the –load-ca-certificate parameter as follows:

```
1 $ certtool --load-ca-certificate ca.pem \
2   --load-certificate cert.pem --load-privkey key.pem \
3   --to-p12 --outder --outfile key.p12
```

Diffie-Hellman parameter generation

To generate parameters for Diffie-Hellman key exchange, use the command:

```
$ certtool --generate-dh-params --outfile dh.pem --sec-param medium
```

Proxy certificate generation

Proxy certificate can be used to delegate your credential to a temporary, typically short-lived, certificate. To create one from the previously created certificate, first create a temporary key and then generate a proxy certificate for it, using the commands:

```
$ certtool --generate-privkey > proxy-key.pem
$ certtool --generate-proxy --load-ca-privkey key.pem \
  --load-privkey proxy-key.pem --load-certificate cert.pem \
  --outfile proxy-cert.pem
```

Certificate revocation list generation

To create an empty Certificate Revocation List (CRL) do:

```
$ certtool --generate-crl --load-ca-privkey x509-ca-key.pem \
        --load-ca-certificate x509-ca.pem
```

To create a CRL that contains some revoked certificates, place the certificates in a file and use `--load-certificate` as follows:

```
$ certtool --generate-crl --load-ca-privkey x509-ca-key.pem \
  --load-ca-certificate x509-ca.pem --load-certificate revoked-certs.pem
```

To verify a Certificate Revocation List (CRL) do:

```
$ certtool --verify-crl --load-ca-certificate x509-ca.pem < crl.pem
```

certtool Files

Certtool's template file format

A template file can be used to avoid the interactive questions of certtool. Initially create a file named 'cert.cfg' that contains the information about the certificate. The template can be used as below:

```
$ certtool --generate-certificate --load-privkey key.pem  \
    --template cert.cfg --outfile cert.pem \
    --load-ca-certificate ca-cert.pem --load-ca-privkey ca-key.pem
```

An example certtool template file that can be used to generate a certificate request or a self signed certificate follows.

```
1   # X.509 Certificate options
2   #
3   # DN options
4
5   # The organization of the subject.
6   organization = "Koko inc."
7
8   # The organizational unit of the subject.
9   unit = "sleeping dept."
10
11  # The locality of the subject.
12  # locality =
13
14  # The state of the certificate owner.
15  state = "Attiki"
16
17  # The country of the subject. Two letter code.
18  country = GR
19
20  # The common name of the certificate owner.
21  cn = "Cindy Lauper"
22
23  # A user id of the certificate owner.
24  #uid = "clauper"
25
26  # Set domain components
27  #dc = "name"
28  #dc = "domain"
29
30  # If the supported DN OIDs are not adequate you can set
31  # any OID here.
32  # For example set the X.520 Title and the X.520 Pseudonym
33  # by using OID and string pairs.
34  #dn_oid = 2.5.4.12 Dr.
35  #dn_oid = 2.5.4.65 jackal
36
37  # This is deprecated and should not be used in new
38  # certificates.
39  # pkcs9_email = "none@none.org"
40
41  # An alternative way to set the certificate's distinguished name directly
42  # is with the "dn" option. The attribute names allowed are:
43  # C (country), street, O (organization), OU (unit), title, CN (common name),
44  # L (locality), ST (state), placeOfBirth, gender, countryOfCitizenship,
45  # countryOfResidence, serialNumber, telephoneNumber, surName, initials,
46  # generationQualifier, givenName, pseudonym, dnQualifier, postalCode, name,
47  # businessCategory, DC, UID, jurisdictionOfIncorporationLocalityName,
48  # jurisdictionOfIncorporationStateOrProvinceName,
49  # jurisdictionOfIncorporationCountryName, XmppAddr, and numeric OIDs.
50
51  #dn = "cn = Nikos,st = New\, Something,C=GR,surName=Mavrogiannopoulos,2.5.4.9=Arkadias"
52
53  # The serial number of the certificate
54  # Comment the field for a time-based serial number.
55  serial = 007
```

```
56
57  # In how many days, counting from today, this certificate will expire.
58  # Use -1 if there is no expiration date.
59  expiration_days = 700
60
61  # Alternatively you may set concrete dates and time. The GNU date string
62  # formats are accepted. See:
63  # http://www.gnu.org/software/tar/manual/html_node/Date-input-formats.html
64
65  #activation_date = "2004-02-29 16:21:42"
66  #expiration_date = "2025-02-29 16:24:41"
67
68  # X.509 v3 extensions
69
70  # A dnsname in case of a WWW server.
71  #dns_name = "www.none.org"
72  #dns_name = "www.morethanone.org"
73
74  # A subject alternative name URI
75  #uri = "http://www.example.com"
76
77  # An IP address in case of a server.
78  #ip_address = "192.168.1.1"
79
80  # An email in case of a person
81  email = "none@none.org"
82
83  # Challenge password used in certificate requests
84  challenge_password = 123456
85
86  # Password when encrypting a private key
87  #password = secret
88
89  # An URL that has CRLs (certificate revocation lists)
90  # available. Needed in CA certificates.
91  #crl_dist_points = "http://www.getcrl.crl/getcrl/"
92
93  # Whether this is a CA certificate or not
94  #ca
95
96  #### Key usage
97
98  # The following key usage flags are used by CAs and end certificates
99
100 # Whether this certificate will be used to sign data (needed
101 # in TLS DHE ciphersuites). This is the digitalSignature flag
102 # in RFC5280 terminology.
103 signing_key
104
105 # Whether this certificate will be used to encrypt data (needed
106 # in TLS RSA ciphersuites). Note that it is preferred to use different
107 # keys for encryption and signing. This is the keyEncipherment flag
108 # in RFC5280 terminology.
109 encryption_key
110
111 # Whether this key will be used to sign other certificates. The
112 # keyCertSign flag in RFC5280 terminology.
113 #cert_signing_key
```

```
114
115  # Whether this key will be used to sign CRLs. The
116  # cRLSign flag in RFC5280 terminology.
117  #crl_signing_key
118
119  # The keyAgreement flag of RFC5280. It's purpose is loosely
120  # defined. Not use it unless required by a protocol.
121  #key_agreement
122
123  # The dataEncipherment flag of RFC5280. It's purpose is loosely
124  # defined. Not use it unless required by a protocol.
125  #data_encipherment
126
127  # The nonRepudiation flag of RFC5280. It's purpose is loosely
128  # defined. Not use it unless required by a protocol.
129  #non_repudiation
130
131  #### Extended key usage (key purposes)
132
133  # The following extensions are used in an end certificate
134  # to clarify its purpose. Some CAs also use it to indicate
135  # the types of certificates they are purposed to sign.
136
137
138  # Whether this certificate will be used for a TLS client;
139  # this sets the id-kp-serverAuth (1.3.6.1.5.5.7.3.1) of
140  # extended key usage.
141  #tls_www_client
142
143  # Whether this certificate will be used for a TLS server;
144  # This sets the id-kp-clientAuth (1.3.6.1.5.5.7.3.2) of
145  # extended key usage.
146  #tls_www_server
147
148  # Whether this key will be used to sign code. This sets the
149  # id-kp-codeSigning (1.3.6.1.5.5.7.3.3) of extended key usage
150  # extension.
151  #code_signing_key
152
153  # Whether this key will be used to sign OCSP data. This sets the
154  # id-kp-OCSPSigning (1.3.6.1.5.5.7.3.9) of extended key usage extension.
155  #ocsp_signing_key
156
157  # Whether this key will be used for time stamping. This sets the
158  # id-kp-timeStamping (1.3.6.1.5.5.7.3.8) of extended key usage extension.
159  #time_stamping_key
160
161  # Whether this key will be used for email protection. This sets the
162  # id-kp-emailProtection (1.3.6.1.5.5.7.3.4) of extended key usage extension.
163  #email_protection_key
164
165  # Whether this key will be used for IPsec IKE operations (1.3.6.1.5.5.7.3.17).
166  #ipsec_ike_key
167
168  ## adding custom key purpose OIDs
169
170  # for microsoft smart card logon
171  # key_purpose_oid = 1.3.6.1.4.1.311.20.2.2
```

```
172
173   # for email protection
174   # key_purpose_oid = 1.3.6.1.5.5.7.3.4
175
176   # for any purpose (must not be used in intermediate CA certificates)
177   # key_purpose_oid = 2.5.29.37.0
178
179   ### end of key purpose OIDs
180
181   # When generating a certificate from a certificate
182   # request, then honor the extensions stored in the request
183   # and store them in the real certificate.
184   #honor_crq_extensions
185
186   # Path length contraint. Sets the maximum number of
187   # certificates that can be used to certify this certificate.
188   # (i.e. the certificate chain length)
189   #path_len = -1
190   #path_len = 2
191
192   # OCSP URI
193   # ocsp_uri = http://my.ocsp.server/ocsp
194
195   # CA issuers URI
196   # ca_issuers_uri = http://my.ca.issuer
197
198   # Certificate policies
199   #policy1 = 1.3.6.1.4.1.5484.1.10.99.1.0
200   #policy1_txt = "This is a long policy to summarize"
201   #policy1_url = http://www.example.com/a-policy-to-read
202
203   #policy2 = 1.3.6.1.4.1.5484.1.10.99.1.1
204   #policy2_txt = "This is a short policy"
205   #policy2_url = http://www.example.com/another-policy-to-read
206
207   # Name constraints
208
209   # DNS
210   #nc_permit_dns = example.com
211   #nc_exclude_dns = test.example.com
212
213   # EMAIL
214   #nc_permit_email = "nmav@ex.net"
215
216   # Exclude subdomains of example.com
217   #nc_exclude_email = .example.com
218
219   # Exclude all e-mail addresses of example.com
220   #nc_exclude_email = example.com
221
222
223   # Options for proxy certificates
224   #proxy_policy_language = 1.3.6.1.5.5.7.21.1
225
226
227   # Options for generating a CRL
228
229   # The number of days the next CRL update will be due.
```

71

```
230 | # next CRL update will be in 43 days
231 | #crl_next_update = 43
232 |
233 | # this is the 5th CRL by this CA
234 | # Comment the field for a time-based number.
235 | #crl_number = 5
236 |
237 | # Specify the update dates more precisely.
238 | #crl_this_update_date = "2004-02-29 16:21:42"
239 | #crl_next_update_date = "2025-02-29 16:24:41"
240 |
241 | # The date that the certificates will be made seen as
242 | # being revoked.
243 | #crl_revocation_date = "2025-02-29 16:24:41"
244 |
```

3.2.6. Invoking ocsptool

Ocsptool is a program that can parse and print information about OCSP requests/responses, generate requests and verify responses.

This section was generated by **AutoGen**, using the `agtexi-cmd` template and the option descriptions for the `ocsptool` program. This software is released under the GNU General Public License, version 3 or later.

ocsptool help/usage ("--help")

This is the automatically generated usage text for ocsptool.

The text printed is the same whether selected with the `help` option ("--help") or the `more-help` option ("--more-help"). `more-help` will print the usage text by passing it through a pager program. `more-help` is disabled on platforms without a working `fork(2)` function. The `PAGER` environment variable is used to select the program, defaulting to "`more`". Both will exit with a status code of 0.

```
1  | ocsptool - GnuTLS OCSP tool
2  | Usage:  ocsptool [ -<flag> [<val>] | --<name>[{=| }<val>] ]...
3  |
4  |   -d, --debug=num         Enable debugging
5  |                            - it must be in the range:
6  |                              0 to 9999
7  |   -V, --verbose           More verbose output
8  |                            - may appear multiple times
9  |       --infile=file       Input file
10 |                            - file must pre-exist
11 |       --outfile=str       Output file
12 |       --ask[=arg]         Ask an OCSP/HTTP server on a certificate validity
13 |                            - requires these options:
14 |                            load-cert
15 |                            load-issuer
16 |   -e, --verify-response   Verify response
17 |   -i, --request-info      Print information on a OCSP request
```

```
18    -j, --response-info       Print information on a OCSP response
19    -q, --generate-request    Generate an OCSP request
20       --nonce                Use (or not) a nonce to OCSP request
21                                - disabled as '--no-nonce'
22       --load-issuer=file     Read issuer certificate from file
23                                - file must pre-exist
24       --load-cert=file       Read certificate to check from file
25                                - file must pre-exist
26       --load-trust=file      Read OCSP trust anchors from file
27                                - prohibits the option 'load-signer'
28                                - file must pre-exist
29       --load-signer=file     Read OCSP response signer from file
30                                - prohibits the option 'load-trust'
31                                - file must pre-exist
32       --inder                Use DER format for input certificates and private keys
33                                - disabled as '--no-inder'
34    -Q, --load-request=file   Read DER encoded OCSP request from file
35                                - file must pre-exist
36    -S, --load-response=file  Read DER encoded OCSP response from file
37                                - file must pre-exist
38    -v, --version[=arg]       output version information and exit
39    -h, --help                display extended usage information and exit
40    -!, --more-help           extended usage information passed thru pager
41
42  Options are specified by doubled hyphens and their name or by a single
43  hyphen and the flag character.
44
45  Ocsptool is a program that can parse and print information about OCSP
46  requests/responses, generate requests and verify responses.
47
```

debug option (-d)

This is the "enable debugging" option. This option takes a number argument. Specifies the debug level.

ask option

This is the "ask an ocsp/http server on a certificate validity" option. This option takes an optional string argument @fileserver name—url.

This option has some usage constraints. It:

- must appear in combination with the following options: load-cert, load-issuer.

Connects to the specified HTTP OCSP server and queries on the validity of the loaded certificate.

ocsptool exit status

One of the following exit values will be returned:

- 0 (EXIT_SUCCESS) Successful program execution.

- 1 (EXIT_FAILURE) The operation failed or the command syntax was not valid.

ocsptool See Also

certtool (1)

ocsptool Examples

Print information about an OCSP request

To parse an OCSP request and print information about the content, the `-i` or `--request-info` parameter may be used as follows. The `-Q` parameter specify the name of the file containing the OCSP request, and it should contain the OCSP request in binary DER format.

```
1  $ ocsptool -i -Q ocsp-request.der
```

The input file may also be sent to standard input like this:

```
1  $ cat ocsp-request.der | ocsptool --request-info
```

Print information about an OCSP response

Similar to parsing OCSP requests, OCSP responses can be parsed using the `-j` or `--response-info` as follows.

```
1  $ ocsptool -j -Q ocsp-response.der
2  $ cat ocsp-response.der | ocsptool --response-info
```

Generate an OCSP request

The `-q` or `--generate-request` parameters are used to generate an OCSP request. By default the OCSP request is written to standard output in binary DER format, but can be stored in a file using `--outfile`. To generate an OCSP request the issuer of the certificate to check needs to be specified with `--load-issuer` and the certificate to check with `--load-cert`. By default PEM format is used for these files, although `--inder` can be used to specify that the input files are in DER format.

```
1  $ ocsptool -q --load-issuer issuer.pem --load-cert client.pem \
2          --outfile ocsp-request.der
```

When generating OCSP requests, the tool will add an OCSP extension containing a nonce. This behaviour can be disabled by specifying `--no-nonce`.

Verify signature in OCSP response

To verify the signature in an OCSP response the `-e` or `--verify-response` parameter is used. The tool will read an OCSP response in DER format from standard input, or from the file specified by `--load-response`. The OCSP response is verified against a set of trust anchors, which are specified using `--load-trust`. The trust anchors are concatenated certificates in PEM format. The certificate that signed the OCSP response needs to be in the set of trust anchors, or the issuer of the signer certificate needs to be in the set of trust anchors and the OCSP Extended Key Usage bit has to be asserted in the signer certificate.

```
1  $ ocsptool -e --load-trust issuer.pem \
2          --load-response ocsp-response.der
```

The tool will print status of verification.

Verify signature in OCSP response against given certificate

It is possible to override the normal trust logic if you know that a certain certificate is supposed to have signed the OCSP response, and you want to use it to check the signature. This is achieved using `--load-signer` instead of `--load-trust`. This will load one certificate and it will be used to verify the signature in the OCSP response. It will not check the Extended Key Usage bit.

```
1  $ ocsptool -e --load-signer ocsp-signer.pem \
2          --load-response ocsp-response.der
```

This approach is normally only relevant in two situations. The first is when the OCSP response does not contain a copy of the signer certificate, so the `--load-trust` code would fail. The second is if you want to avoid the indirect mode where the OCSP response signer certificate is signed by a trust anchor.

Real-world example

Here is an example of how to generate an OCSP request for a certificate and to verify the response. For illustration we'll use the `blog.josefsson.org` host, which (as of writing) uses a certificate from CACert. First we'll use `gnutls-cli` to get a copy of the server certificate chain. The server is not required to send this information, but this particular one is configured to do so.

```
1  $ echo | gnutls-cli -p 443 blog.josefsson.org --print-cert > chain.pem
```

Use a text editor on `chain.pem` to create three files for each separate certificates, called `cert.pem` for the first certificate for the domain itself, secondly `issuer.pem` for the intermediate certificate and `root.pem` for the final root certificate.

The domain certificate normally contains a pointer to where the OCSP responder is located, in the Authority Information Access Information extension. For example, from `certtool -i` `< cert.pem` there is this information:

```
1  Authority Information Access Information (not critical):
2  Access Method: 1.3.6.1.5.5.7.48.1 (id-ad-ocsp)
3  Access Location URI: http://ocsp.CAcert.org/
```

This means the CA support OCSP queries over HTTP. We are now ready to create a OCSP request for the certificate.

```
1  $ ocsptool --ask ocsp.CAcert.org --load-issuer issuer.pem \
2          --load-cert cert.pem --outfile ocsp-response.der
```

The request is sent via HTTP to the OCSP server address specified. If the address is ommited ocsptool will use the address stored in the certificate.

3.2.7. Invoking danetool

Tool to generate and check DNS resource records for the DANE protocol.

This section was generated by **AutoGen**, using the `agtexi-cmd` template and the option descriptions for the `danetool` program. This software is released under the GNU General Public License, version 3 or later.

danetool help/usage ("`--help`")

This is the automatically generated usage text for danetool.

The text printed is the same whether selected with the `help` option ("`--help`") or the `more-help` option ("`--more-help`"). `more-help` will print the usage text by passing it through a pager program. `more-help` is disabled on platforms without a working `fork(2)` function. The `PAGER` environment variable is used to select the program, defaulting to "`more`". Both will exit with a status code of 0.

```
1   danetool - GnuTLS DANE tool
2   Usage:  danetool [ -<flag> [<val>] | --<name>[{=| }<val>] ]...
3
4     -d, --debug=num         Enable debugging
5                               - it must be in the range:
6                               0 to 9999
7     -V, --verbose           More verbose output
8                               - may appear multiple times
9         --infile=file       Input file
10                              - file must pre-exist
11        --outfile=str       Output file
12        --load-pubkey=str   Loads a public key file
13        --load-certificate=str Loads a certificate file
14        --dlv=str           Sets a DLV file
15        --hash=str          Hash algorithm to use for signing
16        --check=str         Check a host's DANE TLSA entry
```

```
17   --check-ee              Check only the end-entity's certificate
18   --check-ca              Check only the CA's certificate
19   --tlsa-rr               Print the DANE RR data on a certificate or public key
20                             - requires the option 'host'
21   --host=str              Specify the hostname to be used in the DANE RR
22   --proto=str             The protocol set for DANE data (tcp, udp etc.)
23   --port=num              Specify the port number for the DANE data
24   --app-proto=str         an alias for the 'starttls-proto' option
25   --starttls-proto=str    The application protocol to be used to obtain the server's certificate
26 (https, ftp, smtp, imap, ldap, xmpp)
27   --ca                    Whether the provided certificate or public key is a Certificate
28 Authority
29   --x509                  Use the hash of the X.509 certificate, rather than the public key
30   --local                 an alias for the 'domain' option
31                             - enabled by default
32   --domain                The provided certificate or public key is issued by the local domain
33                             - disabled as '--no-domain'
34                             - enabled by default
35   --local-dns             Use the local DNS server for DNSSEC resolving
36                             - disabled as '--no-local-dns'
37   --insecure              Do not verify any DNSSEC signature
38   --inder                 Use DER format for input certificates and private keys
39                             - disabled as '--no-inder'
40   --inraw                 an alias for the 'inder' option
41   --print-raw             Print the received DANE data in raw format
42                             - disabled as '--no-print-raw'
43   --quiet                 Suppress several informational messages
44   -v, --version[=arg]     output version information and exit
45   -h, --help              display extended usage information and exit
46   -!, --more-help         extended usage information passed thru pager
47
48 Options are specified by doubled hyphens and their name or by a single
49 hyphen and the flag character.
50
51 Tool to generate and check DNS resource records for the DANE protocol.
52
```

debug option (-d)

This is the "enable debugging" option. This option takes a number argument. Specifies the debug level.

load-pubkey option

This is the "loads a public key file" option. This option takes a string argument. This can be either a file or a PKCS #11 URL

load-certificate option

This is the "loads a certificate file" option. This option takes a string argument. This can be either a file or a PKCS #11 URL

dlv option

This is the "sets a dlv file" option. This option takes a string argument. This sets a DLV file to be used for DNSSEC verification.

hash option

This is the "hash algorithm to use for signing" option. This option takes a string argument. Available hash functions are SHA1, RMD160, SHA256, SHA384, SHA512.

check option

This is the "check a host's dane tlsa entry" option. This option takes a string argument. Obtains the DANE TLSA entry from the given hostname and prints information. Note that the actual certificate of the host can be provided using –load-certificate, otherwise danetool will connect to the server to obtain it. The exit code on verification success will be zero.

check-ee option

This is the "check only the end-entity's certificate" option. Checks the end-entity's certificate only. Trust anchors or CAs are not considered.

check-ca option

This is the "check only the ca's certificate" option. Checks the trust anchor's and CA's certificate only. End-entities are not considered.

tlsa-rr option

This is the "print the dane rr data on a certificate or public key" option.

This option has some usage constraints. It:

- must appear in combination with the following options: host.

This command prints the DANE RR data needed to enable DANE on a DNS server.

host option

This is the "specify the hostname to be used in the dane rr" option. This option takes a string argument "Hostname". This command sets the hostname for the DANE RR.

proto option

This is the "the protocol set for dane data (tcp, udp etc.)" option. This option takes a string argument "Protocol". This command specifies the protocol for the service set in the DANE data.

app-proto option

This is an alias for the `starttls-proto` option, section 3.2.7.

starttls-proto option

This is the "the application protocol to be used to obtain the server's certificate (https, ftp, smtp, imap, ldap, xmpp)" option. This option takes a string argument. When the server's certificate isn't provided danetool will connect to the server to obtain the certificate. In that case it is required to known the protocol to talk with the server prior to initiating the TLS handshake.

ca option

This is the "whether the provided certificate or public key is a certificate authority" option. Marks the DANE RR as a CA certificate if specified.

x509 option

This is the "use the hash of the x.509 certificate, rather than the public key" option. This option forces the generated record to contain the hash of the full X.509 certificate. By default only the hash of the public key is used.

local option

This is an alias for the `domain` option, section 3.2.7.

domain option

This is the "the provided certificate or public key is issued by the local domain" option.

This option has some usage constraints. It:

- can be disabled with –no-domain.
- It is enabled by default.

DANE distinguishes certificates and public keys offered via the DNSSEC to trusted and local entities. This flag indicates that this is a domain-issued certificate, meaning that there could be no CA involved.

local-dns option

This is the "use the local dns server for dnssec resolving" option.

This option has some usage constraints. It:

- can be disabled with –no-local-dns.

This option will use the local DNS server for DNSSEC. This is disabled by default due to many servers not allowing DNSSEC.

insecure option

This is the "do not verify any dnssec signature" option. Ignores any DNSSEC signature verification results.

inder option

This is the "use der format for input certificates and private keys" option.

This option has some usage constraints. It:

- can be disabled with –no-inder.

The input files will be assumed to be in DER or RAW format. Unlike options that in PEM input would allow multiple input data (e.g. multiple certificates), when reading in DER format a single data structure is read.

inraw option

This is an alias for the **inder** option, section 3.2.7.

print-raw option

This is the "print the received dane data in raw format" option.

This option has some usage constraints. It:

- can be disabled with –no-print-raw.

This option will print the received DANE data.

quiet option

This is the "suppress several informational messages" option. In that case on the exit code can be used as an indication of verification success

danetool exit status

One of the following exit values will be returned:

- 0 (EXIT_SUCCESS) Successful program execution.

- 1 (EXIT_FAILURE) The operation failed or the command syntax was not valid.

danetool See Also

certtool (1)

danetool Examples

DANE TLSA RR generation

To create a DANE TLSA resource record for a certificate (or public key) that was issued localy and may or may not be signed by a CA use the following command.

```
1  $ danetool --tlsa-rr --host www.example.com --load-certificate cert.pem
```

To create a DANE TLSA resource record for a CA signed certificate, which will be marked as such use the following command.

```
1  $ danetool --tlsa-rr --host www.example.com --load-certificate cert.pem \
2    --no-domain
```

The former is useful to add in your DNS entry even if your certificate is signed by a CA. That way even users who do not trust your CA will be able to verify your certificate using DANE.

In order to create a record for the CA signer of your certificate use the following.

```
1  $ danetool --tlsa-rr --host www.example.com --load-certificate cert.pem \
2    --ca --no-domain
```

To read a server's DANE TLSA entry, use:

```
1  $ danetool --check www.example.com --proto tcp --port 443
```

To verify a server's DANE TLSA entry, use:

```
1  $ danetool --check www.example.com --proto tcp --port 443 --load-certificate chain.pem
```

3.3. Shared-key and anonymous authentication

In addition to certificate authentication, the TLS protocol may be used with password, shared-key and anonymous authentication methods. The rest of this chapter discusses details of these methods.

3.3.1. SRP authentication

Authentication using SRP

GnuTLS supports authentication via the Secure Remote Password or SRP protocol (see [40, 39] for a description). The SRP key exchange is an extension to the TLS protocol, and it provides an authenticated with a password key exchange. The peers can be identified using a single password, or there can be combinations where the client is authenticated using SRP and the server using a certificate.

The advantage of SRP authentication, over other proposed secure password authentication schemes, is that SRP is not susceptible to off-line dictionary attacks. Moreover, SRP does not require the server to hold the user's password. This kind of protection is similar to the one used traditionally in the UNIX "/etc/passwd" file, where the contents of this file did not cause harm to the system security if they were revealed. The SRP needs instead of the plain password something called a verifier, which is calculated using the user's password, and if stolen cannot be used to impersonate the user.

Typical conventions in SRP are a password file, called "tpasswd" that holds the SRP verifiers (encoded passwords) and another file, "tpasswd.conf", which holds the allowed SRP parameters. The included in GnuTLS helper follow those conventions. The srptool program, discussed in the next section is a tool to manipulate the SRP parameters.

The implementation in GnuTLS is based on [36]. The supported key exchange methods are shown below.

- SRP: Authentication using the SRP protocol.

- SRP_DSS: Client authentication using the SRP protocol. Server is authenticated using a certificate with DSA parameters.

- SRP_RSA: Client authentication using the SRP protocol. Server is authenticated using a certificate with RSA parameters.

---

int **gnutls_srp_base64_encode2** (*const gnutls_datum_t* * **data**, *gnutls_datum_t* * **result**)

int **gnutls_srp_base64_decode2** (*const gnutls_datum_t* * **b64_data**, *gnutls_datum_t* * **result**)

---

int **gnutls_srp_verifier** (*const char* * **username**, *const char* * **password**, *const gnutls_datum_t* * **salt**, *const gnutls_datum_t* * **generator**, *const gnutls_datum_t* * **prime**, *gnutls_datum_t* * **res**)

Description: This function will create an SRP verifier, as specified in RFC2945. The prime and generator should be one of the static parameters defined in gnutls/gnutls.h or may be generated. The verifier will be allocated with gnutls_malloc() and will be stored in res using binary format.

Returns: On success, **GNUTLS_E_SUCCESS** (0) is returned, or an error code.

Invoking srptool

Simple program that emulates the programs in the Stanford SRP (Secure Remote Password) libraries using GnuTLS. It is intended for use in places where you don't expect SRP authentication to be the used for system users.

In brief, to use SRP you need to create two files. These are the password file that holds the users and the verifiers associated with them and the configuration file to hold the group parameters (called tpasswd.conf).

This section was generated by **AutoGen**, using the `agtexi-cmd` template and the option descriptions for the `srptool` program. This software is released under the GNU General Public License, version 3 or later.

srptool help/usage ("`--help`")

This is the automatically generated usage text for srptool.

The text printed is the same whether selected with the `help` option ("`--help`") or the `more-help` option ("`--more-help`"). `more-help` will print the usage text by passing it through a pager program. `more-help` is disabled on platforms without a working `fork(2)` function. The `PAGER` environment variable is used to select the program, defaulting to "`more`". Both will exit with a status code of 0.

```
 1  srptool - GnuTLS SRP tool
 2  Usage:  srptool [ -<flag> [<val>] | --<name>[{=| }<val>] ]...
 3
 4    -d, --debug=num            Enable debugging
 5                                - it must be in the range:
 6                                  0 to 9999
 7    -i, --index=num            specify the index of the group parameters in tpasswd.conf to use
 8    -u, --username=str         specify a username
 9    -p, --passwd=str           specify a password file
10    -s, --salt=num             specify salt size
11        --verify               just verify the password.
12    -v, --passwd-conf=str      specify a password conf file.
```

```
13        --create-conf=str      Generate a password configuration file.
14   -v, --version[=arg]         output version information and exit
15   -h, --help                  display extended usage information and exit
16   -!, --more-help             extended usage information passed thru pager
17
18 Options are specified by doubled hyphens and their name or by a single
19 hyphen and the flag character.
20
21 Simple program that emulates the programs in the Stanford SRP (Secure
22 Remote Password) libraries using GnuTLS.  It is intended for use in places
23 where you don't expect SRP authentication to be the used for system users.
24
25 In brief, to use SRP you need to create two files.  These are the password
26 file that holds the users and the verifiers associated with them and the
27 configuration file to hold the group parameters (called tpasswd.conf).
28
```

debug option (-d)

This is the "enable debugging" option. This option takes a number argument. Specifies the debug level.

verify option

This is the "just verify the password." option. Verifies the password provided against the password file.

passwd-conf option (-v)

This is the "specify a password conf file." option. This option takes a string argument. Specify a filename or a PKCS #11 URL to read the CAs from.

create-conf option

This is the "generate a password configuration file." option. This option takes a string argument. This generates a password configuration file (tpasswd.conf) containing the required for TLS parameters.

srptool exit status

One of the following exit values will be returned:

- 0 (EXIT_SUCCESS) Successful program execution.

- 1 (EXIT_FAILURE) The operation failed or the command syntax was not valid.

srptool See Also

gnutls-cli-debug (1), gnutls-serv (1), srptool (1), psktool (1), certtool (1)

srptool Examples

To create "`tpasswd.conf`" which holds the g and n values for SRP protocol (generator and a large prime), run:

```
1  $ srptool --create-conf /etc/tpasswd.conf
```

This command will create "`/etc/tpasswd`" and will add user 'test' (you will also be prompted for a password). Verifiers are stored by default in the way libsrp expects.

```
1  $ srptool --passwd /etc/tpasswd --passwd-conf /etc/tpasswd.conf -u test
```

This command will check against a password. If the password matches the one in "`/etc/tpasswd`" you will get an ok.

```
1  $ srptool --passwd /etc/tpasswd --passwd\-conf /etc/tpasswd.conf --verify -u test
```

3.3.2. PSK authentication

Authentication using PSK

Authentication using Pre-shared keys is a method to authenticate using usernames and binary keys. This protocol avoids making use of public key infrastructure and expensive calculations, thus it is suitable for constraint clients.

The implementation in GnuTLS is based on [11]. The supported PSK key exchange methods are:

- PSK: Authentication using the PSK protocol.

- DHE-PSK: Authentication using the PSK protocol and Diffie-Hellman key exchange. This method offers perfect forward secrecy.

- ECDHE-PSK: Authentication using the PSK protocol and Elliptic curve Diffie-Hellman key exchange. This method offers perfect forward secrecy.

- RSA-PSK: Authentication using the PSK protocol for the client and an RSA certificate for the server.

Helper functions to generate and maintain PSK keys are also included in GnuTLS.

---

int **gnutls_key_generate** (*gnutls_datum_t* * **key**, *unsigned int* **key_size**)

int **gnutls_hex_encode** (*const gnutls_datum_t* * **data**, *char* * **result**, *size_t* * result_size)

int **gnutls_hex_decode** (*const gnutls_datum_t* * **hex_data**, *void* * **result**, *size_t* * result_size)

Invoking psktool

Program that generates random keys for use with TLS-PSK. The keys are stored in hexadecimal format in a key file.

This section was generated by **AutoGen**, using the `agtexi-cmd` template and the option descriptions for the `psktool` program. This software is released under the GNU General Public License, version 3 or later.

psktool help/usage ("`--help`")

This is the automatically generated usage text for psktool.

The text printed is the same whether selected with the `help` option ("`--help`") or the `more-help` option ("`--more-help`"). `more-help` will print the usage text by passing it through a pager program. `more-help` is disabled on platforms without a working `fork(2)` function. The `PAGER` environment variable is used to select the program, defaulting to "`more`". Both will exit with a status code of 0.

```
 1  psktool - GnuTLS PSK tool
 2  Usage:  psktool [ -<flag> [<val>] | --<name>[{=| }<val>] ]...
 3
 4    -d, --debug=num            Enable debugging
 5                                - it must be in the range:
 6                                  0 to 9999
 7    -s, --keysize=num          specify the key size in bytes
 8                                - it must be in the range:
 9                                  0 to 512
10    -u, --username=str         specify a username
11    -p, --passwd=str           specify a password file
12    -v, --version[=arg]        output version information and exit
13    -h, --help                 display extended usage information and exit
14    -!, --more-help            extended usage information passed thru pager
15
16  Options are specified by doubled hyphens and their name or by a single
17  hyphen and the flag character.
18
19  Program that generates random keys for use with TLS-PSK.  The keys are
20  stored in hexadecimal format in a key file.
21
```

debug option (-d)

This is the "enable debugging" option. This option takes a number argument. Specifies the debug level.

psktool exit status

One of the following exit values will be returned:

- 0 (EXIT_SUCCESS) Successful program execution.

- 1 (EXIT_FAILURE) The operation failed or the command syntax was not valid.

psktool See Also

gnutls-cli-debug (1), gnutls-serv (1), srptool (1), certtool (1)

psktool Examples

To add a user 'psk_identity' in "`passwd.psk`" for use with GnuTLS run:

```
1  $ ./psktool -u psk_identity -p passwd.psk
2  Generating a random key for user 'psk_identity'
3  Key stored to passwd.psk
4  $ cat psks.txt
5  psk_identity:88f3824b3e5659f52d00e959bacab954b6540344
6  $
```

This command will create "`passwd.psk`" if it does not exist and will add user 'psk_identity' (you will also be prompted for a password).

3.3.3. Anonymous authentication

The anonymous key exchange offers encryption without any indication of the peer's identity. This kind of authentication is vulnerable to a man in the middle attack, but can be used even if there is no prior communication or shared trusted parties with the peer. It is useful to establish a session over which certificate authentication will occur in order to hide the indentities of the participants from passive eavesdroppers.

Unless in the above case, it is not recommended to use anonymous authentication. In the cases where there is no prior communication with the peers, an alternative with better properties, such as key continuity, is trust on first use (see section 3.1.3).

The available key exchange algorithms for anonymous authentication are shown below, but note that few public servers support them, and they have to be explicitly enabled.

- ANON_DH: This algorithm exchanges Diffie-Hellman parameters.

- ANON_ECDH: This algorithm exchanges elliptic curve Diffie-Hellman parameters. It is more efficient than ANON_DH on equivalent security levels.

3.4. Selecting an appropriate authentication method

This section provides some guidance on how to use the available authentication methods in GnuTLS in various scenarios.

3.4.1. Two peers with an out-of-band channel

Let's consider two peers who need to communicate over an untrusted channel (the Internet), but have an out-of-band channel available. The latter channel is considered safe from eavesdropping and message modification and thus can be used for an initial bootstrapping of the protocol. The options available are:

- Pre-shared keys (see subsection 3.3.2). The server and a client communicate a shared randomly generated key over the trusted channel and use it to negotiate further sessions over the untrusted channel.

- Passwords (see subsection 3.3.1). The client communicates to the server its username and password of choice and uses it to negotiate further sessions over the untrusted channel.

- Public keys (see section 3.1). The client and the server exchange their public keys (or fingerprints of them) over the trusted channel. On future sessions over the untrusted channel they verify the key being the same (similar to section 3.1.3).

Provided that the out-of-band channel is trusted all of the above provide a similar level of protection. An out-of-band channel may be the initial bootstrapping of a user's PC in a corporate environment, in-person communication, communication over an alternative network (e.g. the phone network), etc.

3.4.2. Two peers without an out-of-band channel

When an out-of-band channel is not available a peer cannot be reliably authenticated. What can be done, however, is to allow some form of registration of users connecting for the first time and ensure that their keys remain the same after that initial connection. This is termed key continuity or trust on first use (TOFU).

The available option is to use public key authentication (see section 3.1). The client and the server store each other's public keys (or fingerprints of them) and associate them with their identity. On future sessions over the untrusted channel they verify the keys being the same (see section 3.1.3).

To mitigate the uncertainty of the information exchanged in the first connection other channels over the Internet may be used, e.g., DNSSEC (see section 3.1.3).

3.4.3. Two peers and a trusted third party

When a trusted third party is available (or a certificate authority) the most suitable option is to use certificate authentication (see section 3.1). The client and the server obtain certificates that associate their identity and public keys using a digital signature by the trusted party and use them to on the subsequent communications with each other. Each party verifies the peer's certificate using the trusted third party's signature. The parameters of the third party's signature are present in its certificate which must be available to all communicating parties.

While the above is the typical authentication method for servers in the Internet by using the commercial CAs, the users that act as clients in the protocol rarely possess such certificates. In that case a hybrid method can be used where the server is authenticated by the client using the commercial CAs and the client is authenticated based on some information the client provided over the initial server-authenticated channel. The available options are:

- Passwords (see subsection 3.3.1). The client communicates to the server its username and password of choice on the initial server-authenticated connection and uses it to negotiate further sessions. This is possible because the SRP protocol allows for the server to be authenticated using a certificate and the client using the password.

- Public keys (see section 3.1). The client sends its public key to the server (or a fingerprint of it) over the initial server-authenticated connection. On future sessions the client verifies the server using the third party certificate and the server verifies that the client's public key remained the same (see section 3.1.3).

enum gnutls_certificate_status_t:

GNUTLS_CERT_INVALID	The certificate is not signed by one of the known authorities or the signature is invalid (deprecated by the flags **GNUTLS_CERT_SIGNATURE_FAILURE** and **GNUTLS_CERT_SIGNER_NOT_FOUND**).
GNUTLS_CERT_REVOKED	Certificate is revoked by its authority. In X.509 this will be set only if CRLs are checked.
GNUTLS_CERT_SIGNER_NOT_FOUND	The certificate's issuer is not known. This is the case if the issuer is not included in the trusted certificate list.
GNUTLS_CERT_SIGNER_NOT_CA	The certificate's signer was not a CA. This may happen if this was a version 1 certificate, which is common with some CAs, or a version 3 certificate without the basic constrains extension.
GNUTLS_CERT_INSECURE_-ALGORITHM	The certificate was signed using an insecure algorithm such as MD2 or MD5. These algorithms have been broken and should not be trusted.
GNUTLS_CERT_NOT_ACTIVATED	The certificate is not yet activated.
GNUTLS_CERT_EXPIRED	The certificate has expired.
GNUTLS_CERT_SIGNATURE_FAILURE	The signature verification failed.
GNUTLS_CERT_REVOCATION_DATA_-SUPERSEDED	The revocation data are old and have been superseded.
GNUTLS_CERT_UNEXPECTED_-OWNER	The owner is not the expected one.
GNUTLS_CERT_REVOCATION_DATA_-ISSUED_IN_FUTURE	The revocation data have a future issue date.
GNUTLS_CERT_SIGNER_-CONSTRAINTS_FAILURE	The certificate's signer constraints were violated.
GNUTLS_CERT_MISMATCH	The certificate presented isn't the expected one (TOFU)
GNUTLS_CERT_PURPOSE_MISMATCH	The certificate or an intermediate does not match the intended purpose (extended key usage).

Table 3.4.: The `gnutls_certificate_status_t` enumeration.

enum **gnutls_certificate_verify_flags**:

GNUTLS_VERIFY_DISABLE_CA_SIGN	If set a signer does not have to be a certificate authority. This flag should normally be disabled, unless you know what this means.
GNUTLS_VERIFY_DO_NOT_ALLOW_-SAME	If a certificate is not signed by anyone trusted but exists in the trusted CA list do not treat it as trusted.
GNUTLS_VERIFY_ALLOW_ANY_X509_-V1_CA_CRT	Allow CA certificates that have version 1 (both root and intermediate). This might be dangerous since those haven't the basicConstraints extension.
GNUTLS_VERIFY_ALLOW_SIGN_RSA_-MD2	Allow certificates to be signed using the broken MD2 algorithm.
GNUTLS_VERIFY_ALLOW_SIGN_RSA_-MD5	Allow certificates to be signed using the broken MD5 algorithm.
GNUTLS_VERIFY_DISABLE_TIME_-CHECKS	Disable checking of activation and expiration validity periods of certificate chains. Don't set this unless you understand the security implications.
GNUTLS_VERIFY_DISABLE_-TRUSTED_TIME_CHECKS	If set a signer in the trusted list is never checked for expiration or activation.
GNUTLS_VERIFY_DO_NOT_ALLOW_-X509_V1_CA_CRT	Do not allow trusted CA certificates that have version 1. This option is to be used to deprecate all certificates of version 1.
GNUTLS_VERIFY_DISABLE_CRL_-CHECKS	Disable checking for validity using certificate revocation lists or the available OCSP data.
GNUTLS_VERIFY_ALLOW_-UNSORTED_CHAIN	A certificate chain is tolerated if unsorted (the case with many TLS servers out there). This is the default since GnuTLS 3.1.4.
GNUTLS_VERIFY_DO_NOT_ALLOW_-UNSORTED_CHAIN	Do not tolerate an unsorted certificate chain.
GNUTLS_VERIFY_DO_NOT_ALLOW_-WILDCARDS	When including a hostname check in the verification, do not consider any wildcards.
GNUTLS_VERIFY_USE_TLS1_RSA	This indicates that a (raw) RSA signature is provided as in the TLS 1.0 protocol. Not all functions accept this flag.

Table 3.5.: The `gnutls_certificate_verify_flags` enumeration.

Purpose	OID	Description
GNUTLS_KP_TLS_WWW_SERVER	1.3.6.1.5.5.7.3.1	The certificate is to be used for TLS WWW authentication. When in a CA certificate, it indicates that the CA is allowed to sign certificates for TLS WWW authentication.
GNUTLS_KP_TLS_WWW_CLIENT	1.3.6.1.5.5.7.3.2	The certificate is to be used for TLS WWW client authentication. When in a CA certificate, it indicates that the CA is allowed to sign certificates for TLS WWW client authentication.
GNUTLS_KP_CODE_SIGNING	1.3.6.1.5.5.7.3.3	The certificate is to be used for code signing. When in a CA certificate, it indicates that the CA is allowed to sign certificates for code signing.
GNUTLS_KP_EMAIL_PROTECTION	1.3.6.1.5.5.7.3.4	The certificate is to be used for email protection. When in a CA certificate, it indicates that the CA is allowed to sign certificates for email users.
GNUTLS_KP_OCSP_SIGNING	1.3.6.1.5.5.7.3.9	The certificate is to be used for signing OCSP responses. When in a CA certificate, it indicates that the CA is allowed to sign certificates which sign OCSP reponses.
GNUTLS_KP_ANY	2.5.29.37.0	The certificate is to be used for any purpose. When in a CA certificate, it indicates that the CA is allowed to sign any kind of certificates.

Table 3.6.: Key purpose object identifiers.

Field	Description
version	The field that indicates the version of the OpenPGP structure.
user ID	An RFC 2822 string that identifies the owner of the key. There may be multiple user identifiers in a key.
public key	The main public key of the certificate.
expiration	The expiration time of the main public key.
public subkey	An additional public key of the certificate. There may be multiple subkeys in a certificate.
public subkey expiration	The expiration time of the subkey.

Table 3.7.: OpenPGP certificate fields.

Key exchange	Public key requirements
RSA	An RSA public key that allows encryption.
DHE_RSA	An RSA public key that is marked for authentication.
ECDHE_RSA	An RSA public key that is marked for authentication.
DHE_DSS	A DSA public key that is marked for authentication.

Table 3.8.: The types of (sub)keys required for the various TLS key exchange methods.

Field	Description
version	The field that indicates the version of the CRL structure.
signature	A signature by the issuing authority.
issuer	Holds the issuer's distinguished name.
thisUpdate	The issuing time of the revocation list.
nextUpdate	The issuing time of the revocation list that will update that one.
revokedCertificates	List of revoked certificates serial numbers.
extensions	Optional CRL structure extensions.

Table 3.9.: Certificate revocation list fields.

Field	Description
version	The OCSP response version number (typically 1).
responder ID	An identifier of the responder (DN name or a hash of its key).
issue time	The time the response was generated.
thisUpdate	The issuing time of the revocation information.
nextUpdate	The issuing time of the revocation information that will update that one.
	Revoked certificates
certificate status	The status of the certificate.
certificate serial	The certificate's serial number.
revocationTime	The time the certificate was revoked.
revocationReason	The reason the certificate was revoked.

Table 3.10.: The most important OCSP response fields.

enum gnutls_x509_crl_reason_t:

GNUTLS_X509_CRLREASON_- UNSPECIFIED	Unspecified reason.
GNUTLS_X509_CRLREASON_- KEYCOMPROMISE	Private key compromised.
GNUTLS_X509_CRLREASON_- CACOMPROMISE	CA compromised.
GNUTLS_X509_CRLREASON_- AFFILIATIONCHANGED	Affiliation has changed.
GNUTLS_X509_CRLREASON_- SUPERSEDED	Certificate superseded.
GNUTLS_X509_CRLREASON_- CESSATIONOFOPERATION	Operation has ceased.
GNUTLS_X509_CRLREASON_- CERTIFICATEHOLD	Certificate is on hold.
GNUTLS_X509_CRLREASON_- REMOVEFROMCRL	Will be removed from delta CRL.
GNUTLS_X509_CRLREASON_- PRIVILEGEWITHDRAWN	Privilege withdrawn.
GNUTLS_X509_CRLREASON_- AACOMPROMISE	AA compromised.

Table 3.11.: The revocation reasons

enum gnutls_pkcs_encrypt_flags_t:

GNUTLS_PKCS_PLAIN	Unencrypted private key.
GNUTLS_PKCS_PKCS12_3DES	PKCS-12 3DES.
GNUTLS_PKCS_PKCS12_ARCFOUR	PKCS-12 ARCFOUR.
GNUTLS_PKCS_PKCS12_RC2_40	PKCS-12 RC2-40.
GNUTLS_PKCS_PBES2_3DES	PBES2 3DES.
GNUTLS_PKCS_PBES2_AES_128	PBES2 AES-128.
GNUTLS_PKCS_PBES2_AES_192	PBES2 AES-192.
GNUTLS_PKCS_PBES2_AES_256	PBES2 AES-256.
GNUTLS_PKCS_NULL_PASSWORD	Some schemas distinguish between an empty and a NULL password.
GNUTLS_PKCS_PBES2_DES	PBES2 single DES.

Table 3.12.: Encryption flags

Abstract keys types and Hardware security modules

In several cases storing the long term cryptographic keys in a hard disk or even in memory poses a significant risk. Once the system they are stored is compromised the keys must be replaced as the secrecy of future sessions is no longer guarranteed. Moreover, past sessions that were not protected by a perfect forward secrecy offering ciphersuite are also to be assumed compromised.

If such threats need to be addressed, then it may be wise storing the keys in a security module such as a smart card, an HSM or the TPM chip. Those modules ensure the protection of the cryptographic keys by only allowing operations on them and preventing their extraction. The purpose of the abstract key API is to provide an API that will allow the handle of keys in memory and files, as well as keys stored in such modules.

In GnuTLS the approach is to handle all keys transparently by the high level API, e.g., the API that loads a key or certificate from a file. The high-level API will accept URIs in addition to files that specify keys on an HSM or in TPM, and a callback function will be used to obtain any required keys. The URI format is defined in [19] and the standardized [26].

More information on the API is provided in the next sections. Examples of a URI of a certificate stored in an HSM, as well as a key stored in the TPM chip are shown below. To discover the URIs of the objects the `p11tool` (see subsection 4.3.6), or `tpmtool` (see subsection 4.4.4) may be used.

```
1  pkcs11:token=Nikos;serial=307521161601031;model=PKCS%2315; \
2  manufacturer=EnterSafe;object=test1;type=cert
3
4  tpmkey:uuid=42309df8-d101-11e1-a89a-97bb33c23ad1;storage=user
```

4.1. Abstract key types

Since there are many forms of a public or private keys supported by GnuTLS such as X.509, OpenPGP, PKCS #11 or TPM it is desirable to allow common operations on them. For these reasons the abstract `gnutls_privkey_t` and `gnutls_pubkey_t` were introduced in `gnutls/-abstract.h` header. Those types are initialized using a specific type of key and then can be used to perform operations in an abstract way. For example in order to sign an X.509 certificate with a key that resides in a token the following steps can be used.

```
1  #inlude <gnutls/abstract.h>
2
3  void sign_cert( gnutls_x509_crt_t to_be_signed)
4  {
5  gnutls_x509_crt_t ca_cert;
6  gnutls_privkey_t abs_key;
7
8    /* initialize the abstract key */
9    gnutls_privkey_init(&abs_key);
10
11   /* keys stored in tokens are identified by URLs */
12   gnutls_privkey_import_url(abs_key, key_url);
13
14   gnutls_x509_crt_init(&ca_cert);
15   gnutls_x509_crt_import_url(&ca_cert, cert_url);
16
17   /* sign the certificate to be signed */
18   gnutls_x509_crt_privkey_sign(to_be_signed, ca_cert, abs_key,
19                       GNUTLS_DIG_SHA256, 0);
20 }
```

4.1.1. Public keys

An abstract `gnutls_pubkey_t` can be initialized using the functions below. It can be imported through an existing structure like `gnutls_x509_crt_t`, or through an ASN.1 encoding of the X.509 `SubjectPublicKeyInfo` sequence.

---

int **gnutls_pubkey_import_x509** (*gnutls_pubkey_t* **key**, *gnutls_x509_crt_t* **crt**, *unsigned int* **flags**)

int **gnutls_pubkey_import_openpgp** (*gnutls_pubkey_t* **key**, *gnutls_openpgp_crt_t* **crt**, *unsigned int* **flags**)

int **gnutls_pubkey_import_pkcs11** (*gnutls_pubkey_t* **key**, *gnutls_pkcs11_obj_t* **obj**, *unsigned int* **flags**)

---

int **gnutls_pubkey_import_url** (*gnutls_pubkey_t* **key**, *const char ** **url**, *unsigned int* **flags**)

int **gnutls_pubkey_import_privkey** (*gnutls_pubkey_t* **key**, *gnutls_privkey_t* **pkey**, *unsigned int* **usage**, *unsigned int* **flags**)

int **gnutls_pubkey_import** (*gnutls_pubkey_t* **key**, *const gnutls_datum_t ** **data**, *gnutls_x509_crt_fmt_t* **format**)

int **gnutls_pubkey_export** (*gnutls_pubkey_t* **key**, *gnutls_x509_crt_fmt_t* **format**, *void ** **output_data**, *size_t ** **output_data_size**)

---

int **gnutls_pubkey_export2** (*gnutls_pubkey_t* **key**, *gnutls_x509_crt_fmt_t* **format**, *gnutls_datum_t ** **out**)

Description: This function will export the public key to DER or PEM format. The contents of the exported data is the SubjectPublicKeyInfo X.509 structure. The output buffer will be allocated using gnutls_malloc(). If the structure is PEM encoded, it will have a header of "BEGIN CERTIFICATE".

Returns: In case of failure a negative error code will be returned, and 0 on success.

Other helper functions that allow directly importing from raw X.509 or OpenPGP structures are shown below.

int **gnutls_pubkey_import_x509_raw** (*gnutls_pubkey_t* **pkey**, *const gnutls_datum_t ** **data**, *gnutls_x509_crt_fmt_t* **format**, *unsigned int* **flags**)

int **gnutls_pubkey_import_openpgp_raw** (*gnutls_pubkey_t* **pkey**, *const gnutls_datum_t ** **data**, *gnutls_openpgp_crt_fmt_t* **format**, *const gnutls_openpgp_keyid_t* **keyid**, *unsigned int* **flags**)

An important function is `gnutls_pubkey_import_url` which will import public keys from URLs that identify objects stored in tokens (see section 4.3 and section 4.4). A function to check for a supported by GnuTLS URL is `gnutls_url_is_supported`.

Additional functions are available that will return information over a public key, such as a unique key ID, as well as a function that given a public key fingerprint would provide a memorable sketch.

Note that `gnutls_pubkey_get_key_id` calculates a SHA1 digest of the public key as a DER-formatted, subjectPublicKeyInfo object. Other implementations use different approaches, e.g.,

---

int **gnutls_url_is_supported** (*const char* * **url**)

Description: Check whether url is supported. Depending on the system libraries GnuTLS may support pkcs11 or tpmkey URLs.

Returns: return non-zero if the given URL is supported, and zero if it is not known.

---

some use the "common method" described in section 4.2.1.2 of [8] which calculates a digest on a part of the subjectPublicKeyInfo object.

---

int **gnutls_pubkey_get_pk_algorithm** (*gnutls_pubkey_t* **key**, *unsigned int* * **bits**)

int **gnutls_pubkey_get_preferred_hash_algorithm** (*gnutls_pubkey_t* **key**, *gnutls_digest_algorithm_t* * **hash**, *unsigned int* * **mand**)

int **gnutls_pubkey_get_key_id** (*gnutls_pubkey_t* **key**, *unsigned int* **flags**, *unsigned char* * **output_data**, *size_t* * **output_data_size**)

int **gnutls_random_art** (*gnutls_random_art_t* **type**, *const char* * **key_type**, *unsigned int* **key_size**, *void* * **fpr**, *size_t* **fpr_size**, *gnutls_datum_t* * **art**)

To export the key-specific parameters, or obtain a unique key ID the following functions are provided.

---

int **gnutls_pubkey_export_rsa_raw** (*gnutls_pubkey_t* **key**, *gnutls_datum_t* * **m**, *gnutls_datum_t* * **e**)

int **gnutls_pubkey_export_dsa_raw** (*gnutls_pubkey_t* **key**, *gnutls_datum_t* * **p**, *gnutls_datum_t* * **q**, *gnutls_datum_t* * **g**, *gnutls_datum_t* * **y**)

int **gnutls_pubkey_export_ecc_raw** (*gnutls_pubkey_t* **key**, *gnutls_ecc_curve_t* * **curve**, *gnutls_datum_t* * **x**, *gnutls_datum_t* * **y**)

int **gnutls_pubkey_export_ecc_x962** (*gnutls_pubkey_t* **key**, *gnutls_datum_t* * **parameters**, *gnutls_datum_t* * **ecpoint**)

4.1.2. Private keys

An abstract `gnutls_privkey_t` can be initialized using the functions below. It can be imported through an existing structure like `gnutls_x509_privkey_t`, but unlike public keys it cannot be exported. That is to allow abstraction over keys stored in hardware that makes available only operations.

---

int **gnutls_privkey_import_x509** (*gnutls_privkey_t* **pkey**, *gnutls_x509_privkey_t* **key**, *unsigned int* **flags**)

int **gnutls_privkey_import_openpgp** (*gnutls_privkey_t* **pkey**, *gnutls_openpgp_privkey_t* **key**, *unsigned int* **flags**)

int **gnutls_privkey_import_pkcs11** (*gnutls_privkey_t* **pkey**, *gnutls_pkcs11_privkey_t* **key**, *unsigned int* **flags**)

Other helper functions that allow directly importing from raw X.509 or OpenPGP structures are shown below. Again, as with public keys, private keys can be imported from a hardware module using URLs.

---

int **gnutls_privkey_import_x509_raw** (*gnutls_privkey_t* **pkey**, *const gnutls_datum_t ** **data**, *gnutls_x509_crt_fmt_t* **format**, *const char ** **password**, *unsigned int* **flags**)

int **gnutls_privkey_import_openpgp_raw** (*gnutls_privkey_t* **pkey**, *const gnutls_datum_t ** **data**, *gnutls_openpgp_crt_fmt_t* **format**, *const gnutls_openpgp_keyid_t* **keyid**, *const char ** **password**)

---

int **gnutls_privkey_import_url** (*gnutls_privkey_t* **key**, *const char ** **url**, *unsigned int* **flags**)

Description: This function will import a PKCS11 or TPM URL as a private key. The supported URL types can be checked using gnutls_url_is_supported().

Returns: On success, **GNUTLS_E_SUCCESS** (0) is returned, otherwise a negative error value.

---

int **gnutls_privkey_get_pk_algorithm** (*gnutls_privkey_t* **key**, *unsigned int ** **bits**)

gnutls_privkey_type_t **gnutls_privkey_get_type** (*gnutls_privkey_t* **key**)

int **gnutls_privkey_status** (*gnutls_privkey_t* **key**)

In order to support cryptographic operations using an external API, the following function is provided. This allows for a simple extensibility API without resorting to PKCS #11.

---

int **gnutls_privkey_import_ext3** (*gnutls_privkey_t* **pkey**, *void* * **userdata**, *gnutls_privkey_sign_func* **sign_fn**, *gnutls_privkey_decrypt_func* **decrypt_fn**, *gnutls_privkey_deinit_func* **deinit_fn**, *gnutls_privkey_info_func* **info_fn**, *unsigned int* **flags**)

Description: This function will associate the given callbacks with the *gnutls_privkey_t* type. At least one of the two callbacks must be non-null. If a deinitialization function is provided then flags is assumed to contain **GNUTLS_PRIVKEY_IMPORT_AUTO_RELEASE**. Note that the signing function is supposed to "raw" sign data, i.e., without any hashing or preprocessing. In case of RSA the DigestInfo will be provided, and the signing function is expected to do the PKCS #1 1.5 padding and the exponentiation. The info_fn must provide information on the algorithms supported by this private key, and should support the flags **GNUTLS_PRIVKEY_INFO_PK_ALGO** and **GNUTLS_PRIVKEY_INFO_SIGN_ALGO**. It must return -1 on unknown flags.

Returns: On success, **GNUTLS_E_SUCCESS** (0) is returned, otherwise a negative error value.

4.1.3. Operations

The abstract key types can be used to access signing and signature verification operations with the underlying keys.

---

int **gnutls_pubkey_verify_data2** (*gnutls_pubkey_t* **pubkey**, *gnutls_sign_algorithm_t* **algo**, *unsigned int* **flags**, *const gnutls_datum_t* * **data**, *const gnutls_datum_t* * **signature**)

Description: This function will verify the given signed data, using the parameters from the certificate.

Returns: In case of a verification failure **GNUTLS_E_PK_SIG_VERIFY_FAILED** is returned, and zero or positive code on success. For known to be insecure signatures this function will return **GNUTLS_E_INSUFFICIENT_SECURITY** unless the flag **GNUTLS_VERIFY_ALLOW_BROKEN** is specified.

Signing existing structures, such as certificates, CRLs, or certificate requests, as well as associating public keys with structures is also possible using the key abstractions.

int **gnutls_pubkey_verify_hash2** (*gnutls_pubkey_t* **key**, *gnutls_sign_algorithm_t* **algo**, *unsigned int* **flags**, *const gnutls_datum_t* * **hash**, *const gnutls_datum_t* * **signature**)

Description: This function will verify the given signed digest, using the parameters from the public key. Note that unlike gnutls_privkey_sign_hash(), this function accepts a signature algorithm instead of a digest algorithm. You can use gnutls_pk_to_sign() to get the appropriate value.

Returns: In case of a verification failure **GNUTLS_E_PK_SIG_VERIFY_FAILED** is returned, and zero or positive code on success.

---

int **gnutls_pubkey_encrypt_data** (*gnutls_pubkey_t* **key**, *unsigned int* **flags**, *const gnutls_datum_t* * **plaintext**, *gnutls_datum_t* * **ciphertext**)

Description: This function will encrypt the given data, using the public key.

Returns: On success, **GNUTLS_E_SUCCESS** (0) is returned, otherwise a negative error value.

---

int **gnutls_x509_crt_privkey_sign** (*gnutls_x509_crt_t* **crt**, *gnutls_x509_crt_t* **issuer**, *gnutls_privkey_t* **issuer_key**, *gnutls_digest_algorithm_t* **dig**, *unsigned int* **flags**)

int **gnutls_x509_crl_privkey_sign** (*gnutls_x509_crl_t* **crl**, *gnutls_x509_crt_t* **issuer**, *gnutls_privkey_t* **issuer_key**, *gnutls_digest_algorithm_t* **dig**, *unsigned int* **flags**)

int **gnutls_x509_crq_privkey_sign** (*gnutls_x509_crq_t* **crq**, *gnutls_privkey_t* **key**, *gnutls_digest_algorithm_t* **dig**, *unsigned int* **flags**)

---

int **gnutls_privkey_sign_data** (*gnutls_privkey_t* **signer**, *gnutls_digest_algorithm_t* **hash**, *unsigned int* **flags**, *const gnutls_datum_t* * **data**, *gnutls_datum_t* * **signature**)

Description: This function will sign the given data using a signature algorithm supported by the private key. Signature algorithms are always used together with a hash functions. Different hash functions may be used for the RSA algorithm, but only the SHA family for the DSA keys. You may use gnutls_pubkey_get_preferred_hash_algorithm() to determine the hash algorithm.

Returns: On success, **GNUTLS_E_SUCCESS** (0) is returned, otherwise a negative error value.

int **gnutls_privkey_sign_hash** (*gnutls_privkey_t* **signer**, *gnutls_digest_algorithm_t* **hash_algo**, *unsigned int* **flags**, *const gnutls_datum_t ** **hash_data**, *gnutls_datum_t ** **signature**)

Description: This function will sign the given hashed data using a signature algorithm supported by the private key. Signature algorithms are always used together with a hash functions. Different hash functions may be used for the RSA algorithm, but only SHA-XXX for the DSA keys. You may use gnutls_pubkey_get_preferred_hash_algorithm() to determine the hash algorithm. Note that if **GNUTLS_PRIVKEY_SIGN_FLAG_TLS1_RSA** flag is specified this function will ignore hash_algo and perform a raw PKCS1 signature.

Returns: On success, **GNUTLS_E_SUCCESS** (0) is returned, otherwise a negative error value.

---

int **gnutls_privkey_decrypt_data** (*gnutls_privkey_t* **key**, *unsigned int* **flags**, *const gnutls_datum_t ** **ciphertext**, *gnutls_datum_t ** **plaintext**)

Description: This function will decrypt the given data using the algorithm supported by the private key.

Returns: On success, **GNUTLS_E_SUCCESS** (0) is returned, otherwise a negative error value.

---

int **gnutls_x509_crq_set_pubkey** (*gnutls_x509_crq_t* **crq**, *gnutls_pubkey_t* **key**)

Description: This function will set the public parameters from the given public key to the request.

Returns: On success, **GNUTLS_E_SUCCESS** (0) is returned, otherwise a negative error value.

---

int **gnutls_x509_crt_set_pubkey** (*gnutls_x509_crt_t* **crt**, *gnutls_pubkey_t* **key**)

Description: This function will set the public parameters from the given public key to the request.

Returns: On success, **GNUTLS_E_SUCCESS** (0) is returned, otherwise a negative error value.

4.2. System and application-specific keys

4.2.1. System-specific keys

In several systems there are keystores which allow to read, store and use certificates and private keys. For these systems GnuTLS provides the system-key API in `gnutls/system-keys.h`. That API provides the ability to iterate through all stored keys, add and delete keys as well as use these keys using a URL which starts with "system:". The format of the URLs is system-specific.

---

int **gnutls_system_key_iter_get_info** (*gnutls_system_key_iter_t* * **iter**, *unsigned* **cert_type**, *char* ** **cert_url**, *char* ** **key_url**, *char* ** **label**, *gnutls_datum_t* * **der**, *unsigned int* **flags**)

Description: This function will return on each call a certificate and key pair URLs, as well as a label associated with them, and the DER-encoded certificate. When the iteration is complete it will return **GNUTLS_E_REQUESTED_DATA_NOT_AVAILABLE**. Typically cert_type should be **GNUTLS_CRT_X509**. All values set are allocated and must be cleared using gnutls_free(),

Returns: On success, **GNUTLS_E_SUCCESS** (0) is returned, otherwise a negative error value.

---

void **gnutls_system_key_iter_deinit** (*gnutls_system_key_iter_t* **iter**)

int **gnutls_system_key_add_x509** (*gnutls_x509_crt_t* **crt**, *gnutls_x509_privkey_t* **privkey**, *const char* * **label**, *char* ** **cert_url**, *char* ** **key_url**)

int **gnutls_system_key_delete** (*const char* * **cert_url**, *const char* * **key_url**)

4.2.2. Application-specific keys

For systems where GnuTLS doesn't provide a system specific store, it may often be desirable to define a custom class of keys that are identified via URLs and available to GnuTLS calls such as `gnutls_certificate_set_x509_key_file2`. Such keys can be registered using the API in `gnutls/urls.h`. The function which registers such keys is `gnutls_register_custom_url`.

The input to this function are three callback functions as well as the prefix of the URL, (e.g., "mypkcs11:") and the length of the prefix. The types of the callbacks are shown below, and

---

int **gnutls_register_custom_url** (*const gnutls_custom_url_st * * **st**)

Description: Register a custom URL. This will affect the following functions: gnutls_-url_is_supported(), gnutls_privkey_import_url(), gnutls_pubkey_import_url, gnutls_x509_crt_-import_url() and all functions that depend on them, e.g., gnutls_certificate_set_x509_-key_file2(). The provided structure and callback functions must be valid throughout the lifetime of the process. The registration of an existing URL type will fail with **GNUTLS_E_INVALID_REQUEST.** This function is not thread safe.

Returns: returns zero if the given structure was imported or a negative value otherwise.

---

are expected to use the exported gnutls functions to import the keys and certificates. E.g., a typical import_key callback should use gnutls_privkey_import_ext3.

```
typedef int (*gnutls_privkey_import_url_func)(gnutls_privkey_t pkey,
                                              const char *url,
                                              unsigned flags);

typedef int (*gnutls_x509_crt_import_url_func)(gnutls_x509_crt_t pkey,
                                               const char *url,
                                               unsigned flags);

/* The following callbacks are optional */

/* This is to enable gnutls_pubkey_import_url() */
typedef int (*gnutls_pubkey_import_url_func)(gnutls_pubkey_t pkey,
                                             const char *url, unsigned flags);

/* This is to allow constructing a certificate chain. It will be provided
 * the initial certificate URL and the certificate to find its issuer, and must
 * return zero and the DER encoding of the issuer's certificate. If not available,
 * it should return GNUTLS_E_REQUESTED_DATA_NOT_AVAILABLE. */
typedef int (*gnutls_get_raw_issuer_func)(const char *url, gnutls_x509_crt_t crt,
                                          gnutls_datum_t *issuer_der, unsigned flags);

typedef struct custom_url_st {
        const char *name;
        unsigned name_size;
        gnutls_privkey_import_url_func import_key;
        gnutls_x509_crt_import_url_func import_crt;
        gnutls_pubkey_import_url_func import_pubkey;
        gnutls_get_raw_issuer_func get_issuer;
} gnutls_custom_url_st;
```

4.3. Smart cards and HSMs

In this section we present the smart-card and hardware security module (HSM) support in GnuTLS using PKCS #11 [2]. Hardware security modules and smart cards provide a way to store private keys and perform operations on them without exposing them. This decouples cryptographic keys from the applications that use them and provide an additional security layer against cryptographic key extraction. Since this can also be achieved in software components such as in Gnome keyring, we will use the term security module to describe any cryptographic key separation subsystem.

PKCS #11 is plugin API allowing applications to access cryptographic operations on a security module, as well as to objects residing on it. PKCS #11 modules exist for hardware tokens such as smart cards[1], cryptographic tokens, as well as for software modules like Gnome Keyring. The objects residing on a security module may be certificates, public keys, private keys or secret keys. Of those certificates and public/private key pairs can be used with GnuTLS. PKCS #11's main advantage is that it allows operations on private key objects such as decryption and signing without exposing the key. In GnuTLS the PKCS #11 functionality is available in gnutls/pkcs11.h.

Moreover PKCS #11 can be (ab)used to allow all applications in the same operating system to access shared cryptographic keys and certificates in a uniform way, as in Figure 4.1. That way applications could load their trusted certificate list, as well as user certificates from a common PKCS #11 module. Such a provider is the p11-kit trust storage module[2].

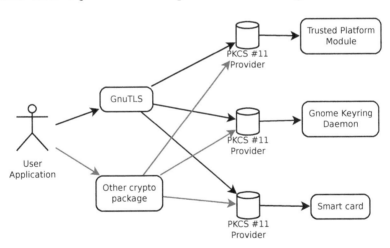

Figure 4.1.: PKCS #11 module usage.

4.3.1. Initialization

To allow all GnuTLS applications to transparently access smard cards and tokens, PKCS #11 is automatically initialized during the first call of a PKCS #11 related function. The initialization

---

[1]For example, OpenSC-supported cards.
[2]http://p11-glue.freedesktop.org/trust-module.html

process, based on p11-kit configuration, loads any appropriate modules. The p11-kit configuration files[3] are typically stored in **/etc/pkcs11/modules/**. For example a file that will instruct GnuTLS to load the OpenSC module, could be named **/etc/pkcs11/modules/opensc.module** and contain the following:

```
1  module: /usr/lib/opensc-pkcs11.so
```

If you use these configuration files, then there is no need for other initialization in GnuTLS, except for the PIN and token callbacks (see next section). In several cases, however, it is desirable to limit badly behaving modules (e.g., modules that add an unacceptable delay on initialization) to single applications. That can be done using the "enable-in:" option followed by the base name of applications that this module should be used.

It is also possible to manually initialize the PKCS #11 subsystem if the default settings are not desirable. To completely disable PKCS #11 support you need to call **gnutls_pkcs11_init** with the flag GNUTLS_PKCS11_FLAG_MANUAL prior to **gnutls_global_init**.

---

int **gnutls_pkcs11_init** (*unsigned int* **flags**, *const char* * **deprecated_config_file**)

Description: This function will initialize the PKCS 11 subsystem in gnutls. It will read configuration files if **GNUTLS_PKCS**11_FLAG_AUTO is used or allow you to independently load PKCS 11 modules using gnutls_pkcs11_add_provider() if **GNUTLS_-PKCS**11_FLAG_MANUAL is specified. You don't need to call this function since GnuTLS 3.3.0 because it is being called during the first request PKCS 11 operation. That call will assume the **GNUTLS_PKCS**11_FLAG_AUTO flag. If another flags are required then it must be called independently prior to any PKCS 11 operation.

Returns: On success, **GNUTLS_E_SUCCESS** (0) is returned, otherwise a negative error value.

Note that, PKCS #11 modules behave in a peculiar way after a fork; they require a reinitialization of all the used PKCS #11 resources. While GnuTLS automates that process, there are corner cases where it is not possible to handle it correctly in an automated way[4]. For that reasons it is recommended not to mix fork() and PKCS #11 module usage. It is recommended to initialize and use any PKCS #11 resources in a single process.

Older versions of GnuTLS required to call **gnutls_pkcs11_reinit** after a fork() call; since 3.3.0 this is no longer required.

---

[3]http://p11-glue.freedesktop.org/
[4]For example when an open session is to be reinitialized, but the PIN is not available to GnuTLS (e.g., it was entered at a pinpad).

4.3.2. Accessing objects that require a PIN

Objects stored in token such as a private keys are typically protected from access by a PIN or password. This PIN may be required to either read the object (if allowed) or to perform operations with it. To allow obtaining the PIN when accessing a protected object, as well as probe the user to insert the token the following functions allow to set a callback.

---

void **gnutls_pkcs11_set_token_function** (*gnutls_pkcs11_token_callback_t* **fn**, *void* *** **userdata**)

void **gnutls_pkcs11_set_pin_function** (*gnutls_pin_callback_t* **fn**, *void* * **userdata**)

int **gnutls_pkcs11_add_provider** (*const char* * **name**, *const char* * **params**)

gnutls_pin_callback_t **gnutls_pkcs11_get_pin_function** (*void* ** **userdata**)

The callback is of type `gnutls_pin_callback_t` and will have as input the provided userdata, the PIN attempt number, a URL describing the token, a label describing the object and flags. The PIN must be at most of `pin_max` size and must be copied to pin variable. The function must return 0 on success or a negative error code otherwise.

```
typedef int (*gnutls_pin_callback_t) (void *userdata, int attempt,
                                      const char *token_url,
                                      const char *token_label,
                                      unsigned int flags,
                                      char *pin, size_t pin_max);
```

The flags are of `gnutls_pin_flag_t` type and are explained below.

```
enum gnutls_pin_flag_t:
```
GNUTLS_PIN_USER	`The PIN for the user.`
GNUTLS_PIN_SO	`The PIN for the security officer (admin).`
GNUTLS_PIN_FINAL_TRY	`This is the final try before blocking.`
GNUTLS_PIN_COUNT_LOW	`Few tries remain before token blocks.`
GNUTLS_PIN_CONTEXT_SPECIFIC	`The PIN is for a specific action and key like signing.`
GNUTLS_PIN_WRONG	`Last given PIN was not correct.`

Table 4.1.: The `gnutls_pin_flag_t` enumeration.

Note that due to limitations of PKCS #11 there are issues when multiple libraries are sharing a module. To avoid this problem GnuTLS uses p11-kit that provides a middleware to control access to resources over the multiple users.

To avoid conflicts with multiple registered callbacks for PIN functions, `gnutls_pkcs11_get_-pin_function` may be used to check for any previously set functions. In addition context specific PIN functions are allowed, e.g., by using functions below.

---

void **gnutls_certificate_set_pin_function** (*gnutls_certificate_credentials_t*   **cred**, *gnutls_pin_callback_t* **fn**, *void* * **userdata**)

void **gnutls_pubkey_set_pin_function** (*gnutls_pubkey_t* **key**, *gnutls_pin_callback_t* **fn**, *void* * **userdata**)

void **gnutls_privkey_set_pin_function** (*gnutls_privkey_t* **key**, *gnutls_pin_callback_t* **fn**, *void* * **userdata**)

void **gnutls_pkcs11_obj_set_pin_function** (*gnutls_pkcs11_obj_t* **obj**, *gnutls_pin_callback_t* **fn**, *void* * **userdata**)

void **gnutls_x509_crt_set_pin_function** (*gnutls_x509_crt_t* **crt**, *gnutls_pin_callback_t* **fn**, *void* * **userdata**)

4.3.3. Reading objects

All PKCS #11 objects are referenced by GnuTLS functions by URLs as described in [26]. This allows for a consistent naming of objects across systems and applications in the same system. For example a public key on a smart card may be referenced as:

```
1  pkcs11:token=Nikos;serial=307521161601031;model=PKCS%2315; \
2  manufacturer=EnterSafe;object=test1;type=public;\
3  id=32f153f3e37990b08624141077ca5dec2d15faed
```

while the smart card itself can be referenced as:

```
1  pkcs11:token=Nikos;serial=307521161601031;model=PKCS%2315;manufacturer=EnterSafe
```

Objects stored in a PKCS #11 token can be extracted if they are not marked as sensitive. Usually only private keys are marked as sensitive and cannot be extracted, while certificates and other data can be retrieved. The functions that can be used to access objects are shown below.

---

int **gnutls_pkcs11_obj_import_url** (*gnutls_pkcs11_obj_t* **obj**, *const char* * **url**, *unsigned int* **flags**)

int **gnutls_pkcs11_obj_export_url** (*gnutls_pkcs11_obj_t* **obj**, *gnutls_pkcs11_url_type_t* **detailed**, *char* ** **url**)

---

int **gnutls_pkcs11_obj_get_info** (*gnutls_pkcs11_obj_t* **obj**, *gnutls_pkcs11_obj_info_t* **itype**, *void* * **output**, *size_t* * **output_size**)

Description: ```This function will return information about the PKCS11 certificate such as the label, id as well as token information where the key is stored. When output is text it returns null terminated string although output_size contains the size of the actual data only.```

Returns: ```GNUTLS_E_SUCCESS (0) on success or a negative error code on error.```

---

int **gnutls_x509_crt_import_pkcs11** (*gnutls_x509_crt_t* **crt**, *gnutls_pkcs11_obj_t* **pkcs11_crt**)

int **gnutls_x509_crt_import_url** (*gnutls_x509_crt_t* **crt**, *const char* * **url**, *unsigned int* **flags**)

int **gnutls_x509_crt_list_import_pkcs11** (*gnutls_x509_crt_t* * **certs**, *unsigned int* **cert_max**, *gnutls_pkcs11_obj_t* * *const* **objs**, *unsigned int* **flags**)

Properties of the physical token can also be accessed and altered with GnuTLS. For example data in a token can be erased (initialized), PIN can be altered, etc.

---

int **gnutls_pkcs11_token_init** (*const char* * **token_url**, *const char* * **so_pin**, *const char* * **label**)

int **gnutls_pkcs11_token_get_url** (*unsigned int* **seq**, *gnutls_pkcs11_url_type_t* **detailed**, *char* ** **url**)

int **gnutls_pkcs11_token_get_info** (*const char* * **url**, *gnutls_pkcs11_token_info_t* **ttype**, *void* * **output**, *size_t* * **output_size**)

int **gnutls_pkcs11_token_get_flags** (*const char* * **url**, *unsigned int* * **flags**)

int **gnutls_pkcs11_token_set_pin** (*const char* * **token_url**, *const char* * **oldpin**, *const char* * **newpin**, *unsigned int* **flags**)

The following examples demonstrate the usage of the API. The first example will list all available PKCS #11 tokens in a system and the latter will list all certificates in a token that have a corresponding private key.

```
1  int i;
```

```
 2  char* url;
 3
 4  gnutls_global_init();
 5
 6  for (i=0;;i++)
 7    {
 8      ret = gnutls_pkcs11_token_get_url(i, &url);
 9      if (ret == GNUTLS_E_REQUESTED_DATA_NOT_AVAILABLE)
10        break;
11
12      if (ret < 0)
13        exit(1);
14
15      fprintf(stdout, "Token[%d]: URL: %s\n", i, url);
16      gnutls_free(url);
17    }
18  gnutls_global_deinit();
```

```
 1  /* This example code is placed in the public domain. */
 2
 3  #include <config.h>
 4  #include <gnutls/gnutls.h>
 5  #include <gnutls/pkcs11.h>
 6  #include <stdio.h>
 7  #include <stdlib.h>
 8
 9  #define URL "pkcs11:URL"
10
11  int main(int argc, char **argv)
12  {
13          gnutls_pkcs11_obj_t *obj_list;
14          gnutls_x509_crt_t xcrt;
15          unsigned int obj_list_size = 0;
16          gnutls_datum_t cinfo;
17          int ret;
18          unsigned int i;
19
20          ret = gnutls_pkcs11_obj_list_import_url4(&obj_list, &obj_list_size, URL,
21                                            GNUTLS_PKCS11_OBJ_FLAG_CRT|
22                                            GNUTLS_PKCS11_OBJ_FLAG_WITH_PRIVKEY);
23          if (ret < 0)
24                  return -1;
25
26          /* now all certificates are in obj_list */
27          for (i = 0; i < obj_list_size; i++) {
28
29                  gnutls_x509_crt_init(&xcrt);
30
31                  gnutls_x509_crt_import_pkcs11(xcrt, obj_list[i]);
32
33                  gnutls_x509_crt_print(xcrt, GNUTLS_CRT_PRINT_FULL, &cinfo);
34
35                  fprintf(stdout, "cert[%d]:\n %s\n\n", i, cinfo.data);
36
37                  gnutls_free(cinfo.data);
38                  gnutls_x509_crt_deinit(xcrt);
39          }
```

```
40
41      for (i = 0; i < obj_list_size; i++)
42              gnutls_pkcs11_obj_deinit(obj_list[i]);
43      gnutls_free(obj_list);
44
45      return 0;
46 }
```

4.3.4. Writing objects

With GnuTLS you can copy existing private keys and certificates to a token. Note that when copying private keys it is recommended to mark them as sensitive using the GNUTLS_PKCS11_OBJ_FLAG_MARK_SENSITIVE to prevent its extraction. An object can be marked as private using the flag GNUTLS_PKCS11_OBJ_FLAG_MARK_PRIVATE, to require PIN to be entered before accessing the object (for operations or otherwise).

---

int **gnutls_pkcs11_copy_x509_privkey2** (*const char* * **token_url**, *gnutls_x509_privkey_t* **key**, *const char* * **label**, *const gnutls_datum_t* * **cid**, *unsigned int* **key_usage**, *unsigned int* **flags**)

Description: This function will copy a private key into a PKCS #11 token specified by a URL. It is highly recommended flags to contain **GNUTLS_PKCS11_OBJ_FLAG_MARK_SENSITIVE** unless there is a strong reason not to.

Returns: On success, **GNUTLS_E_SUCCESS** (0) is returned, otherwise a negative error value.

---

int **gnutls_pkcs11_copy_x509_crt2** (*const char* * **token_url**, *gnutls_x509_crt_t* **crt**, *const char* * **label**, *const gnutls_datum_t* * **cid**, *unsigned int* **flags**)

Description: This function will copy a certificate into a PKCS #11 token specified by a URL. Valid flags to mark the certificate: **GNUTLS_PKCS11_OBJ_FLAG_MARK_TRUSTED**, **GNUTLS_PKCS11_OBJ_FLAG_MARK_SENSITIVE**, **GNUTLS_PKCS11_OBJ_FLAG_MARK_PRIVATE**, **GNUTLS_PKCS11_OBJ_FLAG_MARK_CA**, **GNUTLS_PKCS11_OBJ_FLAG_MARK_ALWAYS_AUTH**.

Returns: On success, **GNUTLS_E_SUCCESS** (0) is returned, otherwise a negative error value.

---

int **gnutls_pkcs11_delete_url** (*const char* * **object_url**, *unsigned int* **flags**)

Description: `This function will delete objects matching the given URL. Note that not all tokens support the delete operation.`

Returns: `On success, the number of objects deleted is returned, otherwise a negative error value.`

4.3.5. Using a PKCS #11 token with TLS

It is possible to use a PKCS #11 token to a TLS session, as shown in subsection 6.1.8. In addition the following functions can be used to load PKCS #11 key and certificates by specifying a PKCS #11 URL instead of a filename.

---

int **gnutls_certificate_set_x509_trust_file** (*gnutls_certificate_credentials_t* **cred**, *const char* * **cafile**, *gnutls_x509_crt_fmt_t* **type**)

int **gnutls_certificate_set_x509_key_file2** (*gnutls_certificate_credentials_t* **res**, *const char* * **certfile**, *const char* * **keyfile**, *gnutls_x509_crt_fmt_t* **type**, *const char* * **pass**, *unsigned int* **flags**)

---

int **gnutls_certificate_set_x509_system_trust** (*gnutls_certificate_credentials_t* **cred**)

Description: `This function adds the system's default trusted CAs in order to verify client or server certificates. In the case the system is currently unsupported` **GNUTLS_-E_UNIMPLEMENTED_FEATURE** `is returned.`

Returns: `the number of certificates processed or a negative error code on error.`

4.3.6. Invoking p11tool

Program that allows operations on PKCS #11 smart cards and security modules.

To use PKCS #11 tokens with GnuTLS the p11-kit configuration files need to be setup. That is create a .module file in /etc/pkcs11/modules with the contents 'module: /path/to/pkcs11.so'. Alternatively the configuration file /etc/gnutls/pkcs11.conf has to exist and contain a number of lines of the form 'load=/usr/lib/opensc-pkcs11.so'.

You can provide the PIN to be used for the PKCS #11 operations with the environment variables GNUTLS_PIN and GNUTLS_SO_PIN.

This section was generated by **AutoGen**, using the `agtexi-cmd` template and the option descriptions for the `p11tool` program. This software is released under the GNU General Public License, version 3 or later.

4.3.7. p11tool help/usage ("`--help`")

This is the automatically generated usage text for p11tool.

The text printed is the same whether selected with the `help` option ("`--help`") or the `more-help` option ("`--more-help`"). `more-help` will print the usage text by passing it through a pager program. `more-help` is disabled on platforms without a working `fork(2)` function. The `PAGER` environment variable is used to select the program, defaulting to "`more`". Both will exit with a status code of 0.

```
1   p11tool - GnuTLS PKCS #11 tool
2   Usage:  p11tool [ -<flag> [<val>] | --<name>[{=| }<val>] ]... [url]
3
4
5   Tokens:
6
7           --list-tokens        List all available tokens
8           --list-token-urls    List the URLs available tokens
9           --list-mechanisms    List all available mechanisms in a token
10          --initialize         Initializes a PKCS #11 token
11          --set-pin=str        Specify the PIN to use on token initialization
12          --set-so-pin=str     Specify the Security Officer's PIN to use on token initialization
13
14  Object listing:
15
16          --list-all           List all available objects in a token
17          --list-all-certs     List all available certificates in a token
18          --list-certs         List all certificates that have an associated private key
19          --list-all-privkeys  List all available private keys in a token
20          --list-privkeys      an alias for the 'list-all-privkeys' option
21          --list-keys          an alias for the 'list-all-privkeys' option
22          --list-all-trusted   List all available certificates marked as trusted
23          --export             Export the object specified by the URL
24          --export-chain       Export the certificate specified by the URL and its chain of trust
25          --export-pubkey      Export the public key for a private key
26          --info               List information on an available object in a token
27
28  Key generation:
29
30          --generate-rsa       Generate an RSA private-public key pair
31          --generate-dsa       Generate a DSA private-public key pair
32          --generate-ecc       Generate an ECDSA private-public key pair
33          --bits=num           Specify the number of bits for key generate
34          --curve=str          Specify the curve used for EC key generation
35          --sec-param=str      Specify the security level
36
37  Writing objects:
38
39          --set-id=str         Set the CKA_ID (in hex) for the specified by the URL object
40                                 - prohibits the option 'write'
41          --set-label=str      Set the CKA_LABEL for the specified by the URL object
```

```
42                            - prohibits these options:
43                              write
44                              set-id
45      --write               Writes the loaded objects to a PKCS #11 token
46      --delete              Deletes the objects matching the given PKCS #11 URL
47      --label=str           Sets a label for the write operation
48      --id=str              Sets an ID for the write operation
49      --mark-wrap           Marks the generated key to be a wrapping key
50                              - disabled as '--no-mark-wrap'
51      --mark-trusted        Marks the object to be written as trusted
52                              - disabled as '--no-mark-trusted'
53      --mark-decrypt        Marks the object to be written for decryption
54                              - disabled as '--no-mark-decrypt'
55   -!, --mark-sign          Marks the object to be written for signature generation
56                              - disabled as '--no-mark-sign'
57   -", --mark-ca            Marks the object to be written as a CA
58                              - disabled as '--no-mark-ca'
59   -#, --mark-private       Marks the object to be written as private
60                              - disabled as '--no-mark-private'
61                              - enabled by default
62   -$, --trusted           an alias for the 'mark-trusted' option
63   -%, --ca                an alias for the 'mark-ca' option
64   -&, --private           an alias for the 'mark-private' option
65                              - enabled by default
66   -', --secret-key=str    Provide a hex encoded secret key
67   -(, --load-privkey=file  Private key file to use
68                              - file must pre-exist
69   -), --load-pubkey=file   Public key file to use
70                              - file must pre-exist
71   -*, --load-certificate=file Certificate file to use
72                              - file must pre-exist
73
74 Other options:
75
76   -d, --debug=num          Enable debugging
77                              - it must be in the range:
78                              0 to 9999
79   -+, --outfile=str        Output file
80   -,, --login              Force (user) login to token
81                              - disabled as '--no-login'
82   --, --so-login           Force security officer login to token
83                              - disabled as '--no-so-login'
84   -., --admin-login        an alias for the 'so-login' option
85   -/, --test-sign          Tests the signature operation of the provided object
86   -0, --generate-random=num Generate random data
87   -8, --pkcs8              Use PKCS #8 format for private keys
88   -1, --inder              Use DER/RAW format for input
89                              - disabled as '--no-inder'
90   -2, --inraw              an alias for the 'inder' option
91   -3, --outder             Use DER format for output certificates, private keys, and DH parameters
92                              - disabled as '--no-outder'
93   -4, --outraw             an alias for the 'outder' option
94   -5, --provider=file      Specify the PKCS #11 provider library
95                              - file must pre-exist
96   -6, --detailed-url       Print detailed URLs
97                              - disabled as '--no-detailed-url'
98   -7, --batch              Disable all interaction with the tool
99
```

114

```
100  Version, usage and configuration options:
101
102     -v, --version[=arg]       output version information and exit
103     -h, --help                display extended usage information and exit
104     -!, --more-help           extended usage information passed thru pager
105
106  Options are specified by doubled hyphens and their name or by a single
107  hyphen and the flag character.
108  Operands and options may be intermixed.  They will be reordered.
109
110  Program that allows operations on PKCS #11 smart cards and security
111  modules.
112
113  To use PKCS #11 tokens with GnuTLS the p11-kit configuration files need to
114  be setup.  That is create a .module file in /etc/pkcs11/modules with the
115  contents 'module: /path/to/pkcs11.so'.  Alternatively the configuration
116  file /etc/gnutls/pkcs11.conf has to exist and contain a number of lines of
117  the form 'load=/usr/lib/opensc-pkcs11.so'.
118
119  You can provide the PIN to be used for the PKCS #11 operations with the
120  environment variables GNUTLS_PIN and GNUTLS_SO_PIN.
121
```

4.3.8. token-related-options options

Tokens.

list-token-urls option.

This is the "list the urls available tokens" option. This is a more compact version of –list-tokens.

set-pin option.

This is the "specify the pin to use on token initialization" option. This option takes a string argument. Alternatively the GNUTLS_PIN environment variable may be used.

set-so-pin option.

This is the "specify the security officer's pin to use on token initialization" option. This option takes a string argument. Alternatively the GNUTLS_SO_PIN environment variable may be used.

4.3.9. object-list-related-options options

Object listing.

list-all-privkeys option.

This is the "list all available private keys in a token" option. Lists all the private keys in a token that match the specified URL.

list-privkeys option.

This is an alias for the `list-all-privkeys` option, section 4.3.9.

list-keys option.

This is an alias for the `list-all-privkeys` option, section 4.3.9.

export-chain option.

This is the "export the certificate specified by the url and its chain of trust" option. Exports the certificate specified by the URL and generates its chain of trust based on the stored certificates in the module.

export-pubkey option.

This is the "export the public key for a private key" option. Exports the public key for the specified private key

4.3.10. keygen-related-options options

Key generation.

generate-rsa option.

This is the "generate an rsa private-public key pair" option. Generates an RSA private-public key pair on the specified token.

generate-dsa option.

This is the "generate a dsa private-public key pair" option. Generates a DSA private-public key pair on the specified token.

generate-ecc option.

This is the "generate an ecdsa private-public key pair" option. Generates an ECDSA private-public key pair on the specified token.

curve option.

This is the "specify the curve used for ec key generation" option. This option takes a string argument. Supported values are secp192r1, secp224r1, secp256r1, secp384r1 and secp521r1.

sec-param option.

This is the "specify the security level" option. This option takes a string argument "`Security parameter`". This is alternative to the bits option. Available options are [low, legacy, medium, high, ultra].

4.3.11. write-object-related-options options

Writing objects.

set-id option.

This is the "set the cka_id (in hex) for the specified by the url object" option. This option takes a string argument.

This option has some usage constraints. It:

- must not appear in combination with any of the following options: write.

Modifies or sets the CKA_ID in the specified by the URL object. The ID should be specified in hexadecimal format without a '0x' prefix.

set-label option.

This is the "set the cka_label for the specified by the url object" option. This option takes a string argument.

This option has some usage constraints. It:

- must not appear in combination with any of the following options: write, set-id.

Modifies or sets the CKA_LABEL in the specified by the URL object

write option.

This is the "writes the loaded objects to a pkcs #11 token" option. It can be used to write private keys, certificates or secret keys to a token. Must be combined with a –load option.

id option.

This is the "sets an id for the write operation" option. This option takes a string argument. Sets the CKA_ID to be set by the write operation. The ID should be specified in hexadecimal format without a '0x' prefix.

mark-wrap option.

This is the "marks the generated key to be a wrapping key" option.

This option has some usage constraints. It:

- can be disabled with –no-mark-wrap.

Marks the generated key with the CKA_WRAP flag.

mark-trusted option.

This is the "marks the object to be written as trusted" option.

This option has some usage constraints. It:

- can be disabled with –no-mark-trusted.

Marks the object to be generated/written with the CKA_TRUST flag.

mark-decrypt option.

This is the "marks the object to be written for decryption" option.

This option has some usage constraints. It:

- can be disabled with –no-mark-decrypt.

Marks the object to be generated/written with the CKA_DECRYPT flag set to true.

mark-sign option.

This is the "marks the object to be written for signature generation" option.

This option has some usage constraints. It:

- can be disabled with –no-mark-sign.

Marks the object to be generated/written with the CKA_SIGN flag set to true.

mark-ca option.

This is the "marks the object to be written as a ca" option.

This option has some usage constraints. It:

- can be disabled with –no-mark-ca.

Marks the object to be generated/written with the CKA_CERTIFICATE_CATEGORY as CA.

mark-private option.

This is the "marks the object to be written as private" option.

This option has some usage constraints. It:

- can be disabled with –no-mark-private.
- It is enabled by default.

Marks the object to be generated/written with the CKA_PRIVATE flag. The written object will require a PIN to be used.

trusted option.

This is an alias for the `mark-trusted` option, section 4.3.11.

ca option.

This is an alias for the `mark-ca` option, section 4.3.11.

private option.

This is an alias for the `mark-private` option, section 4.3.11.

secret-key option.

This is the "provide a hex encoded secret key" option. This option takes a string argument. This secret key will be written to the module if –write is specified.

4.3.12. other-options options

Other options.

debug option (-d).

This is the "enable debugging" option. This option takes a number argument. Specifies the debug level.

so-login option.

This is the "force security officer login to token" option.

This option has some usage constraints. It:

- can be disabled with –no-so-login.

Forces login to the token as security officer (admin).

admin-login option.

This is an alias for the **so-login** option, section 4.3.12.

test-sign option.

This is the "tests the signature operation of the provided object" option. It can be used to test the correct operation of the signature operation. If both a private and a public key are available this operation will sign and verify the signed data.

generate-random option.

This is the "generate random data" option. This option takes a number argument. Asks the token to generate a number of bytes of random bytes.

inder option.

This is the "use der/raw format for input" option.

This option has some usage constraints. It:

- can be disabled with –no-inder.

Use DER/RAW format for input certificates and private keys.

inraw option.

This is an alias for the **inder** option, section 4.3.12.

outder option.

This is the "use der format for output certificates, private keys, and dh parameters" option.

This option has some usage constraints. It:

- can be disabled with –no-outder.

The output will be in DER or RAW format.

outraw option.

This is an alias for the **outder** option, section 4.3.12.

provider option.

This is the "specify the pkcs #11 provider library" option. This option takes a file argument. This will override the default options in /etc/gnutls/pkcs11.conf

batch option.

This is the "disable all interaction with the tool" option. In batch mode there will be no prompts, all parameters need to be specified on command line.

4.3.13. p11tool exit status

One of the following exit values will be returned:

- 0 (EXIT_SUCCESS) Successful program execution.
- 1 (EXIT_FAILURE) The operation failed or the command syntax was not valid.

4.3.14. p11tool See Also

certtool (1)

4.3.15. p11tool Examples

To view all tokens in your system use:

```
$ p11tool --list-tokens
```

To view all objects in a token use:

```
1 $ p11tool --login --list-all "pkcs11:TOKEN-URL"
```

To store a private key and a certificate in a token run:

```
1 $ p11tool --login --write "pkcs11:URL" --load-privkey key.pem \
2         --label "Mykey"
3 $ p11tool --login --write "pkcs11:URL" --load-certificate cert.pem \
4         --label "Mykey"
```

Note that some tokens require the same label to be used for the certificate and its corresponding private key.

To generate an RSA private key inside the token use:

```
1 $ p11tool --login --generate-rsa --bits 1024 --label "MyNewKey" \
2         --outfile MyNewKey.pub "pkcs11:TOKEN-URL"
```

The bits parameter in the above example is explicitly set because some tokens only support limited choices in the bit length. The output file is the corresponding public key. This key can be used to general a certificate request with certtool.

```
1 certtool --generate-request --load-privkey "pkcs11:KEY-URL" \
2    --load-pubkey MyNewKey.pub --outfile request.pem
```

4.4. Trusted Platform Module (TPM)

In this section we present the Trusted Platform Module (TPM) support in GnuTLS.

There was a big hype when the TPM chip was introduced into computers. Briefly it is a co-processor in your PC that allows it to perform calculations independently of the main processor. This has good and bad side-effects. In this section we focus on the good ones; these are the fact that you can use the TPM chip to perform cryptographic operations on keys stored in it, without accessing them. That is very similar to the operation of a PKCS #11 smart card. The chip allows for storage and usage of RSA keys, but has quite some operational differences from PKCS #11 module, and thus require different handling. The basic TPM operations supported and used by GnuTLS, are key generation and signing.

The next sections assume that the TPM chip in the system is already initialized and in a operational state.

In GnuTLS the TPM functionality is available in `gnutls/tpm.h`.

4.4.1. Keys in TPM

The RSA keys in the TPM module may either be stored in a flash memory within TPM or stored in a file in disk. In the former case the key can provide operations as with PKCS #11 and is identified by a URL. The URL is described in [19] and is of the following form.

```
tpmkey:uuid=42309df8-d101-11e1-a89a-97bb33c23ad1;storage=user
```

It consists from a unique identifier of the key as well as the part of the flash memory the key is stored at. The two options for the storage field are 'user' and 'system'. The user keys are typically only available to the generating user and the system keys to all users. The stored in TPM keys are called registered keys.

The keys that are stored in the disk are exported from the TPM but in an encrypted form. To access them two passwords are required. The first is the TPM Storage Root Key (SRK), and the other is a key-specific password. Also those keys are identified by a URL of the form:

```
tpmkey:file=/path/to/file
```

When objects require a PIN to be accessed the same callbacks as with PKCS #11 objects are expected (see subsection 4.3.2). Note that the PIN function may be called multiple times to unlock the SRK and the specific key in use. The label in the key function will then be set to 'SRK' when unlocking the SRK key, or to 'TPM' when unlocking any other key.

4.4.2. Key generation

All keys used by the TPM must be generated by the TPM. This can be done using gnutls_-tpm_privkey_generate.

---

int **gnutls_tpm_privkey_generate** (*gnutls_pk_algorithm_t* **pk**, *unsigned int* **bits**, *const char* * **srk_password**, *const char* * **key_password**, *gnutls_tpmkey_fmt_t* **format**, *gnutls_x509_crt_fmt_t* **pub_format**, *gnutls_datum_t* * **privkey**, *gnutls_datum_t* * **pubkey**, *unsigned int* **flags**)

Description: This function will generate a private key in the TPM chip. The private key will be generated within the chip and will be exported in a wrapped with TPM's master key form. Furthermore the wrapped key can be protected with the provided **password**. Note that bits in TPM is quantized value. If the input value is not one of the allowed values, then it will be quantized to one of 512, 1024, 2048, 4096, 8192 and 16384. Allowed flags are:

Returns: On success, **GNUTLS_E_SUCCESS** (0) is returned, otherwise a negative error value.

---

int **gnutls_tpm_get_registered** (*gnutls_tpm_key_list_t* * **list**)

void **gnutls_tpm_key_list_deinit** (*gnutls_tpm_key_list_t* **list**)

int **gnutls_tpm_key_list_get_url** (*gnutls_tpm_key_list_t* **list**, *unsigned int* **idx**, *char* ** **url**, *unsigned int* **flags**)

---

int **gnutls_tpm_privkey_delete** (*const char* * **url**, *const char* * **srk_password**)

Description: This function will unregister the private key from the TPM chip.

Returns: On success, **GNUTLS_E_SUCCESS** (0) is returned, otherwise a negative error value.

4.4.3. Using keys

Importing keys

The TPM keys can be used directly by the abstract key types and do not require any special structures. Moreover functions like `gnutls_certificate_set_x509_key_file2` can access TPM URLs.

---

int **gnutls_privkey_import_tpm_raw** (*gnutls_privkey_t* **pkey**, *const gnutls_datum_t* * **fdata**, *gnutls_tpmkey_fmt_t* **format**, *const char* * **srk_password**, *const char* * **key_password**, *unsigned int* **flags**)

int **gnutls_pubkey_import_tpm_raw** (*gnutls_pubkey_t* **pkey**, *const gnutls_datum_t* * **fdata**, *gnutls_tpmkey_fmt_t* **format**, *const char* * **srk_password**, *unsigned int* **flags**)

Listing and deleting keys

The registered keys (that are stored in the TPM) can be listed using one of the following functions. Those keys are unfortunately only identified by their UUID and have no label or other human friendly identifier. Keys can be deleted from permanent storage using `gnutls_tpm_privkey_delete`.

int **gnutls_privkey_import_tpm_url** (*gnutls_privkey_t* **pkey**, *const   char   * **url**, *const char* * **srk_password**, *const char* * **key_password**, *unsigned int* **flags**)

Description: This function will import the given private key to the abstract *gnutls_privkey_t* type. Note that unless **GNUTLS_PRIVKEY_DISABLE_CALLBACKS** is specified, if incorrect (or NULL) passwords are given the PKCS11 callback functions will be used to obtain the correct passwords. Otherwise if the SRK password is wrong **GNUTLS_E_TPM_SRK_PASSWORD_ERROR** is returned and if the key password is wrong or not provided then **GNUTLS_E_TPM_KEY_PASSWORD_ERROR** is returned.

Returns: On success, **GNUTLS_E_SUCCESS** (0) is returned, otherwise a negative error value.

---

int **gnutls_pubkey_import_tpm_url** (*gnutls_pubkey_t* **pkey**, *const char* * **url**, *const char* * **srk_password**, *unsigned int* **flags**)

Description: This function will import the given private key to the abstract *gnutls_privkey_t* type. Note that unless **GNUTLS_PUBKEY_DISABLE_CALLBACKS** is specified, if incorrect (or NULL) passwords are given the PKCS11 callback functions will be used to obtain the correct passwords. Otherwise if the SRK password is wrong **GNUTLS_E_TPM_SRK_PASSWORD_ERROR** is returned.

Returns: On success, **GNUTLS_E_SUCCESS** (0) is returned, otherwise a negative error value.

---

int **gnutls_tpm_get_registered** (*gnutls_tpm_key_list_t* * **list**)

void **gnutls_tpm_key_list_deinit** (*gnutls_tpm_key_list_t* **list**)

int **gnutls_tpm_key_list_get_url** (*gnutls_tpm_key_list_t* **list**, *unsigned   int* **idx**, *char* ** **url**, *unsigned int* **flags**)

4.4.4. Invoking tpmtool

Program that allows handling cryptographic data from the TPM chip.

This section was generated by **AutoGen**, using the `agtexi-cmd` template and the option descriptions for the `tpmtool` program. This software is released under the GNU General

---

int **gnutls_tpm_privkey_delete** (*const char* * **url**, *const char* * **srk_password**)

Description: This function will unregister the private key from the TPM chip.

Returns: On success, **GNUTLS_E_SUCCESS** (0) is returned, otherwise a negative error value.

Public License, version 3 or later.

4.4.5. tpmtool help/usage ("--help")

This is the automatically generated usage text for tpmtool.

The text printed is the same whether selected with the `help` option ("--help") or the `more-help` option ("--more-help"). `more-help` will print the usage text by passing it through a pager program. `more-help` is disabled on platforms without a working `fork(2)` function. The `PAGER` environment variable is used to select the program, defaulting to "more". Both will exit with a status code of 0.

```
 1 tpmtool - GnuTLS TPM tool
 2 Usage:  tpmtool [ -<flag> [<val>] | --<name>[{=| }<val>] ]...
 3
 4    -d, --debug=num          Enable debugging
 5                               - it must be in the range:
 6                                 0 to 9999
 7        --infile=file        Input file
 8                               - file must pre-exist
 9        --outfile=str        Output file
10        --generate-rsa       Generate an RSA private-public key pair
11        --register           Any generated key will be registered in the TPM
12                               - requires the option 'generate-rsa'
13        --signing            Any generated key will be a signing key
14                               - requires the option 'generate-rsa'
15                               -- and prohibits the option 'legacy'
16        --legacy             Any generated key will be a legacy key
17                               - requires the option 'generate-rsa'
18                               -- and prohibits the option 'signing'
19        --user               Any registered key will be a user key
20                               - requires the option 'register'
21                               -- and prohibits the option 'system'
22        --system             Any registred key will be a system key
23                               - requires the option 'register'
24                               -- and prohibits the option 'user'
25        --pubkey=str         Prints the public key of the provided key
26        --list               Lists all stored keys in the TPM
27        --delete=str         Delete the key identified by the given URL (UUID).
28        --test-sign=str      Tests the signature operation of the provided object
29        --sec-param=str      Specify the security level [low, legacy, medium, high, ultra].
30        --bits=num           Specify the number of bits for key generate
31        --inder              Use the DER format for keys.
```

```
32                                   - disabled as '--no-inder'
33        --outder               Use DER format for output keys
34                                   - disabled as '--no-outder'
35    -v, --version[=arg]        output version information and exit
36    -h, --help                 display extended usage information and exit
37    -!, --more-help            extended usage information passed thru pager
38
39  Options are specified by doubled hyphens and their name or by a single
40  hyphen and the flag character.
41
42  Program that allows handling cryptographic data from the TPM chip.
43
```

4.4.6. debug option (-d)

This is the "enable debugging" option. This option takes a number argument. Specifies the debug level.

4.4.7. generate-rsa option

This is the "generate an rsa private-public key pair" option. Generates an RSA private-public key pair in the TPM chip. The key may be stored in filesystem and protected by a PIN, or stored (registered) in the TPM chip flash.

4.4.8. user option

This is the "any registered key will be a user key" option.

This option has some usage constraints. It:

- must appear in combination with the following options: register.

- must not appear in combination with any of the following options: system.

The generated key will be stored in a user specific persistent storage.

4.4.9. system option

This is the "any registred key will be a system key" option.

This option has some usage constraints. It:

- must appear in combination with the following options: register.

- must not appear in combination with any of the following options: user.

The generated key will be stored in system persistent storage.

4.4.10. test-sign option

This is the "tests the signature operation of the provided object" option. This option takes a string argument "url". It can be used to test the correct operation of the signature operation. This operation will sign and verify the signed data.

4.4.11. sec-param option

This is the "specify the security level [low, legacy, medium, high, ultra]." option. This option takes a string argument "Security parameter". This is alternative to the bits option. Note however that the values allowed by the TPM chip are quantized and given values may be rounded up.

4.4.12. inder option

This is the "use the der format for keys." option.

This option has some usage constraints. It:

- can be disabled with –no-inder.

The input files will be assumed to be in the portable DER format of TPM. The default format is a custom format used by various TPM tools

4.4.13. outder option

This is the "use der format for output keys" option.

This option has some usage constraints. It:

- can be disabled with –no-outder.

The output will be in the TPM portable DER format.

4.4.14. tpmtool exit status

One of the following exit values will be returned:

- 0 (EXIT_SUCCESS) Successful program execution.
- 1 (EXIT_FAILURE) The operation failed or the command syntax was not valid.

4.4.15. tpmtool See Also

p11tool (1), certtool (1)

4.4.16. tpmtool Examples

To generate a key that is to be stored in filesystem use:

```
$ tpmtool --generate-rsa --bits 2048 --outfile tpmkey.pem
```

To generate a key that is to be stored in TPM's flash use:

```
$ tpmtool --generate-rsa --bits 2048 --register --user
```

To get the public key of a TPM key use:

```
$ tpmtool --pubkey tpmkey:uuid=58ad734b-bde6-45c7-89d8-756a55ad1891;storage=user \
          --outfile pubkey.pem
```

or if the key is stored in the filesystem:

```
$ tpmtool --pubkey tpmkey:file=tmpkey.pem --outfile pubkey.pem
```

To list all keys stored in TPM use:

```
$ tpmtool --list
```

5 How to use GnuTLS in applications

5.1. Introduction

This chapter tries to explain the basic functionality of the current GnuTLS library. Note that there may be additional functionality not discussed here but included in the library. Checking the header files in "`/usr/include/gnutls/`" and the manpages is recommended.

5.1.1. General idea

A brief description of how GnuTLS sessions operate is shown at Figure 5.1. This section will become more clear when it is completely read. As shown in the figure, there is a read-only global state that is initialized once by the global initialization function. This global structure, among others, contains the memory allocation functions used, structures needed for the ASN.1 parser and depending on the system's CPU, pointers to hardware accelerated encryption functions. This structure is never modified by any GnuTLS function, except for the deinitialization function which frees all allocated memory and must be called after the program has permanently finished using GnuTLS.

The credentials structures are used by the authentication methods, such as certificate authentication. They store certificates, privates keys, and other information that is needed to prove the identity to the peer, and/or verify the indentity of the peer. The information stored in the credentials structures is initialized once and then can be shared by many TLS sessions.

A GnuTLS session contains all the required state and information to handle one secure connection. The session communicates with the peers using the provided functions of the transport layer. Every session has a unique session ID shared with the peer.

Since TLS sessions can be resumed, servers need a database back-end to hold the session's parameters. Every GnuTLS session after a successful handshake calls the appropriate back-end function (see subsection 2.5.4) to store the newly negotiated session. The session database is examined by the server just after having received the client hello[1], and if the session ID sent by the client, matches a stored session, the stored session will be retrieved, and the new session will be a resumed one, and will share the same session ID with the previous one.

---

[1]The first message in a TLS handshake

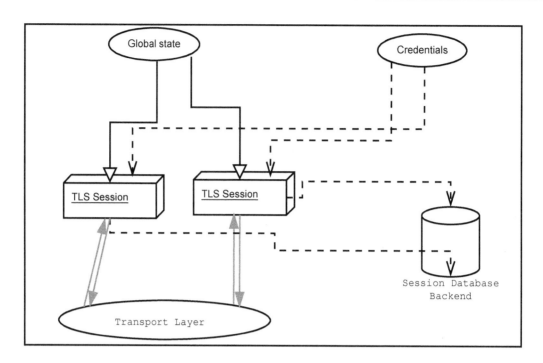

Figure 5.1.: High level design of GnuTLS.

5.1.2. Error handling

In GnuTLS most functions return an integer type as a result. In almost all cases a zero or a positive number means success, and a negative number indicates failure, or a situation that some action has to be taken. Thus negative error codes may be fatal or not.

Fatal errors terminate the connection immediately and further sends and receives will be disallowed. Such an example is GNUTLS_E_DECRYPTION_FAILED. Non-fatal errors may warn about something, i.e., a warning alert was received, or indicate the some action has to be taken. This is the case with the error code GNUTLS_E_REHANDSHAKE returned by **gnutls_record_recv**. This error code indicates that the server requests a re-handshake. The client may ignore this request, or may reply with an alert. You can test if an error code is a fatal one by using the **gnutls_error_is_fatal**. All errors can be converted to a descriptive string using **gnutls_strerror**.

If any non fatal errors, that require an action, are to be returned by a function, these error codes will be documented in the function's reference. For example the error codes GNUTLS_E_WARNING_ALERT_RECEIVED and GNUTLS_E_FATAL_ALERT_RECEIVED that may returned when receiving data, should be handled by notifying the user of the alert (as explained in section 5.9). See Appendix D, for a description of the available error codes.

5.1.3. Common types

All strings that are to provided as input to GnuTLS functions should be in UTF-8 unless otherwise specified. Output strings are also in UTF-8 format unless otherwise specified.

When data of a fixed size are provided to GnuTLS functions then the helper structure `gnutls_datum_t` is often used. Its definition is shown below.

```
typedef struct
{
  unsigned char *data;
  unsigned int size;
} gnutls_datum_t;
```

Other functions that require data for scattered read use a structure similar to `struct iovec` typically used by `readv`. It is shown below.

```
typedef struct
{
  void *iov_base;          /* Starting address */
  size_t iov_len;          /* Number of bytes to transfer */
} giovec_t;
```

5.1.4. Debugging and auditing

In many cases things may not go as expected and further information, to assist debugging, from GnuTLS is desired. Those are the cases where the `gnutls_global_set_log_level` and `gnutls_global_set_log_function` are to be used. Those will print verbose information on the GnuTLS functions internal flow.

---

void **gnutls_global_set_log_level** (*int* level)

void **gnutls_global_set_log_function** (*gnutls_log_func* **log_func**)

Alternatively the environment variable `GNUTLS_DEBUG_LEVEL` can be set to a logging level and GnuTLS will output debugging output to standard error. Other available environment variables are shown in Table 5.1.

When debugging is not required, important issues, such as detected attacks on the protocol still need to be logged. This is provided by the logging function set by `gnutls_global_set_-audit_log_function`. The provided function will receive an message and the corresponding TLS session. The session information might be used to derive IP addresses or other information about the peer involved.

Variable	Purpose
GNUTLS_DEBUG_LEVEL	When set to a numeric value, it sets the default debugging level for GnuTLS applications.
GNUTLS_CPUID_OVERRIDE	That environment variable can be used to explicitly enable/disable the use of certain CPU capabilities. Note that CPU detection cannot be overriden, i.e., VIA options cannot be enabled on an Intel CPU. The currently available options are: @itemize
0x1: Disable all run-time detected optimizations	
0x2: Enable AES-NI	
0x4: Enable SSSE3	
0x8: Enable PCLMUL	
0x100000: Enable VIA padlock	
0x200000: Enable VIA PHE	
0x400000: Enable VIA PHE SHA512 @end itemize	
GNUTLS_FORCE_FIPS_MODE	In setups where GnuTLS is compiled with support for FIPS140-2 (see –enable-fips140-mode in configure), that option if set to one enforces the FIPS140 mode.

Table 5.1.: Environment variables used by the library.

5.1.5. Thread safety

The GnuTLS library is thread safe by design, meaning that objects of the library such as TLS sessions, can be safely divided across threads as long as a single thread accesses a single object. This is sufficient to support a server which handles several sessions per thread. If, however, an object needs to be shared across threads then access must be protected with a mutex. Read-only access to objects, for example the credentials holding structures, is also thread-safe.

A `gnutls_session_t` object can be shared by two threads, one sending, the other receiving. In that case rehandshakes, if required, must only be handled by a single thread being active. The termination of a session should be handled, either by a single thread being active, or by

void **gnutls_global_set_audit_log_function** (*gnutls_audit_log_func* **log_func**)

Description: This is the function to set the audit logging function. This is a function to report important issues, such as possible attacks in the protocol. This is different from gnutls_global_set_log_function() because it will report also session-specific events. The session parameter will be null if there is no corresponding TLS session. gnutls_audit_log_func is of the form, void (*gnutls_audit_log_func)(gnutls_session_t, const char*);

the sender thread using `gnutls_bye` with `GNUTLS_SHUT_WR` and the receiving thread waiting for a return value of zero.

The random generator of the cryptographic back-end, utilizes mutex locks (e.g., pthreads on GNU/Linux and CriticalSection on Windows) which are setup by GnuTLS on library initialization. Prior to version 3.3.0 they were setup by calling `gnutls_global_init`. On special systems you could manually specify the locking system using the function `gnutls_global_set_mutex` before calling any other GnuTLS function. Setting mutexes manually is not recommended. An example of non-native thread usage is shown below.

```
 1  #include <gnutls/gnutls.h>
 2
 3  int main()
 4  {
 5     /* When the system mutexes are not to be used
 6      * gnutls_global_set_mutex() must be called explicitly
 7      */
 8     gnutls_global_set_mutex (mutex_init, mutex_deinit,
 9                              mutex_lock, mutex_unlock);
10  }
```

void **gnutls_global_set_mutex** (*mutex_init_func* **init**, *mutex_deinit_func* **deinit**, *mutex_lock_func* **lock**, *mutex_unlock_func* **unlock**)

Description: With this function you are allowed to override the default mutex locks used in some parts of gnutls and dependent libraries. This function should be used if you have complete control of your program and libraries. Do not call this function from a library, or preferrably from any application unless really needed to. GnuTLS will use the appropriate locks for the running system. This function must be called prior to any other gnutls function.

5.1.6. Sessions and fork

A `gnutls_session_t` object can be shared by two processes after a fork, one sending, the other receiving. In that case rehandshakes, cannot and must not be performed. As with threads, the termination of a session should be handled by the sender process using `gnutls_bye` with `GNUTLS_SHUT_WR` and the receiving process waiting for a return value of zero.

5.1.7. Callback functions

There are several cases where GnuTLS may need out of band input from your program. This is now implemented using some callback functions, which your program is expected to register.

An example of this type of functions are the push and pull callbacks which are used to specify the functions that will retrieve and send data to the transport layer.

---

void **gnutls_transport_set_push_function** (*gnutls_session_t* **session**, *gnutls_push_func* **push_func**)

void **gnutls_transport_set_pull_function** (*gnutls_session_t* **session**, *gnutls_pull_func* **pull_func**)

Other callback functions may require more complicated input and data to be allocated. Such an example is `gnutls_srp_set_server_credentials_function`. All callbacks should allocate and free memory using `gnutls_malloc` and `gnutls_free`.

5.2. Preparation

To use GnuTLS, you have to perform some changes to your sources and your build system. The necessary changes are explained in the following subsections.

5.2.1. Headers

All the data types and functions of the GnuTLS library are defined in the header file "`gnutls/gnutls.h`" This must be included in all programs that make use of the GnuTLS library.

5.2.2. Initialization

The GnuTLS library is initialized on load; prior to 3.3.0 was initialized by calling `gnutls_global_init`. The initialization typically enables CPU-specific acceleration, performs any required precalculations needed, opens any required system devices (e.g., /dev/urandom on Linux) and initializes subsystems that could be used later.

The resources allocated by the initialization process will be released on library deinitialization, or explictly by calling `gnutls_global_deinit`.

Note that during initialization file descriptors may be kept open by GnuTLS (e.g. /dev/urandom) on library load. Applications closing all unknown file descriptors must immediately call `gnutls_global_init`, after that, to ensure they don't disrupt GnuTLS' operation.

5.2.3. Version check

It is often desirable to check that the version of 'gnutls' used is indeed one which fits all requirements. Even with binary compatibility new features may have been introduced but due to problem with the dynamic linker an old version is actually used. So you may want to check that the version is okay right after program start-up. See the function `gnutls_check_version`.

On the other hand, it is often desirable to support more than one versions of the library. In that case you could utilize compile-time feature checks using the the GNUTLS_VERSION_NUMBER macro. For example, to conditionally add code for GnuTLS 3.2.1 or later, you may use:

```
1  #if GNUTLS_VERSION_NUMBER >= 0x030201
2  ...
3  #endif
```

5.2.4. Building the source

If you want to compile a source file including the "gnutls/gnutls.h" header file, you must make sure that the compiler can find it in the directory hierarchy. This is accomplished by adding the path to the directory in which the header file is located to the compilers include file search path (via the "-I" option).

However, the path to the include file is determined at the time the source is configured. To solve this problem, the library uses the external package "pkg-config" that knows the path to the include file and other configuration options. The options that need to be added to the compiler invocation at compile time are output by the "--cflags" option to "pkg-config gnutls". The following example shows how it can be used at the command line:

```
1  gcc -c foo.c `pkg-config gnutls --cflags`
```

Adding the output of pkg-config gnutls –cflags to the compilers command line will ensure that the compiler can find the "gnutls/gnutls.h" header file.

A similar problem occurs when linking the program with the library. Again, the compiler has to find the library files. For this to work, the path to the library files has to be added to the library search path (via the "-L" option). For this, the option "--libs" to "pkg-config gnutls" can be used. For convenience, this option also outputs all other options that are required to link the program with the library (for instance, the -ltasn1 option). The example shows how to link "foo.o" with the library to a program "foo".

```
1  gcc -o foo foo.o `pkg-config gnutls --libs`
```

Of course you can also combine both examples to a single command by specifying both options to "pkg-config":

```
1  gcc -o foo foo.c `pkg-config gnutls --cflags --libs`
```

When a program uses the GNU autoconf system, then the following line or similar can be used to detect the presence of GnuTLS.

```
1  PKG_CHECK_MODULES([LIBGNUTLS], [gnutls >= 3.3.0])
2
3  AC_SUBST([LIBGNUTLS_CFLAGS])
4  AC_SUBST([LIBGNUTLS_LIBS])
```

5.3. Session initialization

In the previous sections we have discussed the global initialization required for GnuTLS as well as the initialization required for each authentication method's credentials (see subsection 2.5.2). In this section we elaborate on the TLS or DTLS session initiation. Each session is initialized using `gnutls_init` which among others is used to specify the type of the connection (server or client), and the underlying protocol type, i.e., datagram (UDP) or reliable (TCP).

---

int **gnutls_init** (*gnutls_session_t* * **session**, *unsigned int* **flags**)

Description: `This function initializes the current session to null. Every session must be initialized before use, so internal structures can be allocated. This function allocates structures which can only be free'd by calling gnutls_deinit(). Returns` **GNUTLS_E-SUCCESS** `(0) on success.` **flags** `can be one of` **GNUTLS_CLIENT, GNUTLS_SERVER, GNUTLS_DATAGRAM, GNUTLS_NONBLOCK** `or` **GNUTLS_NOSIGNAL** `(since 3.4.2). The flag` **GNUTLS_NO_REPLAY_PROTECTION** `will disable any replay protection in DTLS mode. That must only used when replay protection is achieved using other means. Note that since version 3.1.2 this function enables some common TLS extensions such as session tickets and OCSP certificate status request in client side by default. To prevent that use the` **GNUTLS_NO_EXTENSIONS** `flag.`

Returns: `GNUTLS_E_SUCCESS on success, or an error code.`

After the session initialization details on the allowed ciphersuites and protocol versions should be set using the priority functions such as **gnutls_priority_set_direct**. We elaborate on them in section 5.10. The credentials used for the key exchange method, such as certificates or usernames and passwords should also be associated with the session current session using **gnutls_credentials_set**.

5.4. Associating the credentials

Each authentication method is associated with a key exchange method, and a credentials type. The contents of the credentials is method-dependent, e.g. certificates for certificate authentication and should be initialized and associated with a session (see **gnutls_credentials_set**). A mapping of the key exchange methods with the credential types is shown in Table 5.2.

5.4.1. Certificates

Server certificate authentication

When using certificates the server is required to have at least one certificate and private key pair. Clients may not hold such a pair, but a server could require it. In this section we discuss

---

int **gnutls_credentials_set** (*gnutls_session_t* **session**, *gnutls_credentials_type_t* **type**, *void* * **cred**)

Description: Sets the needed credentials for the specified type. Eg username, password - or public and private keys etc. The cred parameter is a structure that depends on the specified type and on the current session (client or server). In order to minimize memory usage, and share credentials between several threads gnutls keeps a pointer to cred, and not the whole cred structure. Thus you will have to keep the structure allocated until you call gnutls_deinit(). For **GNUTLS_CRD_ANON**, cred should be *gnutls_anon_client_credentials_t* in case of a client. In case of a server it should be *gnutls_anon_server_credentials_t*. For **GNUTLS_CRD_SRP**, cred should be *gnutls_srp_client_credentials_t* in case of a client, and *gnutls_srp_server_credentials_t*, in case of a server. For **GNUTLS_CRD_CERTIFICATE**, cred should be *gnutls_certificate_credentials_t*.

Returns: On success, **GNUTLS_E_SUCCESS** (0) is returned, otherwise a negative error code is returned.

---

general issues applying to both client and server certificates. The next section will elaborate on issues arising from client authentication only.

---

int **gnutls_certificate_allocate_credentials** (*gnutls_certificate_credentials_t* * **res**)

void **gnutls_certificate_free_credentials** (*gnutls_certificate_credentials_t* **sc**)

After the credentials structures are initialized, the certificate and key pair must be loaded. This occurs before any TLS session is initialized, and the same structures are reused for multiple sessions. Depending on the certificate type different loading functions are available, as shown below. For X.509 certificates, the functions will accept and use a certificate chain that leads to a trusted authority. The certificate chain must be ordered in such way that every certificate certifies the one before it. The trusted authority's certificate need not to be included since the peer should possess it already.

Authentication method	Key exchange	Client credentials	Server credentials
Certificate	KX_RSA, KX_DHE_RSA, KX_DHE_DSS, KX_ECDHE_RSA, KX_ECDHE_ECDSA, KX_RSA_EXPORT	CRD_CERTIFICATE	CRD_CERTIFICATE
Password and certificate	KX_SRP_RSA, KX_SRP_DSS	CRD_SRP	CRD_CERTIFICATE, CRD_SRP
Password	KX_SRP	CRD_SRP	CRD_SRP
Anonymous	KX_ANON_DH, KX_ANON_ECDH	CRD_ANON	CRD_ANON
Pre-shared key	KX_PSK, KX_DHE_PSK, KX_ECDHE_PSK	CRD_PSK	CRD_PSK

Table 5.2.: Key exchange algorithms and the corresponding credential types.

int **gnutls_certificate_set_x509_key_file2** (*gnutls_certificate_credentials_t* **res**, *const char ** **certfile**, *const char ** **keyfile**, *gnutls_x509_crt_fmt_t* **type**, *const char ** **pass**, *unsigned int* **flags**)

int **gnutls_certificate_set_x509_key_mem2** (*gnutls_certificate_credentials_t* **res**, *const gnutls_datum_t ** **cert**, *const gnutls_datum_t ** **key**, *gnutls_x509_crt_fmt_t* **type**, *const char ** **pass**, *unsigned int* **flags**)

int **gnutls_certificate_set_x509_key** (*gnutls_certificate_credentials_t* **res**, *gnutls_x509_crt_t ** **cert_list**, *int* **cert_list_size**, *gnutls_x509_privkey_t* **key**)

int **gnutls_certificate_set_openpgp_key_file** (*gnutls_certificate_credentials_t* **res**, *const char ** **certfile**, *const char ** **keyfile**, *gnutls_openpgp_crt_fmt_t* **format**)

int **gnutls_certificate_set_openpgp_key_mem** (*gnutls_certificate_credentials_t* **res**, *const gnutls_datum_t ** **cert**, *const gnutls_datum_t ** **key**, *gnutls_openpgp_crt_fmt_t* **format**)

int **gnutls_certificate_set_openpgp_key** (*gnutls_certificate_credentials_t* **res**, *gnutls_openpgp_crt_t* **crt**, *gnutls_openpgp_privkey_t* **pkey**)

It is recommended to use the higher level functions such as `gnutls_certificate_set_x509_key_file2` which accept not only file names but URLs that specify objects stored in token, or system certificates and keys (see section 4.2). For these cases, another important function is `gnutls_certificate_set_pin_function`, that allows setting a callback function to retrieve a PIN if the input keys are protected by PIN.

---

void **gnutls_certificate_set_pin_function** (*gnutls_certificate_credentials_t* **cred**, *gnutls_pin_callback_t* **fn**, *void* * **userdata**)

Description: `This function will set a callback function to be used when required to access a protected object. This function overrides any other global PIN functions. Note that this function must be called right after initialization to have effect.`

If the imported keys and certificates need to be accessed before any TLS session is established, it is convenient to use `gnutls_certificate_set_key` in combination with `gnutls_pcert_import_x509_raw` and `gnutls_privkey_import_x509_raw`.

---

int **gnutls_certificate_set_key** (*gnutls_certificate_credentials_t* **res**, *const char* ** **names**, *int* **names_size**, *gnutls_pcert_st* * **pcert_list**, *int* **pcert_list_size**, *gnutls_privkey_t* **key**)

Description: `This function sets a certificate/private key pair in the gnutls_certificate_credentials_t type. This function may be called more than once, in case multiple keys/certificates exist for the server. For clients that wants to send more than its own end entity certificate (e.g., also an intermediate CA cert) then put the certificate chain in pcert_list. Note that the pcert_list and key will become part of the credentials structure and must not be deallocated. They will be automatically deallocated when the res type is deinitialized. If that function fails to load the res structure is at an undefined state, it must not be reused to load other keys or certificates.`

Returns: `GNUTLS_E_SUCCESS` `(0) on success, or a negative error code.`

If multiple certificates are used with the functions above each client's request will be served with the certificate that matches the requested name (see subsection 2.6.2).

As an alternative to loading from files or buffers, a callback may be used for the server or the client to specify the certificate and the key at the handshake time. In that case a certificate should be selected according the peer's signature algorithm preferences. To get those preferences use `gnutls_sign_algorithm_get_requested`. Both functions are shown below.

---

void **gnutls_certificate_set_retrieve_function** (*gnutls_certificate_credentials_t* **cred**, *gnutls_certificate_retrieve_function* * **func**)

void **gnutls_certificate_set_retrieve_function2** (*gnutls_certificate_credentials_t* **cred**, *gnutls_certificate_retrieve_function2* * **func**)

int **gnutls_sign_algorithm_get_requested** (*gnutls_session_t* **session**, *size_t* **indx**, *gnutls_sign_algorithm_t* * **algo**)

---

c The functions above do not handle the requested server name automatically. A server would need to check the name requested by the client using **gnutls_server_name_get**, and serve the appropriate certificate. Note that some of these functions require the **gnutls_pcert_st** structure to be filled in. Helper functions to fill in the structure are listed below.

```
typedef struct gnutls_pcert_st
{
  gnutls_pubkey_t pubkey;
  gnutls_datum_t cert;
  gnutls_certificate_type_t type;
} gnutls_pcert_st;
```

---

int **gnutls_pcert_import_x509** (*gnutls_pcert_st* * **pcert**, *gnutls_x509_crt_t* **crt**, *unsigned int* **flags**)

int **gnutls_pcert_import_openpgp** (*gnutls_pcert_st* * **pcert**, *gnutls_openpgp_crt_t* **crt**, *unsigned int* **flags**)

int **gnutls_pcert_import_x509_raw** (*gnutls_pcert_st* * **pcert**, *const gnutls_datum_t* * **cert**, *gnutls_x509_crt_fmt_t* **format**, *unsigned int* **flags**)

int **gnutls_pcert_import_openpgp_raw** (*gnutls_pcert_st* * **pcert**, *const gnutls_datum_t* * **cert**, *gnutls_openpgp_crt_fmt_t* **format**, *gnutls_openpgp_keyid_t* **keyid**, *unsigned int* **flags**)

void **gnutls_pcert_deinit** (*gnutls_pcert_st* * **pcert**)

In a handshake, the negotiated cipher suite depends on the certificate's parameters, so some key exchange methods might not be available with all certificates. GnuTLS will disable ciphersuites that are not compatible with the key, or the enabled authentication methods. For example keys marked as sign-only, will not be able to access the plain RSA ciphersuites, that require decryption. It is not recommended to use RSA keys for both signing and encryption. If possible use a different key for the **DHE-RSA** which uses signing and **RSA** that requires decryption. All the key exchange methods shown in Table 3.1 are available in certificate authentication.

Client certificate authentication

If a certificate is to be requested from the client during the handshake, the server will send a certificate request message. This behavior is controlled gnutls_certificate_server_set_request. The request contains a list of the acceptable by the server certificate signers. This list is constructed using the trusted certificate authorities of the server. In cases where the server supports a large number of certificate authorities it makes sense not to advertise all of the names to save bandwidth. That can be controlled using the function gnutls_certificate_send_x509_rdn_sequence. This however will have the side-effect of not restricting the client to certificates signed by server's acceptable signers.

---

void **gnutls_certificate_server_set_request** (*gnutls_session_t* **session**, *gnutls_certificate_request_t* **req**)

Description: This function specifies if we (in case of a server) are going to send a certificate request message to the client. If req is GNUTLS_CERT_REQUIRE then the server will return an error if the peer does not provide a certificate. If you do not call this function then the client will not be asked to send a certificate.

---

void **gnutls_certificate_send_x509_rdn_sequence** (*gnutls_session_t* **session**, *int* **status**)

Description: If status is non zero, this function will order gnutls not to send the rdnSequence in the certificate request message. That is the server will not advertise its trusted CAs to the peer. If status is zero then the default behaviour will take effect, which is to advertise the server's trusted CAs. This function has no effect in clients, and in authentication methods other than certificate with X.509 certificates.

Client or server certificate verification

Certificate verification is possible by loading the trusted authorities into the credentials structure by using the following functions, applicable to X.509 and OpenPGP certificates.

---

int **gnutls_certificate_set_x509_system_trust** (*gnutls_certificate_credentials_t* **cred**)

int **gnutls_certificate_set_x509_trust_file** (*gnutls_certificate_credentials_t* **cred**, *const char *** **cafile**, *gnutls_x509_crt_fmt_t* **type**)

int **gnutls_certificate_set_openpgp_keyring_file** (*gnutls_certificate_credentials_t* **c**, *const char *** **file**, *gnutls_openpgp_crt_fmt_t* **format**)

The peer's certificate will be automatically verified if `gnutls_session_set_verify_cert` is called prior to handshake.

Alternatively, one must set a callback function during the handshake using `gnutls_certificate_-set_verify_function`, which will verify the peer's certificate once received. The verification should happen using `gnutls_certificate_verify_peers3` within the callback. It will verify the certificate's signature and the owner of the certificate. That will provide a brief verification output. If a detailed output is required one should call `gnutls_certificate_get_peers` to obtain the raw certificate of the peer and verify it using the functions discussed in subsection 3.1.1.

In both the automatic and the manual cases, the verification status returned can be printed using `gnutls_certificate_verification_status_print`.

---

void **gnutls_session_set_verify_cert** (*gnutls_session_t* **session**, *const char* * **hostname**, *unsigned* **flags**)

Description: This function instructs GnuTLS to verify the peer's certificate using the provided hostname. If the verification fails the handshake will also fail with **GNUTLS_-E_CERTIFICATE_VERIFICATION_ERROR**. In that case the verification result can be obtained using gnutls_session_get_verify_cert_status(). The hostname pointer provided must remain valid for the lifetime of the session. More precisely it should be available during any subsequent handshakes. If no hostname is provided, no hostname verification will be performed. For a more advanced verification function check gnutls_session_set_verify_-cert2(). The gnutls_session_set_verify_cert() function is intended to be used by TLS clients to verify the server's certificate.

---

int **gnutls_certificate_verify_peers3** (*gnutls_session_t* **session**, *const char* * **hostname**, *unsigned int* * **status**)

void **gnutls_certificate_set_verify_function** (*gnutls_certificate_credentials_t* **cred**, *gnutls_certificate_verify_function* * **func**)

5.4.2. SRP

The initialization functions in SRP credentials differ between client and server. Clients supporting SRP should set the username and password prior to connection, to the credentials structure. Alternatively `gnutls_srp_set_client_credentials_function` may be used instead, to specify a callback function that should return the SRP username and password. The callback is called once during the TLS handshake.

---

int **gnutls_srp_allocate_server_credentials** (*gnutls_srp_server_credentials_t* * **sc**)

int **gnutls_srp_allocate_client_credentials** (*gnutls_srp_client_credentials_t* * **sc**)

void **gnutls_srp_free_server_credentials** (*gnutls_srp_server_credentials_t* **sc**)

void **gnutls_srp_free_client_credentials** (*gnutls_srp_client_credentials_t* **sc**)

int **gnutls_srp_set_client_credentials** (*gnutls_srp_client_credentials_t* **res**, *const char* * **username**, *const char* * **password**)

---

void **gnutls_srp_set_client_credentials_function** (*gnutls_srp_client_credentials_t* **cred**, *gnutls_srp_client_credentials_function* * **func**)

Description: This function can be used to set a callback to retrieve the username and password for client SRP authentication. The callback's function form is: int (*callback)(gnutls_session_t, char** username, char**password); The username and password must be allocated using gnutls_malloc(). username and password should be ASCII strings or UTF-8 strings prepared using the "SASLprep" profile of "stringprep". The callback function will be called once per handshake before the initial hello message is sent. The callback should not return a negative error code the second time called, since the handshake procedure will be aborted. The callback function should return 0 on success. -1 indicates an error.

In server side the default behavior of GnuTLS is to read the usernames and SRP verifiers from password files. These password file format is compatible the with the *Stanford srp libraries* format. If a different password file format is to be used, then **gnutls_srp_set_server_credentials_function** should be called, to set an appropriate callback.

---

int **gnutls_srp_set_server_credentials_file** (*gnutls_srp_server_credentials_t* **res**, *const char* * **password_file**, *const char* * **password_conf_file**)

Description: This function sets the password files, in a *gnutls_srp_server_credentials_t* type. Those password files hold usernames and verifiers and will be used for SRP authentication.

Returns: On success, **GNUTLS_E_SUCCESS** (0) is returned, or an error code.

---

void **gnutls_srp_set_server_credentials_function** (*gnutls_srp_server_credentials_t*
cred, *gnutls_srp_server_credentials_function* * **func**)

Description: This function can be used to set a callback to retrieve the user's SRP
credentials. The callback's function form is: int (*callback)(gnutls_session_t, const
char* username, gnutls_datum_t *salt, gnutls_datum_t *verifier, gnutls_datum_t *generator,
gnutls_datum_t *prime); username contains the actual username. The salt, verifier, generator and prime must be filled in using the gnutls_malloc(). For convenience prime and
generator may also be one of the static parameters defined in gnutls.h. Initially, the
data field is NULL in every *gnutls_datum_t* structure that the callback has to fill in. When
the callback is done GnuTLS deallocates all of those buffers which are non-NULL, regardless
of the return value. In order to prevent attackers from guessing valid usernames, if a
user does not exist, g and n values should be filled in using a random user's parameters.
In that case the callback must return the special value (1). See *gnutls_srp_set_server_fake_-
salt_seed* too. If this is not required for your application, return a negative number from
the callback to abort the handshake. The callback function will only be called once per
handshake. The callback function should return 0 on success, while -1 indicates an error.

5.4.3. PSK

The initialization functions in PSK credentials differ between client and server.

---

int **gnutls_psk_allocate_server_credentials** (*gnutls_psk_server_credentials_t* * **sc**)

int **gnutls_psk_allocate_client_credentials** (*gnutls_psk_client_credentials_t* * **sc**)

void **gnutls_psk_free_server_credentials** (*gnutls_psk_server_credentials_t* **sc**)

void **gnutls_psk_free_client_credentials** (*gnutls_psk_client_credentials_t* **sc**)

Clients supporting PSK should supply the username and key before a TLS session is established. Alternatively gnutls_psk_set_client_credentials_function can be used to specify
a callback function. This has the advantage that the callback will be called only if PSK has
been negotiated.

---

int **gnutls_psk_set_client_credentials** (*gnutls_psk_client_credentials_t* **res**, *const char*
* **username**, *const gnutls_datum_t* * **key**, *gnutls_psk_key_flags* **flags**)

---

void **gnutls_psk_set_client_credentials_function** (*gnutls_psk_client_credentials_t* **cred**, *gnutls_psk_client_credentials_function* * **func**)

Description: This function can be used to set a callback to retrieve the username and password for client PSK authentication. The callback's function form is: int (*callback)(gnutls_session_t, char** username, gnutls_datum_t* key); The username and key→data must be allocated using gnutls_malloc(). username should be ASCII strings or UTF-8 strings prepared using the "SASLprep" profile of "stringprep". The callback function will be called once per handshake. The callback function should return 0 on success. -1 indicates an error.

In server side the default behavior of GnuTLS is to read the usernames and PSK keys from a password file. The password file should contain usernames and keys in hexadecimal format. The name of the password file can be stored to the credentials structure by calling **gnutls_-psk_set_server_credentials_file**. If a different password file format is to be used, then a callback should be set instead by **gnutls_psk_set_server_credentials_function**.

The server can help the client chose a suitable username and password, by sending a hint. Note that there is no common profile for the PSK hint and applications are discouraged to use it. A server, may specify the hint by calling **gnutls_psk_set_server_credentials_hint**. The client can retrieve the hint, for example in the callback function, using **gnutls_psk_client_get_hint**.

---

int **gnutls_psk_set_server_credentials_file** (*gnutls_psk_server_credentials_t*   **res**, *const char* * **password_file**)

Description: This function sets the password file, in a *gnutls_psk_server_credentials_t* type. This password file holds usernames and keys and will be used for PSK authentication.

Returns: On success, **GNUTLS_E_SUCCESS** (0) is returned, otherwise an error code is returned.

---

void **gnutls_psk_set_server_credentials_function** (*gnutls_psk_server_credentials_t* **cred**, *gnutls_psk_server_credentials_function* * **func**)

int **gnutls_psk_set_server_credentials_hint** (*gnutls_psk_server_credentials_t* **res**, *const char* * **hint**)

const char * **gnutls_psk_client_get_hint** (*gnutls_session_t* **session**)

147

5.4.4. Anonymous

The key exchange methods for anonymous authentication might require Diffie-Hellman parameters to be generated by the server and associated with an anonymous credentials structure. Check subsection 5.12.4 for more information. The initialization functions for the credentials are shown below.

---

int **gnutls_anon_allocate_server_credentials** (*gnutls_anon_server_credentials_t* * **sc**)

int **gnutls_anon_allocate_client_credentials** (*gnutls_anon_client_credentials_t* * **sc**)

void **gnutls_anon_free_server_credentials** (*gnutls_anon_server_credentials_t* **sc**)

void **gnutls_anon_free_client_credentials** (*gnutls_anon_client_credentials_t* **sc**)

5.5. Setting up the transport layer

The next step is to setup the underlying transport layer details. The Berkeley sockets are implicitly used by GnuTLS, thus a call to `gnutls_transport_set_int` would be sufficient to specify the socket descriptor.

---

void **gnutls_transport_set_int** (*gnutls_session_t* **session**, *int* **i**)

void **gnutls_transport_set_int2** (*gnutls_session_t* **session**, *int* **recv_int**, *int* **send_int**)

If however another transport layer than TCP is selected, then a pointer should be used instead to express the parameter to be passed to custom functions. In that case the following functions should be used instead.

---

void **gnutls_transport_set_ptr** (*gnutls_session_t* **session**, *gnutls_transport_ptr_t* **ptr**)

void **gnutls_transport_set_ptr2** (*gnutls_session_t* **session**, *gnutls_transport_ptr_t* **recv_ptr**, *gnutls_transport_ptr_t* **send_ptr**)

Moreover all of the following push and pull callbacks should be set.

---

void **gnutls_transport_set_push_function** (*gnutls_session_t* **session**, *gnutls_push_func* **push_func**)

Description: This is the function where you set a push function for gnutls to use in order to send data. If you are going to use berkeley style sockets, you do not need to use this function since the default send(2) will probably be ok. Otherwise you should specify this function for gnutls to be able to send data. The callback should return a positive number indicating the bytes sent, and -1 on error. push_func is of the form, ssize_t (*gnutls_push_func)(gnutls_transport_ptr_t, const void*, size_t);

---

void **gnutls_transport_set_vec_push_function** (*gnutls_session_t* **session**, *gnutls_vec_push_func* **vec_func**)

Description: Using this function you can override the default writev(2) function for gnutls to send data. Setting this callback instead of gnutls_transport_set_push_function() is recommended since it introduces less overhead in the TLS handshake process. vec_func is of the form, ssize_t (*gnutls_vec_push_func) (gnutls_transport_ptr_t, const giovec_t * iov, int iovcnt);

---

void **gnutls_transport_set_pull_function** (*gnutls_session_t* **session**, *gnutls_pull_func* **pull_func**)

Description: This is the function where you set a function for gnutls to receive data. Normally, if you use berkeley style sockets, do not need to use this function since the default recv(2) will probably be ok. The callback should return 0 on connection termination, a positive number indicating the number of bytes received, and -1 on error. gnutls_pull_func is of the form, ssize_t (*gnutls_pull_func)(gnutls_transport_ptr_t, void*, size_t);

The functions above accept a callback function which should return the number of bytes written, or -1 on error and should set **errno** appropriately. In some environments, setting **errno** is unreliable. For example Windows have several errno variables in different CRTs, or in other systems it may be a non thread-local variable. If this is a concern to you, call **gnutls_transport_set_errno** with the intended errno value instead of setting **errno** directly.

GnuTLS currently only interprets the EINTR, EAGAIN and EMSGSIZE errno values and returns the corresponding GnuTLS error codes:

- GNUTLS_E_INTERRUPTED

void **gnutls_transport_set_pull_timeout_function** (*gnutls_session_t* **session,**
gnutls_pull_timeout_func **func**)

Description: This is the function where you set a function for gnutls to know whether
data are ready to be received. It should wait for data a given time frame in milliseconds.
The callback should return 0 on timeout, a positive number if data can be received, and
-1 on error. You'll need to override this function if select() is not suitable for the
provided transport calls. As with select(), if the timeout value is zero the callback
should return zero if no data are immediately available. gnutls_pull_timeout_func is of
the form, int (*gnutls_pull_timeout_func)(gnutls_transport_ptr_t, unsigned int ms); This
callback is necessary when gnutls_handshake_set_timeout() or gnutls_record_set_timeout() are
set. It will not be used when non-blocking sockets are in use. That is, this function
will not operate when **GNUTLS_NONBLOCK** is specified in gnutls_init(), or a custom
pull function is registered without updating the pull timeout function. The helper function
gnutls_system_recv_timeout() is provided to simplify writing callbacks.

void **gnutls_transport_set_errno** (*gnutls_session_t* **session,** *int* **err**)

Description: Store err in the session-specific errno variable. Useful values for err
are EINTR, EAGAIN and EMSGSIZE, other values are treated will be treated as real errors
in the push/pull function. This function is useful in replacement push and pull functions
set by gnutls_transport_set_push_function() and gnutls_transport_set_pull_function() under
Windows, where the replacements may not have access to the same errno variable that is
used by GnuTLS (e.g., the application is linked to msvcr71.dll and gnutls is linked to
msvcrt.dll).

- GNUTLS_E_AGAIN

- GNUTLS_E_LARGE_PACKET

The EINTR and EAGAIN values are returned by interrupted system calls, or when non blocking IO is used. All GnuTLS functions can be resumed (called again), if any of the above error codes is returned. The EMSGSIZE value is returned when attempting to send a large datagram.

In the case of DTLS it is also desirable to override the generic transport functions with functions that emulate the operation of `recvfrom` and `sendto`. In addition DTLS requires timers during the receive of a handshake message, set using the `gnutls_transport_set_pull_timeout_-`
`function` function. To check the retransmission timers the function `gnutls_dtls_get_timeout` is provided, which returns the time remaining until the next retransmission, or better the time until `gnutls_handshake` should be called again.

---

void **gnutls_transport_set_pull_timeout_function** (*gnutls_session_t* **session**, *gnutls_pull_timeout_func* **func**)

Description: This is the function where you set a function for gnutls to know whether data are ready to be received. It should wait for data a given time frame in milliseconds. The callback should return 0 on timeout, a positive number if data can be received, and -1 on error. You'll need to override this function if select() is not suitable for the provided transport calls. As with select(), if the timeout value is zero the callback should return zero if no data are immediately available. gnutls_pull_timeout_func is of the form, int (*gnutls_pull_timeout_func)(gnutls_transport_ptr_t, unsigned int ms); This callback is necessary when gnutls_handshake_set_timeout() or gnutls_record_set_timeout() are set. It will not be used when non-blocking sockets are in use. That is, this function will not operate when **GNUTLS_NONBLOCK** is specified in gnutls_init(), or a custom pull function is registered without updating the pull timeout function. The helper function gnutls_system_recv_timeout() is provided to simplify writing callbacks.

---

unsigned int **gnutls_dtls_get_timeout** (*gnutls_session_t* **session**)

Description: This function will return the milliseconds remaining for a retransmission of the previously sent handshake message. This function is useful when DTLS is used in non-blocking mode, to estimate when to call gnutls_handshake() if no packets have been received.

Returns: the remaining time in milliseconds.

5.5.1. Asynchronous operation

GnuTLS can be used with asynchronous socket or event-driven programming. The approach is similar to using Berkeley sockets under such an environment. The blocking, due to network interaction, calls such as `gnutls_handshake`, `gnutls_record_recv`, can be set to non-blocking by setting the underlying sockets to non-blocking. If other push and pull functions are setup, then they should behave the same way as `recv` and `send` when used in a non-blocking way, i.e., set errno to `EAGAIN`. Since, during a TLS protocol session GnuTLS does not block except for network interaction, the non blocking `EAGAIN` errno will be propagated and GnuTLS functions will return the `GNUTLS_E_AGAIN` error code. Such calls can be resumed the same way as a system call would. The only exception is `gnutls_record_send`, which if interrupted subsequent calls need not to include the data to be sent (can be called with NULL argument).

When using the `select` system call though, one should remember that it is only applicable to the kernel sockets API. To check for any available buffers in a GnuTLS session, utilize `gnutls_record_check_pending`, either before the `select` system call, or after a call to `gnutls_record_recv`. GnuTLS does not keep a write buffer, thus when writing no additional actions are required.

The following paragraphs describe the detailed requirements for non-blocking operation when using the TLS or DTLS protocols.

TLS protocol

There are no special requirements for the TLS protocol operation in non-blocking mode if a non-blocking socket is used.

It is recommended, however, for future compatibility, when in non-blocking mode, to call the `gnutls_init` function with the `GNUTLS_NONBLOCK` flag set (see section 5.3).

Datagram TLS protocol

When in non-blocking mode the function, the `gnutls_init` function must be called with the `GNUTLS_NONBLOCK` flag set (see section 5.3).

In constrast with the TLS protocol, the pull timeout function is required, but will only be called with a timeout of zero. In that case it should indicate whether there are data to be received or not. When not using the default pull function, then `gnutls_transport_set_pull_timeout_-function` should be called.

Although in the TLS protocol implementation each call to receive or send function implies to restoring the same function that was interrupted, in the DTLS protocol this requirement isn't true. There are cases where a retransmission is required, which are indicated by a received message and thus `gnutls_record_get_direction` must be called to decide which direction to check prior to restoring a function call.

---

int **gnutls_record_get_direction** (*gnutls_session_t* **session**)

Description: This function provides information about the internals of the record protocol and is only useful if a prior gnutls function call (e.g. gnutls_handshake()) was interrupted for some reason, that is, if a function returned **GNUTLS_E_INTERRUPTED** or **GNUTLS_E_AGAIN**. In such a case, you might want to call select() or poll() before calling the interrupted gnutls function again. To tell you whether a file descriptor should be selected for either reading or writing, gnutls_record_get_direction() returns 0 if the interrupted function was trying to read data, and 1 if it was trying to write data. This function's output is unreliable if you are using the session in different threads, for sending and receiving.

Returns: 0 if trying to read data, 1 if trying to write data.

When calling **gnutls_handshake** through a multi-plexer, to be able to handle properly the

DTLS handshake retransmission timers, the function `gnutls_dtls_get_timeout` should be used to estimate when to call `gnutls_handshake` if no data have been received.

5.5.2. DTLS sessions

Because datagram TLS can operate over connections where the client cannot be reliably verified, functionality in the form of cookies, is available to prevent denial of service attacks to servers. GnuTLS requires a server to generate a secret key that is used to sign a cookie[2]. That cookie is sent to the client using `gnutls_dtls_cookie_send`, and the client must reply using the correct cookie. The server side should verify the initial message sent by client using `gnutls_dtls_cookie_verify`. If successful the session should be initialized and associated with the cookie using `gnutls_dtls_prestate_set`, before proceeding to the handshake.

---

int **gnutls_key_generate** (*gnutls_datum_t* * **key**, *unsigned int* **key_size**)

int **gnutls_dtls_cookie_send** (*gnutls_datum_t* * **key**, *void* * **client_data**, *size_t* **client_data_size**, *gnutls_dtls_prestate_st* * **prestate**, *gnutls_transport_ptr_t* **ptr**, *gnutls_push_func* **push_func**)

int **gnutls_dtls_cookie_verify** (*gnutls_datum_t* * **key**, *void* * **client_data**, *size_t* **client_data_size**, *void* * **_msg**, *size_t* **msg_size**, *gnutls_dtls_prestate_st* * **prestate**)

void **gnutls_dtls_prestate_set** (*gnutls_session_t* **session**, *gnutls_dtls_prestate_st* * **prestate**)

Note that the above apply to server side only and they are not mandatory to be used. Not using them, however, allows denial of service attacks. The client side cookie handling is part of `gnutls_handshake`.

Datagrams are typically restricted by a maximum transfer unit (MTU). For that both client and server side should set the correct maximum transfer unit for the layer underneath GnuTLS. This will allow proper fragmentation of DTLS messages and prevent messages from being silently discarded by the transport layer. The "correct" maximum transfer unit can be obtained through a path MTU discovery mechanism [21].

---

[2]A key of 128 bits or 16 bytes should be sufficient for this purpose.

---

void **gnutls_dtls_set_mtu** (*gnutls_session_t* **session,** *unsigned int* **mtu**)

unsigned int **gnutls_dtls_get_mtu** (*gnutls_session_t* **session**)

unsigned int **gnutls_dtls_get_data_mtu** (*gnutls_session_t* **session**)

5.6. TLS handshake

Once a session has been initialized and a network connection has been set up, TLS and DTLS protocols perform a handshake. The handshake is the actual key exchange.

---

int **gnutls_handshake** (*gnutls_session_t* **session**)

Description: This function does the handshake of the TLS/SSL protocol, and initializes the TLS connection. This function will fail if any problem is encountered, and will return a negative error code. In case of a client, if the client has asked to resume a session, but the server couldn't, then a full handshake will be performed. The non-fatal errors expected by this function are: **GNUTLS_E_INTERRUPTED, GNUTLS_E_AGAIN, GNUTLS_E_WARNING_ALERT_RECEIVED,** and **GNUTLS_E_GOT_APPLICATION_- DATA,** the latter only in a case of rehandshake. The former two interrupt the handshake procedure due to the lower layer being interrupted, and the latter because of an alert that may be sent by a server (it is always a good idea to check any received alerts). On these errors call this function again, until it returns 0; cf. gnutls_record_get_- direction() and gnutls_error_is_fatal(). In DTLS sessions the non-fatal error **GNUTLS_- E_LARGE_PACKET** is also possible, and indicates that the MTU should be adjusted. If this function is called by a server after a rehandshake request then **GNUTLS_E_GOT_- APPLICATION_DATA** or **GNUTLS_E_WARNING_ALERT_RECEIVED** may be returned. Note that these are non fatal errors, only in the specific case of a rehandshake. Their meaning is that the client rejected the rehandshake request or in the case of **GNUTLS_E_- GOT_APPLICATION_DATA** it could also mean that some data were pending. A client may receive that error code if it initiates the handshake and the server doesn't agreed.

Returns: GNUTLS_E_SUCCESS on success, otherwise a negative error code.

In GnuTLS 3.5.0 and later it is recommended to use `gnutls_session_set_verify_cert` for the handshake process to ensure the verification of the peer's identity.

In older GnuTLS versions it is required to manually verify the peer's certificate during the handshake by using `gnutls_certificate_set_verify_function`, and `gnutls_certificate_- verify_peers2`. See section 3.1 for more information.

---

void **gnutls_handshake_set_timeout** (*gnutls_session_t* **session**, *unsigned int* **ms**)

Description: `This function sets the timeout for the TLS handshake process to the provided value. Use an ms value of zero to disable timeout, or` **GNUTLS_DEFAULT_-HANDSHAKE_TIMEOUT** `for a reasonable default value. For the DTLS protocol, the more detailed gnutls_dtls_set_timeouts() is provided. This function requires to set a pull timeout callback. See gnutls_transport_set_pull_timeout_function().`

---

void **gnutls_session_set_verify_cert** (*gnutls_session_t* **session**, *const char* * **hostname**, *unsigned* **flags**)

int **gnutls_certificate_verify_peers2** (*gnutls_session_t* **session**, *unsigned int* * **status**)

5.7. Data transfer and termination

Once the handshake is complete and peer's identity has been verified data can be exchanged. The available functions resemble the POSIX `recv` and `send` functions. It is suggested to use `gnutls_error_is_fatal` to check whether the error codes returned by these functions are fatal for the protocol or can be ignored.

Although, in the TLS protocol the receive function can be called at any time, when DTLS is used the GnuTLS receive functions must be called once a message is available for reading, even if no data are expected. This is because in DTLS various (internal) actions may be required due to retransmission timers. Moreover, an extended receive function is shown below, which allows the extraction of the message's sequence number. Due to the unreliable nature of the protocol, this field allows distinguishing out-of-order messages.

The `gnutls_record_check_pending` helper function is available to allow checking whether data are available to be read in a GnuTLS session buffers. Note that this function complements but does not replace `select`, i.e., `gnutls_record_check_pending` reports no data to be read, `select` should be called to check for data in the network buffers.

---

int **gnutls_record_get_direction** (*gnutls_session_t* **session**)

Once a TLS or DTLS session is no longer needed, it is recommended to use `gnutls_bye` to terminate the session. That way the peer is notified securely about the intention of termination, which allows distinguishing it from a malicious connection termination. A session can be deinitialized with the `gnutls_deinit` function.

---

ssize_t **gnutls_record_send** (*gnutls_session_t* **session**, *const   void   ** **data**, *size_t* **data_size**)

Description: This function has the similar semantics with send(). The only difference is that it accepts a GnuTLS session, and uses different error codes. Note that if the send buffer is full, send() will block this function. See the send() documentation for more information. You can replace the default push function which is send(), by using gnutls_transport_set_push_function(). If the EINTR is returned by the internal push function then **GNUTLS_E_INTERRUPTED** will be returned. If **GNUTLS_E_INTERRUPTED** or **GNUTLS_E_AGAIN** is returned, you must call this function again, with the exact same parameters; alternatively you could provide a **NULL** pointer for data, and 0 for size. cf. gnutls_record_get_direction(). Note that in DTLS this function will return the **GNUTLS_E_LARGE_PACKET** error code if the send data exceed the data MTU value - as returned by gnutls_dtls_get_data_mtu(). The errno value EMSGSIZE also maps to **GNUTLS_E_LARGE_PACKET**. Note that since 3.2.13 this function can be called under cork in DTLS mode, and will refuse to send data over the MTU size by returning **GNUTLS_E_LARGE_PACKET**.

Returns: The number of bytes sent, or a negative error code. The number of bytes sent might be less than **data_size**. The maximum number of bytes this function can send in a single call depends on the negotiated maximum record size.

---

ssize_t **gnutls_record_recv** (*gnutls_session_t* **session**, *void   ** **data**, *size_t* **data_size**)

Description: This function has the similar semantics with recv(). The only difference is that it accepts a GnuTLS session, and uses different error codes. In the special case that the peer requests a renegotiation, the caller will receive an error code of **GNUTLS_E_REHANDSHAKE**. In case of a client, this message may be simply ignored, replied with an alert **GNUTLS_A_NO_RENEGOTIATION**, or replied with a new handshake, depending on the client's will. A server receiving this error code can only initiate a new handshake or terminate the session. If **EINTR** is returned by the internal push function (the default is recv()) then **GNUTLS_E_INTERRUPTED** will be returned. If **GNUTLS_E_INTERRUPTED** or **GNUTLS_E_AGAIN** is returned, you must call this function again to get the data. See also gnutls_record_get_direction().

Returns: The number of bytes received and zero on EOF (for stream connections). A negative error code is returned in case of an error. The number of bytes received might be less than the requested **data_size**.

---

int **gnutls_error_is_fatal** (*int* error)

Description: If a GnuTLS function returns a negative error code you may feed that value to this function to see if the error condition is fatal to a TLS session (i.e., must be terminated). Note that you may also want to check the error code manually, since some non-fatal errors to the protocol (such as a warning alert or a rehandshake request) may be fatal for your program. This function is only useful if you are dealing with errors from functions that relate to a TLS session (e.g., record layer or handshake layer handling functions).

Returns: Non-zero value on fatal errors or zero on non-fatal.

---

ssize_t **gnutls_record_recv_seq** (*gnutls_session_t* **session**, *void* * **data**, *size_t* **data_size**, *unsigned char* * **seq**)

Description: This function is the same as gnutls_record_recv(), except that it returns in addition to data, the sequence number of the data. This is useful in DTLS where record packets might be received out-of-order. The returned 8-byte sequence number is an integer in big-endian format and should be treated as a unique message identification.

Returns: The number of bytes received and zero on EOF. A negative error code is returned in case of an error. The number of bytes received might be less than **data_size**.

5.8. Buffered data transfer

Although `gnutls_record_send` is sufficient to transmit data to the peer, when many small chunks of data are to be transmitted it is inefficient and wastes bandwidth due to the TLS record overhead. In that case it is preferrable to combine the small chunks before transmission. The following functions provide that functionality.

---

size_t **gnutls_record_check_pending** (*gnutls_session_t* **session**)

Description: This function checks if there are unread data in the gnutls buffers. If the return value is non-zero the next call to gnutls_record_recv() is guaranteed not to block.

Returns: Returns the size of the data or zero.

---

int **gnutls_bye** (*gnutls_session_t* **session**, *gnutls_close_request_t* **how**)

Description: Terminates the current TLS/SSL connection. The connection should have been initiated using gnutls_handshake(). how should be one of **GNUTLS_SHUT_-RDWR**, **GNUTLS_SHUT_WR**. In case of **GNUTLS_SHUT_RDWR** the TLS session gets terminated and further receives and sends will be disallowed. If the return value is zero you may continue using the underlying transport layer. **GNUTLS_SHUT_RDWR** sends an alert containing a close request and waits for the peer to reply with the same message. In case of **GNUTLS_SHUT_WR** the TLS session gets terminated and further sends will be disallowed. In order to reuse the connection you should wait for an EOF from the peer. **GNUTLS_SHUT_WR** sends an alert containing a close request. Note that not all implementations will properly terminate a TLS connection. Some of them, usually for performance reasons, will terminate only the underlying transport layer, and thus not distinguishing between a malicious party prematurely terminating the connection and normal termination. This function may also return **GNUTLS_E_AGAIN** or **GNUTLS_E_-INTERRUPTED**; cf. gnutls_record_get_direction().

Returns: **GNUTLS_E_SUCCESS** on success, or an error code, see function documentation for entire semantics.

---

void **gnutls_deinit** (*gnutls_session_t* **session**)

Description: This function clears all buffers associated with the session. This function will also remove session data from the session database if the session was terminated abnormally.

5.9. Handling alerts

During a TLS connection alert messages may be exchanged by the two peers. Those messages may be fatal, meaning the connection must be terminated afterwards, or warning when something needs to be reported to the peer, but without interrupting the session. The error codes GNUTLS_E_WARNING_ALERT_RECEIVED or GNUTLS_E_FATAL_ALERT_RECEIVED signal those alerts when received, and may be returned by all GnuTLS functions that receive data from the

---

void **gnutls_record_cork** (*gnutls_session_t* **session**)

Description: If called, gnutls_record_send() will no longer send any records. Any sent records will be cached until gnutls_record_uncork() is called. This function is safe to use with DTLS after GnuTLS 3.3.0.

---

int **gnutls_record_uncork** (*gnutls_session_t* **session**, *unsigned int* **flags**)

Description: This resets the effect of gnutls_record_cork(), and flushes any pending data. If the **GNUTLS_RECORD_WAIT** flag is specified then this function will block until the data is sent or a fatal error occurs (i.e., the function will retry on **GNUTLS_E_AGAIN** and **GNUTLS_E_INTERRUPTED**). If the flag **GNUTLS_RECORD_WAIT** is not specified and the function is interrupted then the **GNUTLS_E_AGAIN** or **GNUTLS_E_INTERRUPTED** errors will be returned. To obtain the data left in the corked buffer use gnutls_record_check_corked().

Returns: On success the number of transmitted data is returned, or otherwise a negative error code.

---

peer, being `gnutls_handshake` and `gnutls_record_recv`.

If those error codes are received the alert and its level should be logged or reported to the peer using the functions below.

---

gnutls_alert_description_t **gnutls_alert_get** (*gnutls_session_t* **session**)

Description: This function will return the last alert number received. This function should be called when **GNUTLS_E_WARNING_ALERT_RECEIVED** or **GNUTLS_E_FATAL_ALERT_RECEIVED** errors are returned by a gnutls function. The peer may send alerts if he encounters an error. If no alert has been received the returned value is undefined.

Returns: the last alert received, a *gnutls_alert_description_t* value.

---

const char * **gnutls_alert_get_name** (*gnutls_alert_description_t* **alert**)

Description: This function will return a string that describes the given alert number, or **NULL**. See gnutls_alert_get().

Returns: string corresponding to *gnutls_alert_description_t* value.

The peer may also be warned or notified of a fatal issue by using one of the functions below. All the available alerts are listed in section 2.4.

int **gnutls_alert_send** (*gnutls_session_t* **session**, *gnutls_alert_level_t* **level**, *gnutls_alert_description_t* **desc**)

Description: This function will send an alert to the peer in order to inform him of something important (eg. his Certificate could not be verified). If the alert level is Fatal then the peer is expected to close the connection, otherwise he may ignore the alert and continue. The error code of the underlying record send function will be returned, so you may also receive GNUTLS_E_INTERRUPTED or GNUTLS_E_AGAIN as well.

Returns: On success, GNUTLS_E_SUCCESS (0) is returned, otherwise an error code is returned.

---

int **gnutls_error_to_alert** (*int* **err**, *int* * **level**)

Description: Get an alert depending on the error code returned by a gnutls function. All alerts sent by this function should be considered fatal. The only exception is when err is GNUTLS_E_REHANDSHAKE, where a warning alert should be sent to the peer indicating that no renegotiation will be performed. If there is no mapping to a valid alert the alert to indicate internal error is returned.

Returns: the alert code to use for a particular error code.

5.10. Priority strings

The GnuTLS priority strings specify the TLS session's handshake algorithms and options in a compact, easy-to-use format. That string may contain a single initial keyword such as in Table 5.3 and may be followed by additional algorithm or special keywords. Note that their description is intentionally avoiding specific algorithm details, as the priority strings are not constant between gnutls versions (they are periodically updated to account for cryptographic advances while providing compatibility with old clients and servers).

---

int **gnutls_priority_set_direct** (*gnutls_session_t* **session**, *const char* * **priorities**, *const char* ** **err_pos**)

int **gnutls_priority_set** (*gnutls_session_t* **session**, *gnutls_priority_t* **priority**)

Unless the initial keyword is "NONE" the defaults (in preference order) are for TLS protocols TLS 1.2, TLS1.1, TLS1.0; for compression NULL; for certificate types X.509. In key exchange algorithms when in NORMAL or SECURE levels the perfect forward secrecy algorithms take

Keyword	Description
@KEYWORD	Means that a compile-time specified system configuration file[3] will be used to expand the provided keyword. That is used to impose system-specific policies. It may be followed by additional options that will be appended to the system string (e.g., "@SYSTEM:+SRP"). The system file should have the format 'KEYWORD=VALUE', e.g., 'SYSTEM=NORMAL:+ARCFOUR-128'.
PERFORMANCE	All the known to be secure ciphersuites are enabled, limited to 128 bit ciphers and sorted by terms of speed performance. The message authenticity security level is of 64 bits or more, and the certificate verification profile is set to GNUTLS_PROFILE_LOW (80-bits).
NORMAL	Means all the known to be secure ciphersuites. The ciphers are sorted by security margin, although the 256-bit ciphers are included as a fallback only. The message authenticity security level is of 64 bits or more, and the certificate verification profile is set to GNUTLS_PROFILE_LOW (80-bits). This priority string implicitly enables ECDHE and DHE. The ECDHE ciphersuites are placed first in the priority order, but due to compatibility issues with the DHE ciphersuites they are placed last in the priority order, after the plain RSA ciphersuites.
LEGACY	This sets the NORMAL settings that were used for GnuTLS 3.2.x or earlier. There is no verification profile set, and the allowed DH primes are considered weak today (but are often used by misconfigured servers).
PFS	Means all the known to be secure ciphersuites that support perfect forward secrecy (ECDHE and DHE). The ciphers are sorted by security margin, although the 256-bit ciphers are included as a fallback only. The message authenticity security level is of 80 bits or more, and the certificate verification profile is set to GNUTLS_PROFILE_LOW (80-bits). This option is available since 3.2.4 or later.
SECURE128	Means all known to be secure ciphersuites that offer a security level 128-bit or more. The message authenticity security level is of 80 bits or more, and the certificate verification profile is set to GNUTLS_PROFILE_LOW (80-bits).
SECURE192	Means all the known to be secure ciphersuites that offer a security level 192-bit or more. The message authenticity security level is of 128 bits or more, and the certificate verification profile is set to GNUTLS_PROFILE_HIGH (128-bits).
SECURE256	Currently alias for SECURE192. This option, will enable ciphers which use a 256-bit key but, due to limitations of the TLS protocol, the overall security level will be 192-bits (the security level depends on more factors than cipher key size).
SUITEB128	Means all the NSA Suite B cryptography (RFC5430) ciphersuites with an 128 bit security level, as well as the enabling of the corresponding verification profile.
SUITEB192	Means all the NSA Suite B cryptography (RFC5430) ciphersuites with an 192 bit security level, as well as the enabling of the corresponding verification profile.
NONE	Means nothing is enabled. This disables even protocols and compression methods. It should be followed by the algorithms to be

precedence of the other protocols. In all cases all the supported key exchange algorithms are enabled.

Note that the SECURE levels distinguish between overall security level and message authenticity security level. That is because the message authenticity security level requires the adversary to break the algorithms at real-time during the protocol run, whilst the overall security level refers to off-line adversaries (e.g. adversaries breaking the ciphertext years after it was captured).

The NONE keyword, if used, must followed by keywords specifying the algorithms and protocols to be enabled. The other initial keywords do not require, but may be followed by such keywords. All level keywords can be combined, and for example a level of "SECURE256:+SECURE128" is allowed.

The order with which every algorithm or protocol is specified is significant. Algorithms specified before others will take precedence. The supported algorithms and protocols are shown in Table 5.4. To avoid collisions in order to specify a compression algorithm in the priority string you have to prefix it with "COMP-", protocol versions with "VERS-", signature algorithms with "SIGN-" and certificate types with "CTYPE-". All other algorithms don't need a prefix. Each specified keyword can be prefixed with any of the following characters.

- '!' or '-' appended with an algorithm will remove this algorithm.

- "+" appended with an algorithm will add this algorithm.

Note that the DHE key exchange methods are generally slower[4] than their elliptic curves counterpart (ECDHE). Moreover the plain Diffie-Hellman key exchange requires parameters to be generated and associated with a credentials structure by the server (see subsection 5.12.4).

The available special keywords are shown in Table 5.5 and Table 5.6.

Finally the ciphersuites enabled by any priority string can be listed using the `gnutls-cli` application (see section 7.1), or by using the priority functions as in subsection 6.4.3.

Example priority strings are:

```
1  The system imposed security level:
2      "SYSTEM"
3
4  The default priority without the HMAC-MD5:
5      "NORMAL:-MD5"
6
7  Specifying RSA with AES-128-CBC:
8      "NONE:+VERS-TLS-ALL:+MAC-ALL:+RSA:+AES-128-CBC:+SIGN-ALL:+COMP-NULL"
9
10 Specifying the defaults plus ARCFOUR-128:
11     "NORMAL:+ARCFOUR-128"
12
13 Enabling the 128-bit secure ciphers, while disabling TLS 1.0 and enabling compression:
14     "SECURE128:-VERS-TLS1.0:+COMP-DEFLATE"
15
16 Enabling the 128-bit and 192-bit secure ciphers, while disabling all TLS versions
```

---

[4]It depends on the group used. Primes with lesser bits are always faster, but also easier to break. See section 5.11 for the acceptable security levels.

Type	Keywords
Ciphers	AES-128-CBC, AES-256-CBC, AES-128-GCM, CAMELLIA-128-CBC, CAMELLIA-256-CBC, ARCFOUR-128, 3DES-CBC. Catch all name is CIPHER-ALL which will add all the algorithms from NORMAL priority.
Key exchange	RSA, DHE-RSA, DHE-DSS, SRP, SRP-RSA, SRP-DSS, PSK, DHE-PSK, ECDHE-RSA, ANON-ECDH, ANON-DH. The Catch all name is KX-ALL which will add all the algorithms from NORMAL priority. Add !DHE-RSA:!DHE-DSS to the priority string to disable DHE.
MAC	MD5, SHA1, SHA256, SHA384, AEAD (used with GCM ciphers only). All algorithms from NORMAL priority can be accessed with MAC-ALL.
Compression algorithms	COMP-NULL, COMP-DEFLATE. Catch all is COMP-ALL.
TLS versions	VERS-TLS1.0, VERS-TLS1.1, VERS-TLS1.2, VERS-DTLS1.0, VERS-DTLS1.2. Catch all are VERS-ALL, VERS-TLS-ALL and VERS-DTLS-ALL.
Signature algorithms	SIGN-RSA-SHA1, SIGN-RSA-SHA224, SIGN-RSA-SHA256, SIGN-RSA-SHA384, SIGN-RSA-SHA512, SIGN-DSA-SHA1, SIGN-DSA-SHA224, SIGN-DSA-SHA256, SIGN-RSA-MD5. Catch all is SIGN-ALL. This is only valid for TLS 1.2 and later.
Elliptic curves	CURVE-SECP192R1, CURVE-SECP224R1, CURVE-SECP256R1, CURVE-SECP384R1, CURVE-SECP521R1. Catch all is CURVE-ALL.
Certificate type	CTYPE-OPENPGP, CTYPE-X509. Catch all is CTYPE-ALL.

Table 5.4.: The supported algorithm keywords in priority strings.

```
17  except TLS 1.2:
18      "SECURE128:+SECURE192:-VERS-TLS-ALL:+VERS-TLS1.2"
```

5.11. Selecting cryptographic key sizes

Because many algorithms are involved in TLS, it is not easy to set a consistent security level. For this reason in Table 5.7 we present some correspondence between key sizes of symmetric algorithms and public key algorithms based on [3]. Those can be used to generate certificates with appropriate key sizes as well as select parameters for Diffie-Hellman and SRP authentication.

The first column provides a security parameter in a number of bits. This gives an indication of the number of combinations to be tried by an adversary to brute force a key. For example to test all possible keys in a 112 bit security parameter 2

163

Keyword	Description
%COMPAT	will enable compatibility mode. It might mean that violations of the protocols are allowed as long as maximum compatibility with problematic clients and servers is achieved. More specifically this string would disable TLS record random padding, tolerate packets over the maximum allowed TLS record, and add a padding to TLS Client Hello packet to prevent it being in the 256-512 range which is known to be causing issues with a commonly used firewall.
%DUMBFW	will add a private extension with bogus data that make the client hello exceed 512 bytes. This avoids a black hole behavior in some firewalls. This is a non-standard TLS extension, use with care.
%NO_EXTENSIONS	will prevent the sending of any TLS extensions in client side. Note that TLS 1.2 requires extensions to be used, as well as safe renegotiation thus this option must be used with care.
%NO_TICKETS	will prevent the advertizing of the TLS session ticket extension. This is implied by the PFS keyword.
%NO_SESSION_HASH	will prevent the advertizing the TLS extended master secret (session hash) extension.
%SERVER_PRECEDENCE	The ciphersuite will be selected according to server priorities and not the client's.
%SSL3_RECORD_VERSION	will use SSL3.0 record version in client hello. This is the default.
%LATEST_RECORD_VERSION	will use the latest TLS version record version in client hello.

Table 5.5.: Special priority string keywords.

Keyword	Description
%STATELESS_COMPRESSION	will disable keeping state across records when compressing. This may help to mitigate attacks when compression is used but an attacker is in control of input data. This has to be used only when the data that are possibly controlled by an attacker are placed in separate records.
%DISABLE_WILDCARDS	will disable matching wildcards when comparing hostnames in certificates.
%NO_ETM	will disable the encrypt-then-mac TLS extension (RFC7366). This is implied by the %COMPAT keyword.
%DISABLE_SAFE_RENEGOTIATION	will completely disable safe renegotiation completely. Do not use unless you know what you are doing.
%UNSAFE_RENEGOTIATION	will allow handshakes and re-handshakes without the safe renegotiation extension. Note that for clients this mode is insecure (you may be under attack), and for servers it will allow insecure clients to connect (which could be fooled by an attacker). Do not use unless you know what you are doing and want maximum compatibility.
%PARTIAL_RENEGOTIATION	will allow initial handshakes to proceed, but not re-handshakes. This leaves the client vulnerable to attack, and servers will be compatible with non-upgraded clients for initial handshakes. This is currently the default for clients and servers, for compatibility reasons.
%SAFE_RENEGOTIATION	will enforce safe renegotiation. Clients and servers will refuse to talk to an insecure peer. Currently this causes interoperability problems, but is required for full protection.
%FALLBACK_SCSV	will enable the use of the fallback signaling cipher suite value in the client hello. Note that this should be set only by applications that try to reconnect with a downgraded protocol version. See RFC7507 for details.
%VERIFY_ALLOW_SIGN_RSA_MD5	will allow RSA-MD5 signatures in certificate chains.
%VERIFY_DISABLE_CRL_CHECKS	will disable CRL or OCSP checks in the verification of the certificate chain.
%VERIFY_ALLOW_X509_V1_CA_CRT	will allow V1 CAs in chains.
%PROFILE_(LOW—LEGACY—MEDIUM—HIGH—ULTRA)	require a certificate verification profile the corresponds to the specified security level, see Table 5.7 for the mappings to values.
%PROFILE_(SUITEB128—SUITEB192)	require a certificate verification profile the corresponds to SUITEB. Note that an initial keyword that enables SUITEB auto-

Security bits	RSA, DH and SRP parameter size	ECC key size	Security parameter (profile)	Description
<64	<768	<128	INSECURE	Considered to be insecure
64	768	128	VERY WEAK	Short term protection against individuals
72	1008	160	WEAK	Short term protection against small organizations
80	1024	160	LOW	Very short term protection against agencies (corresponds to ENISA legacy level)
96	1776	192	LEGACY	Legacy standard level
112	2048	224	MEDIUM	Medium-term protection
128	3072	256	HIGH	Long term protection (corresponds to ENISA future level)
192	8192	384	ULTRA	Even longer term protection
256	15424	512	FUTURE	Foreseeable future

Table 5.7.: Key sizes and security parameters.

*textasciicircum*112 combinations have to be tried. For today's technology this is infeasible. The next two columns correlate the security parameter with actual bit sizes of parameters for DH, RSA, SRP and ECC algorithms. A mapping to `gnutls_sec_param_t` value is given for each security parameter, on the next column, and finally a brief description of the level.

Note, however, that the values suggested here are nothing more than an educated guess that is valid today. There are no guarantees that an algorithm will remain unbreakable or that these values will remain constant in time. There could be scientific breakthroughs that cannot be predicted or total failure of the current public key systems by quantum computers. On the other hand though the cryptosystems used in TLS are selected in a conservative way and such catastrophic breakthroughs or failures are believed to be unlikely. The NIST publication SP 800-57 [1] contains a similar table.

When using GnuTLS and a decision on bit sizes for a public key algorithm is required, use of the following functions is recommended:

Those functions will convert a human understandable security parameter of `gnutls_sec_param_t` type, to a number of bits suitable for a public key algorithm.

const char * **gnutls_sec_param_get_name** (*gnutls_sec_param_t* **param**)

The following functions will set the minimum acceptable group size for Diffie-Hellman and SRP

---

unsigned   *int* **gnutls_sec_param_to_pk_bits** (*gnutls_pk_algorithm_t* **algo**, *gnutls_sec_param_t* **param**)

Description: When generating private and public key pairs a difficult question is which size of "bits" the modulus will be in RSA and the group size in DSA. The easy answer is 1024, which is also wrong. This function will convert a human understandable security parameter to an appropriate size for the specific algorithm.

Returns: The number of bits, or (0).

---

gnutls_sec_param_t **gnutls_pk_bits_to_sec_param** (*gnutls_pk_algorithm_t* **algo**, *unsigned int* **bits**)

Description: This is the inverse of gnutls_sec_param_to_pk_bits(). Given an algorithm and the number of bits, it will return the security parameter. This is a rough indication.

Returns: The security parameter.

---

authentication.

---

void **gnutls_dh_set_prime_bits** (*gnutls_session_t* **session**, *unsigned int* **bits**)

void **gnutls_srp_set_prime_bits** (*gnutls_session_t* **session**, *unsigned int* **bits**)

5.12. Advanced topics

5.12.1. Session resumption

Client side

To reduce time and roundtrips spent in a handshake the client can request session resumption from a server that previously shared a session with the client. For that the client has to retrieve and store the session parameters. Before establishing a new session to the same server the parameters must be re-associated with the GnuTLS session using `gnutls_session_set_data`.

---

int **gnutls_session_get_data2** (*gnutls_session_t* **session**, *gnutls_datum_t* * **data**)

int **gnutls_session_get_id2** (*gnutls_session_t* **session**, *gnutls_datum_t* * **session_id**)

int **gnutls_session_set_data** (*gnutls_session_t* **session**, *const void* * **session_data**, *size_t* **session_data_size**)

Keep in mind that sessions will be expired after some time, depending on the server, and a server may choose not to resume a session even when requested to. The expiration is to prevent temporal session keys from becoming long-term keys. Also note that as a client you must enable, using the priority functions, at least the algorithms used in the last session.

---

int **gnutls_session_is_resumed** (*gnutls_session_t* **session**)

Description: Check whether session is resumed or not.

Returns: non zero if this session is resumed, or a zero if this is a new session.

Server side

In order to support resumption a server can store the session security parameters in a local database or by using session tickets (see subsection 2.6.3) to delegate storage to the client. Because session tickets might not be supported by all clients, servers could combine the two methods.

A storing server needs to specify callback functions to store, retrieve and delete session data. These can be registered with the functions below. The stored sessions in the database can be checked using **gnutls_db_check_entry** for expiration.

---

void **gnutls_db_set_retrieve_function** (*gnutls_session_t* **session**, *gnutls_db_retr_func* **retr_func**)

void **gnutls_db_set_store_function** (*gnutls_session_t* **session**, *gnutls_db_store_func* **store_func**)

void **gnutls_db_set_ptr** (*gnutls_session_t* **session**, *void* * **ptr**)

void **gnutls_db_set_remove_function** (*gnutls_session_t* **session**, *gnutls_db_remove_func* **rem_func**)

---

int **gnutls_db_check_entry** (*gnutls_session_t* **session**, *gnutls_datum_t* **session_entry**)

A server utilizing tickets should generate ticket encryption and authentication keys using **gnutls_session_ticket_key_generate**. Those keys should be associated with the GnuTLS session using **gnutls_session_ticket_enable_server**, and should be rotated regularly (e.g., every few hours), to prevent them from becoming long-term keys which if revealed could be used to decrypt all previous sessions.

---

int **gnutls_session_ticket_enable_server** (*gnutls_session_t* **session**, *const gnutls_datum_t* * **key**)

Description: Request that the server should attempt session resumption using SessionTicket. key must be initialized with gnutls_session_ticket_key_generate(), and should be overwritten using gnutls_memset() before being released.

Returns: On success, **GNUTLS_E_SUCCESS** (0) is returned, or an error code.

---

int **gnutls_session_ticket_key_generate** (*gnutls_datum_t* * **key**)

Description: Generate a random key to encrypt security parameters within SessionTicket.

Returns: On success, **GNUTLS_E_SUCCESS** (0) is returned, or an error code.

---

int **gnutls_session_resumption_requested** (*gnutls_session_t* **session**)

Description: Check whether the client has asked for session resumption. This function is valid only on server side.

Returns: non zero if session resumption was asked, or a zero if not.

A server enabling both session tickets and a storage for session data would use session tickets when clients support it and the storage otherwise.

5.12.2. Certificate verification

In this section the functionality for additional certificate verification methods is listed. These methods are intended to be used in addition to normal PKI verification, in order to reduce the risk of a compromised CA being undetected.

Trust on first use

The GnuTLS library includes functionlity to use an SSH-like trust on first use authentication. The available functions to store and verify public keys are listed below.

---

int **gnutls_verify_stored_pubkey** (*const char* * **db_name**, *gnutls_tdb_t* **tdb**, *const char* * **host**, *const char* * **service**, *gnutls_certificate_type_t* **cert_type**, *const gnutls_datum_t* * **cert**, *unsigned int* **flags**)

Description: This function will try to verify the provided (raw or DER-encoded) certificate using a list of stored public keys. The service field if non-NULL should be a port number. The retrieve variable if non-null specifies a custom backend for the retrieval of entries. If it is NULL then the default file backend will be used. In POSIX-like systems the file backend uses the $HOME/.gnutls/known_hosts file. Note that if the custom storage backend is provided the retrieval function should return **GNUTLS_-E_CERTIFICATE_KEY_MISMATCH** if the host/service pair is found but key doesn't match, **GNUTLS_E_NO_CERTIFICATE_FOUND** if no such host/service with the given key is found, and 0 if it was found. The storage function should return 0 on success.

Returns: If no associated public key is found then **GNUTLS_E_NO_CERTIFICATE_-FOUND** will be returned. If a key is found but does not match **GNUTLS_E_-CERTIFICATE_KEY_MISMATCH** is returned. On success, **GNUTLS_E_SUCCESS** (0) is returned, or a negative error value on other errors.

---

int **gnutls_store_pubkey** (*const char* * **db_name**, *gnutls_tdb_t* **tdb**, *const char* * **host**, *const char* * **service**, *gnutls_certificate_type_t* **cert_type**, *const gnutls_datum_t* * **cert**, *time_t* **expiration**, *unsigned int* **flags**)

Description: This function will store the provided (raw or DER-encoded) certificate to the list of stored public keys. The key will be considered valid until the provided expiration time. The store variable if non-null specifies a custom backend for the storage of entries. If it is NULL then the default file backend will be used.

Returns: On success, **GNUTLS_E_SUCCESS** (0) is returned, otherwise a negative error value.

In addition to the above the `gnutls_store_commitment` can be used to implement a key-pinning architecture as in [12]. This provides a way for web server to commit on a public key that is not yet active.

---

int **gnutls_store_commitment** (*const char* * **db_name**, *gnutls_tdb_t* **tdb**, *const char* * **host**, *const char* * **service**, *gnutls_digest_algorithm_t* **hash_algo**, *const gnutls_datum_t* * **hash**, *time_t* **expiration**, *unsigned int* **flags**)

Description: `This function will store the provided hash commitment to the list of stored`
`public keys.  The key with the given hash will be considered valid until the provided`
`expiration time.  The store variable if non-null specifies a custom backend for the storage`
`of entries.  If it is NULL then the default file backend will be used.  Note that this`
`function is not thread safe with the default backend.`

Returns: `On success,` **GNUTLS_E_SUCCESS** `(0) is returned, otherwise a negative error`
`value.`

The storage and verification functions may be used with the default text file based back-end, or another back-end may be specified. That should contain storage and retrieval functions and specified as below.

---

int **gnutls_tdb_init** (*gnutls_tdb_t* * **tdb**)

void **gnutls_tdb_deinit** (*gnutls_tdb_t* **tdb**)

void **gnutls_tdb_set_verify_func** (*gnutls_tdb_t* **tdb**, *gnutls_tdb_verify_func* **verify**)

void **gnutls_tdb_set_store_func** (*gnutls_tdb_t* **tdb**, *gnutls_tdb_store_func* **store**)

void **gnutls_tdb_set_store_commitment_func** (*gnutls_tdb_t* **tdb**, *gnutls_tdb_store_commitment_func* **cstore**)

DANE verification

Since the DANE library is not included in GnuTLS it requires programs to be linked against it. This can be achieved with the following commands.

```
1  gcc -o foo foo.c `pkg-config gnutls-dane --cflags --libs`
```

When a program uses the GNU autoconf system, then the following line or similar can be used to detect the presence of the library.

```
1  PKG_CHECK_MODULES([LIBDANE], [gnutls-dane >= 3.0.0])
2
3  AC_SUBST([LIBDANE_CFLAGS])
4  AC_SUBST([LIBDANE_LIBS])
```

The high level functionality provided by the DANE library is shown below.

---

int **dane_verify_crt** (*dane_state_t* **s**, *const* *gnutls_datum_t* * **chain**, *unsigned* **chain_size**, *gnutls_certificate_type_t* **chain_type**, *const* *char* * **hostname**, *const* *char* * **proto**, *unsigned int* **port**, *unsigned int* **sflags**, *unsigned int* **vflags**, *unsigned int* * **verify**)

Description: This function will verify the given certificate chain against the CA constrains and/or the certificate available via DANE. If no information via DANE can be obtained the flag **DANE_VERIFY_NO_DANE_INFO** is set. If a DNSSEC signature is not available for the DANE record then the verify flag **DANE_VERIFY_NO_DNSSEC_-DATA** is set. Due to the many possible options of DANE, there is no single threat model countered. When notifying the user about DANE verification results it may be better to mention: DANE verification did not reject the certificate, rather than mentioning a successful DANE verication. Note that this function is designed to be run in addition to PKIX - certificate chain - verification. To be run independently the **DANE_VFLAG_-ONLY_CHECK_EE_USAGE** flag should be specified; then the function will check whether the key of the peer matches the key advertized in the DANE entry. If the **q** parameter is provided it will be used for caching entries.

Returns: On success, **DANE_E_SUCCESS** (0) is returned, otherwise a negative error value.

---

int **dane_verify_session_crt** (*dane_state_t* **s**, *gnutls_session_t* **session**, *const* *char* * **hostname**, *const char* * **proto**, *unsigned int* **port**, *unsigned int* **sflags**, *unsigned int* **vflags**, *unsigned int* * **verify**)

const char * **dane_strerror** (*int* **error**)

Note that the **dane_state_t** structure that is accepted by both verification functions is optional. It is required when many queries are performed to facilitate caching. The following flags are returned by the verify functions to indicate the status of the verification.

In order to generate a DANE TLSA entry to use in a DNS server you may use danetool (see subsection 3.2.7).

```
enum dane_verify_status_t:
  DANE_VERIFY_CA_CONSTRAINTS_-        The CA constraints were violated.
  VIOLATED
  DANE_VERIFY_CERT_DIFFERS           The certificate obtained via DNS differs.
  DANE_VERIFY_UNKNOWN_DANE_-         No known DANE data was found in the DNS record.
  INFO
```

Table 5.8.: The DANE verification status flags.

5.12.3. Re-authentication

In TLS there is no distinction between rekey, re-authentication, and re-negotiation. All of these use cases are handled by the TLS' rehandshake process. For that reason in GnuTLS rehandshake is not transparent to the application, and the application must take control of that process. The following paragraphs explain how to safely use the rehandshake process.

Client side

According to the TLS specification a client may initiate a rehandshake at any time. That can be achieved by calling **gnutls_handshake** and rely on its return value for the outcome of the handshake (the server may deny a rehandshake). If a server requests a re-handshake, then a call to **gnutls_record_recv** will return GNUTLS_E_REHANDSHAKE in the client, instructing it to call **gnutls_handshake**. To deny a rehandshake request by the server it is recommended to send a warning alert of type GNUTLS_A_NO_RENEGOTIATION.

Due to limitations of early protocol versions, it is required to check whether safe renegotiation is in place, i.e., using **gnutls_safe_renegotiation_status**, which ensures that the server remains the same as the initial. For older servers, which do not support renegotiation, it is required on the second handshake to verify that their certificate/credentials remained the same as in the initial session.

int **gnutls_safe_renegotiation_status** (*gnutls_session_t* **session**)

Description: Can be used to check whether safe renegotiation is being used in the current session.

Returns: 0 when safe renegotiation is not used and non (0) when safe renegotiation is used.

Server side

A server which wants to instruct the client to re-authenticate, should call gnutls_rehandshake and wait for the client to re-authenticate. It is recommended to only request re-handshake when safe renegotiation is enabled for that session (see gnutls_safe_renegotiation_status and the discussion in subsection 2.6.5).

---

int **gnutls_rehandshake** (*gnutls_session_t* **session**)

Description: This function will renegotiate security parameters with the client. This should only be called in case of a server. This message informs the peer that we want to renegotiate parameters (perform a handshake). If this function succeeds (returns 0), you must call the gnutls_handshake() function in order to negotiate the new parameters. Since TLS is full duplex some application data might have been sent during peer's processing of this message. In that case one should call gnutls_record_recv() until GNUTLS_E_REHANDSHAKE is returned to clear any pending data. Care must be taken, if rehandshake is mandatory, to terminate if it does not start after some threshold. If the client does not wish to renegotiate parameters he should reply with an alert message, thus the return code will be **GNUTLS_E_WARNING_ALERT_RECEIVED** and the alert will be **GNUTLS_A_NO_RENEGOTIATION**. A client may also choose to ignore this message.

Returns: **GNUTLS_E_SUCCESS** on success, otherwise a negative error code.

5.12.4. Parameter generation

Several TLS ciphersuites require additional parameters that need to be generated or provided by the application. The Diffie-Hellman based ciphersuites (ANON-DH or DHE), require the group parameters to be provided. Those can either be be generated on the fly using gnutls_dh_params_generate2 or imported from pregenerated data using gnutls_dh_params_import_pkcs3. The parameters can be used in a TLS session by calling gnutls_certificate_set_dh_params or gnutls_anon_set_server_dh_params for anonymous sessions.

---

int **gnutls_dh_params_generate2** (*gnutls_dh_params_t* **dparams**, *unsigned int* **bits**)

int **gnutls_dh_params_import_pkcs3** (*gnutls_dh_params_t* **params**, *const gnutls_datum_t* * **pkcs3_params**, *gnutls_x509_crt_fmt_t* **format**)

void **gnutls_certificate_set_dh_params** (*gnutls_certificate_credentials_t* **res**, *gnutls_dh_params_t* **dh_params**)

void **gnutls_anon_set_server_dh_params** (*gnutls_anon_server_credentials_t* **res**, *gnutls_dh_params_t* **dh_params**)

Due to the time-consuming calculations required for the generation of Diffie-Hellman parameters we suggest against performing generation of them within an application. The `certtool` tool can be used to generate or export known safe values that can be stored in code or in a configuration file to provide the ability to replace. We also recommend the usage of `gnutls_sec_param_to_pk_bits` (see section 5.11) to determine the bit size of the generated parameters.

Note that the information stored in the generated PKCS #3 structure changed with GnuTLS 3.0.9. Since that version the `privateValueLength` member of the structure is set, allowing the server utilizing the parameters to use keys of the size of the security parameter. This provides better performance in key exchange.

To allow renewal of the parameters within an application without accessing the credentials, which are a shared structure, an alternative interface is available using a callback function.

---

void **gnutls_certificate_set_params_function** (*gnutls_certificate_credentials_t* **res**, *gnutls_params_function* * **func**)

Description: `This function will set a callback in order for the server to get the Diffie-Hellman or RSA parameters for certificate authentication. The callback should return` **GNUTLS_E_SUCCESS** `(0) on success.`

5.12.5. Deriving keys for other applications/protocols

In several cases, after a TLS connection is established, it is desirable to derive keys to be used in another application or protocol (e.g., in an other TLS session using pre-shared keys). The following describe GnuTLS' implementation of RFC5705 to extract keys based on a session's master secret.

The API to use is `gnutls_prf`. The function needs to be provided with a label, and additional context data to mix in the `extra` parameter. Moreover, the API allows to switch the mix of the client and server random nonces, using the `server_random_first` parameter. In typical uses you don't need it, so a zero value should be provided in `server_random_first`.

For example, after establishing a TLS session using **gnutls_handshake**, you can obtain 32-bytes to be used as key, using this call:

```
1  #define MYLABEL "EXPORTER-My-protocol-name"
2  #define MYCONTEXT "my-protocol's-1st-session"
3
4  char out[32];
5  rc = gnutls_prf (session, sizeof(MYLABEL)-1, MYLABEL, 0,
6                   sizeof(MYCONTEXT)-1, MYCONTEXT, 32, out);
```

The output key depends on TLS' master secret, and is the same on both client and server.

If you don't want to use the RFC5705 interface and not mix in the client and server random nonces, there is a low-level TLS PRF interface called **gnutls_prf_raw**.

5.12.6. Channel bindings

In user authentication protocols (e.g., EAP or SASL mechanisms) it is useful to have a unique string that identifies the secure channel that is used, to bind together the user authentication with the secure channel. This can protect against man-in-the-middle attacks in some situations. That unique string is called a "channel binding". For background and discussion see [38].

In GnuTLS you can extract a channel binding using the **gnutls_session_channel_binding** function. Currently only the type **GNUTLS_CB_TLS_UNIQUE** is supported, which corresponds to the **tls-unique** channel binding for TLS defined in [4].

The following example describes how to print the channel binding data. Note that it must be run after a successful TLS handshake.

```
1  {
2    gnutls_datum_t cb;
3    int rc;
4
5    rc = gnutls_session_channel_binding (session,
6                                         GNUTLS_CB_TLS_UNIQUE,
7                                         &cb);
8    if (rc)
9      fprintf (stderr, "Channel binding error: %s\n",
10             gnutls_strerror (rc));
11   else
12     {
13       size_t i;
14       printf ("- Channel binding 'tls-unique': ");
15       for (i = 0; i < cb.size; i++)
16         printf ("%02x", cb.data[i]);
17       printf ("\n");
18     }
19 }
```

5.12.7. Interoperability

The TLS protocols support many ciphersuites, extensions and version numbers. As a result, few implementations are not able to properly interoperate once faced with extensions or version protocols they do not support and understand. The TLS protocol allows for a graceful downgrade to the commonly supported options, but practice shows it is not always implemented correctly.

Because there is no way to achieve maximum interoperability with broken peers without sacrificing security, GnuTLS ignores such peers by default. This might not be acceptable in cases where maximum compatibility is required. Thus we allow enabling compatibility with broken peers using priority strings (see section 5.10). A conservative priority string that would disable certain TLS protocol options that are known to cause compatibility problems, is shown below.

`NORMAL:%COMPAT`

For very old broken peers that do not tolerate TLS version numbers over TLS 1.0 another priority string is:

`NORMAL:-VERS-TLS-ALL:+VERS-TLS1.0:+VERS-SSL3.0:%COMPAT`

This priority string will in addition to above, only enable SSL 3.0 and TLS 1.0 as protocols.

5.12.8. Compatibility with the OpenSSL library

To ease GnuTLS' integration with existing applications, a compatibility layer with the OpenSSL library is included in the **gnutls-openssl** library. This compatibility layer is not complete and it is not intended to completely re-implement the OpenSSL API with GnuTLS. It only provides limited source-level compatibility.

The prototypes for the compatibility functions are in the "**gnutls/openssl.h**" header file. The limitations imposed by the compatibility layer include:

- Error handling is not thread safe.

6

GnuTLS application examples

In this chapter several examples of real-world use cases are listed. The examples are simplified to promote readability and contain little or no error checking.

6.1. Client examples

This section contains examples of TLS and SSL clients, using GnuTLS. Note that some of the examples require functions implemented by another example.

6.1.1. Simple client example with X.509 certificate support

Let's assume now that we want to create a TCP client which communicates with servers that use X.509 or OpenPGP certificate authentication. The following client is a very simple TLS client, which uses the high level verification functions for certificates, but does not support session resumption.

```
1   /* This example code is placed in the public domain. */
2
3   #ifdef HAVE_CONFIG_H
4   #include <config.h>
5   #endif
6
7   #include <stdio.h>
8   #include <stdlib.h>
9   #include <string.h>
10  #include <gnutls/gnutls.h>
11  #include <gnutls/x509.h>
12  #include "examples.h"
13
14  /* A very basic TLS client, with X.509 authentication and server certificate
15   * verification. Note that error checking for missing files etc. is omitted
16   * for simplicity.
17   */
18
19  #define MAX_BUF 1024
20  #define CAFILE "/etc/ssl/certs/ca-certificates.crt"
21  #define MSG "GET / HTTP/1.0\r\n\r\n"
22
```

```
23  extern int tcp_connect(void);
24  extern void tcp_close(int sd);
25
26  int main(void)
27  {
28          int ret, sd, ii;
29          gnutls_session_t session;
30          char buffer[MAX_BUF + 1];
31          gnutls_datum_t out;
32          int type;
33          unsigned status;
34  #if 0
35          const char *err;
36  #endif
37          gnutls_certificate_credentials_t xcred;
38
39          if (gnutls_check_version("3.4.6") == NULL) {
40                  fprintf(stderr, "GnuTLS 3.4.6 or later is required for this example\n");
41                  exit(1);
42          }
43
44          /* for backwards compatibility with gnutls < 3.3.0 */
45          gnutls_global_init();
46
47          /* X509 stuff */
48          gnutls_certificate_allocate_credentials(&xcred);
49
50          /* sets the trusted cas file
51           */
52          gnutls_certificate_set_x509_trust_file(xcred, CAFILE,
53                                               GNUTLS_X509_FMT_PEM);
54
55          /* If client holds a certificate it can be set using the following:
56           *
57           gnutls_certificate_set_x509_key_file (xcred,
58           "cert.pem", "key.pem",
59           GNUTLS_X509_FMT_PEM);
60           */
61
62          /* Initialize TLS session
63           */
64          gnutls_init(&session, GNUTLS_CLIENT);
65
66          gnutls_session_set_ptr(session, (void *) "my_host_name");
67
68          gnutls_server_name_set(session, GNUTLS_NAME_DNS, "my_host_name",
69                                  strlen("my_host_name"));
70
71          /* It is recommended to use the default priorities */
72          gnutls_set_default_priority(session);
73  #if 0
74          /* if more fine-graned control is required */
75          ret = gnutls_priority_set_direct(session,
76                                           "NORMAL", &err);
77          if (ret < 0) {
78                  if (ret == GNUTLS_E_INVALID_REQUEST) {
79                          fprintf(stderr, "Syntax error at: %s\n", err);
80                  }
```

```
81          exit(1);
82       }
83  #endif
84
85       /* put the x509 credentials to the current session
86        */
87       gnutls_credentials_set(session, GNUTLS_CRD_CERTIFICATE, xcred);
88       gnutls_session_set_verify_cert(session, "my_host_name", 0);
89
90       /* connect to the peer
91        */
92       sd = tcp_connect();
93
94       gnutls_transport_set_int(session, sd);
95       gnutls_handshake_set_timeout(session,
96                               GNUTLS_DEFAULT_HANDSHAKE_TIMEOUT);
97
98       /* Perform the TLS handshake
99        */
100      do {
101              ret = gnutls_handshake(session);
102      }
103      while (ret < 0 && gnutls_error_is_fatal(ret) == 0);
104      if (ret < 0) {
105              fprintf(stderr, "*** Handshake failed\n");
106              gnutls_perror(ret);
107              goto end;
108      } else {
109              char *desc;
110
111              desc = gnutls_session_get_desc(session);
112              printf("- Session info: %s\n", desc);
113              gnutls_free(desc);
114      }
115
116      /* check certificate verification status */
117      type = gnutls_certificate_type_get(session);
118      status = gnutls_session_get_verify_cert_status(session);
119      ret =
120          gnutls_certificate_verification_status_print(status, type,
121                                              &out, 0);
122      if (ret < 0) {
123              printf("Error\n");
124              return GNUTLS_E_CERTIFICATE_ERROR;
125      }
126
127      printf("%s", out.data);
128      gnutls_free(out.data);
129
130      /* send data */
131      gnutls_record_send(session, MSG, strlen(MSG));
132
133      ret = gnutls_record_recv(session, buffer, MAX_BUF);
134      if (ret == 0) {
135              printf("- Peer has closed the TLS connection\n");
136              goto end;
137      } else if (ret < 0 && gnutls_error_is_fatal(ret) == 0) {
138              fprintf(stderr, "*** Warning: %s\n", gnutls_strerror(ret));
```

```
139        } else if (ret < 0) {
140                fprintf(stderr, "*** Error: %s\n", gnutls_strerror(ret));
141                goto end;
142        }
143
144        if (ret > 0) {
145                printf("- Received %d bytes: ", ret);
146                for (ii = 0; ii < ret; ii++) {
147                        fputc(buffer[ii], stdout);
148                }
149                fputs("\n", stdout);
150        }
151
152        gnutls_bye(session, GNUTLS_SHUT_RDWR);
153
154    end:
155
156        tcp_close(sd);
157
158        gnutls_deinit(session);
159
160        gnutls_certificate_free_credentials(xcred);
161
162        gnutls_global_deinit();
163
164        return 0;
165 }
```

6.1.2. Simple client example with SSH-style certificate verification

This is an alternative verification function that will use the X.509 certificate authorities for verification, but also assume an trust on first use (SSH-like) authentication system. That is the user is prompted on unknown public keys and known public keys are considered trusted.

```
1  /* This example code is placed in the public domain. */
2
3  #ifdef HAVE_CONFIG_H
4  #include <config.h>
5  #endif
6
7  #include <stdio.h>
8  #include <stdlib.h>
9  #include <string.h>
10 #include <gnutls/gnutls.h>
11 #include <gnutls/x509.h>
12 #include "examples.h"
13
14 /* This function will verify the peer's certificate, check
15  * if the hostname matches. In addition it will perform an
16  * SSH-style authentication, where ultimately trusted keys
17  * are only the keys that have been seen before.
18  */
19 int _ssh_verify_certificate_callback(gnutls_session_t session)
20 {
21        unsigned int status;
```

182

```
22      const gnutls_datum_t *cert_list;
23      unsigned int cert_list_size;
24      int ret, type;
25      gnutls_datum_t out;
26      const char *hostname;
27
28      /* read hostname */
29      hostname = gnutls_session_get_ptr(session);
30
31      /* This verification function uses the trusted CAs in the credentials
32       * structure. So you must have installed one or more CA certificates.
33       */
34      ret = gnutls_certificate_verify_peers3(session, hostname, &status);
35      if (ret < 0) {
36              printf("Error\n");
37              return GNUTLS_E_CERTIFICATE_ERROR;
38      }
39
40      type = gnutls_certificate_type_get(session);
41
42      ret =
43          gnutls_certificate_verification_status_print(status, type,
44                                                       &out, 0);
45      if (ret < 0) {
46              printf("Error\n");
47              return GNUTLS_E_CERTIFICATE_ERROR;
48      }
49
50      printf("%s", out.data);
51
52      gnutls_free(out.data);
53
54      if (status != 0)        /* Certificate is not trusted */
55              return GNUTLS_E_CERTIFICATE_ERROR;
56
57      /* Do SSH verification */
58      cert_list = gnutls_certificate_get_peers(session, &cert_list_size);
59      if (cert_list == NULL) {
60              printf("No certificate was found!\n");
61              return GNUTLS_E_CERTIFICATE_ERROR;
62      }
63
64      /* service may be obtained alternatively using getservbyport() */
65      ret = gnutls_verify_stored_pubkey(NULL, NULL, hostname, "https",
66                                        type, &cert_list[0], 0);
67      if (ret == GNUTLS_E_NO_CERTIFICATE_FOUND) {
68              printf("Host %s is not known.", hostname);
69              if (status == 0)
70                      printf("Its certificate is valid for %s.\n",
71                              hostname);
72
73              /* the certificate must be printed and user must be asked on
74               * whether it is trustworthy. --see gnutls_x509_crt_print() */
75
76              /* if not trusted */
77              return GNUTLS_E_CERTIFICATE_ERROR;
78      } else if (ret == GNUTLS_E_CERTIFICATE_KEY_MISMATCH) {
79              printf
```

```
80              ("Warning: host %s is known but has another key associated.",
81                  hostname);
82          printf
83              ("It might be that the server has multiple keys, or you are under attack\n");
84          if (status == 0)
85                  printf("Its certificate is valid for %s.\n",
86                          hostname);
87
88          /* the certificate must be printed and user must be asked on
89           * whether it is trustworthy. --see gnutls_x509_crt_print() */
90
91          /* if not trusted */
92          return GNUTLS_E_CERTIFICATE_ERROR;
93      } else if (ret < 0) {
94          printf("gnutls_verify_stored_pubkey: %s\n",
95                  gnutls_strerror(ret));
96          return ret;
97      }
98
99      /* user trusts the key -> store it */
100     if (ret != 0) {
101         ret = gnutls_store_pubkey(NULL, NULL, hostname, "https",
102                                     type, &cert_list[0], 0, 0);
103         if (ret < 0)
104                 printf("gnutls_store_pubkey: %s\n",
105                         gnutls_strerror(ret));
106     }
107
108     /* notify gnutls to continue handshake normally */
109     return 0;
110 }
```

6.1.3. Simple client example with anonymous authentication

The simplest client using TLS is the one that doesn't do any authentication. This means no external certificates or passwords are needed to set up the connection. As could be expected, the connection is vulnerable to man-in-the-middle (active or redirection) attacks. However, the data are integrity protected and encrypted from passive eavesdroppers.

Note that due to the vulnerable nature of this method very few public servers support it.

```
1  /* This example code is placed in the public domain. */
2
3  #ifdef HAVE_CONFIG_H
4  #include <config.h>
5  #endif
6
7  #include <stdio.h>
8  #include <stdlib.h>
9  #include <string.h>
10 #include <sys/types.h>
11 #include <sys/socket.h>
12 #include <arpa/inet.h>
13 #include <unistd.h>
```

```
14  #include <gnutls/gnutls.h>
15
16  /* A very basic TLS client, with anonymous authentication.
17   */
18
19  #define MAX_BUF 1024
20  #define MSG "GET / HTTP/1.0\r\n\r\n"
21
22  extern int tcp_connect(void);
23  extern void tcp_close(int sd);
24
25  int main(void)
26  {
27          int ret, sd, ii;
28          gnutls_session_t session;
29          char buffer[MAX_BUF + 1];
30          gnutls_anon_client_credentials_t anoncred;
31          /* Need to enable anonymous KX specifically. */
32
33          gnutls_global_init();
34
35          gnutls_anon_allocate_client_credentials(&anoncred);
36
37          /* Initialize TLS session
38           */
39          gnutls_init(&session, GNUTLS_CLIENT);
40
41          /* Use default priorities */
42          gnutls_priority_set_direct(session,
43                              "PERFORMANCE:+ANON-ECDH:+ANON-DH",
44                              NULL);
45
46          /* put the anonymous credentials to the current session
47           */
48          gnutls_credentials_set(session, GNUTLS_CRD_ANON, anoncred);
49
50          /* connect to the peer
51           */
52          sd = tcp_connect();
53
54          gnutls_transport_set_int(session, sd);
55          gnutls_handshake_set_timeout(session,
56                              GNUTLS_DEFAULT_HANDSHAKE_TIMEOUT);
57
58          /* Perform the TLS handshake
59           */
60          do {
61                  ret = gnutls_handshake(session);
62          }
63          while (ret < 0 && gnutls_error_is_fatal(ret) == 0);
64
65          if (ret < 0) {
66                  fprintf(stderr, "*** Handshake failed\n");
67                  gnutls_perror(ret);
68                  goto end;
69          } else {
70                  char *desc;
71
```

```
72          desc = gnutls_session_get_desc(session);
73          printf("- Session info: %s\n", desc);
74          gnutls_free(desc);
75      }
76
77      gnutls_record_send(session, MSG, strlen(MSG));
78
79      ret = gnutls_record_recv(session, buffer, MAX_BUF);
80      if (ret == 0) {
81          printf("- Peer has closed the TLS connection\n");
82          goto end;
83      } else if (ret < 0 && gnutls_error_is_fatal(ret) == 0) {
84          fprintf(stderr, "*** Warning: %s\n", gnutls_strerror(ret));
85      } else if (ret < 0) {
86          fprintf(stderr, "*** Error: %s\n", gnutls_strerror(ret));
87          goto end;
88      }
89
90      if (ret > 0) {
91          printf("- Received %d bytes: ", ret);
92          for (ii = 0; ii < ret; ii++) {
93              fputc(buffer[ii], stdout);
94          }
95          fputs("\n", stdout);
96      }
97
98      gnutls_bye(session, GNUTLS_SHUT_RDWR);
99
100 end:
101
102     tcp_close(sd);
103
104     gnutls_deinit(session);
105
106     gnutls_anon_free_client_credentials(anoncred);
107
108     gnutls_global_deinit();
109
110     return 0;
111 }
```

6.1.4. Simple datagram TLS client example

This is a client that uses UDP to connect to a server. This is the DTLS equivalent to the TLS example with X.509 certificates.

```
1 /* This example code is placed in the public domain. */
2
3 #ifdef HAVE_CONFIG_H
4 #include <config.h>
5 #endif
6
7 #include <stdio.h>
8 #include <stdlib.h>
9 #include <string.h>
```

```
10   #include <sys/types.h>
11   #include <sys/socket.h>
12   #include <arpa/inet.h>
13   #include <unistd.h>
14   #include <gnutls/gnutls.h>
15   #include <gnutls/dtls.h>
16
17   /* A very basic Datagram TLS client, over UDP with X.509 authentication.
18    */
19
20   #define MAX_BUF 1024
21   #define CAFILE "/etc/ssl/certs/ca-certificates.crt"
22   #define MSG "GET / HTTP/1.0\r\n\r\n"
23
24   extern int udp_connect(void);
25   extern void udp_close(int sd);
26   extern int verify_certificate_callback(gnutls_session_t session);
27
28   int main(void)
29   {
30           int ret, sd, ii;
31           gnutls_session_t session;
32           char buffer[MAX_BUF + 1];
33           const char *err;
34           gnutls_certificate_credentials_t xcred;
35
36           if (gnutls_check_version("3.1.4") == NULL) {
37                   fprintf(stderr, "GnuTLS 3.1.4 or later is required for this example\n");
38                   exit(1);
39           }
40
41           /* for backwards compatibility with gnutls < 3.3.0 */
42           gnutls_global_init();
43
44           /* X509 stuff */
45           gnutls_certificate_allocate_credentials(&xcred);
46
47           /* sets the trusted cas file */
48           gnutls_certificate_set_x509_trust_file(xcred, CAFILE,
49                                                  GNUTLS_X509_FMT_PEM);
50           gnutls_certificate_set_verify_function(xcred,
51                                                  verify_certificate_callback);
52
53           /* Initialize TLS session */
54           gnutls_init(&session, GNUTLS_CLIENT | GNUTLS_DATAGRAM);
55
56           /* Use default priorities */
57           ret = gnutls_priority_set_direct(session,
58                                            "NORMAL", &err);
59           if (ret < 0) {
60                   if (ret == GNUTLS_E_INVALID_REQUEST) {
61                           fprintf(stderr, "Syntax error at: %s\n", err);
62                   }
63                   exit(1);
64           }
65
66           /* put the x509 credentials to the current session */
67           gnutls_credentials_set(session, GNUTLS_CRD_CERTIFICATE, xcred);
```

```
68        gnutls_server_name_set(session, GNUTLS_NAME_DNS, "my_host_name",
69                            strlen("my_host_name"));
70
71        /* connect to the peer */
72        sd = udp_connect();
73
74        gnutls_transport_set_int(session, sd);
75
76        /* set the connection MTU */
77        gnutls_dtls_set_mtu(session, 1000);
78        /* gnutls_dtls_set_timeouts(session, 1000, 60000); */
79
80        /* Perform the TLS handshake */
81        do {
82                ret = gnutls_handshake(session);
83        }
84        while (ret == GNUTLS_E_INTERRUPTED || ret == GNUTLS_E_AGAIN);
85        /* Note that DTLS may also receive GNUTLS_E_LARGE_PACKET */
86
87        if (ret < 0) {
88                fprintf(stderr, "*** Handshake failed\n");
89                gnutls_perror(ret);
90                goto end;
91        } else {
92                char *desc;
93
94                desc = gnutls_session_get_desc(session);
95                printf("- Session info: %s\n", desc);
96                gnutls_free(desc);
97        }
98
99        gnutls_record_send(session, MSG, strlen(MSG));
100
101       ret = gnutls_record_recv(session, buffer, MAX_BUF);
102       if (ret == 0) {
103               printf("- Peer has closed the TLS connection\n");
104               goto end;
105       } else if (ret < 0 && gnutls_error_is_fatal(ret) == 0) {
106               fprintf(stderr, "*** Warning: %s\n", gnutls_strerror(ret));
107       } else if (ret < 0) {
108               fprintf(stderr, "*** Error: %s\n", gnutls_strerror(ret));
109               goto end;
110       }
111
112       if (ret > 0) {
113               printf("- Received %d bytes: ", ret);
114               for (ii = 0; ii < ret; ii++) {
115                       fputc(buffer[ii], stdout);
116               }
117               fputs("\n", stdout);
118       }
119
120       /* It is suggested not to use GNUTLS_SHUT_RDWR in DTLS
121        * connections because the peer's closure message might
122        * be lost */
123       gnutls_bye(session, GNUTLS_SHUT_WR);
124
125   end:
```

188

```
126
127          udp_close(sd);
128
129          gnutls_deinit(session);
130
131          gnutls_certificate_free_credentials(xcred);
132
133          gnutls_global_deinit();
134
135          return 0;
136  }
```

6.1.5. Obtaining session information

Most of the times it is desirable to know the security properties of the current established session. This includes the underlying ciphers and the protocols involved. That is the purpose of the following function. Note that this function will print meaningful values only if called after a successful **gnutls_handshake**.

```
1   /* This example code is placed in the public domain. */
2
3   #ifdef HAVE_CONFIG_H
4   #include <config.h>
5   #endif
6
7   #include <stdio.h>
8   #include <stdlib.h>
9   #include <gnutls/gnutls.h>
10  #include <gnutls/x509.h>
11
12  #include "examples.h"
13
14  /* This function will print some details of the
15   * given session.
16   */
17  int print_info(gnutls_session_t session)
18  {
19          const char *tmp;
20          gnutls_credentials_type_t cred;
21          gnutls_kx_algorithm_t kx;
22          int dhe, ecdh;
23
24          dhe = ecdh = 0;
25
26          /* print the key exchange's algorithm name
27           */
28          kx = gnutls_kx_get(session);
29          tmp = gnutls_kx_get_name(kx);
30          printf("- Key Exchange: %s\n", tmp);
31
32          /* Check the authentication type used and switch
33           * to the appropriate.
34           */
35          cred = gnutls_auth_get_type(session);
```

```
36              switch (cred) {
37              case GNUTLS_CRD_IA:
38                      printf("- TLS/IA session\n");
39                      break;
40
41
42  #ifdef ENABLE_SRP
43              case GNUTLS_CRD_SRP:
44                      printf("- SRP session with username %s\n",
45                              gnutls_srp_server_get_username(session));
46                      break;
47  #endif
48
49              case GNUTLS_CRD_PSK:
50                      /* This returns NULL in server side.
51                       */
52                      if (gnutls_psk_client_get_hint(session) != NULL)
53                              printf("- PSK authentication. PSK hint '%s'\n",
54                                      gnutls_psk_client_get_hint(session));
55                      /* This returns NULL in client side.
56                       */
57                      if (gnutls_psk_server_get_username(session) != NULL)
58                              printf("- PSK authentication. Connected as '%s'\n",
59                                      gnutls_psk_server_get_username(session));
60
61                      if (kx == GNUTLS_KX_ECDHE_PSK)
62                              ecdh = 1;
63                      else if (kx == GNUTLS_KX_DHE_PSK)
64                              dhe = 1;
65                      break;
66
67              case GNUTLS_CRD_ANON:  /* anonymous authentication */
68
69                      printf("- Anonymous authentication.\n");
70                      if (kx == GNUTLS_KX_ANON_ECDH)
71                              ecdh = 1;
72                      else if (kx == GNUTLS_KX_ANON_DH)
73                              dhe = 1;
74                      break;
75
76              case GNUTLS_CRD_CERTIFICATE:   /* certificate authentication */
77
78                      /* Check if we have been using ephemeral Diffie-Hellman.
79                       */
80                      if (kx == GNUTLS_KX_DHE_RSA || kx == GNUTLS_KX_DHE_DSS)
81                              dhe = 1;
82                      else if (kx == GNUTLS_KX_ECDHE_RSA
83                              || kx == GNUTLS_KX_ECDHE_ECDSA)
84                              ecdh = 1;
85
86                      /* if the certificate list is available, then
87                       * print some information about it.
88                       */
89                      print_x509_certificate_info(session);
90
91              }                       /* switch */
92
93          if (ecdh != 0)
```

190

```
 94            printf("- Ephemeral ECDH using curve %s\n",
 95                    gnutls_ecc_curve_get_name(gnutls_ecc_curve_get
 96                                             (session)));
 97        else if (dhe != 0)
 98                printf("- Ephemeral DH using prime of %d bits\n",
 99                    gnutls_dh_get_prime_bits(session));
100
101        /* print the protocol's name (ie TLS 1.0)
102         */
103        tmp =
104            gnutls_protocol_get_name(gnutls_protocol_get_version(session));
105        printf("- Protocol: %s\n", tmp);
106
107        /* print the certificate type of the peer.
108         * ie X.509
109         */
110        tmp =
111            gnutls_certificate_type_get_name(gnutls_certificate_type_get
112                                           (session));
113
114        printf("- Certificate Type: %s\n", tmp);
115
116        /* print the compression algorithm (if any)
117         */
118        tmp = gnutls_compression_get_name(gnutls_compression_get(session));
119        printf("- Compression: %s\n", tmp);
120
121        /* print the name of the cipher used.
122         * ie 3DES.
123         */
124        tmp = gnutls_cipher_get_name(gnutls_cipher_get(session));
125        printf("- Cipher: %s\n", tmp);
126
127        /* Print the MAC algorithms name.
128         * ie SHA1
129         */
130        tmp = gnutls_mac_get_name(gnutls_mac_get(session));
131        printf("- MAC: %s\n", tmp);
132
133        return 0;
134 }
```

6.1.6. Using a callback to select the certificate to use

There are cases where a client holds several certificate and key pairs, and may not want to load all of them in the credentials structure. The following example demonstrates the use of the certificate selection callback.

```
1 /* This example code is placed in the public domain. */
2
3 #ifdef HAVE_CONFIG_H
4 #include <config.h>
5 #endif
6
7 #include <stdio.h>
```

```
 8  #include <stdlib.h>
 9  #include <string.h>
10  #include <sys/types.h>
11  #include <sys/socket.h>
12  #include <arpa/inet.h>
13  #include <unistd.h>
14  #include <gnutls/gnutls.h>
15  #include <gnutls/x509.h>
16  #include <gnutls/abstract.h>
17  #include <sys/types.h>
18  #include <sys/stat.h>
19  #include <fcntl.h>
20
21  /* A TLS client that loads the certificate and key.
22   */
23
24  #define MAX_BUF 1024
25  #define MSG "GET / HTTP/1.0\r\n\r\n"
26
27  #define CERT_FILE "cert.pem"
28  #define KEY_FILE "key.pem"
29  #define CAFILE "/etc/ssl/certs/ca-certificates.crt"
30
31  extern int tcp_connect(void);
32  extern void tcp_close(int sd);
33
34  static int
35  cert_callback(gnutls_session_t session,
36                const gnutls_datum_t * req_ca_rdn, int nreqs,
37                const gnutls_pk_algorithm_t * sign_algos,
38                int sign_algos_length, gnutls_pcert_st ** pcert,
39                unsigned int *pcert_length, gnutls_privkey_t * pkey);
40
41  gnutls_pcert_st pcrt;
42  gnutls_privkey_t key;
43
44  /* Load the certificate and the private key.
45   */
46  static void load_keys(void)
47  {
48          int ret;
49          gnutls_datum_t data;
50
51          ret = gnutls_load_file(CERT_FILE, &data);
52          if (ret < 0) {
53                  fprintf(stderr, "*** Error loading certificate file.\n");
54                  exit(1);
55          }
56
57          ret =
58              gnutls_pcert_import_x509_raw(&pcrt, &data, GNUTLS_X509_FMT_PEM,
59                                           0);
60          if (ret < 0) {
61                  fprintf(stderr, "*** Error loading certificate file: %s\n",
62                          gnutls_strerror(ret));
63                  exit(1);
64          }
65
```

192

```
66          gnutls_free(data.data);
67
68          ret = gnutls_load_file(KEY_FILE, &data);
69          if (ret < 0) {
70                  fprintf(stderr, "*** Error loading key file.\n");
71                  exit(1);
72          }
73
74          gnutls_privkey_init(&key);
75
76          ret =
77              gnutls_privkey_import_x509_raw(key, &data, GNUTLS_X509_FMT_PEM,
78                                             NULL, 0);
79          if (ret < 0) {
80                  fprintf(stderr, "*** Error loading key file: %s\n",
81                          gnutls_strerror(ret));
82                  exit(1);
83          }
84
85          gnutls_free(data.data);
86  }
87
88  int main(void)
89  {
90          int ret, sd, ii;
91          gnutls_session_t session;
92          gnutls_priority_t priorities_cache;
93          char buffer[MAX_BUF + 1];
94          gnutls_certificate_credentials_t xcred;
95
96          if (gnutls_check_version("3.1.4") == NULL) {
97                  fprintf(stderr, "GnuTLS 3.1.4 or later is required for this example\n");
98                  exit(1);
99          }
100
101          /* for backwards compatibility with gnutls < 3.3.0 */
102          gnutls_global_init();
103
104          load_keys();
105
106          /* X509 stuff */
107          gnutls_certificate_allocate_credentials(&xcred);
108
109          /* priorities */
110          gnutls_priority_init(&priorities_cache,
111                               "NORMAL", NULL);
112
113          /* sets the trusted cas file
114           */
115          gnutls_certificate_set_x509_trust_file(xcred, CAFILE,
116                                                 GNUTLS_X509_FMT_PEM);
117
118          gnutls_certificate_set_retrieve_function2(xcred, cert_callback);
119
120          /* Initialize TLS session
121           */
122          gnutls_init(&session, GNUTLS_CLIENT);
123
```

```
124        /* Use default priorities */
125        gnutls_priority_set(session, priorities_cache);
126
127        /* put the x509 credentials to the current session
128         */
129        gnutls_credentials_set(session, GNUTLS_CRD_CERTIFICATE, xcred);
130
131        /* connect to the peer
132         */
133        sd = tcp_connect();
134
135        gnutls_transport_set_int(session, sd);
136
137        /* Perform the TLS handshake
138         */
139        ret = gnutls_handshake(session);
140
141        if (ret < 0) {
142                fprintf(stderr, "*** Handshake failed\n");
143                gnutls_perror(ret);
144                goto end;
145        } else {
146                char *desc;
147
148                desc = gnutls_session_get_desc(session);
149                printf("- Session info: %s\n", desc);
150                gnutls_free(desc);
151        }
152
153        gnutls_record_send(session, MSG, strlen(MSG));
154
155        ret = gnutls_record_recv(session, buffer, MAX_BUF);
156        if (ret == 0) {
157                printf("- Peer has closed the TLS connection\n");
158                goto end;
159        } else if (ret < 0) {
160                fprintf(stderr, "*** Error: %s\n", gnutls_strerror(ret));
161                goto end;
162        }
163
164        printf("- Received %d bytes: ", ret);
165        for (ii = 0; ii < ret; ii++) {
166                fputc(buffer[ii], stdout);
167        }
168        fputs("\n", stdout);
169
170        gnutls_bye(session, GNUTLS_SHUT_RDWR);
171
172    end:
173
174        tcp_close(sd);
175
176        gnutls_deinit(session);
177
178        gnutls_certificate_free_credentials(xcred);
179        gnutls_priority_deinit(priorities_cache);
180
181        gnutls_global_deinit();
```

```
182
183          return 0;
184  }
185
186
187
188  /* This callback should be associated with a session by calling
189   * gnutls_certificate_client_set_retrieve_function( session, cert_callback),
190   * before a handshake.
191   */
192
193  static int
194  cert_callback(gnutls_session_t session,
195                const gnutls_datum_t * req_ca_rdn, int nreqs,
196                const gnutls_pk_algorithm_t * sign_algos,
197                int sign_algos_length, gnutls_pcert_st ** pcert,
198                unsigned int *pcert_length, gnutls_privkey_t * pkey)
199  {
200          char issuer_dn[256];
201          int i, ret;
202          size_t len;
203          gnutls_certificate_type_t type;
204
205          /* Print the server's trusted CAs
206           */
207          if (nreqs > 0)
208                  printf("- Server's trusted authorities:\n");
209          else
210                  printf
211                      ("- Server did not send us any trusted authorities names.\n");
212
213          /* print the names (if any) */
214          for (i = 0; i < nreqs; i++) {
215                  len = sizeof(issuer_dn);
216                  ret = gnutls_x509_rdn_get(&req_ca_rdn[i], issuer_dn, &len);
217                  if (ret >= 0) {
218                          printf("   [%d]: ", i);
219                          printf("%s\n", issuer_dn);
220                  }
221          }
222
223          /* Select a certificate and return it.
224           * The certificate must be of any of the "sign algorithms"
225           * supported by the server.
226           */
227          type = gnutls_certificate_type_get(session);
228          if (type == GNUTLS_CRT_X509) {
229                  *pcert_length = 1;
230                  *pcert = &pcrt;
231                  *pkey = key;
232          } else {
233                  return -1;
234          }
235
236          return 0;
237
238  }
```

6.1.7. Verifying a certificate

An example is listed below which uses the high level verification functions to verify a given certificate list.

```
1  /* This example code is placed in the public domain. */
2
3  #ifdef HAVE_CONFIG_H
4  #include <config.h>
5  #endif
6
7  #include <stdio.h>
8  #include <stdlib.h>
9  #include <string.h>
10 #include <gnutls/gnutls.h>
11 #include <gnutls/x509.h>
12
13 #include "examples.h"
14
15 /* All the available CRLs
16  */
17 gnutls_x509_crl_t *crl_list;
18 int crl_list_size;
19
20 /* All the available trusted CAs
21  */
22 gnutls_x509_crt_t *ca_list;
23 int ca_list_size;
24
25 static int print_details_func(gnutls_x509_crt_t cert,
26                               gnutls_x509_crt_t issuer,
27                               gnutls_x509_crl_t crl,
28                               unsigned int verification_output);
29
30 /* This function will try to verify the peer's certificate chain, and
31  * also check if the hostname matches.
32  */
33 void
34 verify_certificate_chain(const char *hostname,
35                          const gnutls_datum_t * cert_chain,
36                          int cert_chain_length)
37 {
38         int i;
39         gnutls_x509_trust_list_t tlist;
40         gnutls_x509_crt_t *cert;
41
42         unsigned int output;
43
44         /* Initialize the trusted certificate list. This should be done
45          * once on initialization. gnutls_x509_crt_list_import2() and
46          * gnutls_x509_crl_list_import2() can be used to load them.
47          */
48         gnutls_x509_trust_list_init(&tlist, 0);
49
50         gnutls_x509_trust_list_add_cas(tlist, ca_list, ca_list_size, 0);
51         gnutls_x509_trust_list_add_crls(tlist, crl_list, crl_list_size,
52                                 GNUTLS_TL_VERIFY_CRL, 0);
```

196

```
53
54          cert = malloc(sizeof(*cert) * cert_chain_length);
55
56          /* Import all the certificates in the chain to
57           * native certificate format.
58           */
59          for (i = 0; i < cert_chain_length; i++) {
60                  gnutls_x509_crt_init(&cert[i]);
61                  gnutls_x509_crt_import(cert[i], &cert_chain[i],
62                                         GNUTLS_X509_FMT_DER);
63          }
64
65          gnutls_x509_trust_list_verify_named_crt(tlist, cert[0], hostname,
66                                                  strlen(hostname),
67                                                  GNUTLS_VERIFY_DISABLE_CRL_CHECKS,
68                                                  &output,
69                                                  print_details_func);
70
71          /* if this certificate is not explicitly trusted verify against CAs
72           */
73          if (output != 0) {
74                  gnutls_x509_trust_list_verify_crt(tlist, cert,
75                                                    cert_chain_length, 0,
76                                                    &output,
77                                                    print_details_func);
78          }
79
80          if (output & GNUTLS_CERT_INVALID) {
81                  fprintf(stderr, "Not trusted");
82
83                  if (output & GNUTLS_CERT_SIGNER_NOT_FOUND)
84                          fprintf(stderr, ": no issuer was found");
85                  if (output & GNUTLS_CERT_SIGNER_NOT_CA)
86                          fprintf(stderr, ": issuer is not a CA");
87                  if (output & GNUTLS_CERT_NOT_ACTIVATED)
88                          fprintf(stderr, ": not yet activated\n");
89                  if (output & GNUTLS_CERT_EXPIRED)
90                          fprintf(stderr, ": expired\n");
91
92                  fprintf(stderr, "\n");
93          } else
94                  fprintf(stderr, "Trusted\n");
95
96          /* Check if the name in the first certificate matches our destination!
97           */
98          if (!gnutls_x509_crt_check_hostname(cert[0], hostname)) {
99                  printf
100                     ("The certificate's owner does not match hostname '%s'\n",
101                      hostname);
102          }
103
104          gnutls_x509_trust_list_deinit(tlist, 1);
105
106          return;
107  }
108
109  static int
110  print_details_func(gnutls_x509_crt_t cert,
```

```
111                    gnutls_x509_crt_t issuer, gnutls_x509_crl_t crl,
112                    unsigned int verification_output)
113  {
114         char name[512];
115         char issuer_name[512];
116         size_t name_size;
117         size_t issuer_name_size;
118
119         issuer_name_size = sizeof(issuer_name);
120         gnutls_x509_crt_get_issuer_dn(cert, issuer_name,
121                                       &issuer_name_size);
122
123         name_size = sizeof(name);
124         gnutls_x509_crt_get_dn(cert, name, &name_size);
125
126         fprintf(stdout, "\tSubject: %s\n", name);
127         fprintf(stdout, "\tIssuer: %s\n", issuer_name);
128
129         if (issuer != NULL) {
130                 issuer_name_size = sizeof(issuer_name);
131                 gnutls_x509_crt_get_dn(issuer, issuer_name,
132                                        &issuer_name_size);
133
134                 fprintf(stdout, "\tVerified against: %s\n", issuer_name);
135         }
136
137         if (crl != NULL) {
138                 issuer_name_size = sizeof(issuer_name);
139                 gnutls_x509_crl_get_issuer_dn(crl, issuer_name,
140                                               &issuer_name_size);
141
142                 fprintf(stdout, "\tVerified against CRL of: %s\n",
143                         issuer_name);
144         }
145
146         fprintf(stdout, "\tVerification output: %x\n\n",
147                 verification_output);
148
149         return 0;
150  }
```

6.1.8. Using a smart card with TLS

This example will demonstrate how to load keys and certificates from a smart-card or any other PKCS #11 token, and use it in a TLS connection.

```
1  /* This example code is placed in the public domain. */
2
3  #ifdef HAVE_CONFIG_H
4  #include <config.h>
5  #endif
6
7  #include <stdio.h>
8  #include <stdlib.h>
9  #include <string.h>
```

```
10  #include <sys/types.h>
11  #include <sys/socket.h>
12  #include <arpa/inet.h>
13  #include <unistd.h>
14  #include <gnutls/gnutls.h>
15  #include <gnutls/x509.h>
16  #include <gnutls/pkcs11.h>
17  #include <sys/types.h>
18  #include <sys/stat.h>
19  #include <fcntl.h>
20  #include <getpass.h>                /* for getpass() */
21
22  /* A TLS client that loads the certificate and key.
23   */
24
25  #define MAX_BUF 1024
26  #define MSG "GET / HTTP/1.0\r\n\r\n"
27  #define MIN(x,y) (((x)<(y))?(x):(y))
28
29  #define CAFILE "/etc/ssl/certs/ca-certificates.crt"
30
31  /* The URLs of the objects can be obtained
32   * using p11tool --list-all --login
33   */
34  #define KEY_URL "pkcs11:manufacturer=SomeManufacturer;object=Private%20Key" \
35    ";objecttype=private;id=%db%5b%3e%b5%72%33"
36  #define CERT_URL "pkcs11:manufacturer=SomeManufacturer;object=Certificate;" \
37    "objecttype=cert;id=db%5b%3e%b5%72%33"
38
39  extern int tcp_connect(void);
40  extern void tcp_close(int sd);
41
42  static int
43  pin_callback(void *user, int attempt, const char *token_url,
44              const char *token_label, unsigned int flags, char *pin,
45              size_t pin_max)
46  {
47      const char *password;
48      int len;
49
50      printf("PIN required for token '%s' with URL '%s'\n", token_label,
51              token_url);
52      if (flags & GNUTLS_PIN_FINAL_TRY)
53              printf("*** This is the final try before locking!\n");
54      if (flags & GNUTLS_PIN_COUNT_LOW)
55              printf("*** Only few tries left before locking!\n");
56      if (flags & GNUTLS_PIN_WRONG)
57              printf("*** Wrong PIN\n");
58
59      password = getpass("Enter pin: ");
60      if (password == NULL || password[0] == 0) {
61              fprintf(stderr, "No password given\n");
62              exit(1);
63      }
64
65      len = MIN(pin_max - 1, strlen(password));
66      memcpy(pin, password, len);
67      pin[len] = 0;
```

```
68
69          return 0;
70   }
71
72   int main(void)
73   {
74          int ret, sd, ii;
75          gnutls_session_t session;
76          gnutls_priority_t priorities_cache;
77          char buffer[MAX_BUF + 1];
78          gnutls_certificate_credentials_t xcred;
79          /* Allow connections to servers that have OpenPGP keys as well.
80           */
81
82          if (gnutls_check_version("3.1.4") == NULL) {
83                  fprintf(stderr, "GnuTLS 3.1.4 or later is required for this example\n");
84                  exit(1);
85          }
86
87          /* for backwards compatibility with gnutls < 3.3.0 */
88          gnutls_global_init();
89
90          /* The PKCS11 private key operations may require PIN.
91           * Register a callback. */
92          gnutls_pkcs11_set_pin_function(pin_callback, NULL);
93
94          /* X509 stuff */
95          gnutls_certificate_allocate_credentials(&xcred);
96
97          /* priorities */
98          gnutls_priority_init(&priorities_cache,
99                          "NORMAL", NULL);
100
101          /* sets the trusted cas file
102           */
103          gnutls_certificate_set_x509_trust_file(xcred, CAFILE,
104                                          GNUTLS_X509_FMT_PEM);
105
106          gnutls_certificate_set_x509_key_file(xcred, CERT_URL, KEY_URL,
107                                          GNUTLS_X509_FMT_DER);
108
109          /* Initialize TLS session
110           */
111          gnutls_init(&session, GNUTLS_CLIENT);
112
113          /* Use default priorities */
114          gnutls_priority_set(session, priorities_cache);
115
116          /* put the x509 credentials to the current session
117           */
118          gnutls_credentials_set(session, GNUTLS_CRD_CERTIFICATE, xcred);
119
120          /* connect to the peer
121           */
122          sd = tcp_connect();
123
124          gnutls_transport_set_int(session, sd);
125
```

```
126        /* Perform the TLS handshake
127         */
128        ret = gnutls_handshake(session);
129
130        if (ret < 0) {
131                fprintf(stderr, "*** Handshake failed\n");
132                gnutls_perror(ret);
133                goto end;
134        } else {
135                char *desc;
136
137                desc = gnutls_session_get_desc(session);
138                printf("- Session info: %s\n", desc);
139                gnutls_free(desc);
140        }
141
142        gnutls_record_send(session, MSG, strlen(MSG));
143
144        ret = gnutls_record_recv(session, buffer, MAX_BUF);
145        if (ret == 0) {
146                printf("- Peer has closed the TLS connection\n");
147                goto end;
148        } else if (ret < 0) {
149                fprintf(stderr, "*** Error: %s\n", gnutls_strerror(ret));
150                goto end;
151        }
152
153        printf("- Received %d bytes: ", ret);
154        for (ii = 0; ii < ret; ii++) {
155                fputc(buffer[ii], stdout);
156        }
157        fputs("\n", stdout);
158
159        gnutls_bye(session, GNUTLS_SHUT_RDWR);
160
161    end:
162
163        tcp_close(sd);
164
165        gnutls_deinit(session);
166
167        gnutls_certificate_free_credentials(xcred);
168        gnutls_priority_deinit(priorities_cache);
169
170        gnutls_global_deinit();
171
172        return 0;
173 }
```

6.1.9. Client with resume capability example

This is a modification of the simple client example. Here we demonstrate the use of session resumption. The client tries to connect once using TLS, close the connection and then try to establish a new connection using the previously negotiated data.

```
 1   /* This example code is placed in the public domain. */
 2
 3   #ifdef HAVE_CONFIG_H
 4   #include <config.h>
 5   #endif
 6
 7   #include <string.h>
 8   #include <stdio.h>
 9   #include <stdlib.h>
10   #include <gnutls/gnutls.h>
11
12   /* Those functions are defined in other examples.
13    */
14   extern void check_alert(gnutls_session_t session, int ret);
15   extern int tcp_connect(void);
16   extern void tcp_close(int sd);
17
18   #define MAX_BUF 1024
19   #define CAFILE "/etc/ssl/certs/ca-certificates.crt"
20   #define MSG "GET / HTTP/1.0\r\n\r\n"
21
22   int main(void)
23   {
24           int ret;
25           int sd, ii;
26           gnutls_session_t session;
27           char buffer[MAX_BUF + 1];
28           gnutls_certificate_credentials_t xcred;
29
30           /* variables used in session resuming
31            */
32           int t;
33           char *session_data = NULL;
34           size_t session_data_size = 0;
35
36           gnutls_global_init();
37
38           /* X509 stuff */
39           gnutls_certificate_allocate_credentials(&xcred);
40
41           gnutls_certificate_set_x509_trust_file(xcred, CAFILE,
42                                                  GNUTLS_X509_FMT_PEM);
43
44           for (t = 0; t < 2; t++) {        /* connect 2 times to the server */
45
46                   sd = tcp_connect();
47
48                   gnutls_init(&session, GNUTLS_CLIENT);
49
50                   gnutls_priority_set_direct(session,
51                                              "PERFORMANCE:!ARCFOUR-128",
52                                              NULL);
53
54                   gnutls_credentials_set(session, GNUTLS_CRD_CERTIFICATE,
55                                          xcred);
56
57                   if (t > 0) {
```

```
58              /* if this is not the first time we connect */
59              gnutls_session_set_data(session, session_data,
60                                      session_data_size);
61              free(session_data);
62      }
63
64      gnutls_transport_set_int(session, sd);
65      gnutls_handshake_set_timeout(session,
66                                   GNUTLS_DEFAULT_HANDSHAKE_TIMEOUT);
67
68      /* Perform the TLS handshake
69       */
70      do {
71              ret = gnutls_handshake(session);
72      }
73      while (ret < 0 && gnutls_error_is_fatal(ret) == 0);
74
75      if (ret < 0) {
76              fprintf(stderr, "*** Handshake failed\n");
77              gnutls_perror(ret);
78              goto end;
79      } else {
80              printf("- Handshake was completed\n");
81      }
82
83      if (t == 0) {   /* the first time we connect */
84              /* get the session data size */
85              gnutls_session_get_data(session, NULL,
86                                      &session_data_size);
87              session_data = malloc(session_data_size);
88
89              /* put session data to the session variable */
90              gnutls_session_get_data(session, session_data,
91                                      &session_data_size);
92
93      } else {        /* the second time we connect */
94
95              /* check if we actually resumed the previous session */
96              if (gnutls_session_is_resumed(session) != 0) {
97                      printf("- Previous session was resumed\n");
98              } else {
99                      fprintf(stderr,
100                             "*** Previous session was NOT resumed\n");
101             }
102     }
103
104     /* This function was defined in a previous example
105      */
106     /* print_info(session); */
107
108     gnutls_record_send(session, MSG, strlen(MSG));
109
110     ret = gnutls_record_recv(session, buffer, MAX_BUF);
111     if (ret == 0) {
112             printf("- Peer has closed the TLS connection\n");
113             goto end;
114     } else if (ret < 0 && gnutls_error_is_fatal(ret) == 0) {
115             fprintf(stderr, "*** Warning: %s\n",
```

```
116                            gnutls_strerror(ret));
117                   } else if (ret < 0) {
118                           fprintf(stderr, "*** Error: %s\n",
119                                   gnutls_strerror(ret));
120                           goto end;
121                   }
122
123                   if (ret > 0) {
124                           printf("- Received %d bytes: ", ret);
125                           for (ii = 0; ii < ret; ii++) {
126                                   fputc(buffer[ii], stdout);
127                           }
128                           fputs("\n", stdout);
129                   }
130
131                   gnutls_bye(session, GNUTLS_SHUT_RDWR);
132
133            end:
134
135                   tcp_close(sd);
136
137                   gnutls_deinit(session);
138
139          }                            /* for() */
140
141          gnutls_certificate_free_credentials(xcred);
142
143          gnutls_global_deinit();
144
145          return 0;
146  }
```

6.1.10. Simple client example with SRP authentication

The following client is a very simple SRP TLS client which connects to a server and authenticates using a *username* and a *password*. The server may authenticate itself using a certificate, and in that case it has to be verified.

```
1   /* This example code is placed in the public domain. */
2
3   #ifdef HAVE_CONFIG_H
4   #include <config.h>
5   #endif
6
7   #include <stdio.h>
8   #include <stdlib.h>
9   #include <string.h>
10  #include <gnutls/gnutls.h>
11
12  /* Those functions are defined in other examples.
13   */
14  extern void check_alert(gnutls_session_t session, int ret);
15  extern int tcp_connect(void);
16  extern void tcp_close(int sd);
17
```

```
18  #define MAX_BUF 1024
19  #define USERNAME "user"
20  #define PASSWORD "pass"
21  #define CAFILE "/etc/ssl/certs/ca-certificates.crt"
22  #define MSG "GET / HTTP/1.0\r\n\r\n"
23
24  int main(void)
25  {
26          int ret;
27          int sd, ii;
28          gnutls_session_t session;
29          char buffer[MAX_BUF + 1];
30          gnutls_srp_client_credentials_t srp_cred;
31          gnutls_certificate_credentials_t cert_cred;
32
33          if (gnutls_check_version("3.1.4") == NULL) {
34                  fprintf(stderr, "GnuTLS 3.1.4 or later is required for this example\n");
35                  exit(1);
36          }
37
38          /* for backwards compatibility with gnutls < 3.3.0 */
39          gnutls_global_init();
40
41          gnutls_srp_allocate_client_credentials(&srp_cred);
42          gnutls_certificate_allocate_credentials(&cert_cred);
43
44          gnutls_certificate_set_x509_trust_file(cert_cred, CAFILE,
45                                          GNUTLS_X509_FMT_PEM);
46          gnutls_srp_set_client_credentials(srp_cred, USERNAME, PASSWORD);
47
48          /* connects to server
49           */
50          sd = tcp_connect();
51
52          /* Initialize TLS session
53           */
54          gnutls_init(&session, GNUTLS_CLIENT);
55
56
57          /* Set the priorities.
58           */
59          gnutls_priority_set_direct(session,
60                                          "NORMAL:+SRP:+SRP-RSA:+SRP-DSS",
61                                          NULL);
62
63          /* put the SRP credentials to the current session
64           */
65          gnutls_credentials_set(session, GNUTLS_CRD_SRP, srp_cred);
66          gnutls_credentials_set(session, GNUTLS_CRD_CERTIFICATE, cert_cred);
67
68          gnutls_transport_set_int(session, sd);
69          gnutls_handshake_set_timeout(session,
70                                          GNUTLS_DEFAULT_HANDSHAKE_TIMEOUT);
71
72          /* Perform the TLS handshake
73           */
74          do {
75                  ret = gnutls_handshake(session);
```

```
76          }
77          while (ret < 0 && gnutls_error_is_fatal(ret) == 0);
78
79          if (ret < 0) {
80                  fprintf(stderr, "*** Handshake failed\n");
81                  gnutls_perror(ret);
82                  goto end;
83          } else {
84                  char *desc;
85
86                  desc = gnutls_session_get_desc(session);
87                  printf("- Session info: %s\n", desc);
88                  gnutls_free(desc);
89          }
90
91          gnutls_record_send(session, MSG, strlen(MSG));
92
93          ret = gnutls_record_recv(session, buffer, MAX_BUF);
94          if (gnutls_error_is_fatal(ret) != 0 || ret == 0) {
95                  if (ret == 0) {
96                          printf
97                              ("- Peer has closed the GnuTLS connection\n");
98                          goto end;
99                  } else {
100                         fprintf(stderr, "*** Error: %s\n",
101                                 gnutls_strerror(ret));
102                         goto end;
103                 }
104         } else
105                 check_alert(session, ret);
106
107         if (ret > 0) {
108                 printf("- Received %d bytes: ", ret);
109                 for (ii = 0; ii < ret; ii++) {
110                         fputc(buffer[ii], stdout);
111                 }
112                 fputs("\n", stdout);
113         }
114         gnutls_bye(session, GNUTLS_SHUT_RDWR);
115
116     end:
117
118         tcp_close(sd);
119
120         gnutls_deinit(session);
121
122         gnutls_srp_free_client_credentials(srp_cred);
123         gnutls_certificate_free_credentials(cert_cred);
124
125         gnutls_global_deinit();
126
127         return 0;
128 }
```

206

6.1.11. Simple client example using the C++ API

The following client is a simple example of a client client utilizing the GnuTLS C++ API.

```
1   #include <config.h>
2   #include <iostream>
3   #include <stdexcept>
4   #include <gnutls/gnutls.h>
5   #include <gnutls/gnutlsxx.h>
6   #include <cstring> /* for strlen */
7
8   /* A very basic TLS client, with anonymous authentication.
9    * written by Eduardo Villanueva Che.
10   */
11
12  #define MAX_BUF 1024
13  #define SA struct sockaddr
14
15  #define CAFILE "ca.pem"
16  #define MSG "GET / HTTP/1.0\r\n\r\n"
17
18  extern "C"
19  {
20      int tcp_connect(void);
21      void tcp_close(int sd);
22  }
23
24
25  int main(void)
26  {
27      int sd = -1;
28      gnutls_global_init();
29
30      try
31      {
32
33          /* Allow connections to servers that have OpenPGP keys as well.
34           */
35          gnutls::client_session session;
36
37          /* X509 stuff */
38          gnutls::certificate_credentials credentials;
39
40
41          /* sets the trusted cas file
42           */
43          credentials.set_x509_trust_file(CAFILE, GNUTLS_X509_FMT_PEM);
44          /* put the x509 credentials to the current session
45           */
46          session.set_credentials(credentials);
47
48          /* Use default priorities */
49          session.set_priority ("NORMAL", NULL);
50
51          /* connect to the peer
52           */
53          sd = tcp_connect();
```

```
54        session.set_transport_ptr((gnutls_transport_ptr_t) (ptrdiff_t)sd);
55
56        /* Perform the TLS handshake
57         */
58        int ret = session.handshake();
59        if (ret < 0)
60        {
61            throw std::runtime_error("Handshake failed");
62        }
63        else
64        {
65            std::cout << "- Handshake was completed" << std::endl;
66        }
67
68        session.send(MSG, strlen(MSG));
69        char buffer[MAX_BUF + 1];
70        ret = session.recv(buffer, MAX_BUF);
71        if (ret == 0)
72        {
73            throw std::runtime_error("Peer has closed the TLS connection");
74        }
75        else if (ret < 0)
76        {
77            throw std::runtime_error(gnutls_strerror(ret));
78        }
79
80        std::cout << "- Received " << ret << " bytes:" << std::endl;
81        std::cout.write(buffer, ret);
82        std::cout << std::endl;
83
84        session.bye(GNUTLS_SHUT_RDWR);
85    }
86    catch (std::exception &ex)
87    {
88        std::cerr << "Exception caught: " << ex.what() << std::endl;
89    }
90
91    if (sd != -1)
92        tcp_close(sd);
93
94    gnutls_global_deinit();
95
96    return 0;
97 }
```

6.1.12. Helper functions for TCP connections

Those helper function abstract away TCP connection handling from the other examples. It is required to build some examples.

```
1 /* This example code is placed in the public domain. */
2
3 #ifdef HAVE_CONFIG_H
4 #include <config.h>
5 #endif
```

```
 6
 7  #include <stdio.h>
 8  #include <stdlib.h>
 9  #include <string.h>
10  #include <sys/types.h>
11  #include <sys/socket.h>
12  #include <arpa/inet.h>
13  #include <netinet/in.h>
14  #include <unistd.h>
15
16  /* tcp.c */
17  int tcp_connect(void);
18  void tcp_close(int sd);
19
20  /* Connects to the peer and returns a socket
21   * descriptor.
22   */
23  extern int tcp_connect(void)
24  {
25          const char *PORT = "5556";
26          const char *SERVER = "127.0.0.1";
27          int err, sd;
28          struct sockaddr_in sa;
29
30          /* connects to server
31           */
32          sd = socket(AF_INET, SOCK_STREAM, 0);
33
34          memset(&sa, '\0', sizeof(sa));
35          sa.sin_family = AF_INET;
36          sa.sin_port = htons(atoi(PORT));
37          inet_pton(AF_INET, SERVER, &sa.sin_addr);
38
39          err = connect(sd, (struct sockaddr *) &sa, sizeof(sa));
40          if (err < 0) {
41                  fprintf(stderr, "Connect error\n");
42                  exit(1);
43          }
44
45          return sd;
46  }
47
48  /* closes the given socket descriptor.
49   */
50  extern void tcp_close(int sd)
51  {
52          shutdown(sd, SHUT_RDWR);        /* no more receptions */
53          close(sd);
54  }
```

6.1.13. Helper functions for UDP connections

The UDP helper functions abstract away UDP connection handling from the other examples.
It is required to build the examples using UDP.

```
1  /* This example code is placed in the public domain. */
2
3  #ifdef HAVE_CONFIG_H
4  #include <config.h>
5  #endif
6
7  #include <stdio.h>
8  #include <stdlib.h>
9  #include <string.h>
10 #include <sys/types.h>
11 #include <sys/socket.h>
12 #include <arpa/inet.h>
13 #include <netinet/in.h>
14 #include <unistd.h>
15
16 /* udp.c */
17 int udp_connect(void);
18 void udp_close(int sd);
19
20 /* Connects to the peer and returns a socket
21  * descriptor.
22  */
23 extern int udp_connect(void)
24 {
25         const char *PORT = "5557";
26         const char *SERVER = "127.0.0.1";
27         int err, sd, optval;
28         struct sockaddr_in sa;
29
30         /* connects to server
31          */
32         sd = socket(AF_INET, SOCK_DGRAM, 0);
33
34         memset(&sa, '\0', sizeof(sa));
35         sa.sin_family = AF_INET;
36         sa.sin_port = htons(atoi(PORT));
37         inet_pton(AF_INET, SERVER, &sa.sin_addr);
38
39 #if defined(IP_DONTFRAG)
40         optval = 1;
41         setsockopt(sd, IPPROTO_IP, IP_DONTFRAG,
42                     (const void *) &optval, sizeof(optval));
43 #elif defined(IP_MTU_DISCOVER)
44         optval = IP_PMTUDISC_DO;
45         setsockopt(sd, IPPROTO_IP, IP_MTU_DISCOVER,
46                     (const void *) &optval, sizeof(optval));
47 #endif
48
49         err = connect(sd, (struct sockaddr *) &sa, sizeof(sa));
50         if (err < 0) {
51                 fprintf(stderr, "Connect error\n");
52                 exit(1);
53         }
54
55         return sd;
56 }
57
```

```
58  /* closes the given socket descriptor.
59   */
60  extern void udp_close(int sd)
61  {
62          close(sd);
63  }
```

6.2. Server examples

This section contains examples of TLS and SSL servers, using GnuTLS.

6.2.1. Echo server with X.509 authentication

This example is a very simple echo server which supports X.509 authentication.

```
1   /* This example code is placed in the public domain. */
2
3   #ifdef HAVE_CONFIG_H
4   #include <config.h>
5   #endif
6
7   #include <stdio.h>
8   #include <stdlib.h>
9   #include <errno.h>
10  #include <sys/types.h>
11  #include <sys/socket.h>
12  #include <arpa/inet.h>
13  #include <netinet/in.h>
14  #include <string.h>
15  #include <unistd.h>
16  #include <gnutls/gnutls.h>
17
18  #define KEYFILE "key.pem"
19  #define CERTFILE "cert.pem"
20  #define CAFILE "/etc/ssl/certs/ca-certificates.crt"
21  #define CRLFILE "crl.pem"
22
23  /* The OCSP status file contains up to date information about revocation
24   * of the server's certificate. That can be periodically be updated
25   * using:
26   * $ ocsptool --ask --load-cert your_cert.pem --load-issuer your_issuer.pem
27   *            --load-signer your_issuer.pem --outfile ocsp-status.der
28   */
29  #define OCSP_STATUS_FILE "ocsp-status.der"
30
31  /* This is a sample TLS 1.0 echo server, using X.509 authentication and
32   * OCSP stapling support.
33   */
34
35  #define MAX_BUF 1024
36  #define PORT 5556                   /* listen to 5556 port */
37
```

```
38 | /* These are global */
39 | static gnutls_dh_params_t dh_params;
40 |
41 | static int generate_dh_params(void)
42 | {
43 |         unsigned int bits = gnutls_sec_param_to_pk_bits(GNUTLS_PK_DH,
44 |                                                 GNUTLS_SEC_PARAM_LEGACY);
45 |
46 |         /* Generate Diffie-Hellman parameters - for use with DHE
47 |          * kx algorithms. When short bit length is used, it might
48 |          * be wise to regenerate parameters often.
49 |          */
50 |         gnutls_dh_params_init(&dh_params);
51 |         gnutls_dh_params_generate2(dh_params, bits);
52 |
53 |         return 0;
54 | }
55 |
56 | int main(void)
57 | {
58 |         int listen_sd;
59 |         int sd, ret;
60 |         gnutls_certificate_credentials_t x509_cred;
61 |         gnutls_priority_t priority_cache;
62 |         struct sockaddr_in sa_serv;
63 |         struct sockaddr_in sa_cli;
64 |         socklen_t client_len;
65 |         char topbuf[512];
66 |         gnutls_session_t session;
67 |         char buffer[MAX_BUF + 1];
68 |         int optval = 1;
69 |
70 |         /* for backwards compatibility with gnutls < 3.3.0 */
71 |         gnutls_global_init();
72 |
73 |         gnutls_certificate_allocate_credentials(&x509_cred);
74 |         /* gnutls_certificate_set_x509_system_trust(xcred); */
75 |         gnutls_certificate_set_x509_trust_file(x509_cred, CAFILE,
76 |                                                 GNUTLS_X509_FMT_PEM);
77 |
78 |         gnutls_certificate_set_x509_crl_file(x509_cred, CRLFILE,
79 |                                                 GNUTLS_X509_FMT_PEM);
80 |
81 |         ret =
82 |             gnutls_certificate_set_x509_key_file(x509_cred, CERTFILE,
83 |                                                 KEYFILE,
84 |                                                 GNUTLS_X509_FMT_PEM);
85 |         if (ret < 0) {
86 |                 printf("No certificate or key were found\n");
87 |                 exit(1);
88 |         }
89 |
90 |         /* loads an OCSP status request if available */
91 |         gnutls_certificate_set_ocsp_status_request_file(x509_cred,
92 |                                                 OCSP_STATUS_FILE,
93 |                                                 0);
94 |
95 |         generate_dh_params();
```

```
96
97      gnutls_priority_init(&priority_cache,
98                      "PERFORMANCE:%SERVER_PRECEDENCE", NULL);
99
100
101     gnutls_certificate_set_dh_params(x509_cred, dh_params);
102
103     /* Socket operations
104      */
105     listen_sd = socket(AF_INET, SOCK_STREAM, 0);
106
107     memset(&sa_serv, '\0', sizeof(sa_serv));
108     sa_serv.sin_family = AF_INET;
109     sa_serv.sin_addr.s_addr = INADDR_ANY;
110     sa_serv.sin_port = htons(PORT); /* Server Port number */
111
112     setsockopt(listen_sd, SOL_SOCKET, SO_REUSEADDR, (void *) &optval,
113                 sizeof(int));
114
115     bind(listen_sd, (struct sockaddr *) &sa_serv, sizeof(sa_serv));
116
117     listen(listen_sd, 1024);
118
119     printf("Server ready. Listening to port '%d'.\n\n", PORT);
120
121     client_len = sizeof(sa_cli);
122     for (;;) {
123             gnutls_init(&session, GNUTLS_SERVER);
124             gnutls_priority_set(session, priority_cache);
125             gnutls_credentials_set(session, GNUTLS_CRD_CERTIFICATE,
126                                     x509_cred);
127
128             /* We don't request any certificate from the client.
129              * If we did we would need to verify it. One way of
130              * doing that is shown in the "Verifying a certificate"
131              * example.
132              */
133             gnutls_certificate_server_set_request(session,
134                                             GNUTLS_CERT_IGNORE);
135
136             sd = accept(listen_sd, (struct sockaddr *) &sa_cli,
137                         &client_len);
138
139             printf("- connection from %s, port %d\n",
140                     inet_ntop(AF_INET, &sa_cli.sin_addr, topbuf,
141                             sizeof(topbuf)), ntohs(sa_cli.sin_port));
142
143             gnutls_transport_set_int(session, sd);
144
145             do {
146                     ret = gnutls_handshake(session);
147             }
148             while (ret < 0 && gnutls_error_is_fatal(ret) == 0);
149
150             if (ret < 0) {
151                     close(sd);
152                     gnutls_deinit(session);
153                     fprintf(stderr,
```

```
154                            "*** Handshake has failed (%s)\n\n",
155                            gnutls_strerror(ret));
156                    continue;
157            }
158            printf("- Handshake was completed\n");
159
160            /* see the Getting peer's information example */
161            /* print_info(session); */
162
163            for (;;) {
164                    ret = gnutls_record_recv(session, buffer, MAX_BUF);
165
166                    if (ret == 0) {
167                            printf
168                                ("\n- Peer has closed the GnuTLS connection\n");
169                            break;
170                    } else if (ret < 0
171                            && gnutls_error_is_fatal(ret) == 0) {
172                            fprintf(stderr, "*** Warning: %s\n",
173                                    gnutls_strerror(ret));
174                    } else if (ret < 0) {
175                            fprintf(stderr, "\n*** Received corrupted "
176                                    "data(%d). Closing the connection.\n\n",
177                                    ret);
178                            break;
179                    } else if (ret > 0) {
180                            /* echo data back to the client
181                             */
182                            gnutls_record_send(session, buffer, ret);
183                    }
184            }
185            printf("\n");
186            /* do not wait for the peer to close the connection.
187             */
188            gnutls_bye(session, GNUTLS_SHUT_WR);
189
190            close(sd);
191            gnutls_deinit(session);
192
193    }
194    close(listen_sd);
195
196    gnutls_certificate_free_credentials(x509_cred);
197    gnutls_priority_deinit(priority_cache);
198
199    gnutls_global_deinit();
200
201    return 0;
202
203 }
```

6.2.2. Echo server with OpenPGP authentication

The following example is an echo server which supports OpenPGP key authentication. You can easily combine this functionality —that is have a server that supports both X.509 and

214

OpenPGP certificates— but we separated them to keep these examples as simple as possible.

```
1   /* This example code is placed in the public domain. */
2
3   #ifdef HAVE_CONFIG_H
4   #include <config.h>
5   #endif
6
7   #include <stdio.h>
8   #include <stdlib.h>
9   #include <errno.h>
10  #include <sys/types.h>
11  #include <sys/socket.h>
12  #include <arpa/inet.h>
13  #include <netinet/in.h>
14  #include <string.h>
15  #include <unistd.h>
16  #include <gnutls/gnutls.h>
17  #include <gnutls/openpgp.h>
18
19  #define KEYFILE "secret.asc"
20  #define CERTFILE "public.asc"
21  #define RINGFILE "ring.gpg"
22
23  /* This is a sample TLS 1.0-OpenPGP echo server.
24   */
25
26
27  #define SOCKET_ERR(err,s) if(err==-1) {perror(s);return(1);}
28  #define MAX_BUF 1024
29  #define PORT 5556                   /* listen to 5556 port */
30
31  /* These are global */
32  gnutls_dh_params_t dh_params;
33
34  static int generate_dh_params(void)
35  {
36          unsigned int bits = gnutls_sec_param_to_pk_bits(GNUTLS_PK_DH,
37                                               GNUTLS_SEC_PARAM_LEGACY);
38
39          /* Generate Diffie-Hellman parameters - for use with DHE
40           * kx algorithms. These should be discarded and regenerated
41           * once a day, once a week or once a month. Depending on the
42           * security requirements.
43           */
44          gnutls_dh_params_init(&dh_params);
45          gnutls_dh_params_generate2(dh_params, bits);
46
47          return 0;
48  }
49
50  int main(void)
51  {
52          int err, listen_sd;
53          int sd, ret;
54          struct sockaddr_in sa_serv;
55          struct sockaddr_in sa_cli;
56          socklen_t client_len;
```

```
57        char topbuf[512];
58        gnutls_session_t session;
59        gnutls_certificate_credentials_t cred;
60        char buffer[MAX_BUF + 1];
61        int optval = 1;
62        char name[256];
63
64        strcpy(name, "Echo Server");
65
66        if (gnutls_check_version("3.1.4") == NULL) {
67                fprintf(stderr, "GnuTLS 3.1.4 or later is required for this example\n");
68                exit(1);
69        }
70
71        /* for backwards compatibility with gnutls < 3.3.0 */
72        gnutls_global_init();
73
74        gnutls_certificate_allocate_credentials(&cred);
75        gnutls_certificate_set_openpgp_keyring_file(cred, RINGFILE,
76                                        GNUTLS_OPENPGP_FMT_BASE64);
77
78        gnutls_certificate_set_openpgp_key_file(cred, CERTFILE, KEYFILE,
79                                        GNUTLS_OPENPGP_FMT_BASE64);
80
81        generate_dh_params();
82
83        gnutls_certificate_set_dh_params(cred, dh_params);
84
85        /* Socket operations
86         */
87        listen_sd = socket(AF_INET, SOCK_STREAM, 0);
88        SOCKET_ERR(listen_sd, "socket");
89
90        memset(&sa_serv, '\0', sizeof(sa_serv));
91        sa_serv.sin_family = AF_INET;
92        sa_serv.sin_addr.s_addr = INADDR_ANY;
93        sa_serv.sin_port = htons(PORT); /* Server Port number */
94
95        setsockopt(listen_sd, SOL_SOCKET, SO_REUSEADDR, (void *) &optval,
96                        sizeof(int));
97
98        err =
99            bind(listen_sd, (struct sockaddr *) &sa_serv, sizeof(sa_serv));
100       SOCKET_ERR(err, "bind");
101       err = listen(listen_sd, 1024);
102       SOCKET_ERR(err, "listen");
103
104       printf("%s ready. Listening to port '%d'.\n\n", name, PORT);
105
106       client_len = sizeof(sa_cli);
107       for (;;) {
108               gnutls_init(&session, GNUTLS_SERVER);
109               gnutls_priority_set_direct(session,
110                                       "NORMAL:+CTYPE-OPENPGP", NULL);
111
112               /* request client certificate if any.
113                */
114               gnutls_certificate_server_set_request(session,
```

```
115                                              GNUTLS_CERT_REQUEST);
116
117          sd = accept(listen_sd, (struct sockaddr *) &sa_cli,
118                     &client_len);
119
120          printf("- connection from %s, port %d\n",
121                 inet_ntop(AF_INET, &sa_cli.sin_addr, topbuf,
122                           sizeof(topbuf)), ntohs(sa_cli.sin_port));
123
124          gnutls_transport_set_int(session, sd);
125          ret = gnutls_handshake(session);
126          if (ret < 0) {
127                  close(sd);
128                  gnutls_deinit(session);
129                  fprintf(stderr,
130                          "*** Handshake has failed (%s)\n\n",
131                          gnutls_strerror(ret));
132                  continue;
133          }
134          printf("- Handshake was completed\n");
135
136          /* see the Getting peer's information example */
137          /* print_info(session); */
138
139          for (;;) {
140                  ret = gnutls_record_recv(session, buffer, MAX_BUF);
141
142                  if (ret == 0) {
143                          printf
144                              ("\n- Peer has closed the GnuTLS connection\n");
145                          break;
146                  } else if (ret < 0
147                             && gnutls_error_is_fatal(ret) == 0) {
148                          fprintf(stderr, "*** Warning: %s\n",
149                                  gnutls_strerror(ret));
150                  } else if (ret < 0) {
151                          fprintf(stderr, "\n*** Received corrupted "
152                                  "data(%d). Closing the connection.\n\n",
153                                  ret);
154                          break;
155                  } else if (ret > 0) {
156                          /* echo data back to the client
157                           */
158                          gnutls_record_send(session, buffer, ret);
159                  }
160          }
161          printf("\n");
162          /* do not wait for the peer to close the connection.
163           */
164          gnutls_bye(session, GNUTLS_SHUT_WR);
165
166          close(sd);
167          gnutls_deinit(session);
168
169      }
170      close(listen_sd);
171
172      gnutls_certificate_free_credentials(cred);
```

```
173
174        gnutls_global_deinit();
175
176        return 0;
177
178 }
```

6.2.3. Echo server with SRP authentication

This is a server which supports SRP authentication. It is also possible to combine this functionality with a certificate server. Here it is separate for simplicity.

```
1  /* This example code is placed in the public domain. */
2
3  #ifdef HAVE_CONFIG_H
4  #include <config.h>
5  #endif
6
7  #include <stdio.h>
8  #include <stdlib.h>
9  #include <errno.h>
10 #include <sys/types.h>
11 #include <sys/socket.h>
12 #include <arpa/inet.h>
13 #include <netinet/in.h>
14 #include <string.h>
15 #include <unistd.h>
16 #include <gnutls/gnutls.h>
17
18 #define SRP_PASSWD "tpasswd"
19 #define SRP_PASSWD_CONF "tpasswd.conf"
20
21 #define KEYFILE "key.pem"
22 #define CERTFILE "cert.pem"
23 #define CAFILE "/etc/ssl/certs/ca-certificates.crt"
24
25 /* This is a sample TLS-SRP echo server.
26  */
27
28 #define SOCKET_ERR(err,s) if(err==-1) {perror(s);return(1);}
29 #define MAX_BUF 1024
30 #define PORT 5556               /* listen to 5556 port */
31
32 int main(void)
33 {
34        int err, listen_sd;
35        int sd, ret;
36        struct sockaddr_in sa_serv;
37        struct sockaddr_in sa_cli;
38        socklen_t client_len;
39        char topbuf[512];
40        gnutls_session_t session;
41        gnutls_srp_server_credentials_t srp_cred;
42        gnutls_certificate_credentials_t cert_cred;
43        char buffer[MAX_BUF + 1];
```

```
44    int optval = 1;
45    char name[256];
46
47    strcpy(name, "Echo Server");
48
49    if (gnutls_check_version("3.1.4") == NULL) {
50            fprintf(stderr, "GnuTLS 3.1.4 or later is required for this example\n");
51            exit(1);
52    }
53
54    /* for backwards compatibility with gnutls < 3.3.0 */
55    gnutls_global_init();
56
57    /* SRP_PASSWD a password file (created with the included srptool utility)
58     */
59    gnutls_srp_allocate_server_credentials(&srp_cred);
60    gnutls_srp_set_server_credentials_file(srp_cred, SRP_PASSWD,
61                                      SRP_PASSWD_CONF);
62
63    gnutls_certificate_allocate_credentials(&cert_cred);
64    gnutls_certificate_set_x509_trust_file(cert_cred, CAFILE,
65                                      GNUTLS_X509_FMT_PEM);
66    gnutls_certificate_set_x509_key_file(cert_cred, CERTFILE, KEYFILE,
67                                      GNUTLS_X509_FMT_PEM);
68
69    /* TCP socket operations
70     */
71    listen_sd = socket(AF_INET, SOCK_STREAM, 0);
72    SOCKET_ERR(listen_sd, "socket");
73
74    memset(&sa_serv, '\0', sizeof(sa_serv));
75    sa_serv.sin_family = AF_INET;
76    sa_serv.sin_addr.s_addr = INADDR_ANY;
77    sa_serv.sin_port = htons(PORT); /* Server Port number */
78
79    setsockopt(listen_sd, SOL_SOCKET, SO_REUSEADDR, (void *) &optval,
80               sizeof(int));
81
82    err =
83        bind(listen_sd, (struct sockaddr *) &sa_serv, sizeof(sa_serv));
84    SOCKET_ERR(err, "bind");
85    err = listen(listen_sd, 1024);
86    SOCKET_ERR(err, "listen");
87
88    printf("%s ready. Listening to port '%d'.\n\n", name, PORT);
89
90    client_len = sizeof(sa_cli);
91    for (;;) {
92            gnutls_init(&session, GNUTLS_SERVER);
93            gnutls_priority_set_direct(session,
94                              "NORMAL"
95                              ":-KX-ALL:+SRP:+SRP-DSS:+SRP-RSA",
96                              NULL);
97            gnutls_credentials_set(session, GNUTLS_CRD_SRP, srp_cred);
98            /* for the certificate authenticated ciphersuites.
99             */
100           gnutls_credentials_set(session, GNUTLS_CRD_CERTIFICATE,
101                             cert_cred);
```

```
102
103             /* We don't request any certificate from the client.
104              * If we did we would need to verify it. One way of
105              * doing that is shown in the "Verifying a certificate"
106              * example.
107              */
108             gnutls_certificate_server_set_request(session,
109                                            GNUTLS_CERT_IGNORE);
110
111             sd = accept(listen_sd, (struct sockaddr *) &sa_cli,
112                         &client_len);
113
114             printf("- connection from %s, port %d\n",
115                    inet_ntop(AF_INET, &sa_cli.sin_addr, topbuf,
116                              sizeof(topbuf)), ntohs(sa_cli.sin_port));
117
118             gnutls_transport_set_int(session, sd);
119
120             do {
121                     ret = gnutls_handshake(session);
122             }
123             while (ret < 0 && gnutls_error_is_fatal(ret) == 0);
124
125             if (ret < 0) {
126                     close(sd);
127                     gnutls_deinit(session);
128                     fprintf(stderr,
129                             "*** Handshake has failed (%s)\n\n",
130                             gnutls_strerror(ret));
131                     continue;
132             }
133             printf("- Handshake was completed\n");
134             printf("- User %s was connected\n",
135                    gnutls_srp_server_get_username(session));
136
137             /* print_info(session); */
138
139             for (;;) {
140                     ret = gnutls_record_recv(session, buffer, MAX_BUF);
141
142                     if (ret == 0) {
143                             printf
144                                 ("\n- Peer has closed the GnuTLS connection\n");
145                             break;
146                     } else if (ret < 0
147                                && gnutls_error_is_fatal(ret) == 0) {
148                             fprintf(stderr, "*** Warning: %s\n",
149                                     gnutls_strerror(ret));
150                     } else if (ret < 0) {
151                             fprintf(stderr, "\n*** Received corrupted "
152                                     "data(%d). Closing the connection.\n\n",
153                                     ret);
154                             break;
155                     } else if (ret > 0) {
156                             /* echo data back to the client
157                              */
158                             gnutls_record_send(session, buffer, ret);
159                     }
```

```
160                    }
161                    printf("\n");
162                    /* do not wait for the peer to close the connection. */
163                    gnutls_bye(session, GNUTLS_SHUT_WR);
164
165                    close(sd);
166                    gnutls_deinit(session);
167
168             }
169        close(listen_sd);
170
171        gnutls_srp_free_server_credentials(srp_cred);
172        gnutls_certificate_free_credentials(cert_cred);
173
174        gnutls_global_deinit();
175
176        return 0;
177
178 }
```

6.2.4. Echo server with anonymous authentication

This example server supports anonymous authentication, and could be used to serve the example client for anonymous authentication.

```
1  /* This example code is placed in the public domain. */
2
3  #ifdef HAVE_CONFIG_H
4  #include <config.h>
5  #endif
6
7  #include <stdio.h>
8  #include <stdlib.h>
9  #include <errno.h>
10 #include <sys/types.h>
11 #include <sys/socket.h>
12 #include <arpa/inet.h>
13 #include <netinet/in.h>
14 #include <string.h>
15 #include <unistd.h>
16 #include <gnutls/gnutls.h>
17
18 /* This is a sample TLS 1.0 echo server, for anonymous authentication only.
19  */
20
21
22 #define SOCKET_ERR(err,s) if(err==-1) {perror(s);return(1);}
23 #define MAX_BUF 1024
24 #define PORT 5556               /* listen to 5556 port */
25
26 /* These are global */
27 static gnutls_dh_params_t dh_params;
28
29 static int generate_dh_params(void)
30 {
```

```
31         unsigned int bits = gnutls_sec_param_to_pk_bits(GNUTLS_PK_DH,
32                                               GNUTLS_SEC_PARAM_LEGACY);
33         /* Generate Diffie-Hellman parameters - for use with DHE
34          * kx algorithms. These should be discarded and regenerated
35          * once a day, once a week or once a month. Depending on the
36          * security requirements.
37          */
38         gnutls_dh_params_init(&dh_params);
39         gnutls_dh_params_generate2(dh_params, bits);
40
41         return 0;
42 }
43
44 int main(void)
45 {
46         int err, listen_sd;
47         int sd, ret;
48         struct sockaddr_in sa_serv;
49         struct sockaddr_in sa_cli;
50         socklen_t client_len;
51         char topbuf[512];
52         gnutls_session_t session;
53         gnutls_anon_server_credentials_t anoncred;
54         char buffer[MAX_BUF + 1];
55         int optval = 1;
56
57         if (gnutls_check_version("3.1.4") == NULL) {
58                 fprintf(stderr, "GnuTLS 3.1.4 or later is required for this example\n");
59                 exit(1);
60         }
61
62         /* for backwards compatibility with gnutls < 3.3.0 */
63         gnutls_global_init();
64
65         gnutls_anon_allocate_server_credentials(&anoncred);
66
67         generate_dh_params();
68
69         gnutls_anon_set_server_dh_params(anoncred, dh_params);
70
71         /* Socket operations
72          */
73         listen_sd = socket(AF_INET, SOCK_STREAM, 0);
74         SOCKET_ERR(listen_sd, "socket");
75
76         memset(&sa_serv, '\0', sizeof(sa_serv));
77         sa_serv.sin_family = AF_INET;
78         sa_serv.sin_addr.s_addr = INADDR_ANY;
79         sa_serv.sin_port = htons(PORT); /* Server Port number */
80
81         setsockopt(listen_sd, SOL_SOCKET, SO_REUSEADDR, (void *) &optval,
82                     sizeof(int));
83
84         err =
85             bind(listen_sd, (struct sockaddr *) &sa_serv, sizeof(sa_serv));
86         SOCKET_ERR(err, "bind");
87         err = listen(listen_sd, 1024);
88         SOCKET_ERR(err, "listen");
```

```
89
90          printf("Server ready. Listening to port '%d'.\n\n", PORT);
91
92      client_len = sizeof(sa_cli);
93      for (;;) {
94              gnutls_init(&session, GNUTLS_SERVER);
95              gnutls_priority_set_direct(session,
96                                  "NORMAL:+ANON-ECDH:+ANON-DH",
97                                  NULL);
98              gnutls_credentials_set(session, GNUTLS_CRD_ANON, anoncred);
99
100             sd = accept(listen_sd, (struct sockaddr *) &sa_cli,
101                         &client_len);
102
103             printf("- connection from %s, port %d\n",
104                     inet_ntop(AF_INET, &sa_cli.sin_addr, topbuf,
105                             sizeof(topbuf)), ntohs(sa_cli.sin_port));
106
107             gnutls_transport_set_int(session, sd);
108
109             do {
110                     ret = gnutls_handshake(session);
111             }
112             while (ret < 0 && gnutls_error_is_fatal(ret) == 0);
113
114             if (ret < 0) {
115                     close(sd);
116                     gnutls_deinit(session);
117                     fprintf(stderr,
118                             "*** Handshake has failed (%s)\n\n",
119                             gnutls_strerror(ret));
120                     continue;
121             }
122             printf("- Handshake was completed\n");
123
124             /* see the Getting peer's information example */
125             /* print_info(session); */
126
127             for (;;) {
128                     ret = gnutls_record_recv(session, buffer, MAX_BUF);
129
130                     if (ret == 0) {
131                             printf
132                                 ("\n- Peer has closed the GnuTLS connection\n");
133                             break;
134                     } else if (ret < 0
135                             && gnutls_error_is_fatal(ret) == 0) {
136                             fprintf(stderr, "*** Warning: %s\n",
137                                     gnutls_strerror(ret));
138                     } else if (ret < 0) {
139                             fprintf(stderr, "\n*** Received corrupted "
140                                     "data(%d). Closing the connection.\n\n",
141                                     ret);
142                             break;
143                     } else if (ret > 0) {
144                             /* echo data back to the client
145                              */
146                             gnutls_record_send(session, buffer, ret);
```

```
147                          }
148                  }
149                  printf("\n");
150                  /* do not wait for the peer to close the connection.
151                   */
152                  gnutls_bye(session, GNUTLS_SHUT_WR);
153
154                  close(sd);
155                  gnutls_deinit(session);
156
157          }
158          close(listen_sd);
159
160          gnutls_anon_free_server_credentials(anoncred);
161
162          gnutls_global_deinit();
163
164          return 0;
165
166  }
```

6.2.5. DTLS echo server with X.509 authentication

This example is a very simple echo server using Datagram TLS and X.509 authentication.

```
1   /* This example code is placed in the public domain. */
2
3   #ifdef HAVE_CONFIG_H
4   #include <config.h>
5   #endif
6
7   #include <stdio.h>
8   #include <stdlib.h>
9   #include <errno.h>
10  #include <sys/types.h>
11  #include <sys/socket.h>
12  #include <arpa/inet.h>
13  #include <netinet/in.h>
14  #include <sys/select.h>
15  #include <netdb.h>
16  #include <string.h>
17  #include <unistd.h>
18  #include <gnutls/gnutls.h>
19  #include <gnutls/dtls.h>
20
21  #define KEYFILE "key.pem"
22  #define CERTFILE "cert.pem"
23  #define CAFILE "/etc/ssl/certs/ca-certificates.crt"
24  #define CRLFILE "crl.pem"
25
26  /* This is a sample DTLS echo server, using X.509 authentication.
27   * Note that error checking is minimal to simplify the example.
28   */
29
30  #define MAX_BUFFER 1024
```

```
31 | #define PORT 5557
32 |
33 | typedef struct {
34 |         gnutls_session_t session;
35 |         int fd;
36 |         struct sockaddr *cli_addr;
37 |         socklen_t cli_addr_size;
38 | } priv_data_st;
39 |
40 | static int pull_timeout_func(gnutls_transport_ptr_t ptr, unsigned int ms);
41 | static ssize_t push_func(gnutls_transport_ptr_t p, const void *data,
42 |                          size_t size);
43 | static ssize_t pull_func(gnutls_transport_ptr_t p, void *data,
44 |                          size_t size);
45 | static const char *human_addr(const struct sockaddr *sa, socklen_t salen,
46 |                               char *buf, size_t buflen);
47 | static int wait_for_connection(int fd);
48 | static int generate_dh_params(void);
49 |
50 | /* Use global credentials and parameters to simplify
51 |  * the example. */
52 | static gnutls_certificate_credentials_t x509_cred;
53 | static gnutls_priority_t priority_cache;
54 | static gnutls_dh_params_t dh_params;
55 |
56 | int main(void)
57 | {
58 |         int listen_sd;
59 |         int sock, ret;
60 |         struct sockaddr_in sa_serv;
61 |         struct sockaddr_in cli_addr;
62 |         socklen_t cli_addr_size;
63 |         gnutls_session_t session;
64 |         char buffer[MAX_BUFFER];
65 |         priv_data_st priv;
66 |         gnutls_datum_t cookie_key;
67 |         gnutls_dtls_prestate_st prestate;
68 |         int mtu = 1400;
69 |         unsigned char sequence[8];
70 |
71 |         /* this must be called once in the program
72 |          */
73 |         gnutls_global_init();
74 |
75 |         gnutls_certificate_allocate_credentials(&x509_cred);
76 |         gnutls_certificate_set_x509_trust_file(x509_cred, CAFILE,
77 |                                                GNUTLS_X509_FMT_PEM);
78 |
79 |         gnutls_certificate_set_x509_crl_file(x509_cred, CRLFILE,
80 |                                              GNUTLS_X509_FMT_PEM);
81 |
82 |         ret =
83 |             gnutls_certificate_set_x509_key_file(x509_cred, CERTFILE,
84 |                                                  KEYFILE,
85 |                                                  GNUTLS_X509_FMT_PEM);
86 |         if (ret < 0) {
87 |                 printf("No certificate or key were found\n");
88 |                 exit(1);
```

```
 89            }
 90
 91            generate_dh_params();
 92
 93            gnutls_certificate_set_dh_params(x509_cred, dh_params);
 94
 95            gnutls_priority_init(&priority_cache,
 96                                 "PERFORMANCE:-VERS-TLS-ALL:+VERS-DTLS1.0:%SERVER_PRECEDENCE",
 97                                 NULL);
 98
 99            gnutls_key_generate(&cookie_key, GNUTLS_COOKIE_KEY_SIZE);
100
101            /* Socket operations
102             */
103            listen_sd = socket(AF_INET, SOCK_DGRAM, 0);
104
105            memset(&sa_serv, '\0', sizeof(sa_serv));
106            sa_serv.sin_family = AF_INET;
107            sa_serv.sin_addr.s_addr = INADDR_ANY;
108            sa_serv.sin_port = htons(PORT);
109
110            {                             /* DTLS requires the IP don't fragment (DF) bit to be set */
111 #if defined(IP_DONTFRAG)
112                    int optval = 1;
113                    setsockopt(listen_sd, IPPROTO_IP, IP_DONTFRAG,
114                               (const void *) &optval, sizeof(optval));
115 #elif defined(IP_MTU_DISCOVER)
116                    int optval = IP_PMTUDISC_DO;
117                    setsockopt(listen_sd, IPPROTO_IP, IP_MTU_DISCOVER,
118                               (const void *) &optval, sizeof(optval));
119 #endif
120            }
121
122            bind(listen_sd, (struct sockaddr *) &sa_serv, sizeof(sa_serv));
123
124            printf("UDP server ready. Listening to port '%d'.\n\n", PORT);
125
126            for (;;) {
127                    printf("Waiting for connection...\n");
128                    sock = wait_for_connection(listen_sd);
129                    if (sock < 0)
130                            continue;
131
132                    cli_addr_size = sizeof(cli_addr);
133                    ret = recvfrom(sock, buffer, sizeof(buffer), MSG_PEEK,
134                                   (struct sockaddr *) &cli_addr,
135                                   &cli_addr_size);
136                    if (ret > 0) {
137                            memset(&prestate, 0, sizeof(prestate));
138                            ret =
139                                gnutls_dtls_cookie_verify(&cookie_key,
140                                                          &cli_addr,
141                                                          sizeof(cli_addr),
142                                                          buffer, ret,
143                                                          &prestate);
144                            if (ret < 0) {  /* cookie not valid */
145                                    priv_data_st s;
146
```

226

```
147              memset(&s, 0, sizeof(s));
148              s.fd = sock;
149              s.cli_addr = (void *) &cli_addr;
150              s.cli_addr_size = sizeof(cli_addr);
151
152              printf
153                  ("Sending hello verify request to %s\n",
154                   human_addr((struct sockaddr *)
155                              &cli_addr,
156                              sizeof(cli_addr), buffer,
157                              sizeof(buffer)));
158
159              gnutls_dtls_cookie_send(&cookie_key,
160                                      &cli_addr,
161                                      sizeof(cli_addr),
162                                      &prestate,
163                                      (gnutls_transport_ptr_t)
164                                      & s, push_func);
165
166              /* discard peeked data */
167              recvfrom(sock, buffer, sizeof(buffer), 0,
168                       (struct sockaddr *) &cli_addr,
169                       &cli_addr_size);
170              usleep(100);
171              continue;
172          }
173          printf("Accepted connection from %s\n",
174                 human_addr((struct sockaddr *)
175                            &cli_addr, sizeof(cli_addr),
176                            buffer, sizeof(buffer)));
177      } else
178          continue;
179
180  gnutls_init(&session, GNUTLS_SERVER | GNUTLS_DATAGRAM);
181  gnutls_priority_set(session, priority_cache);
182  gnutls_credentials_set(session, GNUTLS_CRD_CERTIFICATE,
183                  x509_cred);
184
185  gnutls_dtls_prestate_set(session, &prestate);
186  gnutls_dtls_set_mtu(session, mtu);
187
188  priv.session = session;
189  priv.fd = sock;
190  priv.cli_addr = (struct sockaddr *) &cli_addr;
191  priv.cli_addr_size = sizeof(cli_addr);
192
193  gnutls_transport_set_ptr(session, &priv);
194  gnutls_transport_set_push_function(session, push_func);
195  gnutls_transport_set_pull_function(session, pull_func);
196  gnutls_transport_set_pull_timeout_function(session,
197                                      pull_timeout_func);
198
199  do {
200          ret = gnutls_handshake(session);
201  }
202  while (ret == GNUTLS_E_INTERRUPTED
203          || ret == GNUTLS_E_AGAIN);
204  /* Note that DTLS may also receive GNUTLS_E_LARGE_PACKET.
```

227

```
205              * In that case the MTU should be adjusted.
206              */
207
208          if (ret < 0) {
209                  fprintf(stderr, "Error in handshake(): %s\n",
210                          gnutls_strerror(ret));
211                  gnutls_deinit(session);
212                  continue;
213          }
214
215          printf("- Handshake was completed\n");
216
217          for (;;) {
218                  do {
219                          ret =
220                              gnutls_record_recv_seq(session, buffer,
221                                                     MAX_BUFFER,
222                                                     sequence);
223                  }
224                  while (ret == GNUTLS_E_AGAIN
225                          || ret == GNUTLS_E_INTERRUPTED);
226
227                  if (ret < 0 && gnutls_error_is_fatal(ret) == 0) {
228                          fprintf(stderr, "*** Warning: %s\n",
229                                  gnutls_strerror(ret));
230                          continue;
231                  } else if (ret < 0) {
232                          fprintf(stderr, "Error in recv(): %s\n",
233                                  gnutls_strerror(ret));
234                          break;
235                  }
236
237                  if (ret == 0) {
238                          printf("EOF\n\n");
239                          break;
240                  }
241
242                  buffer[ret] = 0;
243                  printf
244                      ("received[%.2x%.2x%.2x%.2x%.2x%.2x%.2x%.2x]: %s\n",
245                       sequence[0], sequence[1], sequence[2],
246                       sequence[3], sequence[4], sequence[5],
247                       sequence[6], sequence[7], buffer);
248
249                  /* reply back */
250                  ret = gnutls_record_send(session, buffer, ret);
251                  if (ret < 0) {
252                          fprintf(stderr, "Error in send(): %s\n",
253                                  gnutls_strerror(ret));
254                          break;
255                  }
256          }
257
258          gnutls_bye(session, GNUTLS_SHUT_WR);
259          gnutls_deinit(session);
260
261      }
262      close(listen_sd);
```

228

```
263
264          gnutls_certificate_free_credentials(x509_cred);
265          gnutls_priority_deinit(priority_cache);
266
267          gnutls_global_deinit();
268
269          return 0;
270
271  }
272
273  static int wait_for_connection(int fd)
274  {
275          fd_set rd, wr;
276          int n;
277
278          FD_ZERO(&rd);
279          FD_ZERO(&wr);
280
281          FD_SET(fd, &rd);
282
283          /* waiting part */
284          n = select(fd + 1, &rd, &wr, NULL, NULL);
285          if (n == -1 && errno == EINTR)
286                  return -1;
287          if (n < 0) {
288                  perror("select()");
289                  exit(1);
290          }
291
292          return fd;
293  }
294
295  /* Wait for data to be received within a timeout period in milliseconds
296   */
297  static int pull_timeout_func(gnutls_transport_ptr_t ptr, unsigned int ms)
298  {
299          fd_set rfds;
300          struct timeval tv;
301          priv_data_st *priv = ptr;
302          struct sockaddr_in cli_addr;
303          socklen_t cli_addr_size;
304          int ret;
305          char c;
306
307          FD_ZERO(&rfds);
308          FD_SET(priv->fd, &rfds);
309
310          tv.tv_sec = 0;
311          tv.tv_usec = ms * 1000;
312
313          while (tv.tv_usec >= 1000000) {
314                  tv.tv_usec -= 1000000;
315                  tv.tv_sec++;
316          }
317
318          ret = select(priv->fd + 1, &rfds, NULL, NULL, &tv);
319
320          if (ret <= 0)
```

```
321                     return ret;
322
323             /* only report ok if the next message is from the peer we expect
324              * from
325              */
326             cli_addr_size = sizeof(cli_addr);
327             ret =
328                 recvfrom(priv->fd, &c, 1, MSG_PEEK,
329                         (struct sockaddr *) &cli_addr, &cli_addr_size);
330             if (ret > 0) {
331                     if (cli_addr_size == priv->cli_addr_size
332                         && memcmp(&cli_addr, priv->cli_addr,
333                                 sizeof(cli_addr)) == 0)
334                             return 1;
335             }
336
337             return 0;
338 }
339
340 static ssize_t
341 push_func(gnutls_transport_ptr_t p, const void *data, size_t size)
342 {
343             priv_data_st *priv = p;
344
345             return sendto(priv->fd, data, size, 0, priv->cli_addr,
346                         priv->cli_addr_size);
347 }
348
349 static ssize_t pull_func(gnutls_transport_ptr_t p, void *data, size_t size)
350 {
351             priv_data_st *priv = p;
352             struct sockaddr_in cli_addr;
353             socklen_t cli_addr_size;
354             char buffer[64];
355             int ret;
356
357             cli_addr_size = sizeof(cli_addr);
358             ret =
359                 recvfrom(priv->fd, data, size, 0,
360                         (struct sockaddr *) &cli_addr, &cli_addr_size);
361             if (ret == -1)
362                     return ret;
363
364             if (cli_addr_size == priv->cli_addr_size
365                 && memcmp(&cli_addr, priv->cli_addr, sizeof(cli_addr)) == 0)
366                     return ret;
367
368             printf("Denied connection from %s\n",
369                     human_addr((struct sockaddr *)
370                             &cli_addr, sizeof(cli_addr), buffer,
371                             sizeof(buffer)));
372
373             gnutls_transport_set_errno(priv->session, EAGAIN);
374             return -1;
375 }
376
377 static const char *human_addr(const struct sockaddr *sa, socklen_t salen,
378                             char *buf, size_t buflen)
```

230

```
379  {
380          const char *save_buf = buf;
381          size_t l;
382
383          if (!buf || !buflen)
384                  return NULL;
385
386          *buf = '\0';
387
388          switch (sa->sa_family) {
389  #if HAVE_IPV6
390          case AF_INET6:
391                  snprintf(buf, buflen, "IPv6 ");
392                  break;
393  #endif
394
395          case AF_INET:
396                  snprintf(buf, buflen, "IPv4 ");
397                  break;
398          }
399
400          l = strlen(buf);
401          buf += l;
402          buflen -= l;
403
404          if (getnameinfo(sa, salen, buf, buflen, NULL, 0, NI_NUMERICHOST) !=
405              0)
406                  return NULL;
407
408          l = strlen(buf);
409          buf += l;
410          buflen -= l;
411
412          strncat(buf, " port ", buflen);
413
414          l = strlen(buf);
415          buf += l;
416          buflen -= l;
417
418          if (getnameinfo(sa, salen, NULL, 0, buf, buflen, NI_NUMERICSERV) !=
419              0)
420                  return NULL;
421
422          return save_buf;
423  }
424
425  static int generate_dh_params(void)
426  {
427          int bits = gnutls_sec_param_to_pk_bits(GNUTLS_PK_DH,
428                                          GNUTLS_SEC_PARAM_LEGACY);
429
430          /* Generate Diffie-Hellman parameters - for use with DHE
431           * kx algorithms. When short bit length is used, it might
432           * be wise to regenerate parameters often.
433           */
434          gnutls_dh_params_init(&dh_params);
435          gnutls_dh_params_generate2(dh_params, bits);
436
```

```
437        return 0;
438    }
```

6.3. OCSP example

Generate OCSP request

A small tool to generate OCSP requests.

```
1   /* This example code is placed in the public domain. */
2
3   #ifdef HAVE_CONFIG_H
4   #include <config.h>
5   #endif
6
7   #include <stdio.h>
8   #include <stdlib.h>
9   #include <string.h>
10  #include <gnutls/gnutls.h>
11  #include <gnutls/crypto.h>
12  #include <gnutls/ocsp.h>
13  #ifndef NO_LIBCURL
14  #include <curl/curl.h>
15  #endif
16  #include "read-file.h"
17
18  size_t get_data(void *buffer, size_t size, size_t nmemb, void *userp);
19  static gnutls_x509_crt_t load_cert(const char *cert_file);
20  static void _response_info(const gnutls_datum_t * data);
21  static void
22  _generate_request(gnutls_datum_t * rdata, gnutls_x509_crt_t cert,
23                    gnutls_x509_crt_t issuer, gnutls_datum_t *nonce);
24  static int
25  _verify_response(gnutls_datum_t * data, gnutls_x509_crt_t cert,
26                   gnutls_x509_crt_t signer, gnutls_datum_t *nonce);
27
28  /* This program queries an OCSP server.
29     It expects three files. argv[1] containing the certificate to
30     be checked, argv[2] holding the issuer for this certificate,
31     and argv[3] holding a trusted certificate to verify OCSP's response.
32     argv[4] is optional and should hold the server host name.
33
34     For simplicity the libcurl library is used.
35   */
36
37  int main(int argc, char *argv[])
38  {
39         gnutls_datum_t ud, tmp;
40         int ret;
41         gnutls_datum_t req;
42         gnutls_x509_crt_t cert, issuer, signer;
43  #ifndef NO_LIBCURL
44         CURL *handle;
```

232

```
45          struct curl_slist *headers = NULL;
46 #endif
47          int v, seq;
48          const char *cert_file = argv[1];
49          const char *issuer_file = argv[2];
50          const char *signer_file = argv[3];
51          char *hostname = NULL;
52          unsigned char noncebuf[23];
53          gnutls_datum_t nonce = { noncebuf, sizeof(noncebuf) };
54
55          gnutls_global_init();
56
57          if (argc > 4)
58                  hostname = argv[4];
59
60          ret = gnutls_rnd(GNUTLS_RND_NONCE, nonce.data, nonce.size);
61          if (ret < 0)
62                  exit(1);
63
64          cert = load_cert(cert_file);
65          issuer = load_cert(issuer_file);
66          signer = load_cert(signer_file);
67
68          if (hostname == NULL) {
69
70                  for (seq = 0;; seq++) {
71                          ret =
72                              gnutls_x509_crt_get_authority_info_access(cert,
73                                                                        seq,
74                                                                        GNUTLS_IA_OCSP_URI,
75                                                                        &tmp,
76                                                                        NULL);
77                          if (ret == GNUTLS_E_UNKNOWN_ALGORITHM)
78                                  continue;
79                          if (ret == GNUTLS_E_REQUESTED_DATA_NOT_AVAILABLE) {
80                                  fprintf(stderr,
81                                          "No URI was found in the certificate.\n");
82                                  exit(1);
83                          }
84                          if (ret < 0) {
85                                  fprintf(stderr, "error: %s\n",
86                                          gnutls_strerror(ret));
87                                  exit(1);
88                          }
89
90                          printf("CA issuers URI: %.*s\n", tmp.size,
91                                  tmp.data);
92
93                          hostname = malloc(tmp.size + 1);
94                          memcpy(hostname, tmp.data, tmp.size);
95                          hostname[tmp.size] = 0;
96
97                          gnutls_free(tmp.data);
98                          break;
99                  }
100
101         }
102
```

233

```
103              /* Note that the OCSP servers hostname might be available
104               * using gnutls_x509_crt_get_authority_info_access() in the issuer's
105               * certificate */
106
107              memset(&ud, 0, sizeof(ud));
108              fprintf(stderr, "Connecting to %s\n", hostname);
109
110              _generate_request(&req, cert, issuer, &nonce);
111
112  #ifndef NO_LIBCURL
113              curl_global_init(CURL_GLOBAL_ALL);
114
115              handle = curl_easy_init();
116              if (handle == NULL)
117                      exit(1);
118
119              headers =
120                  curl_slist_append(headers,
121                                    "Content-Type: application/ocsp-request");
122
123              curl_easy_setopt(handle, CURLOPT_HTTPHEADER, headers);
124              curl_easy_setopt(handle, CURLOPT_POSTFIELDS, (void *) req.data);
125              curl_easy_setopt(handle, CURLOPT_POSTFIELDSIZE, req.size);
126              curl_easy_setopt(handle, CURLOPT_URL, hostname);
127              curl_easy_setopt(handle, CURLOPT_WRITEFUNCTION, get_data);
128              curl_easy_setopt(handle, CURLOPT_WRITEDATA, &ud);
129
130              ret = curl_easy_perform(handle);
131              if (ret != 0) {
132                      fprintf(stderr, "curl[%d] error %d\n", __LINE__, ret);
133                      exit(1);
134              }
135
136              curl_easy_cleanup(handle);
137  #endif
138
139              _response_info(&ud);
140
141              v = _verify_response(&ud, cert, signer, &nonce);
142
143              gnutls_x509_crt_deinit(cert);
144              gnutls_x509_crt_deinit(issuer);
145              gnutls_x509_crt_deinit(signer);
146              gnutls_global_deinit();
147
148              return v;
149  }
150
151  static void _response_info(const gnutls_datum_t * data)
152  {
153              gnutls_ocsp_resp_t resp;
154              int ret;
155              gnutls_datum buf;
156
157              ret = gnutls_ocsp_resp_init(&resp);
158              if (ret < 0)
159                      exit(1);
160
```

```
161        ret = gnutls_ocsp_resp_import(resp, data);
162        if (ret < 0)
163                exit(1);
164
165        ret = gnutls_ocsp_resp_print(resp, GNUTLS_OCSP_PRINT_FULL, &buf);
166        if (ret != 0)
167                exit(1);
168
169        printf("%.*s", buf.size, buf.data);
170        gnutls_free(buf.data);
171
172        gnutls_ocsp_resp_deinit(resp);
173 }
174
175 static gnutls_x509_crt_t load_cert(const char *cert_file)
176 {
177        gnutls_x509_crt_t crt;
178        int ret;
179        gnutls_datum_t data;
180        size_t size;
181
182        ret = gnutls_x509_crt_init(&crt);
183        if (ret < 0)
184                exit(1);
185
186        data.data = (void *) read_binary_file(cert_file, &size);
187        data.size = size;
188
189        if (!data.data) {
190                fprintf(stderr, "Cannot open file: %s\n", cert_file);
191                exit(1);
192        }
193
194        ret = gnutls_x509_crt_import(crt, &data, GNUTLS_X509_FMT_PEM);
195        free(data.data);
196        if (ret < 0) {
197                fprintf(stderr, "Cannot import certificate in %s: %s\n",
198                        cert_file, gnutls_strerror(ret));
199                exit(1);
200        }
201
202        return crt;
203 }
204
205 static void
206 _generate_request(gnutls_datum_t * rdata, gnutls_x509_crt_t cert,
207                   gnutls_x509_crt_t issuer, gnutls_datum_t *nonce)
208 {
209        gnutls_ocsp_req_t req;
210        int ret;
211
212        ret = gnutls_ocsp_req_init(&req);
213        if (ret < 0)
214                exit(1);
215
216        ret = gnutls_ocsp_req_add_cert(req, GNUTLS_DIG_SHA1, issuer, cert);
217        if (ret < 0)
218                exit(1);
```

```
219
220
221         ret = gnutls_ocsp_req_set_nonce(req, 0, nonce);
222         if (ret < 0)
223                 exit(1);
224
225         ret = gnutls_ocsp_req_export(req, rdata);
226         if (ret != 0)
227                 exit(1);
228
229         gnutls_ocsp_req_deinit(req);
230
231         return;
232  }
233
234  static int
235  _verify_response(gnutls_datum_t * data, gnutls_x509_crt_t cert,
236                  gnutls_x509_crt_t signer, gnutls_datum_t *nonce)
237  {
238         gnutls_ocsp_resp_t resp;
239         int ret;
240         unsigned verify;
241         gnutls_datum_t rnonce;
242
243         ret = gnutls_ocsp_resp_init(&resp);
244         if (ret < 0)
245                 exit(1);
246
247         ret = gnutls_ocsp_resp_import(resp, data);
248         if (ret < 0)
249                 exit(1);
250
251         ret = gnutls_ocsp_resp_check_crt(resp, 0, cert);
252         if (ret < 0)
253                 exit(1);
254
255         ret = gnutls_ocsp_resp_get_nonce(resp, NULL, &rnonce);
256         if (ret < 0)
257                 exit(1);
258
259         if (rnonce.size != nonce->size || memcmp(nonce->data, rnonce.data,
260                 nonce->size) != 0) {
261                 exit(1);
262         }
263
264         ret = gnutls_ocsp_resp_verify_direct(resp, signer, &verify, 0);
265         if (ret < 0)
266                 exit(1);
267
268         printf("Verifying OCSP Response: ");
269         if (verify == 0)
270                 printf("Verification success!\n");
271         else
272                 printf("Verification error!\n");
273
274         if (verify & GNUTLS_OCSP_VERIFY_SIGNER_NOT_FOUND)
275                 printf("Signer cert not found\n");
276
```

```
277    if (verify & GNUTLS_OCSP_VERIFY_SIGNER_KEYUSAGE_ERROR)
278          printf("Signer cert keyusage error\n");
279
280    if (verify & GNUTLS_OCSP_VERIFY_UNTRUSTED_SIGNER)
281          printf("Signer cert is not trusted\n");
282
283    if (verify & GNUTLS_OCSP_VERIFY_INSECURE_ALGORITHM)
284          printf("Insecure algorithm\n");
285
286    if (verify & GNUTLS_OCSP_VERIFY_SIGNATURE_FAILURE)
287          printf("Signature failure\n");
288
289    if (verify & GNUTLS_OCSP_VERIFY_CERT_NOT_ACTIVATED)
290          printf("Signer cert not yet activated\n");
291
292    if (verify & GNUTLS_OCSP_VERIFY_CERT_EXPIRED)
293          printf("Signer cert expired\n");
294
295    gnutls_free(rnonce.data);
296    gnutls_ocsp_resp_deinit(resp);
297
298    return verify;
299 }
300
301 size_t get_data(void *buffer, size_t size, size_t nmemb, void *userp)
302 {
303    gnutls_datum_t *ud = userp;
304
305    size *= nmemb;
306
307    ud->data = realloc(ud->data, size + ud->size);
308    if (ud->data == NULL) {
309          fprintf(stderr, "Not enough memory for the request\n");
310          exit(1);
311    }
312
313    memcpy(&ud->data[ud->size], buffer, size);
314    ud->size += size;
315
316    return size;
317 }
```

6.4. Miscellaneous examples

6.4.1. Checking for an alert

This is a function that checks if an alert has been received in the current session.

```
1 /* This example code is placed in the public domain. */
2
3 #ifdef HAVE_CONFIG_H
4 #include <config.h>
5 #endif
6
```

```
 7  #include <stdio.h>
 8  #include <stdlib.h>
 9  #include <gnutls/gnutls.h>
10
11  #include "examples.h"
12
13  /* This function will check whether the given return code from
14   * a gnutls function (recv/send), is an alert, and will print
15   * that alert.
16   */
17  void check_alert(gnutls_session_t session, int ret)
18  {
19          int last_alert;
20
21          if (ret == GNUTLS_E_WARNING_ALERT_RECEIVED
22              || ret == GNUTLS_E_FATAL_ALERT_RECEIVED) {
23                  last_alert = gnutls_alert_get(session);
24
25                  /* The check for renegotiation is only useful if we are
26                   * a server, and we had requested a rehandshake.
27                   */
28                  if (last_alert == GNUTLS_A_NO_RENEGOTIATION &&
29                      ret == GNUTLS_E_WARNING_ALERT_RECEIVED)
30                          printf("* Received NO_RENEGOTIATION alert. "
31                                  "Client Does not support renegotiation.\n");
32                  else
33                          printf("* Received alert '%d': %s.\n", last_alert,
34                                  gnutls_alert_get_name(last_alert));
35          }
36  }
```

6.4.2. X.509 certificate parsing example

To demonstrate the X.509 parsing capabilities an example program is listed below. That program reads the peer's certificate, and prints information about it.

```
 1  /* This example code is placed in the public domain. */
 2
 3  #ifdef HAVE_CONFIG_H
 4  #include <config.h>
 5  #endif
 6
 7  #include <stdio.h>
 8  #include <stdlib.h>
 9  #include <gnutls/gnutls.h>
10  #include <gnutls/x509.h>
11
12  #include "examples.h"
13
14  static const char *bin2hex(const void *bin, size_t bin_size)
15  {
16          static char printable[110];
17          const unsigned char *_bin = bin;
18          char *print;
19          size_t i;
```

238

```
20
21          if (bin_size > 50)
22                  bin_size = 50;
23
24          print = printable;
25          for (i = 0; i < bin_size; i++) {
26                  sprintf(print, "%.2x ", _bin[i]);
27                  print += 2;
28          }
29
30          return printable;
31  }
32
33  /* This function will print information about this session's peer
34   * certificate.
35   */
36  void print_x509_certificate_info(gnutls_session_t session)
37  {
38          char serial[40];
39          char dn[256];
40          size_t size;
41          unsigned int algo, bits;
42          time_t expiration_time, activation_time;
43          const gnutls_datum_t *cert_list;
44          unsigned int cert_list_size = 0;
45          gnutls_x509_crt_t cert;
46          gnutls_datum_t cinfo;
47
48          /* This function only works for X.509 certificates.
49           */
50          if (gnutls_certificate_type_get(session) != GNUTLS_CRT_X509)
51                  return;
52
53          cert_list = gnutls_certificate_get_peers(session, &cert_list_size);
54
55          printf("Peer provided %d certificates.\n", cert_list_size);
56
57          if (cert_list_size > 0) {
58                  int ret;
59
60                  /* we only print information about the first certificate.
61                   */
62                  gnutls_x509_crt_init(&cert);
63
64                  gnutls_x509_crt_import(cert, &cert_list[0],
65                                         GNUTLS_X509_FMT_DER);
66
67                  printf("Certificate info:\n");
68
69                  /* This is the preferred way of printing short information about
70                     a certificate. */
71
72                  ret =
73                      gnutls_x509_crt_print(cert, GNUTLS_CRT_PRINT_ONELINE,
74                                            &cinfo);
75                  if (ret == 0) {
76                          printf("\t%s\n", cinfo.data);
77                          gnutls_free(cinfo.data);
```

```
 78              }
 79
 80              /* If you want to extract fields manually for some other reason,
 81                 below are popular example calls. */
 82
 83              expiration_time =
 84                  gnutls_x509_crt_get_expiration_time(cert);
 85              activation_time =
 86                  gnutls_x509_crt_get_activation_time(cert);
 87
 88              printf("\tCertificate is valid since: %s",
 89                      ctime(&activation_time));
 90              printf("\tCertificate expires: %s",
 91                      ctime(&expiration_time));
 92
 93              /* Print the serial number of the certificate.
 94               */
 95              size = sizeof(serial);
 96              gnutls_x509_crt_get_serial(cert, serial, &size);
 97
 98              printf("\tCertificate serial number: %s\n",
 99                      bin2hex(serial, size));
100
101              /* Extract some of the public key algorithm's parameters
102               */
103              algo = gnutls_x509_crt_get_pk_algorithm(cert, &bits);
104
105              printf("Certificate public key: %s",
106                      gnutls_pk_algorithm_get_name(algo));
107
108              /* Print the version of the X.509
109               * certificate.
110               */
111              printf("\tCertificate version: #%d\n",
112                      gnutls_x509_crt_get_version(cert));
113
114              size = sizeof(dn);
115              gnutls_x509_crt_get_dn(cert, dn, &size);
116              printf("\tDN: %s\n", dn);
117
118              size = sizeof(dn);
119              gnutls_x509_crt_get_issuer_dn(cert, dn, &size);
120              printf("\tIssuer's DN: %s\n", dn);
121
122              gnutls_x509_crt_deinit(cert);
123
124          }
125  }
```

6.4.3. Listing the ciphersuites in a priority string

This is a small program to list the enabled ciphersuites by a priority string.

```
 1  /* This example code is placed in the public domain. */
 2
```

```
3  #include <config.h>
4  #include <stdio.h>
5  #include <stdlib.h>
6  #include <string.h>
7  #include <gnutls/gnutls.h>
8
9  static void print_cipher_suite_list(const char *priorities)
10 {
11         size_t i;
12         int ret;
13         unsigned int idx;
14         const char *name;
15         const char *err;
16         unsigned char id[2];
17         gnutls_protocol_t version;
18         gnutls_priority_t pcache;
19
20         if (priorities != NULL) {
21                 printf("Cipher suites for %s\n", priorities);
22
23                 ret = gnutls_priority_init(&pcache, priorities, &err);
24                 if (ret < 0) {
25                         fprintf(stderr, "Syntax error at: %s\n", err);
26                         exit(1);
27                 }
28
29                 for (i = 0;; i++) {
30                         ret =
31                             gnutls_priority_get_cipher_suite_index(pcache,
32                                                                    i,
33                                                                    &idx);
34                         if (ret == GNUTLS_E_REQUESTED_DATA_NOT_AVAILABLE)
35                                 break;
36                         if (ret == GNUTLS_E_UNKNOWN_CIPHER_SUITE)
37                                 continue;
38
39                         name =
40                             gnutls_cipher_suite_info(idx, id, NULL, NULL,
41                                                      NULL, &version);
42
43                         if (name != NULL)
44                                 printf("%-50s\t0x%02x, 0x%02x\t%s\n",
45                                        name, (unsigned char) id[0],
46                                        (unsigned char) id[1],
47                                        gnutls_protocol_get_name(version));
48                 }
49
50                 return;
51         }
52 }
53
54 int main(int argc, char **argv)
55 {
56         if (argc > 1)
57                 print_cipher_suite_list(argv[1]);
58         return 0;
59 }
```

241

6.4.4. PKCS #12 structure generation example

This small program demonstrates the usage of the PKCS #12 API, by generating such a structure.

```
1  /* This example code is placed in the public domain. */
2
3  #ifdef HAVE_CONFIG_H
4  #include <config.h>
5  #endif
6
7  #include <stdio.h>
8  #include <stdlib.h>
9  #include <gnutls/gnutls.h>
10 #include <gnutls/pkcs12.h>
11
12 #include "examples.h"
13
14 #define OUTFILE "out.p12"
15
16 /* This function will write a pkcs12 structure into a file.
17  * cert: is a DER encoded certificate
18  * pkcs8_key: is a PKCS #8 encrypted key (note that this must be
19  *  encrypted using a PKCS #12 cipher, or some browsers will crash)
20  * password: is the password used to encrypt the PKCS #12 packet.
21  */
22 int
23 write_pkcs12(const gnutls_datum_t * cert,
24              const gnutls_datum_t * pkcs8_key, const char *password)
25 {
26      gnutls_pkcs12_t pkcs12;
27      int ret, bag_index;
28      gnutls_pkcs12_bag_t bag, key_bag;
29      char pkcs12_struct[10 * 1024];
30      size_t pkcs12_struct_size;
31      FILE *fd;
32
33      /* A good idea might be to use gnutls_x509_privkey_get_key_id()
34       * to obtain a unique ID.
35       */
36      gnutls_datum_t key_id = { (void *) "\x00\x00\x07", 3 };
37
38      gnutls_global_init();
39
40      /* Firstly we create two helper bags, which hold the certificate,
41       * and the (encrypted) key.
42       */
43
44      gnutls_pkcs12_bag_init(&bag);
45      gnutls_pkcs12_bag_init(&key_bag);
46
47      ret =
48          gnutls_pkcs12_bag_set_data(bag, GNUTLS_BAG_CERTIFICATE, cert);
49      if (ret < 0) {
50              fprintf(stderr, "ret: %s\n", gnutls_strerror(ret));
51              return 1;
52      }
```

```
53
54      /* ret now holds the bag's index.
55       */
56      bag_index = ret;
57
58      /* Associate a friendly name with the given certificate. Used
59       * by browsers.
60       */
61      gnutls_pkcs12_bag_set_friendly_name(bag, bag_index, "My name");
62
63      /* Associate the certificate with the key using a unique key
64       * ID.
65       */
66      gnutls_pkcs12_bag_set_key_id(bag, bag_index, &key_id);
67
68      /* use weak encryption for the certificate.
69       */
70      gnutls_pkcs12_bag_encrypt(bag, password,
71                              GNUTLS_PKCS_USE_PKCS12_RC2_40);
72
73      /* Now the key.
74       */
75
76      ret = gnutls_pkcs12_bag_set_data(key_bag,
77                                    GNUTLS_BAG_PKCS8_ENCRYPTED_KEY,
78                                    pkcs8_key);
79      if (ret < 0) {
80              fprintf(stderr, "ret: %s\n", gnutls_strerror(ret));
81              return 1;
82      }
83
84      /* Note that since the PKCS #8 key is already encrypted we don't
85       * bother encrypting that bag.
86       */
87      bag_index = ret;
88
89      gnutls_pkcs12_bag_set_friendly_name(key_bag, bag_index, "My name");
90
91      gnutls_pkcs12_bag_set_key_id(key_bag, bag_index, &key_id);
92
93
94      /* The bags were filled. Now create the PKCS #12 structure.
95       */
96      gnutls_pkcs12_init(&pkcs12);
97
98      /* Insert the two bags in the PKCS #12 structure.
99       */
100
101     gnutls_pkcs12_set_bag(pkcs12, bag);
102     gnutls_pkcs12_set_bag(pkcs12, key_bag);
103
104
105     /* Generate a message authentication code for the PKCS #12
106      * structure.
107      */
108     gnutls_pkcs12_generate_mac(pkcs12, password);
109
110     pkcs12_struct_size = sizeof(pkcs12_struct);
```

```
111    ret =
112        gnutls_pkcs12_export(pkcs12, GNUTLS_X509_FMT_DER,
113                            pkcs12_struct, &pkcs12_struct_size);
114    if (ret < 0) {
115            fprintf(stderr, "ret: %s\n", gnutls_strerror(ret));
116            return 1;
117    }
118
119    fd = fopen(OUTFILE, "w");
120    if (fd == NULL) {
121            fprintf(stderr, "cannot open file\n");
122            return 1;
123    }
124    fwrite(pkcs12_struct, 1, pkcs12_struct_size, fd);
125    fclose(fd);
126
127    gnutls_pkcs12_bag_deinit(bag);
128    gnutls_pkcs12_bag_deinit(key_bag);
129    gnutls_pkcs12_deinit(pkcs12);
130
131    return 0;
132 }
```

Other included programs

Included with GnuTLS are also a few command line tools that let you use the library for common tasks without writing an application. The applications are discussed in this chapter.

7.1. Invoking gnutls-cli

Simple client program to set up a TLS connection to some other computer. It sets up a TLS connection and forwards data from the standard input to the secured socket and vice versa.

This section was generated by **AutoGen**, using the `agtexi-cmd` template and the option descriptions for the `gnutls-cli` program. This software is released under the GNU General Public License, version 3 or later.

gnutls-cli help/usage ("`--help`")

This is the automatically generated usage text for gnutls-cli.

The text printed is the same whether selected with the `help` option ("`--help`") or the `more-help` option ("`--more-help`"). `more-help` will print the usage text by passing it through a pager program. `more-help` is disabled on platforms without a working `fork(2)` function. The `PAGER` environment variable is used to select the program, defaulting to "`more`". Both will exit with a status code of 0.

```
1  gnutls-cli - GnuTLS client
2  Usage:  gnutls-cli [ -<flag> [<val>] | --<name>[{=| }<val>] ]... [hostname]
3
4     -d, --debug=num            Enable debugging
5                                  - it must be in the range:
6                                    0 to 9999
7     -V, --verbose              More verbose output
8                                  - may appear multiple times
9         --tofu                 Enable trust on first use authentication
10                                 - disabled as '--no-tofu'
11        --strict-tofu          Fail to connect if a known certificate has changed
12                                 - disabled as '--no-strict-tofu'
13        --dane                 Enable DANE certificate verification (DNSSEC)
14                                 - disabled as '--no-dane'
15        --local-dns            Use the local DNS server for DNSSEC resolving
```

```
16                              - disabled as '--no-local-dns'
17        --ca-verification     Enable CA certificate verification
18                              - disabled as '--no-ca-verification'
19                              - enabled by default
20        --ocsp                Enable OCSP certificate verification
21                              - disabled as '--no-ocsp'
22   -r, --resume               Establish a session and resume
23   -e, --rehandshake          Establish a session and rehandshake
24   -s, --starttls             Connect, establish a plain session and start TLS
25        --app-proto=str       an alias for the 'starttls-proto' option
26        --starttls-proto=str  The application protocol to be used to obtain the server's certificate
27   (https, ftp, smtp, imap)
28                              - prohibits the option 'starttls'
29   -u, --udp                  Use DTLS (datagram TLS) over UDP
30        --mtu=num             Set MTU for datagram TLS
31                              - it must be in the range:
32                              0 to 17000
33        --crlf                Send CR LF instead of LF
34        --x509fmtder          Use DER format for certificates to read from
35   -f, --fingerprint          Send the openpgp fingerprint, instead of the key
36        --print-cert          Print peer's certificate in PEM format
37        --save-cert=str       Save the peer's certificate chain in the specified file in PEM format
38        --save-ocsp=str       Save the peer's OCSP status response in the provided file
39        --dh-bits=num         The minimum number of bits allowed for DH
40        --priority=str        Priorities string
41        --x509cafile=str      Certificate file or PKCS #11 URL to use
42        --x509crlfile=file    CRL file to use
43                              - file must pre-exist
44        --pgpkeyfile=file     PGP Key file to use
45                              - file must pre-exist
46        --pgpkeyring=file     PGP Key ring file to use
47                              - file must pre-exist
48        --pgpcertfile=file    PGP Public Key (certificate) file to use
49                              - requires the option 'pgpkeyfile'
50                              - file must pre-exist
51        --x509keyfile=str     X.509 key file or PKCS #11 URL to use
52        --x509certfile=str    X.509 Certificate file or PKCS #11 URL to use
53                              - requires the option 'x509keyfile'
54        --pgpsubkey=str       PGP subkey to use (hex or auto)
55        --srpusername=str     SRP username to use
56        --srppasswd=str       SRP password to use
57        --pskusername=str     PSK username to use
58        --pskkey=str          PSK key (in hex) to use
59   -p, --port=str             The port or service to connect to
60        --insecure            Don't abort program if server certificate can't be validated
61        --ranges              Use length-hiding padding to prevent traffic analysis
62        --benchmark-ciphers   Benchmark individual ciphers
63        --benchmark-tls-kx    Benchmark TLS key exchange methods
64   -!, --benchmark-tls-ciphers  Benchmark TLS ciphers
65   -l, --list                 Print a list of the supported algorithms and modes
66                              - prohibits the option 'port'
67   -", --priority-list        Print a list of the supported priority strings
68   -#, --noticket             Don't allow session tickets
69   -$, --srtp-profiles=str    Offer SRTP profiles
70   -%, --alpn=str             Application layer protocol
71                              - may appear multiple times
72   -b, --heartbeat            Activate heartbeat support
73   -&, --recordsize=num       The maximum record size to advertize
```

```
74 |                                    - it must be in the range:
75 |                                        0 to 4096
76 |   -', --disable-sni          Do not send a Server Name Indication (SNI)
77 |   -(, --disable-extensions   Disable all the TLS extensions
78 |   -), --inline-commands      Inline commands of the form ^<cmd>^
79 |   -*, --inline-commands-prefix=str Change the default delimiter for inline commands.
80 |   -+, --provider=file        Specify the PKCS #11 provider library
81 |                                - file must pre-exist
82 |   -,, --fips140-mode         Reports the status of the FIPS140-2 mode in gnutls library
83 |   -v, --version[=arg]        output version information and exit
84 |   -h, --help                 display extended usage information and exit
85 |   -!, --more-help            extended usage information passed thru pager
86 |
87 | Options are specified by doubled hyphens and their name or by a single
88 | hyphen and the flag character.
89 | Operands and options may be intermixed.  They will be reordered.
90 |
91 | Simple client program to set up a TLS connection to some other computer.  It
92 | sets up a TLS connection and forwards data from the standard input to the
93 | secured socket and vice versa.
94 |
```

debug option (-d)

This is the "enable debugging" option. This option takes a number argument. Specifies the debug level.

tofu option

This is the "enable trust on first use authentication" option.

This option has some usage constraints. It:

- can be disabled with –no-tofu.

This option will, in addition to certificate authentication, perform authentication based on previously seen public keys, a model similar to SSH authentication. Note that when tofu is specified (PKI) and DANE authentication will become advisory to assist the public key acceptance process.

strict-tofu option

This is the "fail to connect if a known certificate has changed" option.

This option has some usage constraints. It:

- can be disabled with –no-strict-tofu.

This option will perform authentication as with option –tofu; however, while –tofu asks whether to trust a changed public key, this option will fail in case of public key changes.

dane option

This is the "enable dane certificate verification (dnssec)" option.

This option has some usage constraints. It:

- can be disabled with –no-dane.

This option will, in addition to certificate authentication using the trusted CAs, verify the server certificates using on the DANE information available via DNSSEC.

local-dns option

This is the "use the local dns server for dnssec resolving" option.

This option has some usage constraints. It:

- can be disabled with –no-local-dns.

This option will use the local DNS server for DNSSEC. This is disabled by default due to many servers not allowing DNSSEC.

ca-verification option

This is the "enable ca certificate verification" option.

This option has some usage constraints. It:

- can be disabled with –no-ca-verification.
- It is enabled by default.

This option can be used to enable or disable CA certificate verification. It is to be used with the –dane or –tofu options.

ocsp option

This is the "enable ocsp certificate verification" option.

This option has some usage constraints. It:

- can be disabled with –no-ocsp.

This option will enable verification of the peer's certificate using ocsp

resume option (-r)

This is the "establish a session and resume" option. Connect, establish a session, reconnect and resume.

rehandshake option (-e)

This is the "establish a session and rehandshake" option. Connect, establish a session and rehandshake immediately.

starttls option (-s)

This is the "connect, establish a plain session and start tls" option. The TLS session will be initiated when EOF or a SIGALRM is received.

app-proto option

This is an alias for the `starttls-proto` option, section 7.1.

starttls-proto option

This is the "the application protocol to be used to obtain the server's certificate (https, ftp, smtp, imap, ldap, xmpp)" option. This option takes a string argument.

This option has some usage constraints. It:

- must not appear in combination with any of the following options: starttls.

Specify the application layer protocol for STARTTLS. If the protocol is supported, gnutls-cli will proceed to the TLS negotiation.

dh-bits option

This is the "the minimum number of bits allowed for dh" option. This option takes a number argument. This option sets the minimum number of bits allowed for a Diffie-Hellman key exchange. You may want to lower the default value if the peer sends a weak prime and you get an connection error with unacceptable prime.

priority option

This is the "priorities string" option. This option takes a string argument. TLS algorithms and protocols to enable. You can use predefined sets of ciphersuites such as PERFORMANCE, NORMAL, PFS, SECURE128, SECURE256. The default is NORMAL.

Check the GnuTLS manual on section "Priority strings" for more information on the allowed keywords

ranges option

This is the "use length-hiding padding to prevent traffic analysis" option. When possible (e.g., when using CBC ciphersuites), use length-hiding padding to prevent traffic analysis.

benchmark-ciphers option

This is the "benchmark individual ciphers" option. By default the benchmarked ciphers will utilize any capabilities of the local CPU to improve performance. To test against the raw software implementation set the environment variable GNUTLS_CPUID_OVERRIDE to 0x1.

benchmark-tls-ciphers option

This is the "benchmark tls ciphers" option. By default the benchmarked ciphers will utilize any capabilities of the local CPU to improve performance. To test against the raw software implementation set the environment variable GNUTLS_CPUID_OVERRIDE to 0x1.

list option (-l)

This is the "print a list of the supported algorithms and modes" option.

This option has some usage constraints. It:

- must not appear in combination with any of the following options: port.

Print a list of the supported algorithms and modes. If a priority string is given then only the enabled ciphersuites are shown.

priority-list option

This is the "print a list of the supported priority strings" option. Print a list of the supported priority strings. The ciphersuites corresponding to each priority string can be examined using -l -p.

alpn option

This is the "application layer protocol" option. This option takes a string argument.

This option has some usage constraints. It:

- may appear an unlimited number of times.

This option will set and enable the Application Layer Protocol Negotiation (ALPN) in the TLS protocol.

disable-extensions option

This is the "disable all the tls extensions" option. This option disables all TLS extensions. Deprecated option. Use the priority string.

inline-commands option

This is the "inline commands of the form
textasciicircum<cmd>
textasciicircum" option. Enable inline commands of the form
textasciicircum<cmd>
textasciicircum. The inline commands are expected to be in a line by themselves. The available commands are: resume and renegotiate.

inline-commands-prefix option

This is the "change the default delimiter for inline commands." option. This option takes a string argument. Change the default delimiter (
textasciicircum) used for inline commands. The delimiter is expected to be a single US-ASCII character (octets 0 - 127). This option is only relevant if inline commands are enabled via the inline-commands option

provider option

This is the "specify the pkcs #11 provider library" option. This option takes a file argument. This will override the default options in /etc/gnutls/pkcs11.conf

gnutls-cli exit status

One of the following exit values will be returned:

- 0 (EXIT_SUCCESS) Successful program execution.

- 1 (EXIT_FAILURE) The operation failed or the command syntax was not valid.

gnutls-cli See Also

gnutls-cli-debug(1), gnutls-serv(1)

gnutls-cli Examples

Connecting using PSK authentication

To connect to a server using PSK authentication, you need to enable the choice of PSK by using a cipher priority parameter such as in the example below.

```
$ ./gnutls-cli -p 5556 localhost --pskusername psk_identity \
    --pskkey 88f3824b3e5659f52d00e959bacab954b6540344 \
    --priority NORMAL:-KX-ALL:+ECDHE-PSK:+DHE-PSK:+PSK
Resolving 'localhost'...
Connecting to '127.0.0.1:5556'...
- PSK authentication.
- Version: TLS1.1
- Key Exchange: PSK
- Cipher: AES-128-CBC
- MAC: SHA1
- Compression: NULL
- Handshake was completed

- Simple Client Mode:
```

By keeping the –pskusername parameter and removing the –pskkey parameter, it will query only for the password during the handshake.

Listing ciphersuites in a priority string

To list the ciphersuites in a priority string:

```
$ ./gnutls-cli --priority SECURE192 -l
Cipher suites for SECURE192
TLS_ECDHE_ECDSA_AES_256_CBC_SHA384        0xc0, 0x24      TLS1.2
TLS_ECDHE_ECDSA_AES_256_GCM_SHA384        0xc0, 0x2e      TLS1.2
TLS_ECDHE_RSA_AES_256_GCM_SHA384          0xc0, 0x30      TLS1.2
TLS_DHE_RSA_AES_256_CBC_SHA256            0x00, 0x6b      TLS1.2
TLS_DHE_DSS_AES_256_CBC_SHA256            0x00, 0x6a      TLS1.2
TLS_RSA_AES_256_CBC_SHA256                0x00, 0x3d      TLS1.2

Certificate types: CTYPE-X.509
Protocols: VERS-TLS1.2, VERS-TLS1.1, VERS-TLS1.0, VERS-SSL3.0, VERS-DTLS1.0
Compression: COMP-NULL
Elliptic curves: CURVE-SECP384R1, CURVE-SECP521R1
PK-signatures: SIGN-RSA-SHA384, SIGN-ECDSA-SHA384, SIGN-RSA-SHA512, SIGN-ECDSA-SHA512
```

Connecting using a PKCS #11 token

To connect to a server using a certificate and a private key present in a PKCS #11 token you need to substitute the PKCS 11 URLs in the x509certfile and x509keyfile parameters.

Those can be found using "p11tool –list-tokens" and then listing all the objects in the needed token, and using the appropriate.

```
1   $ p11tool --list-tokens
2
3   Token 0:
4   URL: pkcs11:model=PKCS15;manufacturer=MyMan;serial=1234;token=Test
5   Label: Test
6   Manufacturer: EnterSafe
7   Model: PKCS15
8   Serial: 1234
9
10  $ p11tool --login --list-certs "pkcs11:model=PKCS15;manufacturer=MyMan;serial=1234;token=Test"
11
12  Object 0:
13  URL: pkcs11:model=PKCS15;manufacturer=MyMan;serial=1234;token=Test;object=client;type=cert
14  Type: X.509 Certificate
15  Label: client
16  ID: 2a:97:0d:58:d1:51:3c:23:07:ae:4e:0d:72:26:03:7d:99:06:02:6a
17
18  $ MYCERT="pkcs11:model=PKCS15;manufacturer=MyMan;serial=1234;token=Test;object=client;type=cert"
19  $ MYKEY="pkcs11:model=PKCS15;manufacturer=MyMan;serial=1234;token=Test;object=client;type=private"
20  $ export MYCERT MYKEY
21
22  $ gnutls-cli www.example.com --x509keyfile $MYKEY --x509certfile $MYCERT
```

Notice that the private key only differs from the certificate in the type.

7.2. Invoking gnutls-serv

Server program that listens to incoming TLS connections.

This section was generated by **AutoGen**, using the `agtexi-cmd` template and the option descriptions for the `gnutls-serv` program. This software is released under the GNU General Public License, version 3 or later.

gnutls-serv help/usage ("`--help`")

This is the automatically generated usage text for gnutls-serv.

The text printed is the same whether selected with the `help` option ("`--help`") or the `more-help` option ("`--more-help`"). `more-help` will print the usage text by passing it through a pager program. `more-help` is disabled on platforms without a working `fork(2)` function. The `PAGER` environment variable is used to select the program, defaulting to "`more`". Both will exit with a status code of 0.

```
1   gnutls-serv - GnuTLS server
2   Usage:  gnutls-serv [ -<flag> [<val>] | --<name>[{=| }<val>] ]...
3
4     -d, --debug=num            Enable debugging
5                                   - it must be in the range:
```

```
 6                                     0 to 9999
 7         --noticket             Don't accept session tickets
 8    -g, --generate              Generate Diffie-Hellman and RSA-export parameters
 9    -q, --quiet                 Suppress some messages
10         --nodb                 Do not use a resumption database
11         --http                 Act as an HTTP server
12         --echo                 Act as an Echo server
13    -u, --udp                   Use DTLS (datagram TLS) over UDP
14         --mtu=num              Set MTU for datagram TLS
15                                    - it must be in the range:
16                                     0 to 17000
17         --srtp-profiles=str    Offer SRTP profiles
18    -a, --disable-client-cert   Do not request a client certificate
19    -r, --require-client-cert   Require a client certificate
20         --verify-client-cert   If a client certificate is sent then verify it.
21    -b, --heartbeat             Activate heartbeat support
22         --x509fmtder           Use DER format for certificates to read from
23         --priority=str         Priorities string
24         --dhparams=file        DH params file to use
25                                    - file must pre-exist
26         --x509cafile=str       Certificate file or PKCS #11 URL to use
27         --x509crlfile=file     CRL file to use
28                                    - file must pre-exist
29         --pgpkeyfile=file      PGP Key file to use
30                                    - file must pre-exist
31         --pgpkeyring=file      PGP Key ring file to use
32                                    - file must pre-exist
33         --pgpcertfile=file     PGP Public Key (certificate) file to use
34                                    - file must pre-exist
35         --x509keyfile=str      X.509 key file or PKCS #11 URL to use
36         --x509certfile=str     X.509 Certificate file or PKCS #11 URL to use
37         --x509dsakeyfile=str   Alternative X.509 key file or PKCS #11 URL to use
38         --x509dsacertfile=str  Alternative X.509 Certificate file or PKCS #11 URL to use
39         --x509ecckeyfile=str   Alternative X.509 key file or PKCS #11 URL to use
40         --x509ecccertfile=str  Alternative X.509 Certificate file or PKCS #11 URL to use
41         --pgpsubkey=str        PGP subkey to use (hex or auto)
42         --srppasswd=file       SRP password file to use
43                                    - file must pre-exist
44         --srppasswdconf=file   SRP password configuration file to use
45                                    - file must pre-exist
46         --pskpasswd=file       PSK password file to use
47                                    - file must pre-exist
48         --pskhint=str          PSK identity hint to use
49         --ocsp-response=file   The OCSP response to send to client
50                                    - file must pre-exist
51    -p, --port=num              The port to connect to
52    -l, --list                  Print a list of the supported algorithms and modes
53         --provider=file        Specify the PKCS #11 provider library
54                                    - file must pre-exist
55    -v, --version[=arg]         output version information and exit
56    -h, --help                  display extended usage information and exit
57    -!, --more-help             extended usage information passed thru pager
58
59 Options are specified by doubled hyphens and their name or by a single
60 hyphen and the flag character.
61
62 Server program that listens to incoming TLS connections.
```

63

debug option (-d)

This is the "enable debugging" option. This option takes a number argument. Specifies the debug level.

verify-client-cert option

This is the "if a client certificate is sent then verify it." option. Do not require, but if a client certificate is sent then verify it and close the connection if invalid.

heartbeat option (-b)

This is the "activate heartbeat support" option. Regularly ping client via heartbeat extension messages

priority option

This is the "priorities string" option. This option takes a string argument. TLS algorithms and protocols to enable. You can use predefined sets of ciphersuites such as PERFORMANCE, NORMAL, SECURE128, SECURE256. The default is NORMAL.

Check the GnuTLS manual on section "Priority strings" for more information on allowed keywords

ocsp-response option

This is the "the ocsp response to send to client" option. This option takes a file argument. If the client requested an OCSP response, return data from this file to the client.

list option (-l)

This is the "print a list of the supported algorithms and modes" option. Print a list of the supported algorithms and modes. If a priority string is given then only the enabled ciphersuites are shown.

provider option

This is the "specify the pkcs #11 provider library" option. This option takes a file argument. This will override the default options in /etc/gnutls/pkcs11.conf

gnutls-serv exit status

One of the following exit values will be returned:

- 0 (EXIT_SUCCESS) Successful program execution.

- 1 (EXIT_FAILURE) The operation failed or the command syntax was not valid.

gnutls-serv See Also

gnutls-cli-debug(1), gnutls-cli(1)

gnutls-serv Examples

Running your own TLS server based on GnuTLS can be useful when debugging clients and/or GnuTLS itself. This section describes how to use **gnutls-serv** as a simple HTTPS server.

The most basic server can be started as:

```
1  gnutls-serv --http --priority "NORMAL:+ANON-ECDH:+ANON-DH"
```

It will only support anonymous ciphersuites, which many TLS clients refuse to use.

The next step is to add support for X.509. First we generate a CA:

```
1  $ certtool --generate-privkey > x509-ca-key.pem
2  $ echo 'cn = GnuTLS test CA' > ca.tmpl
3  $ echo 'ca' >> ca.tmpl
4  $ echo 'cert_signing_key' >> ca.tmpl
5  $ certtool --generate-self-signed --load-privkey x509-ca-key.pem \
6    --template ca.tmpl --outfile x509-ca.pem
7  ...
```

Then generate a server certificate. Remember to change the dns_name value to the name of your server host, or skip that command to avoid the field.

```
1  $ certtool --generate-privkey > x509-server-key.pem
2  $ echo 'organization = GnuTLS test server' > server.tmpl
3  $ echo 'cn = test.gnutls.org' >> server.tmpl
4  $ echo 'tls_www_server' >> server.tmpl
5  $ echo 'encryption_key' >> server.tmpl
6  $ echo 'signing_key' >> server.tmpl
7  $ echo 'dns_name = test.gnutls.org' >> server.tmpl
8  $ certtool --generate-certificate --load-privkey x509-server-key.pem \
9    --load-ca-certificate x509-ca.pem --load-ca-privkey x509-ca-key.pem \
```

```
10    --template server.tmpl --outfile x509-server.pem
11 ...
```

For use in the client, you may want to generate a client certificate as well.

```
1 $ certtool --generate-privkey > x509-client-key.pem
2 $ echo 'cn = GnuTLS test client' > client.tmpl
3 $ echo 'tls_www_client' >> client.tmpl
4 $ echo 'encryption_key' >> client.tmpl
5 $ echo 'signing_key' >> client.tmpl
6 $ certtool --generate-certificate --load-privkey x509-client-key.pem \
7    --load-ca-certificate x509-ca.pem --load-ca-privkey x509-ca-key.pem \
8    --template client.tmpl --outfile x509-client.pem
9 ...
```

To be able to import the client key/certificate into some applications, you will need to convert them into a PKCS#12 structure. This also encrypts the security sensitive key with a password.

```
1 $ certtool --to-p12 --load-ca-certificate x509-ca.pem \
2    --load-privkey x509-client-key.pem --load-certificate x509-client.pem \
3    --outder --outfile x509-client.p12
```

For icing, we'll create a proxy certificate for the client too.

```
1 $ certtool --generate-privkey > x509-proxy-key.pem
2 $ echo 'cn = GnuTLS test client proxy' > proxy.tmpl
3 $ certtool --generate-proxy --load-privkey x509-proxy-key.pem \
4    --load-ca-certificate x509-client.pem --load-ca-privkey x509-client-key.pem \
5    --load-certificate x509-client.pem --template proxy.tmpl \
6    --outfile x509-proxy.pem
7 ...
```

Then start the server again:

```
1 $ gnutls-serv --http \
2           --x509cafile x509-ca.pem \
3           --x509keyfile x509-server-key.pem \
4           --x509certfile x509-server.pem
```

Try connecting to the server using your web browser. Note that the server listens to port 5556 by default.

While you are at it, to allow connections using DSA, you can also create a DSA key and certificate for the server. These credentials will be used in the final example below.

```
1 $ certtool --generate-privkey --dsa > x509-server-key-dsa.pem
2 $ certtool --generate-certificate --load-privkey x509-server-key-dsa.pem \
3    --load-ca-certificate x509-ca.pem --load-ca-privkey x509-ca-key.pem \
4    --template server.tmpl --outfile x509-server-dsa.pem
5 ...
```

The next step is to create OpenPGP credentials for the server.

```
1  gpg --gen-key
2  ...enter whatever details you want, use 'test.gnutls.org' as name...
```

Make a note of the OpenPGP key identifier of the newly generated key, here it was 5D1D14D8. You will need to export the key for GnuTLS to be able to use it.

```
1  gpg -a --export 5D1D14D8 > openpgp-server.txt
2  gpg --export 5D1D14D8 > openpgp-server.bin
3  gpg --export-secret-keys 5D1D14D8 > openpgp-server-key.bin
4  gpg -a --export-secret-keys 5D1D14D8 > openpgp-server-key.txt
```

Let's start the server with support for OpenPGP credentials:

```
1  gnutls-serv --http --priority NORMAL:+CTYPE-OPENPGP \
2              --pgpkeyfile openpgp-server-key.txt \
3              --pgpcertfile openpgp-server.txt
```

The next step is to add support for SRP authentication. This requires an SRP password file created with srptool. To start the server with SRP support:

```
1  gnutls-serv --http --priority NORMAL:+SRP-RSA:+SRP \
2              --srppasswdconf srp-tpasswd.conf \
3              --srppasswd srp-passwd.txt
```

Let's also start a server with support for PSK. This would require a password file created with psktool.

```
1  gnutls-serv --http --priority NORMAL:+ECDHE-PSK:+PSK \
2              --pskpasswd psk-passwd.txt
```

Finally, we start the server with all the earlier parameters and you get this command:

```
1   gnutls-serv --http --priority NORMAL:+PSK:+SRP:+CTYPE-OPENPGP \
2               --x509cafile x509-ca.pem \
3               --x509keyfile x509-server-key.pem \
4               --x509certfile x509-server.pem \
5               --x509dsakeyfile x509-server-key-dsa.pem \
6               --x509dsacertfile x509-server-dsa.pem \
7               --pgpkeyfile openpgp-server-key.txt \
8               --pgpcertfile openpgp-server.txt \
9               --srppasswdconf srp-tpasswd.conf \
10              --srppasswd srp-passwd.txt \
11              --pskpasswd psk-passwd.txt
```

7.3. Invoking gnutls-cli-debug

TLS debug client. It sets up multiple TLS connections to a server and queries its capabilities. It was created to assist in debugging GnuTLS, but it might be useful to extract a TLS server's capabilities. It connects to a TLS server, performs tests and print the server's capabilities. If called with the '-v' parameter more checks will be performed. Can be used to check for servers with special needs or bugs.

This section was generated by **AutoGen**, using the `agtexi-cmd` template and the option descriptions for the `gnutls-cli-debug` program. This software is released under the GNU General Public License, version 3 or later.

gnutls-cli-debug help/usage ("`--help`")

This is the automatically generated usage text for gnutls-cli-debug.

The text printed is the same whether selected with the `help` option ("`--help`") or the `more-help` option ("`--more-help`"). `more-help` will print the usage text by passing it through a pager program. `more-help` is disabled on platforms without a working `fork(2)` function. The `PAGER` environment variable is used to select the program, defaulting to "`more`". Both will exit with a status code of 0.

```
1   gnutls-cli-debug - GnuTLS debug client
2   Usage:  gnutls-cli-debug [ -<flag> [<val>] | --<name>[{=| }<val>] ]...
3
4     -d, --debug=num            Enable debugging
5                                  - it must be in the range:
6                                    0 to 9999
7     -V, --verbose              More verbose output
8                                  - may appear multiple times
9     -p, --port=num             The port to connect to
10                                 - it must be in the range:
11                                   0 to 65536
12        --app-proto=str        an alias for the 'starttls-proto' option
13        --starttls-proto=str   The application protocol to be used to obtain the server's certificate
14    (https, ftp, smtp, imap, ldap, xmpp)
15    -v, --version[=arg]        output version information and exit
16    -h, --help                 display extended usage information and exit
17    -!, --more-help            extended usage information passed thru pager
18
19   Options are specified by doubled hyphens and their name or by a single
20   hyphen and the flag character.
21   Operands and options may be intermixed.  They will be reordered.
22
23   TLS debug client.  It sets up multiple TLS connections to a server and
24   queries its capabilities.  It was created to assist in debugging GnuTLS,
25   but it might be useful to extract a TLS server's capabilities.  It connects
26   to a TLS server, performs tests and print the server's capabilities.  If
27   called with the '-v' parameter more checks will be performed.  Can be used
28   to check for servers with special needs or bugs.
29
```

debug option (-d)

This is the "enable debugging" option. This option takes a number argument. Specifies the debug level.

app-proto option

This is an alias for the `starttls-proto` option, section 7.3.

starttls-proto option

This is the "the application protocol to be used to obtain the server's certificate (https, ftp, smtp, imap, ldap, xmpp)" option. This option takes a string argument. Specify the application layer protocol for STARTTLS. If the protocol is supported, gnutls-cli will proceed to the TLS negotiation.

gnutls-cli-debug exit status

One of the following exit values will be returned:

- 0 (EXIT_SUCCESS) Successful program execution.
- 1 (EXIT_FAILURE) The operation failed or the command syntax was not valid.

gnutls-cli-debug See Also

gnutls-cli(1), gnutls-serv(1)

gnutls-cli-debug Examples

```
1  $ ../src/gnutls-cli-debug localhost
2  GnuTLS debug client 3.5.0
3  Checking localhost:443
4                         for SSL 3.0 (RFC6101) support... yes
5             whether we need to disable TLS 1.2... no
6             whether we need to disable TLS 1.1... no
7             whether we need to disable TLS 1.0... no
8             whether %NO_EXTENSIONS is required... no
9                  whether %COMPAT is required... no
10                   for TLS 1.0 (RFC2246) support... yes
11                   for TLS 1.1 (RFC4346) support... yes
12                   for TLS 1.2 (RFC5246) support... yes
13                       fallback from TLS 1.6 to... TLS1.2
14             for RFC7507 inappropriate fallback... yes
15                       for HTTPS server name... Local
16                  for certificate chain order... sorted
17         for safe renegotiation (RFC5746) support... yes
18          for Safe renegotiation support (SCSV)... no
19          for encrypt-then-MAC (RFC7366) support... no
20          for ext master secret (RFC7627) support... no
21                  for heartbeat (RFC6520) support... no
22             for version rollback bug in RSA PMS... dunno
23          for version rollback bug in Client Hello... no
```

```
24  │         whether the server ignores the RSA PMS version... yes
25  │ whether small records (512 bytes) are tolerated on handshake... yes
26  │     whether cipher suites not in SSL 3.0 spec are accepted... yes
27  │ whether a bogus TLS record version in the client hello is accepted... yes
28  │          whether the server understands TLS closure alerts... partially
29  │          whether the server supports session resumption... yes
30  │                  for anonymous authentication support... no
31  │                   for ephemeral Diffie-Hellman support... no
32  │                for ephemeral EC Diffie-Hellman support... yes
33  │               ephemeral EC Diffie-Hellman group info... SECP256R1
34  │          for AES-128-GCM cipher (RFC5288) support... yes
35  │          for AES-128-CCM cipher (RFC6655) support... no
36  │        for AES-128-CCM-8 cipher (RFC6655) support... no
37  │          for AES-128-CBC cipher (RFC3268) support... yes
38  │     for CAMELLIA-128-GCM cipher (RFC6367) support... no
39  │     for CAMELLIA-128-CBC cipher (RFC5932) support... no
40  │             for 3DES-CBC cipher (RFC2246) support... yes
41  │          for ARCFOUR 128 cipher (RFC2246) support... yes
42  │                            for MD5 MAC support... yes
43  │                           for SHA1 MAC support... yes
44  │                         for SHA256 MAC support... yes
45  │                  for ZLIB compression support... no
46  │           for max record size (RFC6066) support... no
47  │        for OCSP status response (RFC6066) support... no
48  │      for OpenPGP authentication (RFC6091) support... no
```

Internal Architecture of GnuTLS

This chapter is to give a brief description of the way GnuTLS works. The focus is to give an idea to potential developers and those who want to know what happens inside the black box.

8.1. The TLS Protocol

The main use case for the TLS protocol is shown in Figure 8.1. A user of a library implementing the protocol expects no less than this functionality, i.e., to be able to set parameters such as the accepted security level, perform a negotiation with the peer and be able to exchange data.

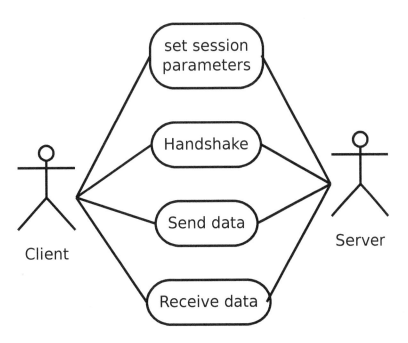

Figure 8.1.: TLS protocol use case.

8.2. TLS Handshake Protocol

The GnuTLS handshake protocol is implemented as a state machine that waits for input or returns immediately when the non-blocking transport layer functions are used. The main idea is shown in Figure 8.2.

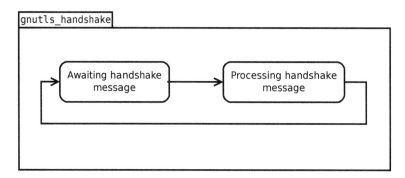

Figure 8.2.: GnuTLS handshake state machine.

Also the way the input is processed varies per ciphersuite. Several implementations of the internal handlers are available and **gnutls_handshake** only multiplexes the input to the appropriate handler. For example a PSK ciphersuite has a different implementation of the **process_client_key_exchange** than a certificate ciphersuite. We illustrate the idea in Figure 8.3.

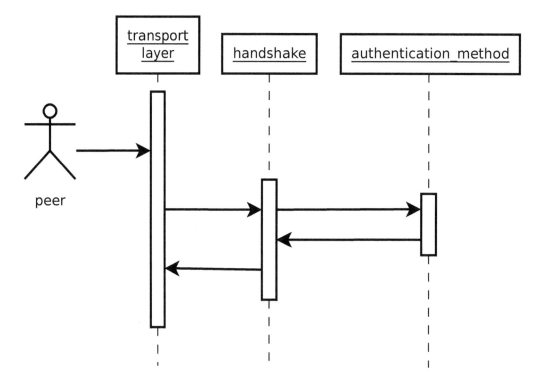

Figure 8.3.: GnuTLS handshake process sequence.

8.3. TLS Authentication Methods

In GnuTLS authentication methods can be implemented quite easily. Since the required changes to add a new authentication method affect only the handshake protocol, a simple interface is used. An authentication method needs to implement the functions shown below.

```
typedef struct
{
  const char *name;
  int (*gnutls_generate_server_certificate) (gnutls_session_t, gnutls_buffer_st*);
  int (*gnutls_generate_client_certificate) (gnutls_session_t, gnutls_buffer_st*);
  int (*gnutls_generate_server_kx) (gnutls_session_t, gnutls_buffer_st*);
  int (*gnutls_generate_client_kx) (gnutls_session_t, gnutls_buffer_st*);
  int (*gnutls_generate_client_cert_vrfy) (gnutls_session_t, gnutls_buffer_st *);
  int (*gnutls_generate_server_certificate_request) (gnutls_session_t,
                                             gnutls_buffer_st *);

  int (*gnutls_process_server_certificate) (gnutls_session_t, opaque *,
                                      size_t);
  int (*gnutls_process_client_certificate) (gnutls_session_t, opaque *,
                                      size_t);
  int (*gnutls_process_server_kx) (gnutls_session_t, opaque *, size_t);
  int (*gnutls_process_client_kx) (gnutls_session_t, opaque *, size_t);
  int (*gnutls_process_client_cert_vrfy) (gnutls_session_t, opaque *, size_t);
  int (*gnutls_process_server_certificate_request) (gnutls_session_t,
                                             opaque *, size_t);
} mod_auth_st;
```

Those functions are responsible for the interpretation of the handshake protocol messages. It is common for such functions to read data from one or more `credentials_t` structures[1] and write data, such as certificates, usernames etc. to `auth_info_t` structures.

Simple examples of existing authentication methods can be seen in `auth/psk.c` for PSK ciphersuites and `auth/srp.c` for SRP ciphersuites. After implementing these functions the structure holding its pointers has to be registered in `gnutls_algorithms.c` in the `_gnutls_kx_algorithms` structure.

8.4. TLS Extension Handling

As with authentication methods, the TLS extensions handlers can be implemented using the interface shown below.

```
typedef int (*gnutls_ext_recv_func) (gnutls_session_t session,
                                const unsigned char *data, size_t len);
typedef int (*gnutls_ext_send_func) (gnutls_session_t session,
```

---

[1]such as the `gnutls_certificate_credentials_t` structures

```
gnutls_buffer_st *extdata);
```

Here there are two functions, one for receiving the extension data and one for sending. These functions have to check internally whether they operate in client or server side.

A simple example of an extension handler can be seen in **ext/srp.c** in GnuTLS' source code. After implementing these functions, together with the extension number they handle, they have to be registered using **_gnutls_ext_register** in **gnutls_extensions.c** typically within **_gnutls_ext_init**.

Adding a new TLS extension

Adding support for a new TLS extension is done from time to time, and the process to do so is not difficult. Here are the steps you need to follow if you wish to do this yourself. For sake of discussion, let's consider adding support for the hypothetical TLS extension **foobar**. The following section is about adding an extension to GnuTLS, for custom application extensions you should check the exported function **gnutls_ext_register**.

Add configure **option like** --enable-foobar **or** --disable-foobar.

This step is useful when the extension code is large and it might be desirable to disable the extension under some circumstances. Otherwise it can be safely skipped.

Whether to chose enable or disable depends on whether you intend to make the extension be enabled by default. Look at existing checks (i.e., SRP, authz) for how to model the code. For example:

```
1   AC_MSG_CHECKING([whether to disable foobar support])
2   AC_ARG_ENABLE(foobar,
3           AS_HELP_STRING([--disable-foobar],
4               [disable foobar support]),
5           ac_enable_foobar=no)
6   if test x$ac_enable_foobar != xno; then
7    AC_MSG_RESULT(no)
8    AC_DEFINE(ENABLE_FOOBAR, 1, [enable foobar])
9   else
10   ac_full=0
11   AC_MSG_RESULT(yes)
12  fi
13  AM_CONDITIONAL(ENABLE_FOOBAR, test "$ac_enable_foobar" != "no")
```

These lines should go in **m4/hooks.m4**.

Add IANA extension value to extensions_t **in** gnutls_int.h.

A good name for the value would be GNUTLS_EXTENSION_FOOBAR. Check with http://www.iana.org/assignments/tls-extensiontype-values for allocated values. For experiments, you could pick a number but remember that some consider it a bad idea to deploy such modified version since it will lead to interoperability problems in the future when the IANA allocates that number to someone else, or when the foobar protocol is allocated another number.

Add an entry to _gnutls_extensions **in** gnutls_extensions.c.

A typical entry would be:

```
1   int ret;
2
3 #if ENABLE_FOOBAR
4   ret = _gnutls_ext_register (&foobar_ext);
5   if (ret != GNUTLS_E_SUCCESS)
6     return ret;
7 #endif
```

Most likely you'll need to add an #include "ext/foobar.h", that will contain something like like:

```
1    extension_entry_st foobar_ext = {
2      .name = "FOOBAR",
3      .type = GNUTLS_EXTENSION_FOOBAR,
4      .parse_type = GNUTLS_EXT_TLS,
5      .recv_func = _foobar_recv_params,
6      .send_func = _foobar_send_params,
7      .pack_func = _foobar_pack,
8      .unpack_func = _foobar_unpack,
9      .deinit_func = NULL
10   }
```

The GNUTLS_EXTENSION_FOOBAR is the integer value you added to gnutls_int.h earlier. In this structure you specify the functions to read the extension from the hello message, the function to send the reply to, and two more functions to pack and unpack from stored session data (e.g. when resumming a session). The deinit function will be called to deinitialize the extension's private parameters, if any.

Note that the conditional ENABLE_FOOBAR definition should only be used if step 1 with the configure options has taken place.

Add new files that implement the extension.

The functions you are responsible to add are those mentioned in the previous step. They should be added in a file such as ext/foobar.c and headers should be placed in ext/foobar.h. As a starter, you could add this:

```
1 int
2 _foobar_recv_params (gnutls_session_t session, const opaque * data,
3                      size_t data_size)
4 {
5   return 0;
6 }
```

```
 7
 8 int
 9 _foobar_send_params (gnutls_session_t session, gnutls_buffer_st* data)
10 {
11   return 0;
12 }
13
14 int
15 _foobar_pack (extension_priv_data_t epriv, gnutls_buffer_st * ps)
16 {
17   /* Append the extension's internal state to buffer */
18   return 0;
19 }
20
21 int
22 _foobar_unpack (gnutls_buffer_st * ps, extension_priv_data_t * epriv)
23 {
24   /* Read the internal state from buffer */
25   return 0;
26 }
```

The _foobar_recv_params function is responsible for parsing incoming extension data (both in the client and server).

The _foobar_send_params function is responsible for sending extension data (both in the client and server).

If you receive length fields that don't match, return GNUTLS_E_UNEXPECTED_PACKET_LENGTH. If you receive invalid data, return GNUTLS_E_RECEIVED_ILLEGAL_PARAMETER. You can use other error codes from the list in Appendix D. Return 0 on success.

An extension typically stores private information in the **session** data for later usage. That can be done using the functions _gnutls_ext_set_session_data and _gnutls_ext_get_session_-data. You can check simple examples at ext/max_record.c and ext/server_name.c extensions. That private information can be saved and restored across session resumption if the following functions are set:

The _foobar_pack function is responsible for packing internal extension data to save them in the session resumption storage.

The _foobar_unpack function is responsible for restoring session data from the session resumption storage.

Recall that both the client and server, send and receive parameters, and your code most likely will need to do different things depending on which mode it is in. It may be useful to make this distinction explicit in the code. Thus, for example, a better template than above would be:

```
1 int
2 _gnutls_foobar_recv_params (gnutls_session_t session,
3                             const opaque * data,
4                             size_t data_size)
5 {
6   if (session->security_parameters.entity == GNUTLS_CLIENT)
7     return foobar_recv_client (session, data, data_size);
```

```
 8    else
 9      return foobar_recv_server (session, data, data_size);
10  }
11
12  int
13  _gnutls_foobar_send_params (gnutls_session_t session,
14                              gnutls_buffer_st * data)
15  {
16    if (session->security_parameters.entity == GNUTLS_CLIENT)
17      return foobar_send_client (session, data);
18    else
19      return foobar_send_server (session, data);
20  }
```

The functions used would be declared as **static** functions, of the appropriate prototype, in the same file. When adding the files, you'll need to add them to **ext/Makefile.am** as well, for example:

```
1  if ENABLE_FOOBAR
2  libgnutls_ext_la_SOURCES += ext/foobar.c ext/foobar.h
3  endif
```

Add API functions to enable/disable the extension.

It might be desirable to allow users of the extension to request use of the extension, or set extension specific data. This can be implemented by adding extension specific function calls that can be added to **includes/gnutls/gnutls.h**, as long as the LGPLv2.1+ applies. The implementation of the function should lie in the **ext/foobar.c** file.

To make the API available in the shared library you need to add the symbol in **lib/-libgnutls.map**, so that the symbol is exported properly.

When writing GTK-DOC style documentation for your new APIs, don't forget to add **Since:** tags to indicate the GnuTLS version the API was introduced in.

Heartbeat extension.

One such extension is HeartBeat protocol (RFC6520: `https://tools.ietf.org/html/rfc6520`) implementation. To enable it use option –heartbeat with example client and server supplied with gnutls:

```
1  ./doc/credentials/gnutls-http-serv --priority "NORMAL:-CIPHER-ALL:+NULL" -d 100 \
2      --heartbeat --echo
3  ./src/gnutls-cli --priority "NORMAL:-CIPHER-ALL:+NULL" -d 100 localhost -p 5556 \
4      --insecure --heartbeat
```

After that pasting

```
1  **HEARTBEAT**
```

command into gnutls-cli will trigger corresponding command on the server and it will send HeartBeat Request with random length to client.

Another way is to run capabilities check with:

```
1  ./doc/credentials/gnutls-http-serv -d 100 --heartbeat
2  ./src/gnutls-cli-debug localhost -p 5556
```

Adding a new Supplemental Data Handshake Message

TLS handshake extensions allow to send so called supplemental data handshake messages [34]. This short section explains how to implement a supplemental data handshake message for a given TLS extension.

First of all, modify your extension foobar in the way, to instruct the handshake process to send and receive supplemental data, as shown below.

```
1  int
2  _gnutls_foobar_recv_params (gnutls_session_t session, const opaque * data,
3                              size_t _data_size)
4  {
5    ...
6    gnutls_supplemental_recv(session, 1);
7    ...
8  }
9
10 int
11 _gnutls_foobar_send_params (gnutls_session_t session, gnutls_buffer_st *extdata)
12 {
13   ...
14   gnutls_supplemental_send(session, 1);
15   ...
16 }
```

Furthermore you'll need two new functions _foobar_supp_recv_params and _foobar_supp_-send_params, which must conform to the following prototypes.

```
1  typedef int (*gnutls_supp_recv_func)(gnutls_session_t session,
2                                       const unsigned char *data,
3                                       size_t data_size);
4  typedef int (*gnutls_supp_send_func)(gnutls_session_t session,
5                                       gnutls_buffer_t buf);
```

The following example code shows how to send a "Hello World" string in the supplemental data handshake message.

```
1  int
2  _foobar_supp_recv_params(gnutls_session_t session, const opaque *data, size_t _data_size)
3  {
4    uint8_t len = _data_size;
5    unsigned char *msg;
6
7    msg = gnutls_malloc(len);
```

270

```
 8     if (msg == NULL) return GNUTLS_E_MEMORY_ERROR;
 9
10     memcpy(msg, data, len);
11     msg[len]='\0';
12
13     /* do something with msg */
14     gnutls_free(msg);
15
16     return len;
17 }
18
19 int
20 _foobar_supp_send_params(gnutls_session_t session, gnutls_buffer_t buf)
21 {
22     unsigned char *msg = "hello world";
23     int len = strlen(msg);
24
25     if (gnutls_buffer_append_data(buf, msg, len) < 0)
26         abort();
27
28     return len;
29 }
```

Afterwards, register the new supplemental data using `gnutls_supplemental_register`, at some point in your program.

8.5. Cryptographic Backend

Today most new processors, either for embedded or desktop systems include either instructions intended to speed up cryptographic operations, or a co-processor with cryptographic capabilities. Taking advantage of those is a challenging task for every cryptographic application or library. GnuTLS handles the cryptographic provider in a modular way, following a layered approach to access cryptographic operations as in Figure 8.4.

The TLS layer uses a cryptographic provider layer, that will in turn either use the default crypto provider – a software crypto library, or use an external crypto provider, if available in the local system. The reason of handling the external cryptographic provider in GnuTLS and not delegating it to the cryptographic libraries, is that none of the supported cryptographic libraries support `/dev/crypto` or CPU-optimized cryptography in an efficient way.

Cryptographic library layer

The Cryptographic library layer, currently supports only libnettle. Older versions of GnuTLS used to support libgcrypt, but it was switched with nettle mainly for performance reasons[2] and secondary because it is a simpler library to use. In the future other cryptographic libraries might be supported as well.

---

[2]See http://lists.gnu.org/archive/html/gnutls-devel/2011-02/msg00079.html.

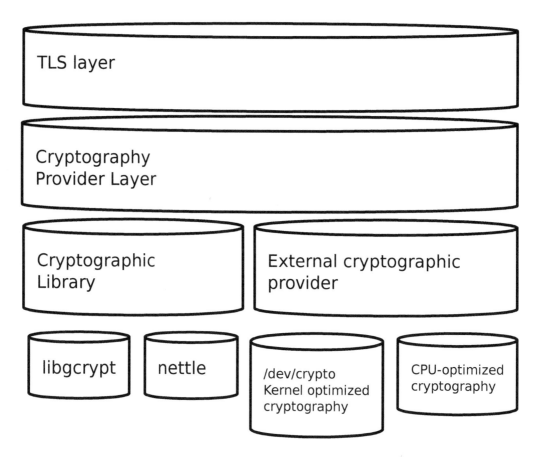

Figure 8.4.: GnuTLS cryptographic back-end design.

External cryptography provider

Systems that include a cryptographic co-processor, typically come with kernel drivers to utilize the operations from software. For this reason GnuTLS provides a layer where each individual algorithm used can be replaced by another implementation, i.e., the one provided by the driver. The FreeBSD, OpenBSD and Linux kernels[3] include already a number of hardware assisted implementations, and also provide an interface to access them, called /dev/crypto. GnuTLS will take advantage of this interface if compiled with special options. That is because in most systems where hardware-assisted cryptographic operations are not available, using this interface might actually harm performance.

In systems that include cryptographic instructions with the CPU's instructions set, using the kernel interface will introduce an unneeded layer. For this reason GnuTLS includes such optimizations found in popular processors such as the AES-NI or VIA PADLOCK instruction sets. This is achieved using a mechanism that detects CPU capabilities and overrides parts of crypto back-end at runtime. The next section discusses the registration of a detected algorithm optimization. For more information please consult the GnuTLS source code in lib/accelerated/.

---

[3]Check http://home.gna.org/cryptodev-linux/ for the Linux kernel implementation of /dev/crypto.

Overriding specific algorithms

When an optimized implementation of a single algorithm is available, say a hardware assisted version of AES-CBC then the following functions, from `crypto.h`, can be used to register those algorithms.

- `gnutls_crypto_register_cipher`: To register a cipher algorithm.

- `gnutls_crypto_register_aead_cipher`: To register an AEAD cipher algorithm.

- `gnutls_crypto_register_mac`: To register a MAC algorithm.

- `gnutls_crypto_register_digest`: To register a hash algorithm.

Those registration functions will only replace the specified algorithm and leave the rest of subsystem intact.

Upgrading from previous versions

The GnuTLS library typically maintains binary and source code compatibility across versions. The releases that have the major version increased break binary compatibility but source compatibility is provided. This section lists exceptional cases where changes to existing code are required due to library changes.

Upgrading to 2.12.x from previous versions

GnuTLS 2.12.x is binary compatible with previous versions but changes the semantics of `gnutls_transport_set_lowat`, which might cause breakage in applications that relied on its default value be 1. Two fixes are proposed:

- Quick fix. Explicitly call `gnutls_transport_set_lowat (session, 1);` after `gnutls_-init`.

- Long term fix. Because later versions of gnutls abolish the functionality of using the system call `select` to check for gnutls pending data, the function `gnutls_record_check_-pending` has to be used to achieve the same functionality as described in subsection 5.5.1.

Upgrading to 3.0.x from 2.12.x

GnuTLS 3.0.x is source compatible with previous versions except for the functions listed below.

Old function	Replacement
gnutls_transport_set_lowat	To replace its functionality the function gnutls_record_check_pending has to be used, as described in subsection 5.5.1
gnutls_session_get_server_random, gnutls_session_get_client_random	They are replaced by the safer function gnutls_session_get_random
gnutls_session_get_master_secret	Replaced by the keying material exporters discussed in subsection 5.12.5
gnutls_transport_set_global_errno	Replaced by using the system's errno facility or gnutls_transport_set_errno.
gnutls_x509_privkey_verify_data	Replaced by gnutls_pubkey_verify_data2.
gnutls_certificate_verify_peers	Replaced by gnutls_certificate_verify_peers2.
gnutls_psk_netconf_derive_key	Removed. The key derivation function was never standardized.
gnutls_session_set_finished_function	Removed.
gnutls_ext_register	Removed. Extension registration API is now internal to allow easier changes in the API.
gnutls_certificate_get_x509_crls, gnutls_certificate_get_x509_cas	Removed to allow updating the internal structures. Replaced by gnutls_certificate_get_issuer.
gnutls_certificate_get_openpgp_keyring	Removed.
gnutls_ia_	Removed. The inner application extensions were completely removed (they failed to be standardized).

Upgrading to 3.1.x from 3.0.x

GnuTLS 3.1.x is source and binary compatible with GnuTLS 3.0.x releases. Few functions have been deprecated and are listed below.

Old function	Replacement
gnutls_pubkey_verify_hash	The function gnutls_pubkey_verify_hash2 is provided and is functionally equivalent and safer to use.
gnutls_pubkey_verify_data	The function gnutls_pubkey_verify_data2 is provided and is functionally equivalent and safer to use.

Upgrading to 3.2.x from 3.1.x

GnuTLS 3.2.x is source and binary compatible with GnuTLS 3.1.x releases. Few functions have been deprecated and are listed below.

Old function	Replacement
gnutls_privkey_sign_-raw_data	The function gnutls_privkey_sign_hash is equivalent when the flag GNUTLS_PRIVKEY_SIGN_FLAG_TLS1_RSA is specified.

Upgrading to 3.3.x from 3.2.x

GnuTLS 3.3.x is source and binary compatible with GnuTLS 3.2.x releases; however there few changes in semantics which are listed below.

Old function	Replacement
gnutls_global_init	No longer required. The library is initialized using a constructor.
gnutls_global_deinit	No longer required. The library is deinitialized using a destructor.

Upgrading to 3.4.x from 3.3.x

GnuTLS 3.4.x is source compatible with GnuTLS 3.3.x releases; however, several deprecated functions were removed, and are listed below.

Old function	Replacement
Priority string "NORMAL" has been modified	The following string emulates the 3.3.x behavior "NORMAL:+VERS-SSL3.0:+ARCFOUR-128:+DHE-DSS:+SIGN-DSA-SHA512:+SIGN-DSA-SHA256:+SIGN-DSA-SHA1"
`gnutls_certificate_client_set_retrieve_function`, `gnutls_certificate_server_set_retrieve_function`	`gnutls_certificate_set_retrieve_function`
`gnutls_certificate_set_rsa_export_params`, `gnutls_rsa_export_get_modulus_bits`, `gnutls_rsa_export_get_pubkey`, `gnutls_rsa_params_cpy`, `gnutls_rsa_params_deinit`, `gnutls_rsa_params_export_pkcs1`, `gnutls_rsa_params_export_raw`, `gnutls_rsa_params_generate2`, `gnutls_rsa_params_import_pkcs1`, `gnutls_rsa_params_import_raw`, `gnutls_rsa_params_init`	No replacement; the library does not support the RSA-EXPORT ciphersuites.
`gnutls_pubkey_verify_hash`,	`gnutls_pubkey_verify_hash2`.
`gnutls_pubkey_verify_data`,	`gnutls_pubkey_verify_data2`.
`gnutls_x509_crt_get_verify_algorithm`,	No replacement; a similar function is `gnutls_x509_crt_get_signature_algorithm`.
`gnutls_pubkey_get_verify_algorithm`,	No replacement; a similar function is `gnutls_pubkey_get_preferred_hash_algorithm`.
`gnutls_certificate_type_set_priority`, `gnutls_cipher_set_priority`, `gnutls_compression_set_priority`, `gnutls_kx_set_priority`, `gnutls_mac_set_priority`, `gnutls_protocol_set_priority`	`gnutls_priority_set_direct`.
`gnutls_sign_callback_get`, `gnutls_sign_callback_set`	`gnutls_privkey_import_ext3`
`gnutls_x509_crt_verify_hash`	`gnutls_pubkey_verify_hash2`
`gnutls_x509_crt_verify_data`	`gnutls_pubkey_verify_data2`
`gnutls_privkey_sign_raw_data`	`gnutls_privkey_sign_hash` with the flag GNUTLS_PRIVKEY_SIGN_FLAG_TLS1_RSA

B

Support

B.1. Getting Help

A mailing list where users may help each other exists, and you can reach it by sending e-mail to gnutls-help@gnutls.org. Archives of the mailing list discussions, and an interface to manage subscriptions, is available through the World Wide Web at `http://lists.gnutls.org/pipermail/gnutls-help/`.

A mailing list for developers are also available, see `http://www.gnutls.org/lists.html`. Bug reports should be sent to bugs@gnutls.org, see section B.3.

B.2. Commercial Support

Commercial support is available for users of GnuTLS. The kind of support that can be purchased may include:

- Implement new features. Such as a new TLS extension.

- Port GnuTLS to new platforms. This could include porting to an embedded platforms that may need memory or size optimization.

- Integrating TLS as a security environment in your existing project.

- System design of components related to TLS.

If you are interested, please write to:

```
Simon Josefsson Datakonsult
Hagagatan 24
113 47 Stockholm
Sweden

E-mail: simon@josefsson.org
```

If your company provides support related to GnuTLS and would like to be mentioned here, contact the authors.

B.3. Bug Reports

If you think you have found a bug in GnuTLS, please investigate it and report it.

- Please make sure that the bug is really in GnuTLS, and preferably also check that it hasn't already been fixed in the latest version.

- You have to send us a test case that makes it possible for us to reproduce the bug.

- You also have to explain what is wrong; if you get a crash, or if the results printed are not good and in that case, in what way. Make sure that the bug report includes all information you would need to fix this kind of bug for someone else.

Please make an effort to produce a self-contained report, with something definite that can be tested or debugged. Vague queries or piecemeal messages are difficult to act on and don't help the development effort.

If your bug report is good, we will do our best to help you to get a corrected version of the software; if the bug report is poor, we won't do anything about it (apart from asking you to send better bug reports).

If you think something in this manual is unclear, or downright incorrect, or if the language needs to be improved, please also send a note.

Send your bug report to:

bugs@gnutls.org

B.4. Contributing

If you want to submit a patch for inclusion – from solving a typo you discovered, up to adding support for a new feature – you should submit it as a bug report, using the process in section B.3. There are some things that you can do to increase the chances for it to be included in the official package.

Unless your patch is very small (say, under 10 lines) we require that you assign the copyright of your work to the Free Software Foundation. This is to protect the freedom of the project. If you have not already signed papers, we will send you the necessary information when you submit your contribution.

For contributions that doesn't consist of actual programming code, the only guidelines are common sense. For code contributions, a number of style guides will help you:

- Coding Style. Follow the GNU Standards document.

  If you normally code using another coding standard, there is no problem, but you should use indent to reformat the code before submitting your work.

- Use the unified diff format diff -u.

- Return errors. No reason whatsoever should abort the execution of the library. Even memory allocation errors, e.g. when malloc return NULL, should work although result in an error code.

- Design with thread safety in mind. Don't use global variables. Don't even write to per-handle global variables unless the documented behaviour of the function you write is to write to the per-handle global variable.

- Avoid using the C math library. It causes problems for embedded implementations, and in most situations it is very easy to avoid using it.

- Document your functions. Use comments before each function headers, that, if properly formatted, are extracted into Texinfo manuals and GTK-DOC web pages.

- Supply a ChangeLog and NEWS entries, where appropriate.

B.5. Certification

Many cryptographic libraries claim certifications from national or international bodies. These certifications are tied on a specific (and often restricted) version of the library or a specific product using the library, and typically in the case of software they assure that the algorithms implemented are correct. The major certifications known are:

- USA's FIPS 140-2 at Level 1 which certifies that approved algorithms are used (see http://en.wikipedia.org/wiki/FIPS_140-2);

- Common Criteria for Information Technology Security Evaluation (CC), an international standard for verification of elaborate security claims (see http://en.wikipedia.org/wiki/Common_Criteria).

Obtaining such a certification is an expensive and elaborate job that has no immediate value for a continuously developed free software library (as the certification is tied to the particular version tested). While, as a free software project, we are not actively pursuing this kind of certification, GnuTLS has been FIPS-140-2 certified in several systems by third parties. If you are, interested, see section B.2.

Supported Ciphersuites

Ciphersuite name	TLS ID	Since
TLS_RSA_NULL_MD5	0x00 0x01	SSL3.0
TLS_RSA_NULL_SHA1	0x00 0x02	SSL3.0
TLS_RSA_NULL_SHA256	0x00 0x3B	TLS1.0
TLS_RSA_ARCFOUR_128_SHA1	0x00 0x05	SSL3.0
TLS_RSA_ARCFOUR_128_MD5	0x00 0x04	SSL3.0
TLS_RSA_3DES_EDE_CBC_SHA1	0x00 0x0A	SSL3.0
TLS_RSA_AES_128_CBC_SHA1	0x00 0x2F	SSL3.0
TLS_RSA_AES_256_CBC_SHA1	0x00 0x35	SSL3.0
TLS_RSA_CAMELLIA_128_CBC_SHA256	0x00 0xBA	TLS1.0
TLS_RSA_CAMELLIA_256_CBC_SHA256	0x00 0xC0	TLS1.0
TLS_RSA_CAMELLIA_128_CBC_SHA1	0x00 0x41	SSL3.0
TLS_RSA_CAMELLIA_256_CBC_SHA1	0x00 0x84	SSL3.0
TLS_RSA_AES_128_CBC_SHA256	0x00 0x3C	TLS1.0
TLS_RSA_AES_256_CBC_SHA256	0x00 0x3D	TLS1.0
TLS_RSA_AES_128_GCM_SHA256	0x00 0x9C	TLS1.2
TLS_RSA_AES_256_GCM_SHA384	0x00 0x9D	TLS1.2
TLS_RSA_CAMELLIA_128_GCM_SHA256	0xC0 0x7A	TLS1.2
TLS_RSA_CAMELLIA_256_GCM_SHA384	0xC0 0x7B	TLS1.2
TLS_RSA_CHACHA20_POLY1305	0xCC 0xA0	TLS1.2
TLS_RSA_AES_128_CCM	0xC0 0x9C	TLS1.2
TLS_RSA_AES_256_CCM	0xC0 0x9D	TLS1.2
TLS_RSA_AES_128_CCM_8	0xC0 0xA0	TLS1.2
TLS_RSA_AES_256_CCM_8	0xC0 0xA1	TLS1.2
TLS_DHE_DSS_ARCFOUR_128_SHA1	0x00 0x66	SSL3.0
TLS_DHE_DSS_3DES_EDE_CBC_SHA1	0x00 0x13	SSL3.0
TLS_DHE_DSS_AES_128_CBC_SHA1	0x00 0x32	SSL3.0
TLS_DHE_DSS_AES_256_CBC_SHA1	0x00 0x38	SSL3.0
TLS_DHE_DSS_CAMELLIA_128_CBC_SHA256	0x00 0xBD	TLS1.0
TLS_DHE_DSS_CAMELLIA_256_CBC_SHA256	0x00 0xC3	TLS1.0
TLS_DHE_DSS_CAMELLIA_128_CBC_SHA1	0x00 0x44	SSL3.0

TLS_DHE_DSS_CAMELLIA_256_CBC_SHA1	0x00	0x87	SSL3.0
TLS_DHE_DSS_AES_128_CBC_SHA256	0x00	0x40	TLS1.0
TLS_DHE_DSS_AES_256_CBC_SHA256	0x00	0x6A	TLS1.0
TLS_DHE_DSS_AES_128_GCM_SHA256	0x00	0xA2	TLS1.2
TLS_DHE_DSS_AES_256_GCM_SHA384	0x00	0xA3	TLS1.2
TLS_DHE_DSS_CAMELLIA_128_GCM_SHA256	0xC0	0x80	TLS1.2
TLS_DHE_DSS_CAMELLIA_256_GCM_SHA384	0xC0	0x81	TLS1.2
TLS_DHE_RSA_3DES_EDE_CBC_SHA1	0x00	0x16	SSL3.0
TLS_DHE_RSA_AES_128_CBC_SHA1	0x00	0x33	SSL3.0
TLS_DHE_RSA_AES_256_CBC_SHA1	0x00	0x39	SSL3.0
TLS_DHE_RSA_CAMELLIA_128_CBC_SHA256	0x00	0xBE	TLS1.0
TLS_DHE_RSA_CAMELLIA_256_CBC_SHA256	0x00	0xC4	TLS1.0
TLS_DHE_RSA_CAMELLIA_128_CBC_SHA1	0x00	0x45	SSL3.0
TLS_DHE_RSA_CAMELLIA_256_CBC_SHA1	0x00	0x88	SSL3.0
TLS_DHE_RSA_AES_128_CBC_SHA256	0x00	0x67	TLS1.0
TLS_DHE_RSA_AES_256_CBC_SHA256	0x00	0x6B	TLS1.0
TLS_DHE_RSA_AES_128_GCM_SHA256	0x00	0x9E	TLS1.2
TLS_DHE_RSA_AES_256_GCM_SHA384	0x00	0x9F	TLS1.2
TLS_DHE_RSA_CAMELLIA_128_GCM_SHA256	0xC0	0x7C	TLS1.2
TLS_DHE_RSA_CAMELLIA_256_GCM_SHA384	0xC0	0x7D	TLS1.2
TLS_DHE_RSA_CHACHA20_POLY1305	0xCC	0xA3	TLS1.2
TLS_DHE_RSA_AES_128_CCM	0xC0	0x9E	TLS1.2
TLS_DHE_RSA_AES_256_CCM	0xC0	0x9F	TLS1.2
TLS_DHE_RSA_AES_128_CCM_8	0xC0	0xA2	TLS1.2
TLS_DHE_RSA_AES_256_CCM_8	0xC0	0xA3	TLS1.2
TLS_ECDHE_RSA_NULL_SHA1	0xC0	0x10	SSL3.0
TLS_ECDHE_RSA_3DES_EDE_CBC_SHA1	0xC0	0x12	SSL3.0
TLS_ECDHE_RSA_AES_128_CBC_SHA1	0xC0	0x13	SSL3.0
TLS_ECDHE_RSA_AES_256_CBC_SHA1	0xC0	0x14	SSL3.0
TLS_ECDHE_RSA_AES_256_CBC_SHA384	0xC0	0x28	TLS1.0
TLS_ECDHE_RSA_ARCFOUR_128_SHA1	0xC0	0x11	SSL3.0
TLS_ECDHE_RSA_CAMELLIA_128_CBC_SHA256	0xC0	0x76	TLS1.0
TLS_ECDHE_RSA_CAMELLIA_256_CBC_SHA384	0xC0	0x77	TLS1.0
TLS_ECDHE_ECDSA_NULL_SHA1	0xC0	0x06	SSL3.0
TLS_ECDHE_ECDSA_3DES_EDE_CBC_SHA1	0xC0	0x08	SSL3.0
TLS_ECDHE_ECDSA_AES_128_CBC_SHA1	0xC0	0x09	SSL3.0
TLS_ECDHE_ECDSA_AES_256_CBC_SHA1	0xC0	0x0A	SSL3.0
TLS_ECDHE_ECDSA_ARCFOUR_128_SHA1	0xC0	0x07	SSL3.0
TLS_ECDHE_ECDSA_CAMELLIA_128_CBC_SHA256	0xC0	0x72	TLS1.0
TLS_ECDHE_ECDSA_CAMELLIA_256_CBC_SHA384	0xC0	0x73	TLS1.0
TLS_ECDHE_ECDSA_AES_128_CBC_SHA256	0xC0	0x23	TLS1.0

TLS_ECDHE_RSA_AES_128_CBC_SHA256	0xC0	0x27	TLS1.0
TLS_ECDHE_ECDSA_CAMELLIA_128_GCM_SHA256	0xC0	0x86	TLS1.2
TLS_ECDHE_ECDSA_CAMELLIA_256_GCM_SHA384	0xC0	0x87	TLS1.2
TLS_ECDHE_ECDSA_AES_128_GCM_SHA256	0xC0	0x2B	TLS1.2
TLS_ECDHE_ECDSA_AES_256_GCM_SHA384	0xC0	0x2C	TLS1.2
TLS_ECDHE_RSA_AES_128_GCM_SHA256	0xC0	0x2F	TLS1.2
TLS_ECDHE_RSA_AES_256_GCM_SHA384	0xC0	0x30	TLS1.2
TLS_ECDHE_ECDSA_AES_256_CBC_SHA384	0xC0	0x24	TLS1.0
TLS_ECDHE_RSA_CAMELLIA_128_GCM_SHA256	0xC0	0x8A	TLS1.2
TLS_ECDHE_RSA_CAMELLIA_256_GCM_SHA384	0xC0	0x8B	TLS1.2
TLS_ECDHE_RSA_CHACHA20_POLY1305	0xCC	0xA1	TLS1.2
TLS_ECDHE_ECDSA_CHACHA20_POLY1305	0xCC	0xA2	TLS1.2
TLS_ECDHE_ECDSA_AES_128_CCM	0xC0	0xAC	TLS1.2
TLS_ECDHE_ECDSA_AES_256_CCM	0xC0	0xAD	TLS1.2
TLS_ECDHE_ECDSA_AES_128_CCM_8	0xC0	0xAE	TLS1.2
TLS_ECDHE_ECDSA_AES_256_CCM_8	0xC0	0xAF	TLS1.2
TLS_ECDHE_PSK_3DES_EDE_CBC_SHA1	0xC0	0x34	SSL3.0
TLS_ECDHE_PSK_AES_128_CBC_SHA1	0xC0	0x35	SSL3.0
TLS_ECDHE_PSK_AES_256_CBC_SHA1	0xC0	0x36	SSL3.0
TLS_ECDHE_PSK_AES_128_CBC_SHA256	0xC0	0x37	TLS1.0
TLS_ECDHE_PSK_AES_256_CBC_SHA384	0xC0	0x38	TLS1.0
TLS_ECDHE_PSK_ARCFOUR_128_SHA1	0xC0	0x33	SSL3.0
TLS_ECDHE_PSK_NULL_SHA1	0xC0	0x39	SSL3.0
TLS_ECDHE_PSK_NULL_SHA256	0xC0	0x3A	TLS1.0
TLS_ECDHE_PSK_NULL_SHA384	0xC0	0x3B	TLS1.0
TLS_ECDHE_PSK_CAMELLIA_128_CBC_SHA256	0xC0	0x9A	TLS1.0
TLS_ECDHE_PSK_CAMELLIA_256_CBC_SHA384	0xC0	0x9B	TLS1.0
TLS_PSK_ARCFOUR_128_SHA1	0x00	0x8A	SSL3.0
TLS_PSK_3DES_EDE_CBC_SHA1	0x00	0x8B	SSL3.0
TLS_PSK_AES_128_CBC_SHA1	0x00	0x8C	SSL3.0
TLS_PSK_AES_256_CBC_SHA1	0x00	0x8D	SSL3.0
TLS_PSK_AES_128_CBC_SHA256	0x00	0xAE	TLS1.0
TLS_PSK_AES_256_GCM_SHA384	0x00	0xA9	TLS1.2
TLS_PSK_CAMELLIA_128_GCM_SHA256	0xC0	0x8E	TLS1.2
TLS_PSK_CAMELLIA_256_GCM_SHA384	0xC0	0x8F	TLS1.2
TLS_PSK_AES_128_GCM_SHA256	0x00	0xA8	TLS1.2
TLS_PSK_NULL_SHA1	0x00	0x2C	SSL3.0
TLS_PSK_NULL_SHA256	0x00	0xB0	TLS1.0
TLS_PSK_CAMELLIA_128_CBC_SHA256	0xC0	0x94	TLS1.0
TLS_PSK_CAMELLIA_256_CBC_SHA384	0xC0	0x95	TLS1.0
TLS_PSK_AES_256_CBC_SHA384	0x00	0xAF	TLS1.0

TLS_PSK_NULL_SHA384	0x00	0xB1	TLS1.0
TLS_RSA_PSK_ARCFOUR_128_SHA1	0x00	0x92	TLS1.0
TLS_RSA_PSK_3DES_EDE_CBC_SHA1	0x00	0x93	TLS1.0
TLS_RSA_PSK_AES_128_CBC_SHA1	0x00	0x94	TLS1.0
TLS_RSA_PSK_AES_256_CBC_SHA1	0x00	0x95	TLS1.0
TLS_RSA_PSK_CAMELLIA_128_GCM_SHA256	0xC0	0x92	TLS1.2
TLS_RSA_PSK_CAMELLIA_256_GCM_SHA384	0xC0	0x93	TLS1.2
TLS_RSA_PSK_AES_128_GCM_SHA256	0x00	0xAC	TLS1.2
TLS_RSA_PSK_AES_128_CBC_SHA256	0x00	0xB6	TLS1.0
TLS_RSA_PSK_NULL_SHA1	0x00	0x2E	TLS1.0
TLS_RSA_PSK_NULL_SHA256	0x00	0xB8	TLS1.0
TLS_RSA_PSK_AES_256_GCM_SHA384	0x00	0xAD	TLS1.2
TLS_RSA_PSK_AES_256_CBC_SHA384	0x00	0xB7	TLS1.0
TLS_RSA_PSK_NULL_SHA384	0x00	0xB9	TLS1.0
TLS_RSA_PSK_CAMELLIA_128_CBC_SHA256	0xC0	0x98	TLS1.0
TLS_RSA_PSK_CAMELLIA_256_CBC_SHA384	0xC0	0x99	TLS1.0
TLS_DHE_PSK_ARCFOUR_128_SHA1	0x00	0x8E	SSL3.0
TLS_DHE_PSK_3DES_EDE_CBC_SHA1	0x00	0x8F	SSL3.0
TLS_DHE_PSK_AES_128_CBC_SHA1	0x00	0x90	SSL3.0
TLS_DHE_PSK_AES_256_CBC_SHA1	0x00	0x91	SSL3.0
TLS_DHE_PSK_AES_128_CBC_SHA256	0x00	0xB2	TLS1.0
TLS_DHE_PSK_AES_128_GCM_SHA256	0x00	0xAA	TLS1.2
TLS_DHE_PSK_NULL_SHA1	0x00	0x2D	SSL3.0
TLS_DHE_PSK_NULL_SHA256	0x00	0xB4	TLS1.0
TLS_DHE_PSK_NULL_SHA384	0x00	0xB5	TLS1.0
TLS_DHE_PSK_AES_256_CBC_SHA384	0x00	0xB3	TLS1.0
TLS_DHE_PSK_AES_256_GCM_SHA384	0x00	0xAB	TLS1.2
TLS_DHE_PSK_CAMELLIA_128_CBC_SHA256	0xC0	0x96	TLS1.0
TLS_DHE_PSK_CAMELLIA_256_CBC_SHA384	0xC0	0x97	TLS1.0
TLS_DHE_PSK_CAMELLIA_128_GCM_SHA256	0xC0	0x90	TLS1.2
TLS_DHE_PSK_CAMELLIA_256_GCM_SHA384	0xC0	0x91	TLS1.2
TLS_PSK_AES_128_CCM	0xC0	0xA4	TLS1.2
TLS_PSK_AES_256_CCM	0xC0	0xA5	TLS1.2
TLS_DHE_PSK_AES_128_CCM	0xC0	0xA6	TLS1.2
TLS_DHE_PSK_AES_256_CCM	0xC0	0xA7	TLS1.2
TLS_PSK_AES_128_CCM_8	0xC0	0xA8	TLS1.2
TLS_PSK_AES_256_CCM_8	0xC0	0xA9	TLS1.2
TLS_DHE_PSK_AES_128_CCM_8	0xC0	0xAA	TLS1.2
TLS_DHE_PSK_AES_256_CCM_8	0xC0	0xAB	TLS1.2
TLS_DHE_PSK_CHACHA20_POLY1305	0xCC	0xA4	TLS1.2
TLS_ECDHE_PSK_CHACHA20_POLY1305	0xCC	0xA6	TLS1.2

TLS_RSA_PSK_CHACHA20_POLY1305	0xCC	0xA7	TLS1.2
TLS_PSK_CHACHA20_POLY1305	0xCC	0xA5	TLS1.2
TLS_DH_ANON_ARCFOUR_128_MD5	0x00	0x18	SSL3.0
TLS_DH_ANON_3DES_EDE_CBC_SHA1	0x00	0x1B	SSL3.0
TLS_DH_ANON_AES_128_CBC_SHA1	0x00	0x34	SSL3.0
TLS_DH_ANON_AES_256_CBC_SHA1	0x00	0x3A	SSL3.0
TLS_DH_ANON_CAMELLIA_128_CBC_SHA256	0x00	0xBF	TLS1.0
TLS_DH_ANON_CAMELLIA_256_CBC_SHA256	0x00	0xC5	TLS1.0
TLS_DH_ANON_CAMELLIA_128_CBC_SHA1	0x00	0x46	SSL3.0
TLS_DH_ANON_CAMELLIA_256_CBC_SHA1	0x00	0x89	SSL3.0
TLS_DH_ANON_AES_128_CBC_SHA256	0x00	0x6C	TLS1.0
TLS_DH_ANON_AES_256_CBC_SHA256	0x00	0x6D	TLS1.0
TLS_DH_ANON_AES_128_GCM_SHA256	0x00	0xA6	TLS1.2
TLS_DH_ANON_AES_256_GCM_SHA384	0x00	0xA7	TLS1.2
TLS_DH_ANON_CAMELLIA_128_GCM_SHA256	0xC0	0x84	TLS1.2
TLS_DH_ANON_CAMELLIA_256_GCM_SHA384	0xC0	0x85	TLS1.2
TLS_ECDH_ANON_NULL_SHA1	0xC0	0x15	SSL3.0
TLS_ECDH_ANON_3DES_EDE_CBC_SHA1	0xC0	0x17	SSL3.0
TLS_ECDH_ANON_AES_128_CBC_SHA1	0xC0	0x18	SSL3.0
TLS_ECDH_ANON_AES_256_CBC_SHA1	0xC0	0x19	SSL3.0
TLS_ECDH_ANON_ARCFOUR_128_SHA1	0xC0	0x16	SSL3.0
TLS_SRP_SHA_3DES_EDE_CBC_SHA1	0xC0	0x1A	SSL3.0
TLS_SRP_SHA_AES_128_CBC_SHA1	0xC0	0x1D	SSL3.0
TLS_SRP_SHA_AES_256_CBC_SHA1	0xC0	0x20	SSL3.0
TLS_SRP_SHA_DSS_3DES_EDE_CBC_SHA1	0xC0	0x1C	SSL3.0
TLS_SRP_SHA_RSA_3DES_EDE_CBC_SHA1	0xC0	0x1B	SSL3.0
TLS_SRP_SHA_DSS_AES_128_CBC_SHA1	0xC0	0x1F	SSL3.0
TLS_SRP_SHA_RSA_AES_128_CBC_SHA1	0xC0	0x1E	SSL3.0
TLS_SRP_SHA_DSS_AES_256_CBC_SHA1	0xC0	0x22	SSL3.0
TLS_SRP_SHA_RSA_AES_256_CBC_SHA1	0xC0	0x21	SSL3.0

Table C.1.: The ciphersuites table

Error Codes and Descriptions

The error codes used throughout the library are described below. The return code `GNUTLS_E_SUCCESS` indicates a successful operation, and is guaranteed to have the value 0, so you can use it in logical expressions.

Code	Name	Description
0	GNUTLS_E_SUCCESS	Success.
-3	GNUTLS_E_UNKNOWN_COMPRESSION_ALGORITHM	Could not negotiate a supported compression method.
-6	GNUTLS_E_UNKNOWN_CIPHER_TYPE	The cipher type is unsupported.
-7	GNUTLS_E_LARGE_PACKET	The transmitted packet is too large (EMSGSIZE).
-8	GNUTLS_E_UNSUPPORTED_VERSION_PACKET	A packet with illegal or unsupported version was received.
-9	GNUTLS_E_UNEXPECTED_PACKET_LENGTH	A TLS packet with unexpected length was received.
-10	GNUTLS_E_INVALID_SESSION	The specified session has been invalidated for some reason.
-12	GNUTLS_E_FATAL_ALERT_RECEIVED	A TLS fatal alert has been received.
-15	GNUTLS_E_UNEXPECTED_PACKET	An unexpected TLS packet was received.
-16	GNUTLS_E_WARNING_ALERT_RECEIVED	A TLS warning alert has been received.
-18	GNUTLS_E_ERROR_IN_FINISHED_PACKET	An error was encountered at the TLS Finished packet calculation.
-19	GNUTLS_E_UNEXPECTED_HANDSHAKE_PACKET	An unexpected TLS handshake packet was received.
-21	GNUTLS_E_UNKNOWN_CIPHER_SUITE	Could not negotiate a supported cipher suite.
-22	GNUTLS_E_UNWANTED_ALGORITHM	An algorithm that is not enabled was negotiated.
-23	GNUTLS_E_MPI_SCAN_FAILED	The scanning of a large integer has failed.
-24	GNUTLS_E_DECRYPTION_FAILED	Decryption has failed.
-25	GNUTLS_E_MEMORY_ERROR	Internal error in memory allocation.
-26	GNUTLS_E_DECOMPRESSION_FAILED	Decompression of the TLS record packet has failed.

-27	GNUTLS_E_COMPRESSION_FAILED	Compression of the TLS record packet has failed.
-28	GNUTLS_E_AGAIN	Resource temporarily unavailable, try again.
-29	GNUTLS_E_EXPIRED	The requested session has expired.
-30	GNUTLS_E_DB_ERROR	Error in Database backend.
-31	GNUTLS_E_SRP_PWD_ERROR	Error in password file.
-32	GNUTLS_E_INSUFFICIENT_CREDENTIALS	Insufficient credentials for that request.
-33	GNUTLS_E_HASH_FAILED	Hashing has failed.
-34	GNUTLS_E_BASE64_DECODING_ERROR	Base64 decoding error.
-35	GNUTLS_E_MPI_PRINT_FAILED	Could not export a large integer.
-37	GNUTLS_E_REHANDSHAKE	Rehandshake was requested by the peer.
-38	GNUTLS_E_GOT_APPLICATION_DATA	TLS Application data were received, while expecting handshake data.
-39	GNUTLS_E_RECORD_LIMIT_REACHED	The upper limit of record packet sequence numbers has been reached. Wow!
-40	GNUTLS_E_ENCRYPTION_FAILED	Encryption has failed.
-43	GNUTLS_E_CERTIFICATE_ERROR	Error in the certificate.
-44	GNUTLS_E_PK_ENCRYPTION_FAILED	Public key encryption has failed.
-45	GNUTLS_E_PK_DECRYPTION_FAILED	Public key decryption has failed.
-46	GNUTLS_E_PK_SIGN_FAILED	Public key signing has failed.
-47	GNUTLS_E_X509_UNSUPPORTED_CRITICAL_EXTENSION	Unsupported critical extension in X.509 certificate.
-48	GNUTLS_E_KEY_USAGE_VIOLATION	Key usage violation in certificate has been detected.
-49	GNUTLS_E_NO_CERTIFICATE_FOUND	No certificate was found.
-50	GNUTLS_E_INVALID_REQUEST	The request is invalid.
-51	GNUTLS_E_SHORT_MEMORY_BUFFER	The given memory buffer is too short to hold parameters.
-52	GNUTLS_E_INTERRUPTED	Function was interrupted.
-53	GNUTLS_E_PUSH_ERROR	Error in the push function.
-54	GNUTLS_E_PULL_ERROR	Error in the pull function.
-55	GNUTLS_E_RECEIVED_ILLEGAL_PARAMETER	An illegal parameter has been received.
-56	GNUTLS_E_REQUESTED_DATA_NOT_AVAILABLE	The requested data were not available.
-57	GNUTLS_E_PKCS1_WRONG_PAD	Wrong padding in PKCS1 packet.
-58	GNUTLS_E_RECEIVED_ILLEGAL_EXTENSION	An illegal TLS extension was received.
-59	GNUTLS_E_INTERNAL_ERROR	GnuTLS internal error.
-60	GNUTLS_E_CERTIFICATE_KEY_MISMATCH	The certificate and the given key do not match.

-61	GNUTLS_E_UNSUPPORTED_-CERTIFICATE_TYPE	The certificate type is not supported.
-62	GNUTLS_E_X509_UNKNOWN_SAN	Unknown Subject Alternative name in X.509 certificate.
-63	GNUTLS_E_DH_PRIME_UNACCEPTABLE	The Diffie-Hellman prime sent by the server is not acceptable (not long enough).
-64	GNUTLS_E_FILE_ERROR	Error while reading file.
-67	GNUTLS_E_ASN1_ELEMENT_NOT_FOUND	ASN1 parser: Element was not found.
-68	GNUTLS_E_ASN1_IDENTIFIER_NOT_-FOUND	ASN1 parser: Identifier was not found
-69	GNUTLS_E_ASN1_DER_ERROR	ASN1 parser: Error in DER parsing.
-70	GNUTLS_E_ASN1_VALUE_NOT_FOUND	ASN1 parser: Value was not found.
-71	GNUTLS_E_ASN1_GENERIC_ERROR	ASN1 parser: Generic parsing error.
-72	GNUTLS_E_ASN1_VALUE_NOT_VALID	ASN1 parser: Value is not valid.
-73	GNUTLS_E_ASN1_TAG_ERROR	ASN1 parser: Error in TAG.
-74	GNUTLS_E_ASN1_TAG_IMPLICIT	ASN1 parser: error in implicit tag
-75	GNUTLS_E_ASN1_TYPE_ANY_ERROR	ASN1 parser: Error in type 'ANY'.
-76	GNUTLS_E_ASN1_SYNTAX_ERROR	ASN1 parser: Syntax error.
-77	GNUTLS_E_ASN1_DER_OVERFLOW	ASN1 parser: Overflow in DER parsing.
-78	GNUTLS_E_TOO_MANY_EMPTY_PACKETS	Too many empty record packets have been received.
-79	GNUTLS_E_OPENPGP_UID_REVOKED	The OpenPGP User ID is revoked.
-80	GNUTLS_E_UNKNOWN_PK_ALGORITHM	An unknown public key algorithm was encountered.
-81	GNUTLS_E_TOO_MANY_HANDSHAKE_-PACKETS	Too many handshake packets have been received.
-84	GNUTLS_E_NO_TEMPORARY_RSA_-PARAMS	No temporary RSA parameters were found.
-86	GNUTLS_E_NO_COMPRESSION_-ALGORITHMS	No supported compression algorithms have been found.
-87	GNUTLS_E_NO_CIPHER_SUITES	No supported cipher suites have been found.
-88	GNUTLS_E_OPENPGP_GETKEY_FAILED	Could not get OpenPGP key.
-89	GNUTLS_E_PK_SIG_VERIFY_FAILED	Public key signature verification has failed.
-90	GNUTLS_E_ILLEGAL_SRP_USERNAME	The SRP username supplied is illegal.
-91	GNUTLS_E_SRP_PWD_PARSING_ERROR	Parsing error in password file.
-93	GNUTLS_E_NO_TEMPORARY_DH_PARAMS	No temporary DH parameters were found.
-94	GNUTLS_E_OPENPGP_FINGERPRINT_-UNSUPPORTED	The OpenPGP fingerprint is not supported.
-95	GNUTLS_E_X509_UNSUPPORTED_-ATTRIBUTE	The certificate has unsupported attributes.

-96	GNUTLS_E_UNKNOWN_HASH_-ALGORITHM	The hash algorithm is unknown.
-97	GNUTLS_E_UNKNOWN_PKCS_CONTENT_-TYPE	The PKCS structure's content type is unknown.
-98	GNUTLS_E_UNKNOWN_PKCS_BAG_TYPE	The PKCS structure's bag type is unknown.
-99	GNUTLS_E_INVALID_PASSWORD	The given password contains invalid characters.
-100	GNUTLS_E_MAC_VERIFY_FAILED	The Message Authentication Code verification failed.
-101	GNUTLS_E_CONSTRAINT_ERROR	Some constraint limits were reached.
-104	GNUTLS_E_IA_VERIFY_FAILED	Verifying TLS/IA phase checksum failed
-105	GNUTLS_E_UNKNOWN_ALGORITHM	The specified algorithm or protocol is unknown.
-106	GNUTLS_E_UNSUPPORTED_SIGNATURE_-ALGORITHM	The signature algorithm is not supported.
-107	GNUTLS_E_SAFE_RENEGOTIATION_-FAILED	Safe renegotiation failed.
-108	GNUTLS_E_UNSAFE_RENEGOTIATION_-DENIED	Unsafe renegotiation denied.
-109	GNUTLS_E_UNKNOWN_SRP_USERNAME	The SRP username supplied is unknown.
-110	GNUTLS_E_PREMATURE_TERMINATION	The TLS connection was non-properly terminated.
-201	GNUTLS_E_BASE64_ENCODING_ERROR	Base64 encoding error.
-202	GNUTLS_E_INCOMPATIBLE_GCRYPT_-LIBRARY	The crypto library version is too old.
-203	GNUTLS_E_INCOMPATIBLE_LIBTASN1_-LIBRARY	The tasn1 library version is too old.
-204	GNUTLS_E_OPENPGP_KEYRING_ERROR	Error loading the keyring.
-205	GNUTLS_E_X509_UNSUPPORTED_OID	The OID is not supported.
-206	GNUTLS_E_RANDOM_FAILED	Failed to acquire random data.
-207	GNUTLS_E_BASE64_UNEXPECTED_-HEADER_ERROR	Base64 unexpected header error.
-208	GNUTLS_E_OPENPGP_SUBKEY_ERROR	Could not find OpenPGP subkey.
-209	GNUTLS_E_CRYPTO_ALREADY_-REGISTERED	There is already a crypto algorithm with lower priority.
-210	GNUTLS_E_HANDSHAKE_TOO_LARGE	The handshake data size is too large.
-211	GNUTLS_E_CRYPTODEV_IOCTL_ERROR	Error interfacing with /dev/crypto
-212	GNUTLS_E_CRYPTODEV_DEVICE_ERROR	Error opening /dev/crypto
-213	GNUTLS_E_CHANNEL_BINDING_NOT_-AVAILABLE	Channel binding data not available
-214	GNUTLS_E_BAD_COOKIE	The cookie was bad.
-215	GNUTLS_E_OPENPGP_PREFERRED_KEY_-ERROR	The OpenPGP key has not a preferred key set.

-216	GNUTLS_E_INCOMPAT_DSA_KEY_WITH_-TLS_PROTOCOL	The given DSA key is incompatible with the selected TLS protocol.
-217	GNUTLS_E_INSUFFICIENT_SECURITY	One of the involved algorithms has insufficient security level.
-292	GNUTLS_E_HEARTBEAT_PONG_-RECEIVED	A heartbeat pong message was received.
-293	GNUTLS_E_HEARTBEAT_PING_RECEIVED	A heartbeat ping message was received.
-300	GNUTLS_E_PKCS11_ERROR	PKCS #11 error.
-301	GNUTLS_E_PKCS11_LOAD_ERROR	PKCS #11 initialization error.
-302	GNUTLS_E_PARSING_ERROR	Error in parsing.
-303	GNUTLS_E_PKCS11_PIN_ERROR	Error in provided PIN.
-305	GNUTLS_E_PKCS11_SLOT_ERROR	PKCS #11 error in slot
-306	GNUTLS_E_LOCKING_ERROR	Thread locking error
-307	GNUTLS_E_PKCS11_ATTRIBUTE_ERROR	PKCS #11 error in attribute
-308	GNUTLS_E_PKCS11_DEVICE_ERROR	PKCS #11 error in device
-309	GNUTLS_E_PKCS11_DATA_ERROR	PKCS #11 error in data
-310	GNUTLS_E_PKCS11_UNSUPPORTED_-FEATURE_ERROR	PKCS #11 unsupported feature
-311	GNUTLS_E_PKCS11_KEY_ERROR	PKCS #11 error in key
-312	GNUTLS_E_PKCS11_PIN_EXPIRED	PKCS #11 PIN expired
-313	GNUTLS_E_PKCS11_PIN_LOCKED	PKCS #11 PIN locked
-314	GNUTLS_E_PKCS11_SESSION_ERROR	PKCS #11 error in session
-315	GNUTLS_E_PKCS11_SIGNATURE_ERROR	PKCS #11 error in signature
-316	GNUTLS_E_PKCS11_TOKEN_ERROR	PKCS #11 error in token
-317	GNUTLS_E_PKCS11_USER_ERROR	PKCS #11 user error
-318	GNUTLS_E_CRYPTO_INIT_FAILED	The initialization of crypto backend has failed.
-319	GNUTLS_E_TIMEDOUT	The operation timed out
-320	GNUTLS_E_USER_ERROR	The operation was cancelled due to user error
-321	GNUTLS_E_ECC_NO_SUPPORTED_CURVES	No supported ECC curves were found
-322	GNUTLS_E_ECC_UNSUPPORTED_CURVE	The curve is unsupported
-323	GNUTLS_E_PKCS11_REQUESTED_-OBJECT_NOT_AVAILBLE	The requested PKCS #11 object is not available
-324	GNUTLS_E_CERTIFICATE_LIST_-UNSORTED	The provided X.509 certificate list is not sorted (in subject to issuer order)
-325	GNUTLS_E_ILLEGAL_PARAMETER	An illegal parameter was found.
-326	GNUTLS_E_NO_PRIORITIES_WERE_SET	No or insufficient priorities were set.
-327	GNUTLS_E_X509_UNSUPPORTED_-EXTENSION	Unsupported extension in X.509 certificate.
-328	GNUTLS_E_SESSION_EOF	Peer has terminated the connection

-329	GNUTLS_E_TPM_ERROR	TPM error.
-330	GNUTLS_E_TPM_KEY_PASSWORD_ERROR	Error in provided password for key to be loaded in TPM.
-331	GNUTLS_E_TPM_SRK_PASSWORD_ERROR	Error in provided SRK password for TPM.
-332	GNUTLS_E_TPM_SESSION_ERROR	Cannot initialize a session with the TPM.
-333	GNUTLS_E_TPM_KEY_NOT_FOUND	TPM key was not found in persistent storage.
-334	GNUTLS_E_TPM_UNINITIALIZED	TPM is not initialized.
-335	GNUTLS_E_TPM_NO_LIB	The TPM library (trousers) cannot be found.
-340	GNUTLS_E_NO_CERTIFICATE_STATUS	There is no certificate status (OCSP).
-341	GNUTLS_E_OCSP_RESPONSE_ERROR	The OCSP response is invalid
-342	GNUTLS_E_RANDOM_DEVICE_ERROR	Error in the system's randomness device.
-343	GNUTLS_E_AUTH_ERROR	Could not authenticate peer.
-344	GNUTLS_E_NO_APPLICATION_PROTOCOL	No common application protocol could be negotiated.
-345	GNUTLS_E_SOCKETS_INIT_ERROR	Error in sockets initialization.
-346	GNUTLS_E_KEY_IMPORT_FAILED	Failed to import the key into store.
-347	GNUTLS_E_INAPPROPRIATE_FALLBACK	A connection with inappropriate fallback was attempted.
-348	GNUTLS_E_CERTIFICATE_-VERIFICATION_ERROR	Error in the certificate verification.
-400	GNUTLS_E_SELF_TEST_ERROR	Error while performing self checks.
-401	GNUTLS_E_NO_SELF_TEST	There is no self test for this algorithm.
-402	GNUTLS_E_LIB_IN_ERROR_STATE	An error has been detected in the library and cannot continue operations.
-403	GNUTLS_E_PK_GENERATION_ERROR	Error in public key generation.

Table D.1.: The error codes table

GNU Free Documentation License

Version 1.3, 3 November 2008

Copyright © 2000, 2001, 2002, 2007, 2008 Free Software Foundation, Inc.

http://fsf.org/

Preamble

The purpose of this License is to make a manual, textbook, or other functional and useful document "free" in the sense of freedom: to assure everyone the effective freedom to copy and redistribute it, with or without modifying it, either commercially or noncommercially. Secondarily, this License preserves for the author and publisher a way to get credit for their work, while not being considered responsible for modifications made by others.

This License is a kind of "copyleft", which means that derivative works of the document must themselves be free in the same sense. It complements the GNU General Public License, which is a copyleft license designed for free software.

We have designed this License in order to use it for manuals for free software, because free software needs free documentation: a free program should come with manuals providing the same freedoms that the software does. But this License is not limited to software manuals; it can be used for any textual work, regardless of subject matter or whether it is published as a printed book. We recommend this License principally for works whose purpose is instruction or reference.

1. APPLICABILITY AND DEFINITIONS

This License applies to any manual or other work, in any medium, that contains a notice placed by the copyright holder saying it can be distributed under the terms of this License. Such a notice grants a world-wide, royalty-free license, unlimited in duration, to use that work under the conditions stated herein. The "**Document**", below, refers to any such manual or work. Any member of the public is a licensee, and is addressed as "**you**". You accept the license if you copy, modify or distribute the work in a way requiring permission under copyright law.

A "**Modified Version**" of the Document means any work containing the Document or a portion of it, either copied verbatim, or with modifications and/or translated into another language.

A "**Secondary Section**" is a named appendix or a front-matter section of the Document that deals exclusively with the relationship of the publishers or authors of the Document to the Document's overall subject (or to related matters) and contains nothing that could fall directly within that overall subject. (Thus, if the Document is in part a textbook of mathematics, a Secondary Section may not explain any mathematics.) The relationship could be a matter of historical connection with the subject or with related matters, or of legal, commercial, philosophical, ethical or political position regarding them.

The "**Invariant Sections**" are certain Secondary Sections whose titles are designated, as being those of Invariant Sections, in the notice that says that the Document is released under this License. If a section does not fit the above definition of Secondary then it is not allowed to be designated as Invariant. The Document may contain zero Invariant Sections. If the Document does not identify any Invariant Sections then there are none.

The "**Cover Texts**" are certain short passages of text that are listed, as Front-Cover Texts or Back-Cover Texts, in the notice that says that the Document is released under this License. A Front-Cover Text may be at most 5 words, and a Back-Cover Text may be at most 25 words.

A "**Transparent**" copy of the Document means a machine-readable copy, represented in a format whose specification is available to the general public, that is suitable for revising the document straightforwardly with generic text editors or (for images composed of pixels) generic paint programs or (for drawings) some widely available drawing editor, and that is suitable for input to text formatters or for automatic translation to a variety of formats suitable for input to text formatters. A copy made in an otherwise Transparent file format whose markup, or absence of markup, has been arranged to thwart or discourage subsequent modification by readers is not Transparent. An image format is not Transparent if used for any substantial amount of text. A copy that is not "Transparent" is called "**Opaque**".

Examples of suitable formats for Transparent copies include plain ASCII without markup, Texinfo input format, LaTeX input format, SGML or XML using a publicly available DTD, and standard-conforming simple HTML, PostScript or PDF designed for human modification. Examples of transparent image formats include PNG, XCF and JPG. Opaque formats include proprietary formats that can be read and edited only by proprietary word processors, SGML or XML for which the DTD and/or processing tools are not generally available, and the machine-generated HTML, PostScript or PDF produced by some word processors for output purposes only.

The "**Title Page**" means, for a printed book, the title page itself, plus such following pages as are needed to hold, legibly, the material this License requires to appear in the title page. For works in formats which do not have any title page as such, "Title Page" means the text near the most prominent appearance of the work's title, preceding the beginning of the body of the text.

The "**publisher**" means any person or entity that distributes copies of the Document to the public.

A section "**Entitled XYZ**" means a named subunit of the Document whose title either is precisely XYZ or contains XYZ in parentheses following text that translates XYZ in another language. (Here XYZ stands for a specific section name mentioned below, such as "**Acknowledgements**", "**Dedications**", "**Endorsements**", or "**History**".) To "**Preserve the Title**" of such a section when you modify the Document means that it remains a section "Entitled XYZ" according to this definition.

The Document may include Warranty Disclaimers next to the notice which states that this License applies to the Document. These Warranty Disclaimers are considered to be included by reference in this License, but only as regards disclaiming warranties: any other implication that these Warranty Disclaimers may have is void and has no effect on the meaning of this License.

2. VERBATIM COPYING

You may copy and distribute the Document in any medium, either commercially or noncommercially, provided that this License, the copyright notices, and the license notice saying this License applies to the Document are reproduced in all copies, and that you add no other conditions whatsoever to those of this License. You may not use technical measures to obstruct or control the reading or further copying of the copies you make or distribute. However, you may accept compensation in exchange for copies. If you distribute a large enough number of copies you must also follow the conditions in section 3.

You may also lend copies, under the same conditions stated above, and you may publicly display copies.

3. COPYING IN QUANTITY

If you publish printed copies (or copies in media that commonly have printed covers) of the Document, numbering more than 100, and the Document's license notice requires Cover Texts, you must enclose the copies in covers that carry, clearly and legibly, all these Cover Texts: Front-Cover Texts on the front cover, and Back-Cover Texts on the back cover. Both covers must also clearly and legibly identify you as the publisher of these copies. The front cover must present the full title with all words of the title equally prominent and visible. You may add other material on the covers in addition. Copying with changes limited to the covers, as long as they preserve the title of the Document and satisfy these conditions, can be treated as verbatim copying in other respects.

If the required texts for either cover are too voluminous to fit legibly, you should put the first ones listed (as many as fit reasonably) on the actual cover, and continue the rest onto adjacent pages.

If you publish or distribute Opaque copies of the Document numbering more than 100, you must either include a machine-readable Transparent copy along with each Opaque copy, or state in or with each Opaque copy a computer-network location from which the general network-using public has access to download using public-standard network protocols a complete Transparent copy of the Document, free of added material. If you use the latter option, you must take reasonably prudent steps, when you begin distribution of Opaque copies in quantity, to ensure that this Transparent copy will remain thus accessible at the stated location until at least one year after the last time you distribute an Opaque copy (directly or through your agents or retailers) of that edition to the public.

It is requested, but not required, that you contact the authors of the Document well before redistributing any large number of copies, to give them a chance to provide you with an updated version of the Document.

4. MODIFICATIONS

You may copy and distribute a Modified Version of the Document under the conditions of sections 2 and 3 above, provided that you release the Modified Version under precisely this License, with the Modified Version filling the role of the Document, thus licensing distribution and modification of the Modified Version to whoever possesses a copy of it. In addition, you must do these things in the Modified Version:

A. Use in the Title Page (and on the covers, if any) a title distinct from that of the Document, and from those of previous versions (which should, if there were any, be listed in the History section of the Document). You may use the same title as a previous version if the original publisher of that version gives permission.

B. List on the Title Page, as authors, one or more persons or entities responsible for authorship of the modifications in the Modified Version, together with at least five of the principal authors of the Document (all of its principal authors, if it has fewer than five), unless they release you from this requirement.

C. State on the Title page the name of the publisher of the Modified Version, as the publisher.

D. Preserve all the copyright notices of the Document.

E. Add an appropriate copyright notice for your modifications adjacent to the other copyright notices.

F. Include, immediately after the copyright notices, a license notice giving the public permission to use the Modified Version under the terms of this License, in the form shown in the Addendum below.

G. Preserve in that license notice the full lists of Invariant Sections and required Cover Texts given in the Document's license notice.

H. Include an unaltered copy of this License.

I. Preserve the section Entitled "History", Preserve its Title, and add to it an item stating at least the title, year, new authors, and publisher of the Modified Version as given on the Title Page. If there is no section Entitled "History" in the Document, create one stating the title, year, authors, and publisher of the Document as given on its Title Page, then add an item describing the Modified Version as stated in the previous sentence.

J. Preserve the network location, if any, given in the Document for public access to a Transparent copy of the Document, and likewise the network locations given in the Document for previous versions it was based on. These may be placed in the "History" section. You may omit a network location for a work that was published at least four years before the Document itself, or if the original publisher of the version it refers to gives permission.

K. For any section Entitled "Acknowledgements" or "Dedications", Preserve the Title of the section, and preserve in the section all the substance and tone of each of the contributor acknowledgements and/or dedications given therein.

L. Preserve all the Invariant Sections of the Document, unaltered in their text and in their titles. Section numbers or the equivalent are not considered part of the section titles.

M. Delete any section Entitled "Endorsements". Such a section may not be included in the Modified Version.

N. Do not retitle any existing section to be Entitled "Endorsements" or to conflict in title with any Invariant Section.

O. Preserve any Warranty Disclaimers.

If the Modified Version includes new front-matter sections or appendices that qualify as Secondary Sections and contain no material copied from the Document, you may at your option designate some or all of these sections as invariant. To do this, add their titles to the list of Invariant Sections in the Modified Version's license notice. These titles must be distinct from any other section titles.

You may add a section Entitled "Endorsements", provided it contains nothing but endorsements of your Modified Version by various parties—for example, statements of peer review or that the text has been approved by an organization as the authoritative definition of a standard.

You may add a passage of up to five words as a Front-Cover Text, and a passage of up to 25 words as a Back-Cover Text, to the end of the list of Cover Texts in the Modified Version. Only one passage of Front-Cover Text and one of Back-Cover Text may be added by (or through arrangements made by) any one entity. If the Document already includes a cover text for the same cover, previously added by you or by arrangement made by the same entity you are acting on behalf of, you may not add another; but you may replace the old one, on explicit permission from the previous publisher that added the old one.

The author(s) and publisher(s) of the Document do not by this License give permission to use their names for publicity for or to assert or imply endorsement of any Modified Version.

5. COMBINING DOCUMENTS

You may combine the Document with other documents released under this License, under the terms defined in section 4 above for modified versions, provided that you include in the combination all of the Invariant Sections of all of the original documents, unmodified, and list them all as Invariant Sections of your combined work in its license notice, and that you preserve all their Warranty Disclaimers.

The combined work need only contain one copy of this License, and multiple identical Invariant Sections may be replaced with a single copy. If there are multiple Invariant Sections with the same name but different contents, make the title of each such section unique by adding at the end of it, in parentheses, the name of the original author or publisher of that section if known, or else a unique number. Make the same adjustment to the section titles in the list of Invariant Sections in the license notice of the combined work.

In the combination, you must combine any sections Entitled "History" in the various original documents, forming one section Entitled "History"; likewise combine any sections Entitled "Acknowledgements", and any sections Entitled "Dedications". You must delete all sections Entitled "Endorsements".

6. COLLECTIONS OF DOCUMENTS

You may make a collection consisting of the Document and other documents released under this License, and replace the individual copies of this License in the various documents with a single copy that is included in the collection, provided that you follow the rules of this License for verbatim copying of each of the documents in all other respects.

You may extract a single document from such a collection, and distribute it individually under this License, provided you insert a copy of this License into the extracted document, and follow this License in all other respects regarding verbatim copying of that document.

7. AGGREGATION WITH INDEPENDENT WORKS

A compilation of the Document or its derivatives with other separate and independent documents or works, in or on a volume of a storage or distribution medium, is called an "aggregate" if the copyright resulting from the compilation is not used to limit the legal rights of the compilation's users beyond what the individual works permit. When the Document is included in an aggregate, this License does not apply to the other works in the aggregate which are not themselves derivative works of the Document.

If the Cover Text requirement of section 3 is applicable to these copies of the Document, then if the Document is less than one half of the entire aggregate, the Document's Cover Texts may be placed on covers that bracket the Document within the aggregate, or the electronic equivalent of covers if the Document is in electronic form. Otherwise they must appear on printed covers that bracket the whole aggregate.

8. TRANSLATION

Translation is considered a kind of modification, so you may distribute translations of the Document under the terms of section 4. Replacing Invariant Sections with translations requires special permission from their copyright holders, but you may include translations of some or all Invariant Sections in addition to the original versions of these Invariant Sections. You may include a translation of this License, and all the license notices in the Document, and any Warranty Disclaimers, provided that you also include the original English version of this License and the original versions of those notices and disclaimers. In case of a disagreement between the translation and the original version of this License or a notice or disclaimer, the original version will prevail.

If a section in the Document is Entitled "Acknowledgements", "Dedications", or "History", the requirement (section 4) to Preserve its Title (section 1) will typically require changing the actual title.

9. TERMINATION

You may not copy, modify, sublicense, or distribute the Document except as expressly provided under this License. Any attempt otherwise to copy, modify, sublicense, or distribute it is void, and will automatically terminate your rights under this License.

However, if you cease all violation of this License, then your license from a particular copyright holder is reinstated (a) provisionally, unless and until the copyright holder explicitly and finally terminates your license, and (b) permanently, if the copyright holder fails to notify you of the violation by some reasonable means prior to 60 days after the cessation.

Moreover, your license from a particular copyright holder is reinstated permanently if the copyright holder notifies you of the violation by some reasonable means, this is the first time you have received notice of violation of this License (for any work) from that copyright holder, and you cure the violation prior to 30 days after your receipt of the notice.

Termination of your rights under this section does not terminate the licenses of parties who have received copies or rights from you under this License. If your rights have been terminated and not permanently reinstated, receipt of a copy of some or all of the same material does not give you any rights to use it.

10. FUTURE REVISIONS OF THIS LICENSE

The Free Software Foundation may publish new, revised versions of the GNU Free Documentation License from time to time. Such new versions will be similar in spirit to the present version, but may differ in detail to address new problems or concerns. See http://www.gnu.org/copyleft/.

Each version of the License is given a distinguishing version number. If the Document specifies that a particular numbered version of this License "or any later version" applies to it, you have the option of following the terms and conditions either of that specified version or of any later version that has been published (not as a draft) by the Free Software Foundation. If the Document does not specify a version number of this License, you may choose any version ever published (not as a draft) by the Free Software Foundation. If the Document specifies that a proxy can decide which future versions of this License can be used, that proxy's public statement of acceptance of a version permanently authorizes you to choose that version for the Document.

11. RELICENSING

"Massive Multiauthor Collaboration Site" (or "MMC Site") means any World Wide Web server that publishes copyrightable works and also provides prominent facilities for anybody to edit those works. A public wiki that anybody can edit is an example of such a server. A "Massive Multiauthor Collaboration" (or "MMC") contained in the site means any set of copyrightable works thus published on the MMC site.

"CC-BY-SA" means the Creative Commons Attribution-Share Alike 3.0 license published by Creative Commons Corporation, a not-for-profit corporation with a principal place of business in San Francisco, California, as well as future copyleft versions of that license published by that same organization.

"Incorporate" means to publish or republish a Document, in whole or in part, as part of another Document.

An MMC is "eligible for relicensing" if it is licensed under this License, and if all works that were first published under this License somewhere other than this MMC, and subsequently incorporated in whole or in part into the MMC, (1) had no cover texts or invariant sections, and (2) were thus incorporated prior to November 1, 2008.

The operator of an MMC Site may republish an MMC contained in the site under CC-BY-SA on the same site at any time before August 1, 2009, provided the MMC is eligible for relicensing.

ADDENDUM: How to use this License for your documents

To use this License in a document you have written, include a copy of the License in the document and put the following copyright and license notices just after the title page:

> Copyright © YEAR YOUR NAME. Permission is granted to copy, distribute and/or modify this document under the terms of the GNU Free Documentation License, Version 1.3 or any later version published by the Free Software Foundation; with no Invariant Sections, no Front-Cover Texts, and no Back-Cover Texts. A copy of the license is included in the section entitled "GNU Free Documentation License".

If you have Invariant Sections, Front-Cover Texts and Back-Cover Texts, replace the "with ... Texts." line with this:

> with the Invariant Sections being LIST THEIR TITLES, with the Front-Cover Texts being LIST, and with the Back-Cover Texts being LIST.

If you have Invariant Sections without Cover Texts, or some other combination of the three, merge those two alternatives to suit the situation.

If your document contains nontrivial examples of program code, we recommend releasing these examples in parallel under your choice of free software license, such as the GNU General Public License, to permit their use in free software.

Bibliography

[1] NIST Special Publication 800-57, Recommendation for Key Management - Part 1: General (Revised), March 2007.

[2] PKCS #11 Base Functionality v2.30: Cryptoki Draft 4, July 2009.

[3] ECRYPT II Yearly Report on Algorithms and Keysizes (2009-2010), 2010.

[4] J. Altman, N. Williams, and L. Zhu. Channel bindings for TLS, July 2010. Available from `http://www.ietf.org/rfc/rfc5929`.

[5] R. J. Anderson. *Security Engineering: A Guide to Building Dependable Distributed Systems*. John Wiley & Sons, Inc., New York, NY, USA, 1st edition, 2001.

[6] S. Blake-Wilson, M. Nystrom, D. Hopwood, J. Mikkelsen, and T. Wright. Transport layer security (TLS) extensions, June 2003. Available from `http://www.ietf.org/rfc/rfc3546`.

[7] J. Callas, L. Donnerhacke, H. Finney, D. Shaw, and R. Thayer. OpenPGP message format, November 2007. Available from `http://www.ietf.org/rfc/rfc4880`.

[8] D. Cooper, S. Santesson, S. Farrell, S. Boeyen, R. Housley, and W. Polk. Internet X.509 Public Key Infrastructure Certificate and Certificate Revocation List (CRL) Profile. RFC 5280 (Proposed Standard), May 2008. Available from `http://www.ietf.org/rfc/rfc5280`.

[9] T. Dierks and E. Rescorla. The TLS protocol version 1.1, April 2006. Available from `http://www.ietf.org/rfc/rfc4346`.

[10] T. Dierks and E. Rescorla. The TLS Protocol Version 1.2, August 2008. Available from `http://www.ietf.org/rfc/rfc5246`.

[11] P. Eronen and H. Tschofenig. Pre-shared key ciphersuites for TLS, December 2005. Available from http://www.ietf.org/rfc/rfc4279.

[12] C. Evans and C. Palmer. Public Key Pinning Extension for HTTP, December 2011. Available from `http://tools.ietf.org/html/draft-ietf-websec-key-pinning-01`.

[13] A. Freier, P. Karlton, and P. Kocher. The secure sockets layer (ssl) protocol version 3.0, August 2011. Available from `http://www.ietf.org/rfc/rfc6101`.

[14] P. Gutmann. Everything you never wanted to know about PKI but were forced to find out, 2002. Available from `http://www.cs.auckland.ac.nz/~pgut001/pubs/pkitutorial.pdf`.

[15] S. Hollenbeck. Transport layer security protocol compression methods, May 2004. Available from `http://www.ietf.org/rfc/rfc3749`.

[16] R. Housley, T. Polk, W. Ford, and D. Solo. Internet X.509 public key infrastructure

certificate and certificate revocation list (CRL) profile, April 2002. Available from `http://www.ietf.org/rfc/rfc3280`.

[17] R. Khare and S. Lawrence. Upgrading to TLS within HTTP/1.1, May 2000. Available from `http://www.ietf.org/rfc/rfc2817`.

[18] R. Laboratories. PKCS 12 v1.0: Personal information exchange syntax, June 1999.

[19] C. Latze and N. Mavrogiannopoulos. The TPMKEY URI Scheme, January 2013. Work in progress, available from `http://tools.ietf.org/html/draft-mavrogiannopoulos-tpmuri-01`.

[20] A. Lenstra, X. Wang, and B. de Weger. Colliding X.509 Certificates, 2005. Available from `http://eprint.iacr.org/2005/067`.

[21] M. Mathis and J. Heffner. Packetization Layer Path MTU Discovery, March 2007. Available from `http://www.ietf.org/rfc/rfc4821`.

[22] D. McGrew and E. Rescorla. Datagram Transport Layer Security (DTLS) Extension to Establish Keys for the Secure Real-time Transport Protocol (SRTP), May 2010. Available from `http://www.ietf.org/rfc/rfc5764`.

[23] B. Moeller. Security of CBC ciphersuites in SSL/TLS: Problems and countermeasures, 2002. Available from `http://www.openssl.org/~bodo/tls-cbc.txt`.

[24] M. Myers, R. Ankney, A. Malpani, S. Galperin, and C. Adams. X.509 Internet Public Key Infrastructure Online Certificate Status Protocol - OCSP, June 1999. Available from `http://www.ietf.org/rfc/rfc2560`.

[25] M. Nystrom and B. Kaliski. PKCS 10 v1.7: certification request syntax specification, November 2000. Available from `http://www.ietf.org/rfc/rfc2986`.

[26] J. Pechanec and D. J. Moffat. The PKCS 11 URI Scheme. RFC 7512 (Standards Track), Apr. 2015.

[27] M. T. R. Seggelmann and M. Williams. Transport Layer Security (TLS) and Datagram Transport Layer Security (DTLS) Heartbeat Extension, February 2012. Available from `http://www.ietf.org/rfc/rfc6520`.

[28] E. Rescola. HTTP over TLS, May 2000. Available from `http://www.ietf.org/rfc/rfc2818`.

[29] E. Rescorla and N. Modadugu. Datagram transport layer security, April 2006. Available from `http://www.ietf.org/rfc/rfc4347`.

[30] E. Rescorla, M. Ray, S. Dispensa, and N. Oskov. Transport layer security (TLS) renegotiation indication extension, February 2010. Available from `http://www.ietf.org/rfc/rfc5746`.

[31] R. L. Rivest. Can We Eliminate Certificate Revocation Lists?, February 1998. Available from `http://people.csail.mit.edu/rivest/Rivest-CanWeEliminateCertificateRevocationLists.pdf`.

[32] P. Saint-Andre and J. Hodges. Representation and Verification of Domain-Based Application Service Identity within Internet Public Key Infrastructure Using X.509 (PKIX) Certificates in the Context of Transport Layer Security (TLS), March 2011. Available from http://www.ietf.org/rfc/rfc6125.

[33] J. Salowey, H. Zhou, P. Eronen, and H. Tschofenig. Transport layer security (TLS) session resumption without server-side state, January 2008. Available from http://www.ietf.org/rfc/rfc5077.

[34] S. Santesson. TLS Handshake Message for Supplemental Data, September 2006. Available from http://www.ietf.org/rfc/rfc4680.

[35] W. R. Stevens. *UNIX Network Programming, Volume 1.* Prentice Hall, 1998.

[36] D. Taylor, T. Perrin, T. Wu, and N. Mavrogiannopoulos. Using SRP for TLS authentication, November 2007. Available from http://www.ietf.org/rfc/rfc5054.

[37] S. Tuecke, V. Welch, D. Engert, L. Pearlman, and M. Thompson. Internet X.509 public key infrastructure (PKI) proxy certificate profile, June 2004. Available from http://www.ietf.org/rfc/rfc3820.

[38] N. Williams. On the use of channel bindings to secure channels, November 2007. Available from http://www.ietf.org/rfc/rfc5056.

[39] T. Wu. The stanford SRP authentication project. Available from http://srp.stanford.edu/.

[40] T. Wu. The SRP authentication and key exchange system, September 2000. Available from http://www.ietf.org/rfc/rfc2945.

[41] K. D. Zeilenga. Lightweight Directory Access Protocol (LDAP): String Representation of Distinguished Names, June 2006. Available from http://www.ietf.org/rfc/rfc4514.

Index

abstract types, 95
alert protocol, 9
ALPN, 17
anonymous authentication, 87
Application Layer Protocol Negotiation, 17
Application-specific keys, 103
authentication methods, 21

bad_record_mac, 9

callback functions, 135
certificate authentication, 21, 41
certificate requests, 41
certificate revocation lists, 44
certificate status, 47
Certificate status request, 15
Certificate verification, 38
certification, 281
certtool, 55
certtool help, 56
channel bindings, 176
ciphersuites, 283
client certificate authentication, 11
compression algorithms, 8
contributing, 280
CRL, 44

DANE, 39, 170
dane_strerror, 172
dane_verify_crt, 172
dane_verify_session_crt, 172
dane_verify_status_t, 173
danetool, 76
danetool help, 76
deriving keys, 175
digital signatures, 39
DNSSEC, 39, 170
download, 1

Encrypted keys, 51
error codes, 289

example programs, 179
examples, 179
exporting keying material, 175

fork, 135

generating parameters, 174
gnutls-cli, 245
gnutls-cli help, 245
gnutls-cli-debug, 258
gnutls-cli-debug help, 259
gnutls-serv, 253
gnutls-serv help, 253
gnutls_alert_get, 159
gnutls_alert_get_name, 159
gnutls_alert_send, 160
gnutls_alpn_get_selected_protocol, 17
gnutls_alpn_set_protocols, 17
gnutls_anon_allocate_client_credentials, 148
gnutls_anon_allocate_server_credentials, 148
gnutls_anon_free_client_credentials, 148
gnutls_anon_free_server_credentials, 148
gnutls_anon_set_server_dh_params, 175
gnutls_bye, 158
gnutls_certificate_allocate_credentials, 139
gnutls_certificate_free_credentials, 139
gnutls_certificate_send_x509_rdn_sequence, 143
gnutls_certificate_server_set_request, 143
gnutls_certificate_set_dh_params, 175
gnutls_certificate_set_key, 141
gnutls_certificate_set_ocsp_status_request_file, 15
gnutls_certificate_set_ocsp_status_request_function, 15
gnutls_certificate_set_openpgp_key, 140
gnutls_certificate_set_openpgp_key_file, 140
gnutls_certificate_set_openpgp_key_mem, 140
gnutls_certificate_set_openpgp_keyring_file, 38, 143
gnutls_certificate_set_params_function, 175

gnutls_certificate_set_pin_function, 108, 141
gnutls_certificate_set_retrieve_function, 142
gnutls_certificate_set_retrieve_function2, 142
gnutls_certificate_set_verify_function, 144
gnutls_certificate_set_x509_crl_file, 35
gnutls_certificate_set_x509_key, 140
gnutls_certificate_set_x509_key_file2, 112, 140
gnutls_certificate_set_x509_key_mem2, 140
gnutls_certificate_set_x509_system_trust, 35,
    112, 143
gnutls_certificate_set_x509_trust_dir, 35
gnutls_certificate_set_x509_trust_file, 35, 112,
    143
gnutls_certificate_status_t, 90
gnutls_certificate_verify_flags, 34, 91, 170
gnutls_certificate_verify_peers2, 155
gnutls_certificate_verify_peers3, 144
gnutls_compression_method_t, 8
gnutls_credentials_set, 139
gnutls_db_check_entry, 169
gnutls_db_set_ptr, 168
gnutls_db_set_remove_function, 168
gnutls_db_set_retrieve_function, 168
gnutls_db_set_store_function, 168
gnutls_deinit, 158
gnutls_dh_params_generate2, 175
gnutls_dh_params_import_pkcs3, 175
gnutls_dh_set_prime_bits, 167
gnutls_dtls_cookie_send, 153
gnutls_dtls_cookie_verify, 153
gnutls_dtls_get_data_mtu, 154
gnutls_dtls_get_mtu, 154
gnutls_dtls_get_timeout, 151
gnutls_dtls_prestate_set, 153
gnutls_dtls_set_mtu, 154
gnutls_error_is_fatal, 157
gnutls_error_to_alert, 160
gnutls_global_set_audit_log_function, 134
gnutls_global_set_log_function, 133
gnutls_global_set_log_level, 133
gnutls_global_set_mutex, 135
gnutls_handshake, 154
gnutls_handshake_set_timeout, 155
gnutls_heartbeat_allowed, 13
gnutls_heartbeat_enable, 13
gnutls_heartbeat_get_timeout, 13

gnutls_heartbeat_ping, 13
gnutls_heartbeat_pong, 13
gnutls_heartbeat_set_timeouts, 13
gnutls_hex_decode, 86
gnutls_hex_encode, 86
gnutls_init, 138
gnutls_key_generate, 86, 153
gnutls_ocsp_req_add_cert, 49
gnutls_ocsp_req_add_cert_id, 49
gnutls_ocsp_req_deinit, 49
gnutls_ocsp_req_export, 49
gnutls_ocsp_req_get_cert_id, 49
gnutls_ocsp_req_get_extension, 49
gnutls_ocsp_req_get_nonce, 50
gnutls_ocsp_req_import, 49
gnutls_ocsp_req_init, 49
gnutls_ocsp_req_print, 49
gnutls_ocsp_req_randomize_nonce, 50
gnutls_ocsp_req_set_extension, 49
gnutls_ocsp_req_set_nonce, 50
gnutls_ocsp_resp_check_crt, 51
gnutls_ocsp_resp_deinit, 50
gnutls_ocsp_resp_export, 50
gnutls_ocsp_resp_get_single, 51
gnutls_ocsp_resp_import, 50
gnutls_ocsp_resp_init, 50
gnutls_ocsp_resp_print, 50
gnutls_ocsp_resp_verify, 51
gnutls_ocsp_resp_verify_direct, 51
gnutls_ocsp_status_request_enable_client, 15
gnutls_ocsp_status_request_is_checked, 15
gnutls_openpgp_crt_verify_ring, 38
gnutls_openpgp_crt_verify_self, 38
gnutls_pcert_deinit, 142
gnutls_pcert_import_openpgp, 142
gnutls_pcert_import_openpgp_raw, 142
gnutls_pcert_import_x509, 142
gnutls_pcert_import_x509_raw, 142
gnutls_pin_flag_t, 107
gnutls_pk_bits_to_sec_param, 167
gnutls_pkcs11_add_provider, 107
gnutls_pkcs11_copy_x509_crt2, 111
gnutls_pkcs11_copy_x509_privkey2, 111
gnutls_pkcs11_delete_url, 112
gnutls_pkcs11_get_pin_function, 107
gnutls_pkcs11_init, 106

gnutls_pkcs11_obj_export_url, 108
gnutls_pkcs11_obj_get_info, 109
gnutls_pkcs11_obj_import_url, 108
gnutls_pkcs11_obj_set_pin_function, 108
gnutls_pkcs11_set_pin_function, 107
gnutls_pkcs11_set_token_function, 107
gnutls_pkcs11_token_get_flags, 109
gnutls_pkcs11_token_get_info, 109
gnutls_pkcs11_token_get_url, 109
gnutls_pkcs11_token_init, 109
gnutls_pkcs11_token_set_pin, 109
gnutls_pkcs12_bag_decrypt, 53
gnutls_pkcs12_bag_encrypt, 55
gnutls_pkcs12_bag_get_count, 53
gnutls_pkcs12_bag_get_data, 54
gnutls_pkcs12_bag_get_friendly_name, 54
gnutls_pkcs12_bag_get_key_id, 54
gnutls_pkcs12_bag_set_crl, 55
gnutls_pkcs12_bag_set_crt, 55
gnutls_pkcs12_bag_set_data, 55
gnutls_pkcs12_bag_set_friendly_name, 55
gnutls_pkcs12_bag_set_key_id, 55
gnutls_pkcs12_generate_mac, 55
gnutls_pkcs12_get_bag, 53
gnutls_pkcs12_set_bag, 55
gnutls_pkcs12_simple_parse, 54
gnutls_pkcs12_verify_mac, 53
gnutls_pkcs_encrypt_flags_t, 94
gnutls_priority_set, 160
gnutls_priority_set_direct, 160
gnutls_privkey_decrypt_data, 102
gnutls_privkey_get_pk_algorithm, 99
gnutls_privkey_get_type, 99
gnutls_privkey_import_ext3, 100
gnutls_privkey_import_openpgp, 99
gnutls_privkey_import_openpgp_raw, 99
gnutls_privkey_import_pkcs11, 99
gnutls_privkey_import_tpm_raw, 124
gnutls_privkey_import_tpm_url, 125
gnutls_privkey_import_url, 99
gnutls_privkey_import_x509, 99
gnutls_privkey_import_x509_raw, 52, 99
gnutls_privkey_set_pin_function, 108
gnutls_privkey_sign_data, 101
gnutls_privkey_sign_hash, 102
gnutls_privkey_status, 99

gnutls_psk_allocate_client_credentials, 146
gnutls_psk_allocate_server_credentials, 146
gnutls_psk_client_get_hint, 147
gnutls_psk_free_client_credentials, 146
gnutls_psk_free_server_credentials, 146
gnutls_psk_set_client_credentials, 146
gnutls_psk_set_client_credentials_function, 147
gnutls_psk_set_server_credentials_file, 147
gnutls_psk_set_server_credentials_function, 147
gnutls_psk_set_server_credentials_hint, 147
gnutls_pubkey_encrypt_data, 101
gnutls_pubkey_export, 97
gnutls_pubkey_export2, 97
gnutls_pubkey_export_dsa_raw, 98
gnutls_pubkey_export_ecc_raw, 98
gnutls_pubkey_export_ecc_x962, 98
gnutls_pubkey_export_rsa_raw, 98
gnutls_pubkey_get_key_id, 98
gnutls_pubkey_get_pk_algorithm, 98
gnutls_pubkey_get_preferred_hash_algorithm, 98
gnutls_pubkey_import, 97
gnutls_pubkey_import_openpgp, 96
gnutls_pubkey_import_openpgp_raw, 97
gnutls_pubkey_import_pkcs11, 96
gnutls_pubkey_import_privkey, 97
gnutls_pubkey_import_tpm_raw, 124
gnutls_pubkey_import_tpm_url, 125
gnutls_pubkey_import_url, 97
gnutls_pubkey_import_x509, 96
gnutls_pubkey_import_x509_raw, 97
gnutls_pubkey_set_pin_function, 108
gnutls_pubkey_verify_data2, 100
gnutls_pubkey_verify_hash2, 101
gnutls_random_art, 98
gnutls_record_check_pending, 157
gnutls_record_cork, 158
gnutls_record_get_direction, 152, 155
gnutls_record_get_max_size, 12
gnutls_record_recv, 156
gnutls_record_recv_seq, 157
gnutls_record_send, 156
gnutls_record_set_max_size, 12
gnutls_record_uncork, 159
gnutls_register_custom_url, 104
gnutls_rehandshake, 174

gnutls_safe_renegotiation_status, 173
gnutls_sec_param_get_name, 166
gnutls_sec_param_to_pk_bits, 167
gnutls_server_name_get, 12
gnutls_server_name_set, 12
gnutls_session_get_data2, 168
gnutls_session_get_id2, 168
gnutls_session_is_resumed, 168
gnutls_session_resumption_requested, 169
gnutls_session_set_data, 168
gnutls_session_set_verify_cert, 144, 155
gnutls_session_ticket_enable_server, 169
gnutls_session_ticket_key_generate, 169
gnutls_sign_algorithm_get_requested, 142
gnutls_srp_allocate_client_credentials, 145
gnutls_srp_allocate_server_credentials, 145
gnutls_srp_base64_decode2, 82
gnutls_srp_base64_encode2, 82
gnutls_srp_free_client_credentials, 145
gnutls_srp_free_server_credentials, 145
gnutls_srp_set_client_credentials, 145
gnutls_srp_set_client_credentials_function, 145
gnutls_srp_set_prime_bits, 167
gnutls_srp_set_server_credentials_file, 145
gnutls_srp_set_server_credentials_function, 146
gnutls_srp_verifier, 83
gnutls_srtp_get_keys, 17
gnutls_srtp_get_profile_id, 17
gnutls_srtp_get_profile_name, 17
gnutls_srtp_get_selected_profile, 17
gnutls_srtp_profile_t, 16
gnutls_srtp_set_profile, 16
gnutls_srtp_set_profile_direct, 16
gnutls_store_commitment, 171
gnutls_store_pubkey, 170
gnutls_subject_alt_names_get, 25
gnutls_subject_alt_names_init, 25
gnutls_subject_alt_names_set, 25
gnutls_system_key_add_x509, 103
gnutls_system_key_delete, 103
gnutls_system_key_iter_deinit, 103
gnutls_system_key_iter_get_info, 103
gnutls_tdb_deinit, 171
gnutls_tdb_init, 171
gnutls_tdb_set_store_commitment_func, 171
gnutls_tdb_set_store_func, 171

gnutls_tdb_set_verify_func, 171
gnutls_tpm_get_registered, 124, 125
gnutls_tpm_key_list_deinit, 124, 125
gnutls_tpm_key_list_get_url, 124, 125
gnutls_tpm_privkey_delete, 124, 126
gnutls_tpm_privkey_generate, 123
gnutls_transport_set_errno, 150
gnutls_transport_set_int, 148
gnutls_transport_set_int2, 148
gnutls_transport_set_ptr, 148
gnutls_transport_set_ptr2, 148
gnutls_transport_set_pull_function, 136, 149
gnutls_transport_set_pull_timeout_function, 150, 151
gnutls_transport_set_push_function, 136, 149
gnutls_transport_set_vec_push_function, 149
gnutls_url_is_supported, 98
gnutls_verify_stored_pubkey, 170
gnutls_x509_crl_export, 45
gnutls_x509_crl_get_crt_count, 46
gnutls_x509_crl_get_crt_serial, 45
gnutls_x509_crl_get_issuer_dn, 46
gnutls_x509_crl_get_issuer_dn2, 46
gnutls_x509_crl_get_next_update, 46
gnutls_x509_crl_get_this_update, 46
gnutls_x509_crl_get_version, 46
gnutls_x509_crl_import, 45
gnutls_x509_crl_init, 45
gnutls_x509_crl_privkey_sign, 47, 101
gnutls_x509_crl_reason_t, 94
gnutls_x509_crl_set_authority_key_id, 47
gnutls_x509_crl_set_crt, 46
gnutls_x509_crl_set_crt_serial, 46
gnutls_x509_crl_set_next_update, 46
gnutls_x509_crl_set_number, 47
gnutls_x509_crl_set_this_update, 46
gnutls_x509_crl_set_version, 46
gnutls_x509_crl_sign2, 47
gnutls_x509_crq_privkey_sign, 101
gnutls_x509_crq_set_basic_constraints, 42
gnutls_x509_crq_set_dn, 42
gnutls_x509_crq_set_dn_by_oid, 42
gnutls_x509_crq_set_key, 42
gnutls_x509_crq_set_key_purpose_oid, 42
gnutls_x509_crq_set_key_usage, 42
gnutls_x509_crq_set_pubkey, 102

gnutls_x509_crq_set_version, 42
gnutls_x509_crq_sign2, 42
gnutls_x509_crt_deinit, 24
gnutls_x509_crt_get_authority_info_access, 48
gnutls_x509_crt_get_basic_constraints, 30
gnutls_x509_crt_get_dn, 25
gnutls_x509_crt_get_dn2, 25
gnutls_x509_crt_get_dn_by_oid, 25
gnutls_x509_crt_get_dn_oid, 25
gnutls_x509_crt_get_extension_by_oid2, 27
gnutls_x509_crt_get_extension_data2, 27
gnutls_x509_crt_get_extension_info, 27
gnutls_x509_crt_get_issuer, 26
gnutls_x509_crt_get_issuer_dn, 26
gnutls_x509_crt_get_issuer_dn2, 26
gnutls_x509_crt_get_issuer_dn_by_oid, 26
gnutls_x509_crt_get_issuer_dn_oid, 26
gnutls_x509_crt_get_key_id, 30
gnutls_x509_crt_get_key_usage, 30
gnutls_x509_crt_get_subject, 26
gnutls_x509_crt_get_subject_alt_name2, 24
gnutls_x509_crt_import, 24
gnutls_x509_crt_import_pkcs11, 109
gnutls_x509_crt_import_url, 109
gnutls_x509_crt_init, 24
gnutls_x509_crt_list_import, 24
gnutls_x509_crt_list_import2, 24
gnutls_x509_crt_list_import_pkcs11, 109
gnutls_x509_crt_privkey_sign, 101
gnutls_x509_crt_set_basic_constraints, 30
gnutls_x509_crt_set_key_usage, 30
gnutls_x509_crt_set_pin_function, 108
gnutls_x509_crt_set_pubkey, 102
gnutls_x509_crt_set_subject_alt_name, 24
gnutls_x509_dn_get_rdn_ava, 26
gnutls_x509_ext_export_basic_constraints, 27
gnutls_x509_ext_export_key_usage, 27
gnutls_x509_ext_export_name_constraints, 28
gnutls_x509_ext_import_basic_constraints, 27
gnutls_x509_ext_import_key_usage, 27
gnutls_x509_ext_import_name_constraints, 28
gnutls_x509_name_constraints_add_excluded, 28
gnutls_x509_name_constraints_add_permitted, 28
gnutls_x509_name_constraints_check, 28

gnutls_x509_name_constraints_check_crt, 28
gnutls_x509_name_constraints_deinit, 28
gnutls_x509_name_constraints_get_excluded, 28
gnutls_x509_name_constraints_get_permitted, 28
gnutls_x509_name_constraints_init, 28
gnutls_x509_privkey_export2_pkcs8, 53
gnutls_x509_privkey_export_dsa_raw, 31
gnutls_x509_privkey_export_ecc_raw, 31
gnutls_x509_privkey_export_pkcs8, 53
gnutls_x509_privkey_export_rsa_raw2, 31
gnutls_x509_privkey_get_key_id, 31
gnutls_x509_privkey_get_pk_algorithm2, 31
gnutls_x509_privkey_import2, 52
gnutls_x509_privkey_import_openssl, 56
gnutls_x509_privkey_import_pkcs8, 53
gnutls_x509_trust_list_add_cas, 31
gnutls_x509_trust_list_add_crls, 32
gnutls_x509_trust_list_add_named_crt, 32
gnutls_x509_trust_list_add_system_trust, 34
gnutls_x509_trust_list_add_trust_file, 34
gnutls_x509_trust_list_add_trust_mem, 34
gnutls_x509_trust_list_verify_crt, 32
gnutls_x509_trust_list_verify_crt2, 33
gnutls_x509_trust_list_verify_named_crt, 33

hacking, 280
handshake protocol, 10
hardware security modules, 105
hardware tokens, 105
heartbeat, 13

installation, 1, 2
internal architecture, 263

key extraction, 175
Key pinning, 39, 170
key sizes, 163
keying material exporters, 175

maximum fragment length, 12

OCSP, 47
OCSP status request, 15
ocsptool, 72
ocsptool help, 72

Online Certificate Status Protocol, 47
OpenPGP certificates, 36
OpenPGP server, 214
OpenSSL, 177
OpenSSL encrypted keys, 55

p11tool, 112
p11tool help, 113
parameter generation, 174
PCT, 20
PKCS #10, 41
PKCS #11 tokens, 105
PKCS #12, 53
PKCS #8, 52
Priority strings, 160
PSK authentication, 85
psktool, 86
psktool help, 86

reauthentication, 173
record padding, 9
record protocol, 6
renegotiation, 14, 173
reporting bugs, 280
resuming sessions, 11, 167

safe renegotiation, 14
Secure RTP, 16
server name indication, 12
session resumption, 11, 167
session tickets, 13
Smart card example, 198
smart cards, 105
SRP authentication, 82
srptool, 83
srptool help, 83
SRTP, 16
SSH-style authentication, 39, 170
SSL 2, 20
Supplemental data, 18
symmetric encryption algorithms, 6
System-specific keys, 103

thread safety, 134
tickets, 13
TLS extensions, 12, 13
TLS layers, 5

TPM, 122
tpmtool, 125
tpmtool help, 126
transport layer, 5
transport protocol, 5
Trust on first use, 39, 170
trusted platform module, 122

upgrading, 275

verifying certificate paths, 31, 34, 39
verifying certificate with pkcs11, 35

X.509 certificate name, 24
X.509 certificates, 21
X.509 distinguished name, 25
X.509 extensions, 27